U0038134

全新修訂版

完勝大考！英語7000單字

中高級篇 4501~7000字

空中英語教室編輯群／著

笛藤出版

推薦序

近年來，坊間其實已經有眾多紙本、甚至是電腦化的字彙學習輔助教材，提供英語教師和學生許多字彙學習上的選擇。但是在選擇適當教材時，教師和學生最常問的一個問題就是哪一本或是那一種教材才是最有效的學習資源。但是坊間教材之間就形式內容而言，大致是大同小異（譬如大都是按照字母順序編排，都有例句）。但是如何產生、挑選、編纂字彙教材內容才往往是區隔教材良劣的關鍵。坊間紙本字彙學習書往往可以分成四個類型：

（一）按照字母或是字根字首順序編排、無前後文、無例句，但提供音標、詞性、中文解釋。

（二）和前面第一類型內容幾乎一樣，但不再是無前後文；但在大部分的情況下每一單字僅搭配一個例句。

（三）含有第二類型的內容，且多了英文同（反）義字 ，提供學生類同字的聯想。

（四）在最新的含有字頻資訊，提供學生對於字彙重要性判斷的參考。

其中，第二類型的字彙學習資源書雖然補足了第一種類型資源書沒有的例句，但是單一例句往往無法精確地幫助學生釐清許多英語字彙（尤其是一字多義）之間的精確語用資訊。第三種字彙資源書，雖然提供了同義字，但是根據 Alan Baddeley (2003) 對於人類短期記憶的研究，在遭遇到陌生的初學字彙時，同時間呈現與初學字彙意義、概念上互相關聯（但是沒前後文的）字串（如：huge, big, long, tall, large）並不會特別幫助學生對這些初學字彙的立即回想（immediate recall）。Baddeley 發現意義、概念上互相關聯的同義字只有在被打散時（譬如：呈現在不同的例句、或情境中，才能有效的幫助學生記得初學字彙的學習。若字彙只提供單一例句，有點像把一隻鑰匙跟很多其他類似的鑰匙放在一起；這樣的安排，會讓學生事後得單憑記憶，在很多類似的鑰匙中找出他們所需要的鑰匙。但是若是透過不同的（兩個或兩個以上）例句，就像給予學生不同的情境記憶標籤，幫助學生將新學的字彙和其他的同義字在不同情境的記憶中做連結與代換，進而幫助學生建立新學字彙與同義字之間的記憶標籤。空英這次編纂的紙本字彙資源書中，針對一字多義的字彙提供至少兩種例句，提供學生不同的前後文情境來連結初學字彙與對應同義字。此外，空英編纂的字彙資源書並參酌字庫、歷屆學測指考內容，補充最常用同義字及重要搭配語，進而達到上述第四類型字彙學習資源書的優點。

不同於坊間字彙學習資源書僅有紙本或是僅有 app 版本，空中英語教室所編製的字彙學習書同時具有紙本與手機 app 版本。有了 app 版本最大的好處，除了提供行動學習的工具，最重要的是 app 補足了紙本字彙資源學習書所無法提供的發音。同時，除了單字本身的發音，在 app 中更提供例句的發音。這樣的好處是可以讓學生同時接觸到單字單獨呈現與在有前後文的例句中的發音（不論在中文與英語中，有許多字在單獨發音及有前後文句子當中的發音是有細微差異的，例如連音與局部變音）。藉由空英老師字正腔圓的道地發音音檔，學生可以在課室內與課室外的環境中，得到更多的輔助。當然學生更可以在 app 版本中，標示自己覺得最困難、最重要、或是最喜歡的單字，提供日後複習時的電子書籤。以上這些用心的特點，讓空英的單字書所匯集的 7000 英文單字能更有效地深植在學生的腦海中，成為輔助英語字彙學習有效工具。

國立台灣師範大學英語學系 副教授 劉宇挺

本書特色

1. 本書收錄實用中高級字彙，其中包括相同拚法，不同詞性的字彙等約 2500 字。以點、線、面擴展方式學習該單字用法，使用讀者能夠有效率增加字彙量。
2. 收錄衍生單字詞彙，如同義字、反義字、搭配詞及實用片語等，使讀者快速了解該單字的延伸用法，進而在語言學習上更加活用單字。
3. 特別強調《搭配詞 Collocation》的彙集補充，有效使讀者在口說或寫作時，語感自然又道地。
4. 以單元學習的方式，分為 76 回，每回 25 個單字組，並在每回結束時，設計 10 題練習題，包含【配合題】、【文意字彙】、【字類變化】及【選擇題】等四種基本題型，有效評核學習狀況，循序漸進學會新的單字。
5. 另附有完勝大考 7000 單字雲 _ 中高級 -- 專屬序號，幫助讀者學習不間斷，充份利用零碎時間，走到哪聽到哪，走到哪背到哪。

※ 完勝大考 7000 單字雲及單字書內容的差異：

單字雲：主要單字及例句，並附音檔。

1. ◆提供多樣互動練習題　◆聽發音猜中文意思
◆聽發音猜英文拚法　◆聽發音猜單字

單字書：提供主要單字及例句，並補充實用片語、搭配詞並搭配詞例句。

2. 單字書另提供 76 回，每回 10 題，便於讀者更深入學習單字的使用情境。

本書使用導覽

◎ 詞性縮寫

v. = Verb 動詞
n. = Noun 名詞
adj. = Adjective 形容詞
adv. = Adverb 副詞
prep. = Preposition 介系詞
conj. = Conjunction 連接詞

◎音標參考 DICT.TW 線上字典 / Macmillan Dictionary / Cambridge Dictionary

同：同義詞
搭：搭配詞
▶：例句
99：學測或指考或統測年度

considerate [kən'sɪd.ɚ.ət]

adj. 考慮周到的；體貼的

同 **thoughtful**

反 **inconsiderate**

實用片語與搭配詞

considerate towards others
體貼 / 為人著想的

▶ Be considerate of others when you are in public.
當你身處公共場所時，請為他人著想。

▶ My friend is very considerate towards others and will always help whenever there is need.
我的朋友非常為別人著想，並且每當他人有困難，他總是提供協助。

目次 Contents

完勝大考 7000 單字雲開通說明

親愛的讀者 您好：

恭喜您獲得【完勝大考 7000 單字雲】專屬 QR Code，請按以下步驟開通：

➡ 請掃下方 QR Code 進入【完勝大考 7000 單字雲服務首頁】，輸入空英官網會員帳號及密碼直接登入。若非空英官網會員，請按【註冊】，並填妥相關欄位成為空英會員。

序號：6U8g150Qbj4K
對象：購完勝大考7000單字書中高級附贈
級別：中高

★注意事項：

(1) 完勝大考 7000 單字雲 - 中高級服務網址：https://7000wh.studioclassroom.com

(2) 完勝大考 7000 單字雲的音檔服務係為雲端服務，無離線收聽的功能。

(3) 任何可上網的裝置，都可以使用服務網址收聽音檔。

(4) 序號開通後，若書籍轉給他人使用，只能以原帳號接續使用，無法轉移。

若您在操作上有任何疑問，或完勝大考 7000 單字雲無法正常使用，請洽空中英語教室客服專線 (02)2533-9123。

單字
Vocabulary

收錄 2528 字

► 76 回單字（每回 25 字）

每回 25 個實用單字，附上音標、詞性、例句、同義字、反義字、實用片語與搭配詞等説明，循序漸進增加字彙量。

► 76 回練習題（每回 10 題）

每回單字後面皆有練習題，馬上驗收前面所學，加深學習印象。

Unit 1

99

abbreviate [ə'bri:.vi.eɪt]

v. 使簡短；縮短；縮寫

同 **shorten**

反 **lengthen**

▶ He made the speech shorter by abbreviating parts of it.
他縮短了演講的部份內容，使演講變短。

99

abbreviation [ə,bri:.vi'eɪ.ʃən]

n. 簡短；縮短；縮寫（字）

實用片語與搭配詞

abbreviation for 代表

▶ The play was an abbreviation from the original.
那部戲是原劇的精簡版。

▶ We use abbreviations for long English words like United Nations, so we just say U.N.
我們會將如 United Nation（聯合國）這樣較長的字詞，以其首字母縮寫，因此我們稱之為 UN。

---

abide [ə'baɪd] *v.* 容忍

同 **endure; obey**

反 **leave**

▶ He couldn't abide such foolishness.
他無法容忍如此的愚蠢。

---

abnormal [æb'nɔ:r.məl]

adj. 反常的；不正常的

同 **odd**

反 **normal**

▶ The health problem was abnormal and needed a special surgery.
那種健康上的問題相當反常，需要進行特殊的手術。

abolish [ə'bɑ:.lɪʃ] *v.* 廢除

同 **destroy**

反 **establish**

▶ The government finally abolished the luxury tax.
政府終於廢除了奢侈稅。

---

aboriginal [,æbə'rɪdʒ(ə)n(ə)l]

① *adj.* 原住民的

同 **native**

② *n.* 原住民

同 **inhabitant**

▶ His aboriginal parents told him about their old traditions.
他的原住民父母告訴他古老的傳統。

▶ His people have been here for ages. He is an aboriginal.
他的族人定居此地已經很久了。他是原住民。

實用片語與搭配詞

aboriginal inhabitant 土著

▶ Aboriginal inhabitants of Australia arrived on the continent thousands of years ago.
澳洲的原住民在數千年前就抵達了這個大陸。

---

aborigine [ˌæb.əˈrɪdʒ.ən.i] *n.* 原住民

▶ Aborigines have lived in this area for thousands of years.
原住民定居在這個地區好幾千年了。

---

abortion [əˈbɔːr.ʃən] *n.* 墮胎；流產

同 **miscarriage**

實用片語與搭配詞

have an abortion 墮胎

▶ Abortion is illegal in many South American countries.
墮胎在許多南美洲國家是違法的。

▶ In many countries it is illegal to have an abortion because it is viewed as murder.
在許多國家墮胎是非法的，因為它被視同於謀殺。

---

abound [əˈbaʊnd] *v.* 充滿；有很多

同 **fill**

反 **lack**

實用片語與搭配詞

abound for / in / with sth.
滿溢／大量的某物

▶ Blame and excuses abounded between the fighting children.
爭吵的孩子們彼此以大量指責和藉口相互攻擊。

▶ In the rainy season the African savannah abounds with food for wild animals
在雨季，非洲的稀樹草原提供野生動物充足的食物。

---

abrupt [əˈbrʌpt] *adj.* 突然的；魯莽的

搭 **curt; hasty**

▶ The bus made an abrupt turn to avoid the scooter.
公車為了閃避機車而突然轉彎。

---

absent-minded [ˌæb.səntˈmaɪn.dɪd]
adj. 心不在焉的；茫茫然的

反 **attentive; wide-awake**

▶ He was so absent-minded that he forgot his keys and phone.
他心不在焉到連鑰匙和手機都忘記帶了。

---

abstraction [æbˈstræk.ʃən]
n. 抽象的概念；抽象

實用片語與搭配詞

abstraction of sth.
某事物的抽象

▶ The professor spoke in many abstractions about the topic.
教授針對那個主題講了很多抽象的概念。

▶ Jonathan asked for an abstraction of adoption records to help find his birth mother.
喬納森要求領取他的領養記錄以幫助他找到他的親生母親。

absurd [əbˈsɝːd] *adj.* 不合理的；荒謬的

同 ridiculous

反 reasonable

▶ The teacher assigned an absurd amount of work.
老師給的作業多到不合理。

---

abundance [əˈbʌn.dəns] *n.* 大量；很多

同 plenty

反 shortage

▶ There is an abundance of oil in the Middle East.
中東地區盛產原油。

104

abundant [əˈbʌn.dənt] *adj.* 豐富的；大量的

同 rich; flourish

反 short

▶ The farmer has an abundant amount of wheat.
這名農夫有大量的小麥。

102

abuse [əˈbjuːz] *v.* 虐待；濫用

同 injure; ill-use

反 heal

▶ The owner abused the dog by hitting it.
飼主虐待那條狗的方式是毆打牠。

102

abuse [əˈbjuːs] *n.* 辱罵；謾罵；虐待；濫用

同 damage; mistreat

▶ He suffered a lot of abuse for his beliefs.
他為著自己的信念而承受了很多辱罵。

---

academy [əˈkæd.ə.mi]
n. 學院；研究院；學會

同 college; school

▶ Pam hopes to study at the military academy.
潘希望讀軍校。

104

accelerate [əkˈsel.ə.eɪt] *v.* 加速；增進

同 speed up

反 decelerate

▶ The bike accelerated down the hill.
那輛自行車下坡時速度加快了。

---

acceleration [əkˌsel.əˈreɪ.ʃən]
n. 加速性能；加速；促進

反 deceleration / retardation

▶ A sports car has a high acceleration.
跑車的加速性能很強。

accessible [əkˈses.ə.bəl]

adj. 可進入的；可接近的；可得到的

反 **inaccessible**

▶ You have to enter in the front. The back is not accessible.
你必須從前方進入，因為後方無法進入。

accessory [əkˈses.ər.i]

① *n.* 配件

同 **supplement**

實用片語與搭配詞

accessory apartment 配套公寓

② *adj.* 輔助的；非主要的；附加的

同 **additional**

實用片語與搭配詞

accessory to a crime 協助犯罪

▶ She loves buying accessories to wear to parties.
她喜歡買配件好穿戴著參加派對。

▶ They created an accessory apartment next door so their elderly parents could live closeby.
他們在隔壁設置了一個附屬公寓，讓他們年邁的父母能就近居住。

▶ Everything else was accessory to this plan.
其他一切都只是這項計畫案附加的非主要部份。

▶ If you knew about a crime and did not report it, you would be an accessory to the crime and can go to jail.
如果你知曉一個犯罪活動卻不通報，你就等同於幫兇並且會因此入獄。

103

accommodate [əˈkɑː.mə.deɪt]

v. 照顧到；提供；可容納；使適應

同 **conform; supply**

實用片語與搭配詞

can / could accommodate 能夠容納

▶ She accommodated all of their needs.
她照顧到他們的一切需求。

▶ This house is very expensive, but the landlord could accommodate you and lower the price.
這間房子所費不貲，但是房東可以通融你並且降價。

accommodation [əˌkɑː.məˈdeɪ.ʃən]

n. 變通；調節；住宿；適應

同 **adjustment; fitting**

實用片語與搭配詞

look for / seek accommodation 找住所

▶ The owner was very busy but made accommodations to meet us.
那位主人雖然非常忙碌，卻為了和我們見面而做了變通。

▶ You better seek accommodation before you leave or you might sleep on the street.
你最好在離開前先找好住處，否則你可能會流落街頭。

accord [əˈkɔːrd]

① *v.* 調解；使一致；給予（特殊待遇）

同 **agree; conform**

實用片語與搭配詞

accord with 合乎；符合；與…相符

② *n.* 協議；一致；和諧

同 **agreement**

實用片語與搭配詞

accord was signed 簽署協定

▶ The teacher accorded between the two fighting boys.
老師調解了吵架的兩個男孩之間的紛爭。

▶ Amazon tribes live in accord with nature and they only take what they need to survive.
亞馬遜部族順應自然環境而居，他們只索取他們生存所需之物。

▶ I will go tomorrow, and you will help me. Do we have an accord?
我明天出發，而你也會協助我。我們達成協議了嗎？

▶ In 1945 a peace accord was signed among world leaders to end World War II.
在 1945 年，國家領導人們簽署了一個和平協議以終止第二次世界大戰。

accordance [əˈkɔːr.dəns]

n. 依照；一致；和諧；符合

同 **accordance; conformity**

實用片語與搭配詞

in accordance with 依照

▶ The game will be played in accordance to the rules.
比賽將按照規則來進行。

▶ The game must be played in accordance with the rules.
這遊戲必須按照規則進行。

99

accordingly [əˈkɔːr.dɪŋ.li]

adv. 照著；因此；於是

同 **consequently**

實用片語與搭配詞

act accordingly 按照指示行動

▶ Accordingly, they did exactly what was expected of them.
他們完全照著外界對他們的期許行事。

▶ You are a representative of your school and you must act accordingly by behaving well.
身為貴校的代表，你的舉止理當相應得宜。

Exercise 1

I. Derivatives

1. Airbnb is becoming more and more popular nowadays because it does not only provide affordable ______________ (accommodate), but also socially connect with travelers and the people who manage on behalf of vendors.
2. The concept of Lihiya, a cross-cultural collaborated fashion brand, is not only to work with the ____________ (aborigine) communities in Taiwan, but also to develop sustainable growth for them.
3. After watching a documentary film about homelessness, he felt very thankful for having an _________ (abundance) life and wanted to provide financial support for the homeless.
4. The purpose of today's meeting will be focused on strategies to create sales ________________ (accelerate) in our business.
5. Dena tries to elaborate some philosophical ____________ (abstract) in the textbook to her classmates.

II. Choices

1. After the election of the United States of America in 2016, there is considerable debate within the cities across the country about whether the Electoral College should be ________.
   (A) accomplished (B) abolished (C) achieved (D) approached

2. He thought that was an _________ idea because he's never heard of it.
   (A) absent (B) absurd (C) abrupt (D) abundant

3. Some hiking maniacs are obsessed with the hiking trails in Taipei because many of them are conveniently _________ by public transportations.
   (A) acceptable (B) affordable (C) accidental (D) accessible

4. PMS is the _________ for pre-menstrual syndrome, which includes breast tenderness, body aches, or irritability that happens in a period of time before women's menstrual cycle.
   (A) abbreviation (B) depletion (C) reduction (D) contraction

5. In December 2015, nearly 200 countries have ratified the Paris _________ on climate change, which comes into effect on 4 November 2016, and it commits all the governments to keep global warming to no greater than 2C threshold.
   (A) acceptance (B) account (C) accord (D) access

Unit 2

accountable [əˈkaʊn.t̬ə.bəl]

adj. 應負責的；可說明的

實用片語與搭配詞

accountable for sth. 為某行為負責

▶ When you get older, you will need to be accountable.
等你年紀大一點時，就必須為自己負責。

▶ You are the team leader and you will be held accountable for the failure of this project.
你身為團隊領袖，對於本次專案計畫的失敗應將負起責任。

---

accounting [əˈkaʊn.t̬ɪŋ] *n.* 會計（學）

同 **accounting**

▶ Payments will be taken care of by the accounting department.
會計部會負責支付款項。

accumulate [əˈkjuː.mjə.leɪt] *v.* 累積；積聚

同 **store up**

反 **dissipate**

▶ The old car seems to accumulate more problems every year.
那輛舊車每年出的問題似乎越積越多。

---

accumulation [əˌkjuː.mjəˈleɪ.ʃən]

n. 累積；積聚

實用片語與搭配詞

lead to / prevent accumulation
導致／預防囤積

▶ The roof collapsed due to the extreme snow accumulation.
屋頂由於積雪過多而坍塌了。

▶ Saving money every month is a good habit and will lead to the accumulation of your funds.
每月儲蓄是一個好習慣並且將能累積你的資金。

---

accusation [ˌæk.jəˈzeɪ.ʃən] *n.* 指控

同 **charge; dissipate**

實用片語與搭配詞

make an accusation against sb.
指控某人

▶ He had to go to court due to certain accusations.
他因為被人控告而必須出庭。

▶ She made an accusation against the restaurant owner for selling food that made her sick.
她對那家餐廳老闆作出指控，因其販售讓她身體不適的食物。

accustom [ə'kʌs·təm] *v.* 使…習慣於…

同 **familiarize; get used to**

實用片語與搭配詞

accustom sb. to sth. 使某人習慣於某事物

- I am accustomed to waking up early.
  我習慣早起。
- Change is not easy, but if you slowly accustom people to it, it will happen eventually.
  改變並不容易，但是如果你慢慢讓人們習慣它，改變終將會實現。

---

ace [eɪs]

① *n.* (骰子、紙牌 A) 王牌；傑出人才；帶來成功的人或事

同 **champion; hotshot**

② *adj.* 第一流的

同 **first-rate; virtuoso**

- He played his ace at the end of the card game.
  他在牌局尾聲打出了他的王牌。
- He is an ace player at tennis.
  他是一流的網球好手。

---

acknowledge [ək'nɑː.lɪdʒ] *v.* 承認

同 **admit**

反 **deny**

實用片語與搭配詞

fail / refuse to acknowledge sth. / sb.
拒絕承認某人或某事

- He finally acknowledged that he stole the money.
  他終於承認他偷了錢。
- Many Americans refuse to acknowledge Donald Trump as president.
  很多美國人拒絕承認川普是他們的總統。

---

acknowledgement [ək'nɑː.lɪdʒ] *n.* 承認

同 **recognition**

反 **disregard**

- The hotel sent guests an acknowledgement that its service was poor.
  飯店致信給房客，承認他們服務不周。

---

acne ['æk.ni] *n.* 粉刺

- He asked the doctor to treat his acne.
  他請了醫生治療粉刺。

---

acquisition [ˌæk.wə'zɪʃ.ən]

n. 收購；獲得；取得；習得

同 **acquirement; learning skill**

實用片語與搭配詞

make / complete an acquisition
收購

- The company now owns the building after the acquisition.
  那家公司在收購案完成之後，成為擁有那棟建築的業主。
- When shopping online, most people complete their acquisition by paying with a credit card.
  線上購物時，大多數人用信用卡付款以完成訂購程序。

activist [ˈæk.tə.vɪst]
n. 積極支持者；行動主義者；活躍份子
同 **militant**

▶ Animal rights activists demanded changes to the law.
積極維護動物權益的人士要求修改法律。

104

acute [əˈkjuːt] *adj.* 洞悉的；尖銳的；敏銳的
同 **astute**
反 **dull**

▶ He was acute to all of his patients' health problems.
他能洞悉所有患者的健康問題。

---

adaptation [ˌæd.əpˈteɪ.ʃən]
n. 做出調整；改編；適應
同 **adaption; adjustment version**

▶ They made a quick adaptation to the equipment which made it work.
他們很快地調整設備，而成功地讓它運作了。

101

addict [ˈæd.ɪkt]
① *v.* 使沉溺於…；上癮
同 **hook**
② *n.* 成癮者；狂熱愛好者
同 **junkie; junky**

▶ He never left his room because he was addicted to computer games.
他從不離開房間，因為他對電玩遊戲上癮了。

▶ She joined a group that helps addicts.
她加入了一個協助成癮者戒癮的團體。

103

addiction [əˈdɪk·ʃən] *n.* 上癮；入迷
同 **dependence; habituation**

▶ The addiction was so strong that he needed professional help to quit.
他上癮很嚴重，所以需要專業的協助才能戒癮。

---

administer [ədˈmɪn.ə.stɚ]
v. 給予；施用；管理
同 **apply; manage**

▶ The doctor administered what he thought best for the patient.
醫師依照對患者最有幫助的方式施藥。

---

administration [ədˌmɪn.əˈstreɪ.ʃən]
n. 管理階層；管理部門；管理
同 **governance; management**

▶ All decisions were made through the school's administration.
所有決定都是透過學校的管理階層定奪的。

---

administrative [ədˈmɪn.ə.strə.t̬ɪv]
adj. 行政的；管理的
同 **governing; managing**

▶ She was hired for her administrative experience.
她因為擁有管理方面的經驗而被雇用。

administrator [əd'mɪn.ə.streɪ.t̬ɚ]

n. 管理人員；行政人員；系統管理員

同 **decision maker; executive**

▶ He knew how the agency worked because he was an administrator for many years.

他清楚這家機構的運作方式，因為他擔任管理者多年。

---

admiral ['æd.mər.əl] *n.* 海軍上將

▶ The admiral was in charge of all the ships in the Pacific area.

這名海軍上將負責管理所有太平洋地區的船艦。

---

adolescence [ˌæd.ə'les.əns]

n. 青春期；青少年期

同 **puberty; teenage**

▶ A boy's body changes a lot during adolescence.

男孩的身體在青春期會出現許多變化。

---

adolescent [ˌæd.ə'les.ənt]

① *adj.* 青春期的；青少年的

同 **teenaged; puerile**

② *n.* 青少年

同 **teen; teenager**

▶ Her adolescent years were challenging for her parents.

她青春期時，令她父母頗傷腦筋。

▶ As an adolescent, I was unable to rent a car.

我當時是青少年，不能租車。

---

adore [ə'dɔːr]

v. 愛慕；崇拜

同 **admire**

反 **abominate**

▶ Christians sing hymns because they adore Jesus.

基督徒吟唱讚美詩是因為他們愛耶穌。

---

adulthood ['æd.ʌlt.hʊd] *n.* 成年期

同 **maturation**

▶ Many people get married after they reach adulthood.

許多人在成年後結婚。

Exercise 2

I. Derivatives

1. The famous musician has been struggling with his ___________ (addict) to cocaine for many years.
2. Fiona has over 5 years of experience working as an ___________ (administration) assistant in Duke University.
3. I'm so surprised that she can readily ___________ (adaptation) to this new environment in such a short time.
4. One of the best strategies for leading technology companies to grow business is to depend on ___________ (acquire).
5. Brad Pitt denied all the ___________ (accuse) of child abuse, drug-taking and poor parenting that had been flying around.

II. Vocabulary Choices

(A) acknowledgement	(B) accountable	(C) adulthood	(D) accumulate
(E) admiral	(F) administrative	(G) accustom	(H) acute
(I) adore	(J) adolescence		

1. She becomes ________ ed to staying up late to finish house core ever since she started to have the second baby.
2. Darren didn't have parents to hold him ________ for misbehavior when he's very little.
3. I'm writing this letter in ________ of your help with the improvement of our customer service.
4. He had suffered so much from teen depression in his ________ .
5. Monica is a bibliophile who likes to ________ quite a collection of books over recent years.

Unit 3

advertiser [ˈædvətaɪzər]

n. 刊登廣告者；廣告客戶

▶ The advertiser introduced a new product on TV.
廣告主在電視上介紹了一項新產品。

---

advocate [ˈæd.və.kət]

n. 辯護律師；提倡者；擁護者

同 **lawyer; attorney**

▶ He hired the lawyer to be his advocate in court.
他僱請那名律師擔任他出庭的辯護律師。

advocate [ˈæd.və.keɪt]

v. 主張；擁護；支持；提倡

同 **defend**

反 **impugn**

▶ My mom always advocates eating healthier food.
我媽媽總是主張攝食更有益健康的食物。

98

affection [əˈfek.ʃən] *n.* 感情；影響；感染

同 **admiration**

反 **contempt**

▶ The boy showed his affection for the puppy.
男孩展現了他對小狗的感情。

102

affectionate [əˈfek.ʃən.ət] *adj.* 充滿深情的

同 **fond; tender**

▶ The affectionate puppy ran to meet him at the door.
那隻充滿溫情的小狗跑到門前迎接他回來。

---

affirm [əˈfɝːm] *v.* 確認；證實；斷言

同 **assert**

反 **negate**

▶ The teacher affirmed the student's progress.
那位老師確認了學生的進度。

---

agenda [əˈdʒen.də] *n.* 待議事項；議程

同 **business schedule**

▶ We have a long agenda of items to discuss.
我們有一長串的待議事項要討論。

---

aggression [əˈgreʃ.ən] *n.* 攻擊；侵略

同 **invasion**

反 **repulsion**

▶ You could see that he was holding back his aggression.
你可以看出他正在忍住不讓自己做出攻擊行為。

agony [ˈæg.ə.ni] *n.* 極度的痛苦；苦惱

同 **anguish**

反 **relief**

▶ Liz was in agony after her surgery.
麗茲手術後非常痛苦。

---

agricultural [ˌæg.rəˈkʌl.tʃɚ.əl] *adj.* 農業的

同 **farming**

▶ Many agricultural products are grown in the midwestern part of America.
許多農產品都是在美國中西部栽種的。

AI / artificial intelligence
[ˌɑːr.t̬ə.fɪʃ.əl ɪnˈtel.ə.dʒəns] *n.* 人工智慧

▶ The robot is programmed to use artificial intelligence.
機器人經設定使用人工智慧。

---

airtight [ˈer.taɪt] *adj.* 密閉的

同 **air-tight; gas-tight**

▶ The jar was airtight, so nothing could get in or out.
罐子是密封的，所以沒有任何東西能進去或出來。

---

airway [ˈer.weɪ] *n.* 通風道；航線

▶ The airway to the room was blocked, so it got very hot.
房間的通風道阻塞了，所以裡面變得很熱。

---

aisle [aɪl] *n.* 走道；通道

同 **corridor; walkway**

▶ The bride walked down the aisle to the front of the church.
新娘沿著走道走到了教堂的前方。

---

alcoholic [ˌæl.kəˈhɑː.lɪk]

① *adj.* 含酒精的

同 **inebriate**

反 **nonalcoholic**

② *n.* 酗酒者；酒鬼

同 **drunkard; tippler**

▶ Please do not bring alcoholic drinks into the theater.
請不要把含酒精飲料帶到電影院裡。

▶ She became an alcoholic after the divorce.
她離婚後變成酗酒者。

---

algebra [ˈæl.dʒə.brə] *n.* 代數學

▶ Tony likes math and got a good grade in algebra.
湯尼喜歡數學，而且代數考得很高分。

---

alien [ˈeɪ.li.ən]

① *adj.* 外國的；外國僑民的

同 **foreign**

反 **national**

▶ Anna was an alien resident of Japan for two years.
安娜以外國居民身分在日本住了兩年。

② *n.* 外國人；僑民；外星人

同 **foreigner; stranger**

▶ Albert was an alien in America before getting his green card.
亞伯特拿到綠卡前，以外國人身份住在美國。

alienate [ˈeɪ.li.ə.neɪt] *v.* 使疏遠

同 **disaffect; estrange**

▶ That terrible experience alienated her from the rest of the group.
那個可怕的經驗使她和團體中的其他人疏遠了。

97

allergic [əˈlɝː.dʒɪk] *adj.* 過敏的

同 **hypersensitive; supersensitive**

▶ She had an allergic reaction to the bee sting.
她對蜂螫起了過敏反應。

allergy [ˈæl.ɚ.dʒi] *n.* 過敏症

同 **allergic; reaction**

▶ Her allergy to cats caused her to sneeze.
因為她對貓過敏，所以打了噴嚏。

alliance [əˈlaɪ.əns] *n.* 聯盟；結盟

同 **league; union**

▶ The two political parties formed an alliance and worked together.
那兩個政黨組成聯盟，攜手合作。

alligator [ˈæl.ə.geɪ.t̬ɚ] *n.* 短吻鱷魚

同 **gator**

▶ This swamp is filled with alligators.
沼澤裡滿是鱷魚。

allocate [ˈæl.ə.keɪt] *v.* 分配；分派

同 **distribute; assign**

▶ The mother allocated the same amount of food to each child.
媽媽分配給每個孩子等量的食物。

ally [ˈæl.aɪ]

① *n.* 結盟者；同盟者

反 **enemy; rival**

② *v.* 使結盟

同 **unite**

反 **divide**

▶ The two countries were allies during the war.
這兩個國家在戰爭期間是結盟國。

▶ He allied himself with Mark, and they became a team.
他和馬克結盟，組成了一隊。

alongside [əˈlɑːŋ.saɪd]

① *adv.* 在旁邊；沿著

同 **along**

反 **aboard**

▶ He parked alongside the building.
他把車停在那棟建築旁邊。

② *prep.* 在…旁邊；沿著…的邊

▶ The house stood alongside the river.
那棟屋子矗立在河邊。

---

alter [ˈɑːl.tɚ] *v.* 改變；修改

同 **vary; modify**

▶ We altered our plans because of the rain.
因為下雨，所以我們改變了計畫。

Exercise 3

I. Choices

1. Mike has been becoming a(an) ________ for going on a vegan diet since he was 20 because he strongly believes that eating non-dairy products and no meat will prevent heart disease and stroke.
   (A) advertiser (B) agenda (C) advocate (D) alliance

2. Some companies will build a collaborative ________ in order to broaden greater business and create a mutually beneficial bond in the new partnership.
   (A) alliance (B) affection (C) allocation (D) alignment

3. Evan's irrational behaviors gradually ________ our respect and trust from him and it seems like no one wants to be friends with him.
   (A) avoid (B) align (C) alleviate (D) alienate

4. Gina and Brian exchanged their wedding vows that they would stay faithful to walk ________ one another through the difficult and the easy, in sickness and in health, until parted by death.
   (A) below (B) between (C) alongside (D) alone

5. After Serena and Ronald got married, they purchased a fancy apartment, which included an ________ parking space below the building.
   (A) accepted (B) allocated (C) alternative (D) applicable

II. Derivatives

1. Marsha knew that she would like to spend the rest of her life with Nick when Nick smiled ____________ (affection) at her upon first sight.
2. Vincent was told to consider psychotherapy because people found that he has expressed his ____________ (aggress) by taking cocaine.
3. Scott has been preparing for the college-entrance exam for a long time and he is determined to study ____________ (agriculture) engineering in National Taiwan University.
4. The law required people to show ID when purchasing ____________ (alcohol) beverages in the United States.
5. Monica had a severe ____________ (allergy) reaction to nuts once before to a level so extreme that she could barely breathe and fainted on the ground.

Unit 4

alternate [ˈɑːl.tɚ.neɪt] *v.* 使輪流；交替

同 **take turns; switch**

反 **conserve; preserve**

▶ The two players alternated hitting the ball.

這兩名球員輪流擊球。

alternate [ˈɑːl.tɝː.nət]

① *adj.* 交替；輪流的

反 **consecutive**

② *n.* 候補者；代理人

同 **interchange; substitute**

▶ Maria loves desserts with alternate layers of strawberries and cream.

瑪利亞喜愛草莓和奶油層層交疊的甜點。

▶ Mike got hurt, so an alternate played for him.

麥克受了傷，因此有個候補代替他出賽。

---

100 97

alternative [ɑːlˈtɝː.nə.t̬ɪv]

① *adj.* 二選一的；另類的

實用片語與搭配詞

provide / offer an alternative

提供替代性方案

② *n.* 選擇；可供選擇的事物

同 **choice; option**

▶ Due to heavy traffic, I took an alternative route.

由於這裡交通壅塞，所以我決定走另一條路。

▶ If you cannot accept this agreement, you need to provide an alternative solution.

如果你無法接受這個協議，你必須提供替代的解決方案。

▶ I found myself with no alternative but to make this choice.

我發現自己沒有任何其他選項可言，只能做出這個選擇。

---

altitude [ˈæl.tə.tuːd] *n.* 海拔；高度

同 **elevation; height**

▶ Skiing at high altitudes can be tiring.

在高海拔滑雪可能會令人疲倦。

103

ambiguity [ˌæm.bɪˈgjuː.ə.t̬i] *n.* 意義不明確

反 **crystal clear**

▶ There was some ambiguity whether the flight would arrive on time.

究竟班機會不會準時抵達，仍不清楚。

---

ambiguous [æmˈbɪg.ju.əs] *adj.* 含糊不清的

同 **vague**

反 **definite**

▶ He gave me an ambiguous answer for his return.

有關他回來的情況，他只給了我含糊不清的答案。

ambulance [ˈæm.bjə.ləns] *n.* 救護車

實用片語與搭配詞

phone / ring / telephone for an ambulance 叫救護車

▶ The ambulance arrived shortly after the accident.
事故發生之後不久，救護車就開來了。

▶ This man is having a heart attack. Could someone please phone for an ambulance?
這個男人心臟病發作了。誰能誰打電話叫救護車嗎？

---

ambush [ˈæm.bʊʃ]

① *n.* 伏擊；埋伏突襲

同 **trap**

實用片語與搭配詞

set up / lay / prepare / an ambush 設下埋伏

② *v.* 埋伏突襲；伏擊

實用片語與搭配詞

ambush on 伏擊…

▶ The police set an ambush to catch him.
警方設下伏擊想要捉拿他。

▶ Police set up an ambush for the drug dealer and caught him red-handed.
警方埋伏突擊那位毒販，並且當場將其逮捕。

▶ The lion ambushed the animal from behind a tree.
獅子躲在樹後方埋伏突擊那隻動物。

▶ There was an ambush on the soldiers, but they escaped unharmed.
那些士兵們在一次突擊行動中毫髮無傷地脫逃了。

---

amiable [ˈeɪ.mi.ə.bəl] *adj.* 親切的；和藹的

反 **detestable**

▶ Mom became quite amiable after resting.
媽媽休息過後就變得相當和藹可親。

---

ample [ˈæm.pəl] *adj.* 充裕的；足夠的

同 **abundant; sufficient**

實用片語與搭配詞

ample time 足夠的時間

▶ There is ample room for everyone.
每個人都有充裕的空間。

▶ The entrance exam will take place next year, so there is ample time for me to study.
入學考試將在明年舉行，所以我還有充裕的時間讀書。

104

amplify [ˈæm.plə.faɪ] *v.* 擴大；放大

同 **exaggerate; magnify**

實用片語與搭配詞

amplify the sound / electric current / signal 增強聲音 / 電流 / 信號

▶ Use the speaker to amplify the guitar.
用喇叭來擴大吉他的樂音。

▶ We need bigger speakers to amplify the computers' sound during the conference.
在會議中，我們需要更大的喇叭來擴大電腦上的音訊。

analects [ˌænəˈlɛkts] *n.* 文選

▶ Many students read analects from Shakespeare in school.
在學校裡，很多學生都會讀莎士比亞文選。

---

analogy [əˈnæl.ə.dʒi] *n.* 類推；類比；比擬

實用片語與搭配詞
draw / make / use an analogy 打比方

▶ The teacher used an analogy to help the students understand.
老師用類推的方式來協助學生理解。

▶ Use an analogy to explain difficult concepts so that people can understand better.
不妨使用類推的方法來解釋困難的概念，如此人們比較容易理解。

---

analyst [ˈæn.ə.lɪst] *n.* 分析者

實用片語與搭配詞
a leading analyst 一流的分析師

▶ He likes studying data because he is an analyst.
他喜歡研究資料，因為他是分析師。

▶ That Harvard professor is a leading analyst on investment; you can trust him.
那位哈佛教授是一個頂尖的投資分析家；你可以信任他。

---

analytical [ˌæn.əˈlɪṭ.ɪ.kəl] *adj.* 分析的

同 **analytic**

▶ There are many analytical jobs that use numbers.
有很多要運用數字的分析職務。

---

anchor [ˈæŋ.kɚ]

① *n.* 錨

實用片語與搭配詞
cast / drop anchor off... 在…拋錨

② *v.* 停泊

同 **fasten; attach**

▶ The captain dropped the ship's anchor.
船長放下了船錨。

▶ After sailing for days, we dropped anchor near a nice village.
經過幾日的航行，我們在一個不錯的村莊附近拋錨停船。

▶ He anchored the ship.
他下錨停船。

---

anecdote [ˈæn.ɪk.doʊt] *n.* 趣聞；軼事

同 **story; tale**

實用片語與搭配詞
tell an anecdote
說故事

▶ Please give us an anecdote from your trip.
請告訴我們，你這次旅行所發生的趣事。

▶ When doing a presentation, tell an anecdote; people like to hear true-life stories.
在進行簡報時，不妨講段趣聞；人們喜歡聽真實故事。

animate [ˈæn.ə.mət] *adj.* 有生命的

同 **alive**

反 **lifeless**

▶ All animate creatures need food to eat.
所有有生命的生物都需要進食。

---

animate [ˈæn.ə.meɪt]

v. 使生氣勃勃；使有活力；賦予生命

反 **depress**

實用片語與搭配詞

animate sb. to 激勵某人做某事

▶ The fresh air animated him, and he was able to continue.
新鮮空氣使他生氣勃勃，所以他就能繼續進行了。

▶ To animate Trudy to get involved in charity, we went to see a Feed the World exhibition.
為了驅使特魯迪參與慈善活動，我們參觀了Feed the World的展覽。

---

annoyance [əˈnɔɪ.əns]

n. 討厭的事物；煩惱；惱怒

同 **irritation**

實用片語與搭配詞

show one's annoyance 表達某人的不滿

▶ Wearing wet socks is a terrible annoyance.
穿著溼襪子是很討厭的事。

▶ Chinese consumer showed their annoyance over a French insult by boycotting French luxury goods' stores.
中國的消費者藉著抵制法國精品商店，對法國的屈辱表達惱怒之情。

---

anonymous [əˈnɑː.nə.məs] *adj.* 匿名的

同 **nameless; unidentified**

實用片語與搭配詞

prefer / wish to remain anonymous
希望保持匿名的狀態

▶ She wondered who gave her the anonymous gift.
她想知道究竟是誰匿名送她禮物。

▶ People who give money to politicians in return for favors wish to remain anonymous.
那些以政治獻金回報政客幫助的人們希望繼續保持匿名。

---

antarctic [ænˈtɑːrk.tɪk] *adj.* 南極的

反 **arctic**

▶ The antarctic winds caused the weather to become cold.
來自南極的風導致氣候變冷了。

Antarctica [ænˈtɑːrk.tɪ.kə] *n.* 南極洲

▶ Antarctica is a very cold continent.
南極洲是酷寒的大洲。

---

antenna [ænˈten.ə] *n.* 天線；觸角

同 **aerial**

▶ Please fix the antenna so we can listen to the radio.
請幫忙修天線，好讓我們能聽收音機。

anthem [ˈæn.θəm] *n.* 聖歌；讚美詩

同 **hymn**

▶ The church choir sang their anthem.
教會詩班吟唱聖歌。

---

antibiotic [ˌæn.t̬i.baɪˈɑː.t̬ɪk]

① *n.* 抗生素

實用片語與搭配詞

put sb. on / give sb. / prescribe antibiotics 吩咐採用抗生素療法

② *adj.* 抗生素的

▶ The doctor gave her antibiotics for the infection.
醫師給她開了抗生素來治療感染。

▶ Don't put children on antibiotics to treat a simple cold; they will develop resistance.
不要用抗生素治療孩童們的小感冒；他們自己會產生抵抗力。

▶ Use antibiotic cream on that cut.
用抗生素藥膏來塗抹在割傷的部位。

---

antibody [ˈæn.t̬iˌbɑː.di] *n.* 抗體

▶ Antibodies protect our bodies from illnesses.
抗生素能保護人體對抗疾病。

Exercise 4

I. Derivatives

1. She will get back to you later to discuss more about it if there is another ___________ (alternate) option for this customized case.
2. Students are taught to undertake an ___________ (analyze) survey with a certain project management tool for this class.
3. Life of Pi is one of the popular novels, which has been shelved as a book ending on an ___________ (ambiguity) note on Goodreads.
4. You are allowed to remain ___________ (anonym) to leave a comment in this forum if you prefer to.
5. It increasingly becomes an ___________ (annoy) to me when he complains about almost everything over our dinner.

II. Vocabulary Choices

(A) ambush	(B) anecdote	(C) animate	(D) ample
(E) amiable	(F) amplify	(G) analogy	(H) apology
(I) altitude	(J) attitude		

1. Ken is such an interesting person that he always has some personal ________ s to entertain people around him.
2. She has spent over 20 years studying how to ________ positive feelings and to increase happiness.
3. The devastating news of a young student getting ________ ed by a gunman on campus has become the headline on the press today.
4. Even though Anita passed away, her radiant smile is always there to ________ us and to bless us.
5. My first impression of Amy is that she has an ________ personality and is very friendly to everyone.

Unit 5

anticipate [æn'tɪs.ə.peɪt] *v.* 預期；期望

同 **expect; foresee**

▶ Anticipate a cake at any birthday party.
任何慶生會都可以期待一定會看到蛋糕。

---

anticipation [æn͵tɪs.ə'peɪ.ʃən]

n. 預期；期望

同 **expectation; prevision**

▶ He was full of excited anticipation for the vacation.
他對度假充滿了興奮的期待。

---

antique [æn'ti:k]

① *n.* 古董

實用片語與搭配詞

collect antiques 收藏古董

② *adj.* 古董的；陳舊的

同 **ancient; archaic**

反 **modern**

▶ This table is considered an antique.
這張桌子被視為古董。

▶ I collect antiques, but it is expensive because the older something is, the more it costs.
我收集古董，但這所費不貲，因為物品的年代越久遠，其要價越高。

▶ The antique car was built in 1920.
這輛古董車製造於一九二〇年。

---

antonym ['æn.tən.ɪm] *n.* 反義字

反 **synonym**

▶ The word "sad" is the antonym of the word "happy".
「悲傷」一詞是「快樂」這個詞的反義字。

---

applaud [ə'plɑ:d] *v.* 向…鼓掌；向…喝采

同 **approve; clap**

▶ The crowd applauded for five minutes when the singer finished.
歌手演唱完後，觀眾鼓掌了五分鐘。

99

applause [ə'plɑ:z] *n.* 鼓掌；喝采

同 **clapping**

實用片語與搭配詞

break / burst into applause
迸出掌聲

▶ The audience gave great applause to the winning team.
觀眾對勝利隊伍報以熱烈掌聲。

▶ Following Adele's performance at the national theatre, the audience burst into applause.
在國家戲劇院欣賞愛黛兒演出的觀眾們爆出了掌聲。

---

applicable [ə'plɪk.ə.bəl]

adj. 可應用的；適用的

同 **applicative; appropriate**

▶ His outdoor experience became quite applicable during the camping trip.
他的戶外活動經驗剛好能充分應用在這次露營之旅中。

apprentice [ə'pren.t̬ɪs]

① *n.* 見習生；學徒

同 **trainee; beginner learner**

實用片語與搭配詞

work as an apprentice 給某人當學徒

② *v.* 當學徒

► He is learning a lot as an apprentice at this company.
他在公司擔任見習生學到了很多。

► Nursing students must work as apprentices in a hospital for six months before graduation.
護校學生在畢業前必須在醫院擔任長達六個月的實習護理人員。

► Is she going to apprentice at a company after graduating?
她畢業之後會不會在企業當見習生？

---

approximate [ə'prɑ:k.sə.mət]

adj. 大約的；近似的

同 **close; roughly**

► What is the approximate cost of owning a car?
買一部車大約要花多少錢？

approximate [ə'prɑ:k.sə.meɪt]

v. 粗估；大致估計

同 **estimate; approach**

實用片語與搭配詞

approximate to sth. 與某事物幾乎相同

► Please approximate the number of people that will attend.
請粗估一下參加的人數。

► The flight time from Taipei to Beijing is approximate to that of Taipei to Tokyo.
從台北到北京的飛行時間幾乎等同從台北到東京。

---

apt [æpt] *adj.* 恰當的；易於…的；貼切的

同 **appropriate; suitable**

實用片語與搭配詞

apt at doing sth. 學得快的；善於做某事

► She gave an apt response to his question.
針對他的問題，她給了恰當的回答。

► Mary is quite apt at designing websites, so if you need help, just give her a call.
瑪莉相當會設計網站，所以如果你需要協助可以打電話給她。

---

aptitude ['æp.tə.tu:d]

n. 天賦；資質；傾向

同 **talent; gift**

實用片語與搭配詞

have / display / show an aptitude for sth. 有做某事的天分

► She impressed her teacher with her aptitude to play instruments.
她彈奏樂器的天分讓老師印象深刻。

► He has shown an aptitude for music since he was three years old.
他自從三歲起便展現了音樂上的才能。

architect ['ɑ:r.kə.tekt] *n.* 建築師；設計師

同 **designer; draftsman**

▶ The architect designed the building.
那位建築師設計了這座建築物。

97

architecture ['ɑ:r.kə.tek.tʃɚ] *n.* 建築（學）

同 **building / structure construction**

▶ Teri studied architecture in college.
泰瑞在大學攻讀建築學。

Arctic / arctic ['ɑ:rk.tɪk]

① *adj.* （大寫）北極的
（小寫）嚴寒的；酷寒的

反 **antarctic**

② *n.* （大寫）北極 /（小寫）禦寒防水套鞋

反 **antarctic**

▶ The ship could endure arctic conditions.
那艘船可以耐受酷寒的天候狀況。

▶ He planned an expedition to the Arctic.
他計畫到北極探險。

---

arena [ə'ri:.nə] *n.* 體育館；競技場

同 **field; sports stadium**

▶ The rock concert was held at the arena.
那場搖滾演唱會在體育館舉行。

---

armor ['ɑ:r.mɚ]

① *n.* 盔甲

實用片語與搭配詞

put on / take off an armor
穿戴 / 脫去盔甲

② *v.* 為…提供防禦；為…穿盔甲

同 **armour**

▶ The knight wore armor into battle.
那名騎士穿戴盔甲上戰場。

▶ When people get hurt by love, they will put on armor to prevent being hurt again.
當人們在愛情裡受傷，他們會披上盔甲，防止再度被傷害。

▶ He armored himself with a shield.
他用盾牌自我防禦。

103

arrogant ['er.ə.gənt]

adj. 傲慢的；自大的

同 **insolent**

反 **modest**

▶ She was very talented but also very arrogant.
她資賦優異，卻也相當傲慢。

artery [ˈɑːr.t̬ɚ.i] *n.* 動脈

同 **blood vessel**

反 **vein**

▶ The nurse put the needle into the artery.
護士把針頭刺入動脈中。

---

articulate [ɑːrˈtɪk.jə.lət]

adj. 能表達清楚的；有口才的；能言善道的

反 **inarticulate**

▶ Everyone agreed the speaker was very articulate about this issue.
大家都一致同意，演講者把這個議題闡述得淋漓盡致。

articulate [ɑːrˈtɪk.jə.leɪt]

v. 清楚地表達；清晰地發音

實用片語與搭配詞

articulate the words carefully
仔細說清楚

▶ She couldn't articulate how she felt about him.
她難以清楚表達出對他的感覺。

▶ When talking to your angry husband, you better articulate what you want to say very carefully.
在跟你盛怒的丈夫說話時，你最好非常小心地把你想說的話明確地表達出來。

---

artifact [ˈɑːr.t̬ə.fækt] *n.* 人工製品；手工藝品

同 **work of art**

▶ There are many old artifacts at the museum.
博物館裡有很多歷史悠久的手工藝品。

---

ascend [əˈsend] *v.* 上升

同 **rise**

反 **descend**

實用片語與搭配詞

ascend steeply 陡峭的上升

▶ The balloon ascended into the sky.
氣球上升到空中。

▶ The road up the mountain is narrow and ascends steeply towards the top, so be careful.
這條通往山頂的路很狹窄，並且坡度上升幅度極陡，所以務必要小心。

---

ass [æs] *n.* 驢子

同 **donkey; mule**

▶ We rode an ass through the valley.
我們騎一隻驢子穿過了山谷。

---

assassinate [əˈsæs.ə.neɪt] *v.* 行刺；暗殺

同 **kill; murder**

實用片語與搭配詞

attempt / try / plan / plot to assassinate
企圖 / 密謀暗殺 / 行刺

▶ Many guards protect the leader so no one can assassinate him.
有好多保鏢保衛著領袖，以免他遭人暗殺。

▶ The shooter who plotted to assassinate the president was sent to jail for life.
這位密謀暗殺總統的槍手被終身監禁。

assault [ə'sɑːlt]

① *n.* 攻擊；抨擊

同 **attack; offense**

② *v.* 攻擊；譴責

同 **attack; offense**

▶ The violent assault shocked everyone on campus.
這起暴力攻擊震驚全校。

▶ The burglar assaulted the couple after entering their home.
竊賊進入屋內後，攻擊了這對夫妻。

---

assert [ə'sɝːt] *v.* 主張；堅持；斷言

同 **declare; insist on**

實用片語與搭配詞

assert her innocence 堅稱自己的清白

▶ Dad asserted his reasons why I should study harder.
爸爸說出了他主張我應該更用功讀書的理由。

▶ In order to assert her innocence in the murder case, the girl provided a very good alibi.
為了主張自己在這起謀殺案中的清白，這位女孩提供了極佳的不在場證明。

Exercise 5

I. Choices

1. Alisha demonstrated a remarkable and early ________ at her age of 16 for computer science.
   (A) attitude (B) aptitude (C) altitude (D) gratitude
2. Stacey told me that she was stuck in traffic but her ________ time of arrival would be roughly around 6 o'clock.
   (A) appealing (B) appropriate (C) approaching (D) approximate
3. Max was too terrified to ________ what has been hanging over his head for several months.
   (A) activate (B) anticipate (C) articulate (D) alienate
4. 13 February 2017, Kim Jong Nam, the half-brother of the North Korean leader, was reportedly ________ and poisoned by two women at Kuala Lumpur airport in Malaysia.
   (A) assembled (B) asserted (C) associated (D) assassinated
5. During the Lantern Festival, hundreds and thousands of tourists come to Pingxi to write down all the wishes for the new year and make sky lanterns ________ into the sky.
   (A) accede (B) ascend (C) access (D) accent

I. Derivatives

1. Henry stood up to ____________ (assertion) himself that he was completely innocent.
2. Spain is well-known worldwide for its ____________ (architecture) and Gaudí is one of the leading ones.
3. My parents ____________ (applause) the achievement that I have received an award for.
4. The sense of ____________ (anticipate) was slightly shown on her face when she was told that she would be going on a business trip to New York.
5. This rule now doesn't seem equally ____________ (application) to all the employees in this case.

Unit 6

assess [ə'ses] *v.* 估價；估計；評估

同 **evaluate; measure**

實用片語與搭配詞

attempt / try to 嘗試評估

▸ The mechanic assessed the damage would cost $300 to fix.
技師估價受損部份要花三百美元來修理。

▸ Mary attempted to become a dentist, but failed because she could not stand the sight of blood.
瑪莉試圖成為牙醫，但是因為害怕見血而失敗。

---

assessment [ə'ses.mənt]

n. 評估；估價；估計

同 **appraisal; judgment**

▸ The doctors discussed their assessment of her health problems.
醫生們一起討論他們對她健康問題的評估。

---

asset ['æs.et]

n. 有用的人；財產；資產

同 **capital; property**

▸ Ellen is a valuable asset to the company.
艾倫是公司的寶貴人才。

---

assumption [ə'sʌmp.ʃən]

n. 設想；假定

同 **supposition**

反 **conclusion**

▸ She was aware of her parents' assumption that she would get married.
她知道她的爸媽假定她會結婚。

---

asthma ['æz.mə] *n.* 氣喘

▸ He can't do some types of exercise due to his asthma.
他因為罹患氣喘的關係，而不能做某些類型的運動。

---

astonish [ə'stɑ:.nɪʃ] *v.* 使…吃驚；驚訝

同 **astound; surprise**

實用片語與搭配詞

look astonished
顯得很吃驚

▸ My parents were astonished by the prices in Japan.
我父母對日本的物價驚訝不已。

▸ After learning that he won the national lottery, Paul looks astonished.
在得知自己贏得國營彩券後，保羅看上去很吃驚。

astonishment [ə'stɑː.nɪʃ.mənt] *n.* 驚訝

反 **ease relief**

▸ He had a look of astonishment on his face after I spoke Chinese to him.
我跟他說了中文後，他一臉驚訝。

---

astray [ə'streɪ] *adv.* 離開正道地；迷路地

同 **wide**

▸ The balloon went astray, and we chased it through the park.
氣球飛走了，我們穿過公園一路追逐。

---

astronaut ['æs.trə.nɑːt] *n.* 太空人

同 **cosmonaut; spaceman**

▸ The astronauts rocketed into space.
這些太空人迅速登入太空中。

---

astronomer [ə'strɑː.nə.mɚ] *n.* 天文學家

同 **stargazer**

▸ A team of astronomers is studying how stars are formed.
一群天文學家正在研究星星是如何形成的。

---

astronomy [ə'strɑː.nə.mi] *n.* 天文學

▸ She went to Harvard to study astronomy.
她上哈佛大學讀天文學。

---

asylum [ə'saɪ.ləm] *n.* 政治庇護；收容所

同 **refuge; shelter**

▸ The refugees received asylum upon entering the country.
那名難民在進入該國時，獲得了政治庇護。

---

attain [ə'teɪn] *v.* 獲得；達成；實現

同 **achieve**

反 **fail**

實用片語與搭配詞

attain one's goal / objective / ambition 實現目標

▸ He asked his teacher first to attain permission.
他先問了老師以獲得允許。

▸ If you want to attain your goals in life, you have to work hard. Nothing is for free.
如果想要達到人生目標，你就必須努力工作。天下沒有白吃的午餐。

---

attainment [ə'teɪn.mənt]

n. 獲得；贏得；實現

同 **accomplishment**

反 **failure**

▸ Her parents congratulated her for her attainment of a good job.
她爸媽都對她獲得了好工作而恭喜她。

---

attendance [ə'ten.dəns] *n.* 出席

反 **absence**

▸ Attendance in this class is required.
這堂課要求出席率。

98

attendant [əˈten.dənt]

① *n.* 服務員；隨從

同 **attendee**

② *adj.* 在場的；隨行的

同 **accompanying; incidental**

▸ Ask an attendant for any needs.
若有任何需要，可以詢問服務員。

▸ The attendant students were informed about the upcoming test.
在場的學生都被告知即將會有考試。

---

attic [ˈæt̬.ɪk] *n.* 閣樓

▸ Mom put most of Dad's old clothes in the attic.
媽媽把爸爸的舊衣服存放在閣樓裡。

---

auction [ˈɑːk.ʃən]

① *n.* 拍賣

同 **sale**

② *v.* 拍賣

同 **sell**

實用片語與搭配詞

put sth. up for auction 把某物拍賣

▸ Many expensive paintings are sold at an auction.
很多昂貴的畫作都在一場拍賣會中售出了。

▸ The family decided to auction off most things from the home.
那家人決定把家裡大多數物品都拍賣掉。

▸ When the company went bankrupt, everything it owned was put up for auction to pay its debts.
當這間公司破產時，它所擁有的全數物品被交付拍賣以付清它的債款。

---

audible [ˈɑː.də.bəl] *adj.* 聽得見的

反 **inaudible**

▸ The man's voice was barely audible from across the busy street.
從車水馬龍的街道對面，幾乎聽不見那名男子的聲音。

---

auditorium [ˌɑː.dəˈtɔːr.i.əm] *n.* 禮堂；觀眾席

同 **hall**

▸ The lecture was held in the auditorium.
那場演講是在禮堂舉行的。

103

authentic [ɑːˈθen.t̬ɪk]

adj. 道地的；正宗的；真品的

同 **genuine**

反 **spurious**

▸ They ate authentic sushi in Tokyo.
他們在東京嚐到了道地的壽司。

authorize [ˈɑː.θɚ.aɪz] *v.* 批准；准許；授權

同 **assign**

反 **forbid**

實用片語與搭配詞

authorize sb. for sth. to do sth.
為了什麼目的授權某人做某事

▶ Only the boss can authorize vacation leave.
只有老闆有權批准員工休假去度假。

▶ My boss was not able to attend the meeting, so he authorized me to take his place.
我的老闆無法參加會議，所以他委託我代表他出席。

---

autograph [ˈɑː.t̬ə.græf]

① *n.* 親筆簽名

同 **endorse; sign**

實用片語與搭配詞

sign one's autograph for sb.
為某人簽名留念

② *v.* 親筆簽名

同 **endorse; sign**

▶ Many asked the celebrity for an autograph.
很多人都問那位名人要親筆簽名。

▶ The movie star signed his autograph for his fans for three hours.
這位電影明星幫他的影迷們簽名簽了三小時。

▶ The baseball player autographed things for the fans.
棒球選手為粉絲簽名在物品上。

---

autonomy [ɑːˈtɑː.nə.mi]

n. 自主（權）；自治（權）

同 **self-reliance; self-sufficiency**

▶ He did what he wanted with his new found autonomy.
他擁有了全新的自主權，就得以隨心所欲。

---

auxiliary [ɑːgˈzɪl.i.er.i] *n.* 輔助者；助手

同 **assistant**

▶ The school auxiliary served as a support to the teachers.
學校的輔助人員是老師的後援。

Exercise 6

I. Choices

1. I got a strong feeling of nostalgia for the ________ Chinese food that this restaurant served when I spent my college life in New York.
   (A) authoritative (B) authentic (C) fictitious (D) synthetic
2. In a healthy and strong relationship or marriage, couples would have to learn how to balance the need of ________ and intimacy.
   (A) anatomy (B) autograph (C) autonomy (D) authority
3. You can make a huge difference for our healthcare community by applying volunteer and ________ services in this hospital.
   (A) auxiliary (B) anticipate (C) necessary (D) obligatory
4. My supervisor has ________ d me to sign the contract on his behalf during his leave of absence.
   (A) accessorize (B) promise (C) authorize (D) categorize
5. His sigh of relief is clearly ________ over the disturbing noise of renovations above.
   (A) workable (B) accessible (C) attachable (D) audible

II. Derivatives

1. Some studies show that parental participation and family structure have a significant impact on a student's educational ___________ (attain).
2. A group of tourists stood gazing at the enchanting scenery in ___________ (astonish).
3. I don't think you can make this ___________ (assume) underlying your feelings- things are not black and white.
4. Once you have enrolled in this class, please keep in mind that full-time ___________ (attend) is required.
5. No detailed ___________ (assess) of costs has been made but yet the court will have it to be carried out as soon as possible.

Unit 7

aviation [ˌeɪ.viˈeɪ.ʃən] *n.* 飛行；航空（業）

同 **air travel; airmanship**

▶ She has always been interested in aviation. That's why she became a pilot.

她一直對飛行相當感興趣，那就是她之所以成為飛行員的原因。

---

awe [ɑː]

① *n.* 敬畏

同 **respect**

反 **scorn**

② *v.* 使敬佩；使敬畏

實用片語與搭配詞

be awed into silence 嚇得說不出話來

▶ We stood in awe at the top of the Grand Canyon.

我們滿懷敬畏地站在大峽谷的最高處。

▶ John was awed by his sister's singing ability.

約翰的姊妹的歌唱功力令他感到相當敬佩。

▶ The crowd was awed into silence when Adele started singing in her deep, powerful voice.

當愛黛兒以她低沈渾厚的嗓音開唱時，群眾們屏氣凝神地嘆服著。

---

awesome [ˈɑː.səm]

adj. 令人讚嘆的；令人敬畏的；極好的

同 **amazing**

▶ They saw an awesome sunset from the beach.

他們在海灘看到了令人讚嘆的日落景象。

---

awhile [əˈwaɪl] *adv.* 一會兒；片刻

反 **forever**

▶ He waited awhile for the doctor to see him.

他等醫生看病等了一會兒。

---

bachelor [ˈbætʃ.əl.ɚ] *n.* 單身漢

反 **married man**

▶ Trey is a bachelor and has no plans to get married.

崔伊是個單身漢，而且沒有打算結婚。

---

backbone [ˈbæk.boʊn] *n.* 脊椎骨

同 **spinal; spine**

▶ She injured her backbone in the bike accident.

她在那起自行車事故中傷到了脊椎骨。

---

badge [bædʒ] *n.* 徽章；獎章

▶ The police officer showed us his badge to prove his identity.

這名員警給我們看他的警徽來證明他的身份。

ballot [ˈbæl.ət]

① *n.* 選票

同 **poll vote**

② *v.* 投票表決

同 **poll vote**

實用片語與搭配詞

put it to / carry out / hold / organize / cast a ballot 舉行投票

▶ We counted all the ballots after the election.
選舉後，我們計算了所有的選票。

▶ The citizens will ballot next Tuesday and choose a new mayor.
市民將在下星期二投票選出新市長。

▶ If you don't cast your ballot during an election, you have no right to complain afterwards.
如果你不在選舉期間投下你的一票，你事後就沒有權利抱怨。

---

ban [bæn]

① *v.* 禁止

同 **forbid**

反 **permit**

實用片語與搭配詞

call for / demand a ban 要求禁止

② *n.* 禁止；禁令

反 **approval; permission**

▶ The city banned smoking in all parks.
這個城市禁止在所有公園內吸菸。

▶ Following the oil spill in the Atlantic Ocean, people demanded a ban on oil exploration there.
民眾密切關注著大西洋的漏油事件，要求禁止在該地進行石油勘探。

▶ The priest was given a lifetime ban by the church.
教會對這名神父下了終生禁令。

---

bandit [ˈbæn.dɪt] *n.* 強盜；土匪

同 **gangster; robber**

▶ The bandits robbed everyone on the train.
強盜洗劫了火車上的所有人。

---

banner [ˈbæn.ɚ] *n.* 旗幟；橫幅廣告

同 **streamer**

▶ The soldiers carried the banner into battle.
士兵們舉著旗幟上了戰場。

---

banquet [ˈbæŋ.kwət]

① *n.* 宴會；盛宴

同 **feast**

② *v.* 參加宴會；宴請

同 **affair feast**

實用片語與搭配詞

attend a banquet 參加宴會

▶ Two hundred guests attended the wedding banquet.
兩百名賓客參加了這場婚宴。

▶ The family banqueted to celebrate their son's wedding.
這家人設宴慶祝兒子結婚。

▶ I can't go camping this weekend; I have to attend my best friend's wedding banquet.
本週末我無法去露營；我必須參加我摯友的婚宴。

B

barbarian [bɑːrˈber.i.ən]

① *n.* 野蠻人

同 **primitive; savage**

② *adj.* 野蠻的

同 **primitive**

反 **civilized**

▶ The barbarians raided the village.
野蠻人襲擊了村莊。

▶ His barbarian act shocked the people.
他野蠻的行徑令人震驚。

---

barbershop [ˈbɑːr.bɚ.ʃɑːp] *n.* 理髮店

▶ Curt got his hair cut at the barbershop.
科特在理髮店理了頭髮。

---

barefoot [ˈber.fʊt]

① *adj.* 赤足的

同 **shoeless**

② *adv.* 打赤腳地

實用片語與搭配詞

pad / walk barefoot 打赤腳走著

▶ The barefoot girl couldn't kick the ball very well.
這個赤腳女孩無法把球踢好。

▶ Alex walked barefoot on the beach.
艾力克斯打赤腳在沙灘上散步。

▶ Nothing beats walking barefoot on the beach with water rolling over your feet.
沒有事情比赤腳漫步在海水沖刷的沙灘上更美好的了。

---

barometer [bəˈrɑː.mə.t̬ɚ] *n.* 氣壓計

同 **indicator; gauge**

▶ The barometer will tell you if the weather is going to be nice.
氣壓計能讓人知道天氣是否會變好。

---

barren [ˈber.ən] *adj.* 不生育的

同 **unfertile**

反 **fertile**

▶ The barren woman prayed to God to give her a child.
這個不孕婦女向上帝祈求賜給她一個孩子。

---

bass [beɪs]

① *n.* 鱸魚；男低音

反 **alto tenor**

② *adj.* 低沉的

反 **alto tenor**

▶ We went fishing for bass in the lake.
我們去湖邊釣鱸魚。

▶ He plays bass guitar in the band.
他在樂團裡彈低音吉他。

---

batch [bætʃ] *n.* 一批生產量

同 **flock; lot**

▶ Jean made a batch of cookies for the party.
珍為派對烤了一批餅乾。

batter [ˈbæt̬.ɚ]

① *v.* 重擊；連續猛擊；打碎

同 **beat; smash**

② *n.* 盤子上的缺損；（麵粉為底的）糊狀物

▶ The wind battered the boat against the dock.
風重重地吹擊停靠在船塢的船隻。

▶ The plate's batter could not be fixed.
這個盤子的缺損修不好。

---

bazaar [bəˈzɑːr] *n.* 市集

同 **fair**

▶ We went shopping for souvenirs at the bazaar.
我們去了市集買紀念品。

---

beautify [ˈbjuː.t̬ə.faɪ] *v.* 美化

同 **decorate; embellish**

▶ The new mayor pledged to beautify the city.
新市長承諾了要美化市容。

---

beckon [ˈbek.ən] *v.* 向…示意；召喚

同 **gesture; invite**

實用片語與搭配詞

beckon to one to do sth.
招手要某人做某事

▶ The mother beckoned her child to come back to her.
媽媽示意要孩子回到她身邊。

▶ The mother beckoned to her child to more away from the store.
這位母親示意她的孩子離開那家商店。

---

beforehand [bɪˈfɔːr.hænd] *adv.* 預先；事前

反 **afterward**

▶ Mary let me know beforehand that she was coming for the weekend.
瑪麗事先通知了我，說她週末要來。

---

behalf [bɪˈhæf] *n.* 利益；支持；代表

同 **benefit; welfare**

▶ We donated money to the orphanage for the children's behalf.
我們捐錢給這家孤兒院以嘉惠孩童。

Exercise 7

I. Choices

1. The U.S. government allows citizens who are residing outside the United States or unwilling to vote at polling stations to vote through absentee ________ s during an election period.
   (A) bullet (B) ballot (C) ballet (D) ballad
2. Samuel has decided to gain a ________ degree in business from the University of Pennsylvania.
   (A) program (B) curriculum (C) bachelor (D) bachelorette
3. I feel mindfully engaged in the present to walk ________ along a sandy beach.
   (A) barefoot (B) barely (C) beforehand (D) underfoot
4. You can receive a 30% discount off at this restaurant by simply showing your identification ________ at the time of purchase.
   (A) beverage (B) badge (C) barrage (D) baggage
5. Dianna has shown her ________ and perseverance in healing the traumas of her divorce.
   (A) backlash (B) background (C) backbone (D) backfire

II. Vocabulary Choices

(A) barren	(B) bazaar	(C) batter	(D) beckon
(E) awhile	(F) beforehand	(G) bandit	(H) batch
(I) behalf	(J) barbarian		

1. When you are ready for order in a restaurant, you can ________ the waiter to come over to the table.
2. A surreal and thriving oasis town, Huacachina, is amazingly located in a ________ desert in Peru.
3. He was lashing out by ________ ing on the wall with his fists.
4. I'm honored to speak on ________ of our director for she is unable to come today.
5. I think I need some headspace to process the whole new ________ problems that have been coming up in my life recently.

Unit 8

belongings [bɪˈlɑːŋ.ɪŋz]

n. 所有物；財產；攜帶物品

同 **property**

▸ When Jane moved to Australia, she took all her belongings.
珍搬到澳洲時，帶走了自己的所有財物。

---

beloved [bɪˈlʌvd]

① *adj.* 心愛的；親愛的

同 **cherished; dear**

② *n.* （稱呼語）心愛的人

同 **darling; dearest**

▸ She was sad to leave her beloved country.
離開她心愛的國家，她感到很悲傷。

▸ Tiffany kissed her beloved goodbye and boarded the train.
蒂芬妮吻別了她的愛人，登上了火車。

---

beneficial [ˌben.əˈfɪʃ.əl] *adj.* 有利的；有益的

同 **advantageous**

反 **fruitless**

▸ The agreement was beneficial to both parties.
這項協議對雙方都有利。

---

besiege [bɪˈsiːdʒ] *v.* 糾纏不休；圍攻

同 **assault**

反 **release**

實用片語與搭配詞

besiege sb. with sth.
以某事 / 物纏著某人使他應接不暇

▸ The news reporter besieged the speaker after his controversial statements.
演講者發表了爭議性的言論後，有個新聞記者就開始對他糾纏不休。

▸ John was besieged with guilt after his friend was injured in a car accident he caused.
約翰的朋友因一起他釀成的車禍而受傷後，約翰被罪惡感籠罩著。

---

betray [bɪˈtreɪ] *v.* 背叛；出賣

同 **be disloyal to**

反 **protect**

▸ Timmy's little sister betrayed him, telling their mom everything.
提米的小妹出賣了他，向媽媽全盤托出一切內情。

---

beverage [ˈbev.ɚ.ɪdʒ] *n.* 飲料

同 **drink**

▸ What beverage would you like to drink?
你想喝哪種飲料？

---

beware [bɪˈwer] *v.* 當心；小心

同 **look out; watch out**

▸ Beware of falling rocks in this area.
當心這個地區有落石。

B

bias ['baɪ.əs]

① *n.* 偏心；偏見

同 **partiality; prejudice**

② *v.* 存有偏見

同 **sway; lean**

實用片語與搭配詞

be biased in one's favor 偏向某人的

▶ The professor held a bias against students who were not science majors.
那名教授對於非主修理科的學生抱持偏見。

▶ She biased his decision by offering to buy dinner.
她提議付晚餐的錢，而影響了他的決定。

▶ The judge's decision was biased in the mother's favor, because she was a single parent.
法官偏頗的決策是有利於那位母親的，因為法官也是位單親媽媽。

---

bid [bɪd]

① *v.* 吩咐；出價

同 **ask; offer**

② *n.* 出價；投標

同 **ask; offer**

實用片語與搭配詞

bid against sb. 與某人競買 / 競標

▶ We bid on the item during the auction.
我們在拍賣會中對這項物品出了價。

▶ They made a bid to buy the house.
他們開了價買這棟房子。

▶ The rivals bid against each other for the painting at the auction.
在拍賣會上，出價者們為了那幅畫作與對手喊價競爭。

---

binoculars [bə'nɑː.kjə.lɚz]

n. 雙筒望遠鏡

同 **field glasses; opera glasses**

▶ Take a look at the bird through the binoculars.
用望遠鏡來看看那隻鳥。

---

biochemistry [ˌbaɪ.oʊ'kem.ɪ.stri]

n. 生物化學

▶ He studied biochemistry in graduate school.
他在研究所研修生物化學。

---

biological [ˌbaɪ.ə'lɑː.dʒɪ.kəl]

adj. 生理的；生物（學）的

同 **biologic**

▶ His illness was a biological problem, no matter what other reason he might believe.
無論他自以為病因出在哪裡，他的疾病都純屬生理上的問題。

---

bizarre [bə'zɑːr] *adj.* 奇異的；古怪的

同 **peculiar; weird**

▶ Why is there an elephant in the street? That's bizarre.
街上為什麼有隻大象？那真的很怪！

---

blacksmith ['blæk.smɪθ] *n.* 鐵匠

反 **whitesmith**

▶ The blacksmith made horseshoes out of iron.
鐵匠用鐵鑄造馬蹄鐵。

blast [blæst]

① *n.* 爆炸；疾風

同 **burst; explosion**

② *v.* 轟開；爆發出

同 **blowout; burst**

- The storm's blast caused our windows to rattle.
  暴風強勁的風勢吹得窗戶嘎嘎作響。
- The tornado blasted a hole in the roof.
  颶風在屋頂上轟開了一個洞。

---

blaze [bleɪz]

① *v.* 燃燒；閃耀

同 **flame; glow**

② *n.* 火焰；熊熊燃燒

同 **fire; flame**

實用片語與搭配詞

the blaze spread / sweep through sth. 火焰延燒到某物

- The fire blazed brightly.
  火光熊熊。
- The blaze from the fire could be seen for miles.
  大火的熊熊火焰可在數英里外就看見。
- The blaze spread through the park and everything was burned to the ground in minutes.
  大火蔓延至公園各處，全部的東西在數分鐘內被燃燒殆盡。

---

bleach [bliːtʃ]

① *v.* 將…漂白

同 **whiten**

反 **dye**

② *n.* 漂白（劑）

同 **whitener**

- The sunlight bleaches his hair in the summer.
  夏天的陽光把他的髮色曬淡了。
- Wash your white clothes with bleach and water.
  用水加漂白劑清洗你的白色衣服。

---

bleak [ˋblik] *adj.* 淒涼的；荒涼的；慘淡的

同 **dismal**

反 **animated**

- The rainy and cold weather made life seem bleak.
  多雨又寒冷的天候使得生活似乎變得淒涼起來。

---

blizzard [ˋblɪz.ɚd] *n.* 暴風雪

同 **snowstorm**

- The roads were closed because of the blizzard.
  道路因暴風雪的緣故都封閉了。

---

blond / blonde [blɑːnd]

① *adj.* 白皙的；亞麻色的；金黃色的

同 **light-haired; light-colored**

② *n.* 膚色白皙的人；金髮的人

- Since he is blond, he sunburns easily.
  他膚色白皙，容易曬傷。
- Anna is a blond and needs to wear sunscreen.
  安娜膚色白皙，因此需要擦防曬乳。

blot [blɑ:t]

① *n.* 污漬

同 **erase; wipe out**

② *v.* 弄乾；沾污；玷污

同 **stain; tarnish**

實用片語與搭配詞

blot out 塗改

▶ He spilled a blot of paint on his shirt.
他把油漆污漬濺到了襯衫上。

▶ Mom blotted the spilled wine with a napkin.
媽媽用餐巾紙弄乾潑灑出來的酒。

▶ The accident blotted out the woman's memory and she could not remember her name.
這起意外消除了這位女士的記憶，而她記不起自己的名字。

---

blues [blu:z]

n. 憂鬱

同 **sadness; depress**

▶ Pete has the blues after his breakup with Sandy.
比德跟女友姍蒂分手後，變得鬱鬱寡歡。

102

blunder [ˈblʌn.dɚ]

① *n.* 一不小心出的差錯；因疏忽而犯的錯誤

同 **error; mistake**

② *v.* 出錯；犯錯

同 **slip up; stumble**

實用片語與搭配詞

commit / make a blunder 犯大錯

▶ He was embarrassed by his blunder made in front of the whole class.
他在全班面前一不小心出了差錯而出糗。

▶ The man blundered through the speech, causing his manager to gasp.
那名男子在演講中一不小心出錯了，導致他的經理嚇得倒抽一口氣。

▶ He made a big blunder when he argued with his boss in front of the whole company.
他犯了一個大錯，他在全公司同仁面前與他的老闆爭執。

---

blunt [ˈblʌnt]

① *adj.* 鈍的

同 **dull**

反 **sharp**

② *v.* 變鈍

同 **dampen**

反 **sharpen**

▶ The knife can't cut anything. It is too blunt.
那把刀子根本沒辦法切東西，太鈍了。

▶ Use a cutting board to not blunt the knife.
用切菜板吧，以免把刀弄鈍了。

---

blur [ˈblɝ]

① *v.* 使模糊不清；弄髒

同 **smear**

反 **clear**

▶ The sunlight blurred his vision.
陽光模糊了他的視線。

② *n.* 模糊；汙點

同 **smear**

▸ The boy ran by me in a blur.

男孩像一團影子般地跑過我身邊。

Exercise 8

I. Derivatives

1. Eugene has acknowledged that what he has done to Amy was a ___________ (betray).
2. Some studies claims that rooibos tea is not only a lower caffeine intake; but has a ___________ (benefit) side effect of reducing the risk of heart disease.
3. You can ___________ (blurry) photos and create clarity in certain areas that you want by using this image-editing tool.
4. Cindy is extremely anxious and her ___________ (biology) clock is ticking because she just turned 45.
5. The travel hotspot was ___________ (besiege) with numerous tourists from all over the world.

II. Choices

1. Jeff already made a serious ________ that he knew he shouldn't have done.
   (A) blunt (B) blender (C) blond (D) blunder
2. The prospects in global economy remain ________ and the global growth continues to be weak.
   (A) bleak (B) blunt (C) beneficial (D) blurry
3. The organization that Tanya works for ultimately succeeded in a ________ for fundraising.
   (A) blot (B) blaze (C) bill (D) bid
4. There are some ________ natural phenomena which are beyond imagination and that may blow you away when you actually see them.
   (A) bizarre (B) bazaar (C) blizzard (D) blazing
5. Please ________ of your steps! It's easy to fall when the floor is wet and slippery.
   (A) swear (B) adware (C) beware (D) aware

Unit 9

bodily ['bɑː.dəl.i]

① *adj.* 身體上的；肉體的

反 **mental; spiritual**

② *adv.* 親身地

反 **mentally; spiritually**

▶ The car accident didn't cause any bodily harm.
這起車禍並未造成任何身體上的傷害。

▶ I may be in class bodily, but my mind is elsewhere.
也許我人在教室，但我的心卻飄到別的地方去了。

---

bodyguard ['bɑː.di.gɑːrd]

n. 護衛者；保鏢

同 **escort; guard**

▶ The bodyguards are responsible for protecting the governor.
保鏢負責保護州長。

---

bog [bɑːg]

① *n.* 沼澤

同 **swamp; marshland**

② *v.* 使陷入泥沼

實用片語與搭配詞

got bogged down 陷入困境不能前進

▶ The soft, wet ground in the bog made it difficult to walk.
沼澤裡濕軟的土壤令行走困難。

▶ The truck got bogged down in the mud.
卡車深陷淤泥之中。

▶ If you procrastinate on your homework you will get bogged down by too much to do later.
如果你遲遲不完成你的回家作業，你之後將會因為待做份量太多而陷入困境。

---

bolt [boʊlt]

① *n.* 門栓；閂

同 **fastener; lock**

② *v.* 拴上

同 **lock**

反 **unlock**

▶ Turn the bolt to lock the door.
轉動門拴把門鎖上。

▶ Patty bolted the door and turned off the lights.
派蒂拴上門，然後把燈關上。

---

bombard [bɑːm'bɑːrd] *v.* 轟炸

同 **attack; assail**

▶ The small island was bombarded during war, which caused great destruction.
那座小島在戰爭中遭到轟炸，而產生了極大的破壞。

bondage [ˈbɑːn.dɪdʒ] *n.* 奴役

同 **slavery; repression**

▶ The slave was in bondage.
那名奴隸處於被奴役的狀態。

---

bonus [ˈboʊ.nəs] *n.* 獎金；額外津貼（好處）

同 **extra; premium**

▶ Tammy received a bonus beyond her normal salary.
譚美收到了正常薪水以外的獎金。

---

boom [buːm]

① *n.* 隆隆聲；澎湃聲

同 **rumble**

反 **slump**

② *v.* 發出低沉有力的聲音；發出隆隆聲

同 **roar; grumble**

反 **slump**

實用片語與搭配詞

speak in a booming voice
深沉宏亮的聲音

▶ The boom of the thunder scared the baby.
打雷的隆隆聲，嚇壞了嬰兒。

▶ His deep voice boomed across the room.
他深沈的嗓音大聲傳到了房間的另一頭。

▶ The foreigner's booming voice disturbed the quiet atmosphere in the restaurant.
那位外國人宏亮的聲音破壞了這間餐廳裡安靜的氣氛。

---

boost [buːst]

① *v.* 向上推；提升；促進

同 **thrust**

② *n.* 提振及促進

同 **enhancement**

▶ Please boost me up so I can see over the wall.
請把我向上推，好讓我能看到牆外的景象。

▶ The cup of coffee gave her the boost she needed.
那杯咖啡讓她提振了所需的活力。

---

booth [buːθ] *n.* 小亭；貨攤

同 **stall**

▶ He stepped inside the phone booth to make a call.
他走進了電話亭打電話。

---

boredom [ˈbɔːr.dəm] *n.* 無聊

同 **tediousness; dullness**

▶ His boredom forced him to leave the classroom.
他無聊到只好離開教室。

---

bosom [ˈbʊz.əm] *n.* 胸懷；胸部

同 **breast**

▶ The mother held her child close to her bosom.
母親把孩子抱在懷裡。

---

botany [ˈbɑː.t̬ən.i] *n.* 植物學

▶ Alice loves gardening and wants to study botany.
愛麗絲喜愛園藝，想要攻讀植物學。

boulevard [ˈbʊl.ə.vɑːrd] *n.* 林蔭大道

同 **avenue**

▶ The city planted new trees along the boulevard.
這個城市沿著林蔭大道種植新樹。

---

bound [baʊnd]

① *v.* 跳躍

同 **jump**

反 **unbound**

實用片語與搭配詞

bound for someplace 前往某地

② *n.* 跳躍；界線

同 **leap; limit**

▶ The boy bounded across the room.
男孩蹦蹦跳跳地穿過房間。

▶ The students boarded a plane bound for Hawaii two hours ago.
兩小時前，學生們登上了飛往夏威夷的飛機。

▶ Her bound was farther than the boy's.
她跳得比這個男孩遠。

---

boundary [ˈbaʊn.dər.i] *n.* 邊界；分界線

同 **border; limit**

▶ The ball cannot go beyond the boundary.
球不可以出界。

---

bout [ˈbaʊt] *n.* 一回；一場次

同 **session; round**

▶ That was a fun game. Would you like one more bout?
那真是好玩的比賽。你要不要再來一回合？

---

bowel [ˈbaʊ.əl] *n.* 腸子

同 **gut; intestine**

▶ The doctor operated on Jim's bowel.
醫生為吉姆動腸道手術。

---

boxer [ˈbɑːk.sɚ] *n.* 拳擊手

▶ Boxers need strength and agility.
拳擊手需要有力氣和靈活度。

---

boxing [ˈbɑːk.sɪŋ] *n.* 把…裝箱；拳擊

同 **packing**

反 **unpacking**

▶ Will is boxing up his office on his last day.
威爾在他上班的最後一天把辦公室的東西給裝箱。

---

boycott [ˈbɔɪˌkɑt]

① *v.* 拒絕（作某事）；抵制；杯葛

同 **repel; revolt**

② *n.* 抵制

▶ The boy hated the mall and boycotted going there.
那男孩痛恨購物中心，而且拒絕去那裡。

▶ The boycott against beef imports only lasted a week.
抵制進口牛肉的行動只持續了一週。

實用片語與搭配詞

impose a boycott of / on sth
抵制 / 拒絕某事物

▶ Shoppers imposed a boycott on the company because of its unfair treatment of employees.
該公司對員工的不公平待遇讓消費者抵制這間公司。

---

boyhood [ˈbɔɪ.hʊd]

n. （男性）童年；少年期；男孩們

反 **girlhood**

▶ Since boyhood, Max has wanted to be a pilot.
從童年起，麥克斯就一直想當飛行員。

---

brace [breɪs]

① *n.* 支架；支撐物

同 **prop; support**

② *v.* 加固；支撐

同 **strengthen; tighten**

實用片語與搭配詞

brace up 打起精神振作起來

▶ The man used a brace to hold the pieces in place.
男子用支架把碎片固定住。

▶ Donna braced the old table with some wood.
唐納用一些木頭來強化這張舊桌子。

▶ To confront a bully, you need to brace up and be brave.
面對一個惡霸，你必須做好準備並變得勇敢。

---

braid [breɪd]

① *n.* 辮子

同 **braiding**

② *v.* 把（頭髮）編成辮子

同 **plait**

▶ The girl's braid went down her back.
女孩的辮子垂在她的背後。

▶ Harriet asked her mom to braid her hair for the dance.
哈莉葉請媽媽幫她編參加舞會的辮子。

---

breadth [bredθ]

n. 寬度；幅度

反 **length**

▶ Measure the breadth of the box to see if the toy fits.
量一量箱子的寬度，看玩具是否裝得下。

Exercise 9

I. Choices

1. Ken just established his own company few years ago and it has been expanding in leaps and ________ s.

   (A) board (B) bond (C) bund (D) bound

2. You can follow this guide to not only ________ website traffic but also increase sales for your business.

   (A) dwindle (B) shrink (C) boost (D) balance

3. E-commerce has made most of business transactions happen across geographic ________ .

   (A) boundaries (B) bondage (C) bundles (D) bonds

4. Sherry is satisfied with her job because the company has been offering generous holiday ________ annually in different forms—paid time off and gift cards.

   (A) biases (B) bonuses (C) blasts (D) blunders

5. To alleviate ________ and loneliness, I was binge-watching many episodes of a TV series.

   (A) anticipation (B) excitement (C) entertainment (D) boredom

II. Vocabulary Choices

(A) booth	(B) bout	(C) bonus	(D) brace
(E) boycott	(F) boyhood	(G) breadth	(H) bowel
(I) bombard	(J) boom		

1. Since Starbucks announced to raise prices ranging from NT$5 to NT$20, some people have organized a business ________ .
2. Every time when typhoons come, please make sure to ________ outdoor objects and secure the windows from breaking.
3. Ben had been going through a ________ of depression for the past 10 years but one day he realized that what he got to hold on was faith.
4. Managing to win a beauty pageant is pretty competitive but Laura did by a hair's ________ .
5. The creative songwriter added the ________ of the sea to the original song, which made it sound like a completely different remix.

breakdown [ˈbreɪk.daʊn] *n.* 故障

同 **crack-up; equipment failure**

▶ The tour came to a halt after the bus breakdown.
巴士故障之後，導致旅行暫時停止。

---

98 95

breakthrough [ˈbreɪk.θruː]

n. 重大進展；突破

同 **advance; step forward**

▶ Starting to walk again was a huge breakthrough in his recovery.
重新開始能走路是他康復過程中的重大進展。

---

breakup [ˈbreɪk͵ʌp] *n.* 中斷；分手

同 **divide**

▶ She cried for days after the breakup.
分手後，她一連哭了好幾天。

---

brew [bruː]

① *v.* 泡；煮；釀

同 **condense**

實用片語與搭配詞

brewed up sth.
沖泡某物；醞釀（壞事）；即將來臨（暴風雨）

② *n.* 釀製的飲料；茶

▶ Let's brew some tea.
我們泡茶來喝吧。

▶ The criminals brewed up a plan to get rid of a witness who could send them to jail.
那些罪犯們醞釀了一個計畫，打算處理掉一個可能會讓他們坐牢的目擊者。

▶ The brew sat in the pot for days.
那壺飲料已經放了好多天了。

101

bribe [ˈbraɪb]

① *v.* 行賄；收買

同 **buy off**

② *n.* 賄賂；行賄物

實用片語與搭配詞

give / offer / pay sb. a bribe 向某人行賄

▶ The company bribed the official to win the contract.
這家公司行賄這名官員來取得合約。

▶ Jon refused to accept a bribe from the criminal.
強拒絕接受這個罪犯的賄賂。

▶ Some people willingly pay bribes to police to avoid a traffic fine.
有些人情願賄賂警方以避免支付交通罰款。

---

briefcase [ˈbriːf.keɪs] *n.* 公事包

▶ Jack carries a briefcase to work most days.
傑克大部分的日子都帶著公事包上班。

brink [brɪŋk] *n.* 邊；邊緣

同 **threshold; verge**

▶ The bird landed on the brink of the cliff.
那隻鳥飛落在懸崖邊上。

---

brisk [ˈbrɪsk]

adj. 輕快的；活潑的；生氣勃勃的

同 **energetic**

反 **invigorating**

▶ They went for a brisk walk.
他們一起去快步走路。

103

broaden [ˈbrɑː.dən]

v. 使…加寬；變寬；擴大

同 **extend; widen**

▶ We broadened our search for the lost ring.
我們擴大找尋遺失的戒指。

---

brochure [broʊˈʃʊr] *n.* 手冊；小冊子

同 **booklet**

實用片語與搭配詞

browse / leaf / look through a brochure 翻看小冊子

▶ Let's look at some brochures about hotels there.
我們來看看那裡一些飯店的簡介手冊吧。

▶ If you leaf through this travel brochure, you might get ideas for your next trip.
如果你翻閱這本旅遊手冊，你對於下趟旅行可能會有些想法。

---

bronze [brɑːnz]

① *n.* 青銅；青銅製品

實用片語與搭配詞

be cast in bronze 以青銅鑄造而成的

② *adj.* 青銅（色）的

同 **bronzy**

▶ The statue was made out of bronze.
這座雕像是青銅製的。

▶ Many statues are cast in bronze because it can withstand any weather.
許多雕像是以青銅鑄造，因為它禁得起日曬雨淋。

▶ She won a bronze medal in the Olympics.
她在奧運會中贏得了一面銅牌。

---

brooch [ˈbroʊtʃ] *n.* 女用胸針

同 **breastpin**

▶ Michelle fastened a brooch to her blouse.
蜜雪兒在她的襯衫上別了一枚女用胸針。

---

brood [bruːd]

① *n.* 一窩孵出的雛雞

▶ The mother hen watched over her brood.
母雞保護牠的一窩小雞。

② *v.* 憂思；擔憂；孵蛋；孵出

同 **consider; contemplate**

▶ The boy brooded over the mean things his sister had said.
這個男孩因姊妹說的惡毒話而鬱悶不已。

---

broth [brɑ:θ] *n.* 清湯；高湯

同 **potage**

▶ Louis put some chicken bones into the broth.
路易絲加了一些雞骨到高湯裡。

---

brotherhood [ˈbrʌð.ɚ.hʊd]

n. 兄弟會；兄弟關係

同 **fellowship**

▶ Mark and Mike have a special bond through brotherhood.
馬克和麥克加入兄弟會而培養出特殊的緊密情誼。

---

browse [ˈbraʊz]

① *v.* 瀏覽；（牲畜）吃葉、草

同 **graze; scan**

實用片語與搭配詞

browse through a book 瀏覽書籍

② *n.* （牲畜吃的）嫩草；嫩葉

實用片語與搭配詞

have a browse 瀏覽

▶ The couple browsed through a bookstore after dinner.
這對夫妻吃了晚飯後，到一家書店逛逛。

▶ She nervously browsed through a book as she waited for the interviewer to call her.
在她等著被面試官叫到名字的期間，她緊張地隨意翻看著一本書。

▶ The cattle ate the browse.
牛群吃了嫩草。

▶ I often have a browse through online store catalogues, but I usually don't buy anything.
我時常瀏覽線上商店的型錄，但是我通常不買任何東西。

---

bruise [bru:z]

① *n.* 瘀傷；青腫

同 **injure; wound**

② *v.* 使受瘀傷；碰傷

同 **injure; wound**

實用片語與搭配詞

black / dark / purple bruise 瘀青

▶ The accident left a purple bruise on her arm.
這起意外事故害她的手臂上留下了紫色瘀傷。

▶ Noah punched his brother, and it bruised his arm.
諾亞打了兄弟一拳，對方的手臂因此瘀傷了。

▶ I fell down the stairs at home and now I have purple bruises all over my body.
我在家時從樓梯上跌下來，而現在我全身都是紫色的瘀青。

brute [bru:t]

① *n.* 殘暴的人

② *adj.* 蠻橫的；殘忍的

▶ The brute killed another man and was put in jail.
那個殘暴的人殺害了一名男子，結果被關進牢裡了。

▶ John won the contest by brute strength.
約翰靠著蠻力而贏得了比賽。

---

buckle [ˈbʌk.əl]

① *n.* 扣環

同 **hook**

② *v.* （用扣環）扣住

同 **clip; hook**

實用片語與搭配詞

buckle down to sth. 下決心做某事

▶ That belt has a buckle in the shape of Texas.
那條皮帶上有個德州造型的扣環。

▶ Always buckle your seatbelt when driving.
開車時務必扣上安全帶。

▶ If you want to finish that project on time, you have to buckle down and work faster.
如果你想要如期完成那份企劃，你必須開始努力工作並提高效率。

---

bulge [bʌldʒ]

① *n.* 腫塊；凸塊

同 **swell; lump**

② *v.* 膨脹；凸起

實用片語與搭配詞

bulge out 鼓起；凸起

▶ Jane asked the doctor to look at the bulge in her neck.
珍請醫生看看她脖子上的腫塊。

▶ Simon's muscles bulged under his tight shirt.
賽門的肌肉在緊身襯衫下鼓起。

▶ The puppies drank so much milk that their tummies are bulging out.
那些小狗們喝了很多奶，以致於牠們的肚子都鼓起來了。

---

bulk [bʌlk] *n.* 大量；巨大的東西

同 **mass**

▶ Josh removed the bulk of the letters from his desk.
喬許把大堆信件從桌上移走。

---

bulky [ˈbʌl.ki] *adj.* 龐大的

同 **massive**

反 **tight**

▶ It was difficult to carry that bulky thing up the stairs.
實在很難把那麼龐大的東西抬上樓梯。

bully ['bʊl.i]

① *n.* 霸凌者；恃強欺弱者

同 **oppressor; persecutor**

② *v.* 霸凌

同 **intimidate; oppress**

實用片語與搭配詞

bully sb. into doing sth. 脅迫某人做某事

▶ The bully picked on the small boy.
霸凌者欺負了這個小男孩。

▶ Terry bullied the new student and made her cry.
泰瑞霸凌新學生，把她弄哭了。

▶ My friends bullied me into going camping even though they knew I did not want to go.
儘管我的朋友們知道我並不想去露營，他們依然逼迫我參加。

---

bureau ['bjʊr.oʊ] *n.* 局；處

同 **agency office**

▶ Tina is a public servant. She works at the labor bureau.
提娜是公務員，她在勞工處上班。

---

bureaucracy [bjʊ'rɑː.krə.si]

n. 官僚體制；官僚主義

同 **bureaucratism**

▶ The bureaucracy manages government tasks.
官僚體制管理著政府的事務。

B

Exercise 10

I. Choices

1. Once you ________ your spectrum of happiness, you will never live the life in the same way as you did.
   (A) brighten (B) straighten (C) broaden (D) unfasten
2. Some particular surveys and data will be annually or quarterly published from the Census ________ .
   (A) Desk (B) Agency (C) Branch (D) Bureau
3. Those of public officials in the U.S. who receive ________ s or any items of value will be under the FBI's investigation.
   (A) bribe (B) bride (C) bridle (D) bridge
4. In 2016, Apple announced the newest MacBook Pro with a ________ and revolutionary feature that is called the Touch Bar.
   (A) breakout (B) breakdown (C) breakthrough (D) breakaway
5. I wonder how much it will cost to deliver such a ________ and heavy package from Taipei to London.
   (A) brisk (B) bully (C) bulky (D) bullish

II. Vocabulary Choices

(A) buckle	(B) bulk	(C) bruise	(D) bronze
(E) bulge	(F) brute	(G) broth	(H) brochure
(I) brew	(J) browse		

1. While she was ________ ing through the magazine at the newsstand, a stranger came to talk to her.
2. I asked Jack to help me with my seatbelt ________ repair.
3. My mom's homemade chicken ________ is the best medicine for recovery from illness.
4. The statistical report provides policymakers evidence and new insights on youth ________ and youth unemployment.
5. Brandon has tried all the possible passwords to ________ force his way into Nick's computer, but he failed.

burial [ˈber.i.əl] *n.* 葬禮；埋葬

同 **entombment; interment**

▶ The burial took place last Saturday.
葬禮是在上週六舉行的。

---

butcher [ˈbʊtʃ.ɚ]

① *n.* 肉販；肉店老闆；屠夫

同 **slaughter**

② *v.* 屠宰（牲口）；屠殺

同 **slaughter**

▶ I asked the butcher to give me two pounds of pork.
我請肉販給我兩磅豬肉。

▶ My aunt butchered a pig for the feast.
我阿姨為宴席宰殺了一頭豬。

---

byte [ˈbaɪt] *n.* 位元組

▶ How many bytes of data is that?
那共有幾個位元組？

---

cactus [ˈkæk.təs] *n.* 仙人掌

▶ The cactus can survive in the desert despite the high temperatures.
儘管沙漠氣溫高，但仙人掌仍能存活。

---

caffeine [ˈkæf.iːn] *n.* 咖啡因

▶ Coffee contains quite a bit of caffeine.
咖啡含有相當多的咖啡因。

---

calcium [ˈkæl.si.əm] *n.* 鈣

▶ Bones are made of calcium.
骨骼的成份是鈣。

---

calf [kæf]

① *n.* 小牛

實用片語與搭配詞

graze / rear the calf 飼養小牛

② *n.* 小腿

▶ The cow gave birth to a calf.
母牛生了一隻小牛。

▶ The farmer reared many calves on his farm.
那位農夫在他的農場中飼養了許多牛。

▶ Her calves were sore after the marathon.
跑完馬拉松後，她的小腿酸痛。

---

calligraphy [kəˈlɪg.rə.fi] *n.* 書法；筆跡

同 **chirography**

▶ Carol studied ancient Chinese calligraphy.
卡蘿研究中國古代的書法。

canal [kə'næl] *n.* 運河

同 **tube; waterway**

▶ The large ship barely fit through the canal.
這艘大船差一點就通不過運河。

---

cannon ['kæn.ən]

① *n.* 大砲

② *v.* 砲轟；炮擊

▶ The pirate ship fired its cannon at the enemy.
這艘海盜船向敵人發射大砲。

▶ The sailors cannoned the enemy's battleship.
水手們砲轟了敵人的戰艦。

---

canvas ['kæn.vəs] *n.* 畫布；帆布

同 **picture; image**

▶ The artist mainly paints on canvas.
那位藝術家大都在畫布上作畫。

---

capability [ˌkeɪ.pə'bɪl.ə.t̬i] *n.* 能力

同 **ability; competency**

▶ The capability of two people is much greater than that of one.
兩個人的力量遠大於一個人的。

---

capsule ['kæp.səl] *n.* 膠囊

實用片語與搭配詞

swallow / take a capsule 吞膠囊

▶ The medicine is in a capsule that you swallow.
藥被裝進膠囊中讓人吞嚥服用。

▶ The most common way to take antibiotics is in capsule form, but babies get a liquid form.
抗生素最常以膠囊的形式被服用，但是嬰兒們得到的是液體的形式。

---

caption ['kæp.ʃən]

① *n.* 標題；字幕；照片說明

同 **heading; title**

② *v.* 加標題於

▶ What does the caption on that newspaper say?
那份報紙的標題上寫什麼？

▶ Sally captions updates about what is happening.
莎莉替現在發生的事情的更新資訊加標題。

---

captive ['kæp.tɪv]

① *n.* 俘虜

同 **prisoner; hostage**

實用片語與搭配詞

be held / kept captive 被俘虜

▶ There were five captives set free from the enemy.
五名俘虜被從敵營獲釋。

▶ The soldier escaped from a enemy camp after being held captive for seven years.
那位士兵在被俘虜七年之後，逃出了敵軍的陣營。

② *adj.* 被俘的

同 **imprisoned; enslaved**

反 **free**

▶ The solders were captive for seven days by the enemy.
那些士兵被敵軍俘虜了七天。

---

captivity [kæpˈtɪv.ə.t̬i] *n.* 囚禁；被俘

同 **imprisonment; custody**

▶ She was held in captivity for six years.
她被囚禁了六年。

---

carbohydrate [ˌkɑːr.boʊˈhaɪ.dreɪt] *n.* 碳水化合物

▶ Does that meal have a lot of carbohydrates in it?
那餐飯裡含有很多碳水化合物嗎？

99

carbon [ˈkɑːr.bən] *n.* 碳

▶ Graphite is a form of carbon used to make pencils.
石墨是一種碳，用來製作鉛筆。

---

cardboard [ˈkɑːrd.bɔːrd] *n.* 硬紙板

同 **composition board**

▶ Cardboard is a popular material for making boxes.
硬紙板是製作箱子的普遍材料。

---

carefree [ˈker.friː] *adj.* 無憂無慮的

同 **jolly; lighthearted**

▶ Holly feels carefree after finishing her exams.
荷莉考完試後感到無憂無慮。

---

caress [kəˈres]

① *v.* 撫摸

同 **fondle; touch**

② *n.* 撫摸

▶ She liked to caress the little kitten.
她喜歡撫摸那隻小貓。

▶ The baby fell asleep in his mother's caress.
嬰兒在媽媽的撫摸下睡著了。

---

caretaker [ˈkerˌteɪ.kɚ] *n.* 照顧者；管理人

▶ The Smiths hired a caretaker to watch over their property.
史密斯一家雇用了一名管理人來看管他們的產業。

---

carnation [kɑːrˈneɪ.ʃən] *n.* 康乃馨

▶ Uncle Joe planted red carnations in the garden.
喬伊叔叔在花園裡種了紅色康乃馨。

---

carnival [ˈkɑːr.nə.vəl] *n.* 嘉年華會

同 **fair; festival**

▶ The carnival features rides, games and delicious food.
這場嘉年華會有遊樂設施、遊戲和美食饗宴。

carol [ˈker.əl] *n.* （聖誕）頌歌；詩歌

同 **hymn; song**

▶ I love singing carols around Christmas.
我喜歡在聖誕節前後唱詩歌。

Exercise 11

I. Choices

1. Rebecca ________ ed gently the sleeping baby and put her to sleep with a lullaby.
   (A) regress (B) aggress (C) address (D) caress
2. Closed ________ s are automatically generated for viewers on YouTube videos, which can be read when audio can't be heard in a noisy environment.
   (A) account (B) caption (C) capture (D) capital
3. Gina has demonstrated her ________ of multimedia to the maximum.
   (A) certainty (B) capacity (C) capability (D) creativity
4. Steve reminisced about his ________ youth over the good old days when he flipped through the photo album.
   (A) cheerless (B) carefree (C) careful (D) careworn
5. Many beneficial efficacies of ________ have been shown to reduce sleepiness when driving, help focus on work, and offer relief for headaches.
   (A) carbohydrate (B) gluten (C) calories (D) caffeine

II. Vocabulary Choices

(A) calf	(B) capsule	(C) cannon	(D) canal
(E) calligraphy	(F) canvas	(G) captive	(H) carbon
(I) carol	(J) carnival		

1. My family and I had a good time in the ________ and enjoyed the parades, the snow park, and some signature events.
2. One of the traditions to do during Christmas season is to sing Christmas ________ in public places.
3. The task of the escape room game is to solve the killer's mystery and rescue victims kept ________ .
4. A ________ coffee machine is the best invention ever to a coffee enthusiast like me because I can have a homemade espresso by just conveniently pressing a button.
5. The ________ footprint calculator enables individuals to take actions on climate changes by living a lifestyle of shrinking greenhouse gases emissions.

Unit 12

carp [kɑːrp] *n.* 鯉魚

實用片語與搭配詞

carp (v.) at / about sb. /sth.
吹毛求疵 / 挑毛病

▶ My father breeds carp in this pond for his restaurant.
我父親在池子裡養殖鯉魚，供應他的餐廳所需。

▶ You should stop carping about everything and try to be more positive about your life.
你應該要停止在每件事上吹毛求疵，並且試著積極面對人生。

---

carton [ˈkɑːr.t̬ən] *n.* 紙盒；紙板箱

同 **cardboard box**

▶ Please stop at the store and buy three cartons of eggs.
請順便到店裡去買三盒蛋。

---

cashier [kæʃˈɪr] *n.* 收銀員；出納員

同 **clerk**

▶ Take your items to the cashier to buy them.
請把你要買的品項拿去給收銀員結帳。

---

casualty [ˈkæʒ.ju.əl.ti] *n.* 傷亡人員

同 **injury; mishap**

實用片語與搭配詞

cause / inflict casualties
造成傷亡

▶ There were five casualties from the accident.
那場意外事故共有五人傷亡。

▶ The attack on the village inflicted hundreds of casualties mostly women and children.
那起攻擊事件造成此村莊上百人傷亡，多數是婦女與孩童。

---

catastrophe [kəˈtæs.trə.fi] *n.* 大災難

同 **calamity; disaster**

實用片語與搭配詞

cause / lead sth. to catastrophe
造成某事物的大災難

▶ The town took three months to recover from the catastrophe.
那個鎮花了三個月才從那場大災難中復原。

▶ Global warming could lead us to catastrophe and wipe out many species.
全球暖化可能帶給我們大災難並且使許多物種滅絕。

---

category [ˈkæt̬.ə.ɡri] *n.* 種類；部屬

同 **class**

▶ The exam tested our knowledge of many categories of species.
這項考試測驗了我們對許多物種類別的認識。

C

cater [ˈkeɪ.t̬ɚ] *v.* 辦外燴；迎合

同 **calamity; disaster**

實用片語與搭配詞

cater for sb. / sth.
為某人或某事提供酒席 / 外燴的服務

▶ Will you cater the party this weekend?
你願意幫這個週末舉行的派對辦外燴嗎？

▶ The luxury hotel caters for wealthy families.
豪華飯店迎合富裕的家庭。

---

cathedral [kəˈθiː.drəl] *n.* 大教堂

實用片語與搭配詞

magnificent / baroque / Gothic / medieval cathedral
宏偉的 / 巴洛克 / 歌德 / 中世紀式的大教堂

▶ Matt and Pam got married in a large cathedral.
麥特和潘在大教堂裡結婚了。

▶ In Prague, you can visit a medieval cathedral to escape the hustle and bustle of the city.
在布拉格，造訪一個中世紀的天主教堂可幫助你逃離城市的喧囂。

---

caution [ˈkɑː.ʃən]

① *n.* 謹慎

同 **prudence; carefulness**

② *v.* 警告；使小心

同 **warning; rebuke**

實用片語與搭配詞

proceed with caution 小心行事

▶ I took caution when walking over the narrow bridge.
我小心翼翼地走過這座狹窄的橋。

▶ Tammy cautioned us not to swim in the river.
譚美警告我們不要在這條河裡游泳。

▶ After the earthquake, the building is unstable, and you should proceed with caution.
這棟建築物在地震後很不穩固，你前進時必須謹慎小心。

cautious [ˈkɑː.ʃəs] *adj.* 謹慎的

同 **careful**

反 **careless**

▶ Mia is very cautious when driving her car.
米雅開車時非常小心謹慎。

---

cavalry [ˈkæv.əl.ri] *n.* 騎兵

▶ The cavalry fought against the natives.
騎兵和原住民奮戰。

---

cavity [ˈkæv.ə.t̬i] *n.* 蛀牙洞；洞穴

同 **hole; pit**

▶ Go to the dentist when you have a cavity.
有蛀牙的話，就該去看牙醫。

celebrity [sə'leb.rə.t̬i] *n.* 名人；名流；名聲

同 **notable**

實用片語與搭配詞

overnight celebrity 一夜成名

▶ Many celebrities appear in TV commercials.
許多名人都拍過電視廣告。

▶ After saving the president's life, the bodyguard became an overnight celebrity.
在拯救了總統的性命後，這名保鑣在一夕之間成為了名人。

---

celery ['sel.ɚ.i] *n.* 芹菜

▶ She put celery and carrots into the soup.
她把芹菜和胡蘿蔔放進了湯裡。

---

cellar ['sel.ɚ]

① *n.* 地窖；酒窖

同 **basement**

② *v.* 放入地窖

▶ My uncle stores wine down in the cellar.
我叔叔把紅酒儲藏在地窖裡。

▶ Mom cellars her pickles for several months before we can eat them.
媽媽把醃黃瓜放入地窖中幾個月，然後我們才能吃。

---

cello ['tʃel.oʊ] *n.* 大提琴

▶ Tanya wants someone to play the cello at her wedding.
譚雅希望有人能在她的婚禮上演奏大提琴。

---

cellphone / cellular phone

['sel foʊn / 'sel·jə·lər 'foʊn] *n.* 行動電話

▶ Cellphones make communication very convenient.
手機讓通訊非常方便。

Celsius / Centigrade / centigrade

['sel.si.əs / 'sen.t̬ə.greɪd / 'sen.t̬ə.greɪd] *n.* 攝氏度

▶ The temperature was forty degrees Celsius.
那時的氣溫是攝氏四十度。

---

cemetery ['sem.ə.ter.i] *n.* 墓園

同 **graveyard**

▶ Her ancestors are buried in the cemetery.
她的祖先都埋葬在那處墓園裡。

95

ceremony ['ser.ə.mə.ni] *n.* 儀式；典禮

同 **ritual**

▶ The wedding ceremony was held at the church.
婚禮是在教堂舉行的。

實用片語與搭配詞

conduct / hold / perform a wedding ceremony 舉行婚禮

▶ Tammy and John held their wedding ceremony at a church.
譚美跟約翰在一座教堂裡舉行了他們的結婚儀式。

---

certainty ['sɝː.tən.ti]

n. 確實；必然

同 **assurance**

反 **doubt**

實用片語與搭配詞

with absolute certainty 肯定 / 有把握

▶ It is a certainty that the world has been getting hotter the past few years.
過去幾年來，全球氣溫確實越來越炎熱。

▶ Scientists can prove, with absolute certainty, that the effects of global warming are real.
科學家們絕對能夠保證全球暖化的效應是真實的。

---

certificate [sɚ'tɪf.ə.kət]

① *n.* 證明書；執照

同 **credential; diploma**

實用片語與搭配詞

award / issue sb. a certificate
發證書 / 證照

② *v.* 發證書

▶ His birth certificate shows he was born in the United States.
他的出生證明顯示他是在美國出生的。

▶ Once you complete this course, you will be issued a certificate of completion.
一旦你修完了這門課，你將會被授予一張結業證書。

▶ The school certificated that Brandon had finished his degree.
學校發給證書，證明布蘭登完成了學位。

---

certify ['sɝː.t̬ə.faɪ] *v.* 證明；證實

同 **affirm testify**

實用片語與搭配詞

certify sb. / sth. as sth.
書面證明某人 / 事為 ...

▶ The health department certifies the product is safe.
衛生部證實那項產品安全無虞。

▶ To be certified as a chartered accountant, you need to write several examinations.
為了成為持有皇家執照的會計師，你需要接受許多不同的考試。

---

chairperson / chair / chairman / chairwoman

['tʃer͵pɝː.sən / tʃer / 'tʃer.mən / 'tʃer͵wʊm.ən]

n. 主席；議長 / （男）主席 / 女主席

同 **speaker**

▶ The chairman of the board voted to fire the CEO.
董事會的主席投票表決開除執行長。

champagne [ʃæm`peɪn] *n.* 香檳酒

▶ I only have champagne on special occasions.
我只在特殊場合才喝香檳。

Exercise 12

I. Derivatives

1. I can't give you the answer with any degree of ___________ (certain), but I can promise you that I will go all out.
2. The city hospital has been deliberately ___________ (caution) about giving the treatment of inflammatory disease.
3. My grandma was employed as a ___________ (cash) at the age of 18, and it was the one and only job she had in her life.
4. The earthquake that happened in Japan was an appalling ___________ (catastrophic) that led to severe damage and enormous effects.
5. I hereby ___________ (certificate) that I have fully understood the above statements and the signature of participant below is authentic.

II. Choices

1. My favorite tourist attraction in Spain is the ________ of Barcelona, which is fascinating from outside to inside.
   (A) Capital (B) Cathedral (C) Crystal (D) Center
2. Shawn has decided to go for his dream to invest his savings in the business of vineyard and wine ________ .
   (A) cellar (B) cell (C) carnet (D) cabin
3. One of the most significant challenges for teachers is to ________ for students their diverse needs.
   (A) withdraw (B) withhold (C) meet (D) cater
4. The news reported that traffic ________ figures have noticeably increased in the past years.
   (A) cavity (B) casualty (C) cavalry (D) celery
5. Kina has been swamped with work recently and yet she hasn't have time to plan the wedding ________ .
   (A) cemetery (B) celebrity (C) ceremony (D) conference

Unit 13

chant [ˈtʃænt]

① *n.* 歌

同 **psalm; song**

② *v.* 唱

▶ The crowd's chant filled the stadium.
群眾的歌唱聲充滿了整座體育場。

▶ The monks chanted their prayers.
修道士吟唱禱詞。

---

chaos [ˈkeɪ.ɑːs] *n.* 混亂

同 **confusion; mix-up**

反 **cosmos**

▶ The home was a chaos when all seven children were there.
七個孩子全員到齊時，家裡簡直變得一團混亂。

---

characterize [ˈkær.ək.tə.raɪz]

v. 描述…的特性；具有…的特性；歸納…的特徵

同 **depict; describe**

實用片語與搭配詞

characterize sb. / sth. as sth.
將某人 / 事物的特點描述成某事物

▶ I would characterize her as hard-working.
我會用努力工作來形容她。

▶ Politicians are usually characterized as cunning, self-absorbed and corrupt.
政客通常都被認為擁有狡猾、只顧自身利益以及貪腐的特質。

95

charcoal [ˈtʃɑːr.koʊl] *n.* 炭

同 **wood coal**

▶ Use charcoal for the grill.
應該用炭來作燒烤。

---

chariot [ˈtʃer.i.ət]

① *n.* 雙輪戰車或馬車

② *v.* 駕或乘雙輪戰車或馬車

▶ Important people in history rode in chariots.
歷史上一些重要的人物都曾乘駕戰車。

▶ They charioted to the next town.
他們駕馬車去下一個城鎮。

---

charitable [ˈtʃer.ə.t̬ə.bəl]

adj. 仁慈的；樂善好施的

同 **generous; giving kindly**

▶ He is known as a charitable man in the community.
他樂善好施，在社區裡人盡皆知。

---

chatter [ˈtʃæt̬.ɚ]

① *v.* 喋喋不休；嘮叨

同 **babble; jabber**

▶ The two girls chattered all night and hardly slept.
這兩個女孩徹夜聊天，幾乎沒睡。

② *n.* 閒言閒語；流言；嘮叨

同 **babble; jabber**

▶ Bryan tried to ignore the chatter about him.
布萊恩試著不去理會那些談論他的閒言閒語。

---

check-in [ˈtʃek.ɪn] *n.* 入宿登記；報到

同 **sign in**

▶ Check-in at the hotel is at 3 p.m.
這家飯店的入宿登記時間是下午三點。

---

check-out [ˈtʃek.aʊt] *n.* 退房；檢查

▶ Check-out at the hotel must be done by noon.
這家飯店的退房手續一定得在中午前完成。

---

checkbook [ˈtʃek.bʊk] *n.* 支票簿

▶ Carl used his checkbook to pay for the clothes.
卡爾用支票簿來付衣服錢。

---

checkup [ˈtʃekˌʌp] *n.* 檢查；核對

同 **examination**

▶ His dental checkup lasted an hour.
他檢查牙齒檢查了一個小時。

---

chef [ʃef] *n.* 主廚；廚師

實用片語與搭配詞

master chef 大師主廚

▶ Marc works as a chef at a new restaurant.
馬克在一家新餐廳擔任主廚。

▶ Every master chef wants their own restaurant where they can design their own dishes.
每位主廚都想開自己的餐廳，以自行設計菜色。

---

chemist [ˈkem.ɪst] *n.* 化學家

▶ The chemist is working on a new vaccine.
這名化學家正在研發一種新疫苗。

---

chestnut [ˈtʃes.nʌt]

① *n.* 栗樹；栗子

② *adj.* 栗色的

▶ We planted a chestnut in our backyard.
我們在後院種了一顆栗樹。

▶ His briefcase was a dark chestnut color.
他的公事包是深栗色的。

---

chili [ˈtʃɪl.i] *n.* 辣椒

▶ She used chilis to make the dish spicy.
她用紅辣椒增添這道菜的辣味。

chimpanzee [ˌtʃɪm.pænˈziː] *n.* 黑猩猩

同 **ape; chimp**

▶ We went to the zoo to see the chimpanzees.
我們去了動物園看黑猩猩。

---

choir [ˈkwaɪ.ɚ] *n.* 詩班；合唱團

同 **chorus; consort**

▶ The choir at our church is looking for singers.
我們教會的詩班正在徵求歌者。

---

cholesterol [kəˈles.tə.rɑːl] *n.* 膽固醇

▶ He should eat more vegetables because of his high cholesterol.
他有高血壓，所以應該多吃蔬菜。

---

chord [kɔːrd] *n.* 和弦；琴弦

實用片語與搭配詞

chord progression / change 和絃進程

▶ Luke learned several new chords on the guitar.
路克學會好幾個吉他新和弦。

▶ “Chord progression” is a musical term used in western music to refer to harmony.
「和弦進程」在西方音樂中是一個被用來指稱和聲的音樂相關詞彙。

95

chronic [ˈkrɑː.nɪk] *adj.* 慢性的

同 **unceasing; unremitting**

實用片語與搭配詞

chronic arthritis 慢性關節炎

▶ My grandpa has chronic back pain.
我祖父有慢性背痛。

▶ Elderly people often suffer from chronic arthritis, a disease that affects joints.
上了年紀的人通常受慢性關節炎而苦，它是一個會影響關節功能的疾病。

---

chubby [ˈtʃʌb.i] *adj.* 圓胖的

同 **plump; tubby**

▶ Nat's chubby fingers didn't fit into the glove.
奈特圓圓胖胖的手指戴不進這隻手套。

---

chuckle [ˈtʃʌk.əl]

① *v.* 咯咯地笑

同 **giggle**

② *n.* 咯咯聲

同 **giggle**

實用片語與搭配詞

let out / give / have a chuckle
笑出聲來 / 竊笑

▶ The two students chuckled in the back of class.
那兩名學生在教室後面咯咯笑。

▶ The joke gave us a chuckle.
那個笑話讓我們笑呵呵。

▶ Looking at animals and their funny antics usually gives me a chuckle.
看著動物們滑稽的舉動往往會讓我發笑。

chunk [tʃʌŋk] *n.* 厚塊

同 **bulk; lump**

實用片語與搭配詞

cut sth. up into chunks 切成一塊塊的

▶ The ax took a chunk out of the tree.
斧頭把那棵樹砍下了一塊。

▶ That meat will take too long to cook; you need to cut it up into smaller chunks.
煮那塊肉將會花很長的時間；你必須把它切成小塊。

---

circuit [ˋsɝːkɪt] *n.* 外圍；周邊；電路

▶ They followed the circuit around the track.
他們沿著跑道周邊繞行。

---

cite [saɪt] *v.* 引用；引述

同 **quote; refer**

實用片語與搭配詞

cite sth. as an example
引述某事 / 物作為例子

▶ The study cited several trusted sources to make its claims.
這份研究引用了幾個可靠的來源來支持其主張。

▶ When writing an academic paper, you have to cite many examples to prove your argument.
當你在寫一篇學術論文時，必須引用許多範例來證明你的論點。

Exercise 13

I. Derivatives

1. How Elise learned English was to compose ___________ (chant) poems with the vocabularies that she memorized.
2. I would ___________ (character) our different religions as a deal breaker in the relationship.
3. Bill and Melinda Gates Foundation is the largest ___________ (charity) trust on earth, which has been making philanthropic contributions to many aspects in developing countries, such as healthcare, education, and poverty reduction.
4. Emma has fulfilled the educational requirements to become a ___________ (chemistry) but she wants to pursue an advanced degree for teaching positions.
5. Before the band got started with the performance, the entire room was buzzing with ___________ (chat).

II. Choices

1. The studies have indicated that there is a ________ shortage of trained teachers in some disadvantaged areas.
   (A) chronicle (B) bionic (C) botanic (D) chronic
2. Lack of time management and self-discipline are usually ________ as the reasons for insufficient exercises.
   (A) cited (B) confirmed (C) committed (D) connected
3. She ________ d in high glee when she learnt that she was pregnant with twins.
   (A) truckle (B) pickle (C) buckle (D) chuckle
4. In Eason's later years, he has come to realize that he can't buy happiness and health with a big ________ of money.
   (A) chunk (B) choke (C) chip (D) coin
5. Nick Vujicic has gone to many speech ________ and has shared his incredible stories that resonated with hundreds of thousands of people.
   (A) circumstances (B) circuits (C) circuses (D) codes

Unit 14

civic [ˈsɪv.ɪk] *adj.* 市民的；城市的

同 **civil**

▶ The protest was held in the civic center.
這場抗議活動在市民中心舉行。

---

civilize [ˈsɪv.əl.aɪz] *v.* 使有教養；教化

同 **cultivate; educate**

▶ My mother tries to civilize me at the dinner table.
我媽媽試圖讓我在晚餐桌上表現得更有教養。

---

clam [klæm] *n.* 蛤蜊

實用片語與搭配詞

clam up (v.) 閉口不言；沉默不語

▶ Esther added fresh clams to the seafood stew.
伊絲特在燉海鮮裡加了新鮮蛤蜊。

▶ The new girl is so shy she clams up every time I try to talk to her, so I haven't been able to ask her out.
這位新來的女孩十分害羞，以致我每次試著和她攀談，她都閉口不語，所以我一直苦無機會約她出去。

---

clamp [klæmp]

① *v.* 夾住；鉗緊

同 **clasp; fasten**

實用片語與搭配詞

clamp down on sb. / sth.
箝制 / 防止 / 壓制某事

② *n.* 夾子；夾具；夾鉗

同 **brace; clasp**

▶ Clamp down that flap.
把袋蓋固定夾好。

▶ In order to clamp down on crime, the police department appointed 100 more officers.
為了防止犯罪，警察局任命了一百多位警官。

▶ Use a clamp to close that bag.
用夾子來緊閉那個包包。

---

clan [klæn] *n.* 部族

同 **group; tribe**

▶ Wayne can trace his family history to a Scottish clan.
偉恩的家族歷史可追溯至一個蘇格蘭部族。

---

clarity [ˈkler.ə.t̬i] *n.* 清楚；清澈

同 **clearness; limpidity**

▶ She asked her boss for some clarity about the assignment.
她要求老闆把工作任務講清楚。

---

clasp [klæsp]

① *n.* 扣子；緊握

同 **buckle; hook**

▶ The clasp on his jacket was difficult to fasten.
他夾克上的扣子很難扣上。

② *v.* 扣住；緊抱；緊握

同 **buckle; hook**

▸ Marie needed help clasping the back of her dress.
瑪麗需要人幫她把洋裝背後扣好。

---

clause [klɑ:z] *n.* 子句；條款

實用片語與搭配詞

confidentiality clause 保密條款

▸ The sentence contained two clauses.
這個句子包含了兩個子句。

▸ Employees at the tech company must sign a confidentiality clause to protect company secrets.
科技公司的職員必須簽一份保密條款以保護公司機密。

---

cleanse [klenz] *v.* 清洗；淨化

同 **purify**

反 **stain**

▸ The rain cleanses the city air.
雨淨化了都市內的空氣。

---

clearance [ˈklɪr.əns] *n.* 清理；清掃

同 **headroom; headway**

實用片語與搭配詞

clearance sale 清倉大拍賣

▸ The clearance after the storm took a while.
暴風雨肆虐過後，花了一段時間才清理完成。

▸ After the winter season, many stores have clearance sales to get rid of old stock.
冬季過後，許多商店舉行清倉大拍賣以傾銷存貨。

---

clench [klentʃ]

① *v.* 握緊；緊抓

同 **clutch; grip**

實用片語與搭配詞

clench one's fist 握緊拳頭

② *n.* 握緊；緊抓

▸ He clenched his fist when he felt the pain.
他感覺痛時就握緊了拳頭。

▸ In order to stay calm during the argument, I just clenched my fists and did not say anything.
為了在爭論期間保持冷靜，我握緊拳頭閉口不語。

▸ She left a mark after she released her clench.
她鬆脫了緊抓的手之後，仍留有抓痕。

---

cling [klɪŋ] *v.* 黏著；緊握不放

同 **adhere; stick**

▸ The frightened child clung to her mother's dress.
這個害怕的孩子緊抓母親的洋裝不放。

實用片語與搭配詞

cling on / to sb./sth.
緊抓住 / 抱住某人 / 事物

▶ It is not a good idea to cling to your boyfriend if he does not love you anymore.
如果你的男朋友不再愛你，緊抓著他並不是一個好主意。

---

clinical [ˈklɪn.ɪ.kəl] *adj.* 臨床的；診所的

▶ She went to the doctor for some clinical advice.
她去看醫生，尋求臨床上的建議。

---

clockwise [ˈklɑːk.waɪz]

① *adv.* 順時針方向地；右旋地
反 **anti-clockwise**
② *adj.* 順時針方向的；右旋的
反 **anti-clockwise**

▶ The children walked clockwise around the circle.
孩子們順時針繞著圓圈走。

▶ Should I deal the cards in a clockwise order?
我應該按順時針方向來發牌嗎？

---

clone [kloʊn]

① *n.* 複製品
同 **replica; copy**
② *v.* 複製出
同 **duplicate; copy**

▶ The sheep looked like a clone because it was so similar.
那隻綿羊看起來好像是複製羊，因為外觀神似。

▶ The scientist worked hard to clone the cells.
那名科學家努力複製細胞。

---

closure [ˈkloʊ.ʒɚ] *n.* 關閉；結束
同 **end; closing**

▶ My dad told me about the closure of my favorite restaurant.
我爸爸告訴我，我最喜歡的那家餐廳結束營業了。

---

clover [ˈkloʊ.vɚ] *n.* 苜蓿

▶ She kept the four-leaf clover in her pocket.
她把四片葉的苜蓿幸運草放進她的口袋裡。

---

cluster [ˈklʌs.tɚ]

① *n.* 串；簇；群
同 **bunch; group**
② *v.* 聚集成群
同 **bunch; gather**

實用片語與搭配詞

cluster around sb. / sth.
團團圍住某人 / 事

▶ Diane brought a cluster of grapes to the picnic.
黛安帶了一串葡萄來野餐。

▶ The boys clustered around the TV.
男孩們聚集在電視機前。

▶ In our solar system there are several planets clustered around the sun.
在我們的太陽系中，有數個行星聚集在太陽周圍。

clutch [klʌtʃ]

① *v.* 抓住；攫取

同 **grasp; grap**

② *n.* 爪子；掌握；抓住

實用片語與搭配詞

fell into the clutches 落入爪牙

- The baby clutched her blanket in her hands.
  嬰兒把毯子抓在手中。
- The toy was tight in the child's clutch.
  玩具緊緊握在這個孩子的手裡。
- Once you fall into the clutches of drugs and alcohol, it is not easy to escape without help.
  一但你落入毒品與酒精的掌控之中，自救並非易事。

---

coastline [ˈkoʊst.laɪn] *n.* 海岸線

同 **shoreline**

- We drove along the coastline of California.
  我們沿著加州的海岸線開車。

---

cocoon [kəˈkuːn]

① *n.* 繭

② *v.* 把…緊緊包住

同 **insulate; wrap**

實用片語與搭配詞

cocooned in sth. 包裹在某事 / 物之中

- The butterfly broke through the cocoon.
  這隻蝴蝶破繭而出了。
- My son cocooned himself in his blankets.
  我兒子用毛毯把自己緊緊裹住。
- Babies feel safest when they are fed and cocooned in warm blankets.
  當嬰兒被餵飽並且被溫暖的毯子包裹時，是他們覺得最有安全感的時刻。

---

coffin [ˈkɑː.fɪn] *n.* 棺材

同 **tomb**

- Many people are buried in coffins.
  很多人都是被放在棺材裡埋葬的。

---

coherent [koʊˈhɪr.ənt]

adj. 前後一致的；連貫的

同 **consistent; logical**

- I couldn't understand the book. Its ideas were not coherent.
  我看不懂那本書，裡面的觀點前後不一致。

---

coil [kɔɪl]

① *n.* 線圈；圈

同 **loop; spiral**

② *v.* 把…捲成圈；盤繞

同 **curl; loop**

- We stretched the coil of wire across the room.
  我們把線圈拉到房間的另一端。
- Mark coiled the long rope.
  馬克把這條長繩索盤成圈。

coincide [ˌkoʊ.ɪnˈsaɪd] *v.* 同時發生

同 **co-occur**

實用片語與搭配詞

coincide with sth. 和某事同時發生

► This year my birthday coincides with Easter.

今年我的生日和復活節同天。

► My brother's wedding coincides with my graduation ceremony, so I need to choose which one to go to.

我哥哥的婚禮與我的畢業典禮都在同一天，因此我必須擇一參加。

C

Exercise 14

I. Derivatives

1. Low birth rate has put many schools under the threat of ___________ (close) over the past years.
2. You should go to your doctor for opinions before you take part in a ___________ (clinic) trial as a treatment.
3. To Simon's excitement, his baby's arrival day merrily ___________ (coincidence) with his mother's birthday.
4. I bought the doormat when the store went on a ___________ (clearing) sale last summer.
5. Susan has been putting a lot of effort into deriving a ___________ (coherence) strategy from her team.

II. Vocabulary Choices

(A) clause	(B) cling	(C) cocoon	(D) cluster
(E) clone	(F) coincide	(G) clockwise	(H) civilize
(I) clasp	(J) coherent		

1. Sarah's parents ________ d her by cultivating her musical talent since she was only 5.
2. I usually ________ myself in bed and drink hot chocolate during a cold spell.
3. Just because you spent a lot of time on something, it doesn't mean you have to ________ to the past.
4. When people heard the crash outside, they ________ ed around to watch what exactly happened.
5. I always wonder if water spins ________ or in the opposite direction when flushing the toilet.

Unit 15

coincidence [koʊˈɪn.sɪ.dəns] *n.* 巧合

同 **co-occurrence; concurrence**

實用片語與搭配詞

sheer / pure coincidence
純然 / 全然的意外 / 巧合

▶ Running into my old teacher at the airport was pure coincidence.
會在機場遇到我以前的老師，純屬巧合。

▶ It was pure coincidence that I met my best friend on a trip to Spain; we did not plan it.
我在西班牙的旅途中遇見我的摯友實在純屬巧合；我們並沒有事先計畫。

---

colleague [ˈkɑː.liːg] *n.* 同事；同僚

同 **associate; partner**

▶ Dr. Smith was respected by all his colleagues at the hospital.
史密斯醫師在醫院裡受所有同事敬重。

---

collective [kəˈlek.tɪv]

① *adj.* 共同的；集體的

同 **corporate**

實用片語與搭配詞

collective bargaining 勞資雙方的集體談判

② *n.* 企業集團；聯合組織

同 **corporation**

▶ The family made a collective decision to eat out today.
那家人一致決定今天出去吃。

▶ Collective bargaining gives employees power to negotiate with employers because there is strength in numbers.
因為人多勢眾的緣故，勞資雙方集體談判賦予員工權力以與其雇主協商。

▶ The collective worked on the project.
那個企業集團著手進行專案。

---

collector [kəˈlek.tɚ] *n.* 收藏家；收集者

同 **gatherer; accumulator**

▶ He is a collector of fine art.
他是藝術品收藏家。

---

collide [kəˈlaɪd] *v.* 相撞；碰撞

同 **bang; bump**

實用片語與搭配詞

collide with sb. / sth. 和某人或某物相撞

▶ The two players collided on the field. Both were injured.
兩名選手在賽場上相撞，兩個人都受傷了。

▶ It is feared that when a huge asteroid collides with earth, it could be the end of life as we know it.
人們擔憂當巨大的小行星與地球相撞時，可能便是世界末日了。

---

collision [kəˈlɪʒ.ən] *n.* 相撞；碰撞

同 **hit**

▶ There was a car collision on Fifth street.
第五街發生了汽車相撞事故。

colloquial [kə'loʊ.kwi.əl] *adj.* 口語的

反 **literary**

▶ Colloquial phrases should not be used in writing your thesis.
不應該用口語的用語來寫論文。

---

colonel ['kɝː.nəl] *n.* （陸軍或空軍）上校

▶ Earl was promoted to colonel in the army.
厄爾在軍中獲得晉升為上校。

---

colonial [kə'loʊ.ni.əl]

① *adj.* 殖民地的；殖民的

② *n.* 殖民地居民

▶ Tara is studying the American colonial period.
塔拉正在研讀美國殖民時期的歷史。

▶ This town was originally inhabited by the colonials.
這個城鎮最早本來住著殖民地居民。

---

columnist ['kɑː.ləm.nɪst] *n.* 專欄作家

同 **editorialist**

▶ He is a famous columnist for the Times newspaper.
他是泰晤士報的著名專欄作家。

---

combat ['kɑːm.bæt] *n.* 戰鬥 / 與…戰鬥；反對

同 **battle; conflict**

實用片語與搭配詞

combat against / with sb. / sth.
與某人 / 事 / 物搏鬥

▶ The ship was damaged in combat.
這艘船艦在戰鬥中受損了。

▶ Police in the U.S. are in constant combat against drug smugglers from Mexico, but they can't win this war.
美國警方持續打擊墨西哥毒品走私犯，但他們是無法贏得這場鬥爭的。

101

comedian [kə'miː.di.ən] *n.* 喜劇演員

實用片語與搭配詞

stand-up comedian 脫口秀喜劇演員

▶ We hired a comedian to host our company party.
我們雇用了一名喜劇演員來主持公司的派對。

▶ One of my favorite stand-up comedians is Trevor Noah because his performances are full of wit.
特雷弗諾亞是我最喜歡的單口相聲演員之一，因為他的表演幽默風趣。

---

comet ['kɑː.mɪt] *n.* 彗星

▶ The comet only appears every 75 years.
這顆彗星每七十五年才出現一次。

---

commemorate [kə'mem.ə.reɪt]

v. 紀念；慶祝

同 **celebrate; memorialize**

▶ The mayor came to commemorate the new building.
市長蒞臨慶祝新大樓的落成。

commence [kə'mens] *v.* 開始

同 **begin; start**

反 **end; finish**

▶ Class commenced once the bell rang.
鈴響後，就開始上課了。

---

commentary ['kɑː.mən.ter.i] *n.* 評論

同 **review; essay**

實用片語與搭配詞

live commentary on / of sth.
某事物的實況報導

▶ I always enjoy listening to the commentary during sports.
我向來喜歡收聽運動賽事過程中的講評分析。

▶ The live commentary on the sports channel is excellent and it makes the game much easier to understand.
體育頻道的實況報導簡直太棒了，而且它讓賽事更淺顯易懂。

---

commentator ['kɑː.mən.teɪ.t̬ɚ]

n. 時事評論家；實況播音員

▶ The news commentator criticized the government.
這名新聞評論家批評政府。

---

commission [kə'mɪʃ.ən] *v.* 委託；任命

同 **appoint; authorize**

實用片語與搭配詞

commission sb. to do sth.
委託

▶ The president commissioned a review of the situation.
董事長委派人來審查這個情況。

▶ The famous artist was commissioned to create a memorial for those who died in the attack.
這位知名的藝術家被委託創作一個紀念碑，以緬懷該攻擊事件中的罹難者。

commitment [kə'mɪt.mənt] *n.* 承諾；獻身

同 **promise; pledge**

實用片語與搭配詞

take on the commitment 承攬 / 承攬承諾

▶ A wedding ring shows commitment to their partner.
婚戒能展現出對伴侶的承諾。

▶ If you take on the commitment to do this project, you should keep to the deadline.
如果你承攬了這個計畫，你要明白你將會很難脫身。

---

commodity [kə'mɑː.də.t̬i]

n. 商品；有價之物

同 **article of trade; product**

實用片語與搭配詞

export commodity 出口商品

▶ Oil is a valuable commodity.
原油是相當有價值的商品。

▶ Tea and fruit are some of Taiwan's best export commodities and can be found all over the world.
台灣最佳的出口商品其中包含茶葉及水果，它們被銷往全世界各地。

commonplace [ˈkɑː.mən.pleɪs]

adj. 司空見慣的；普通的

同 **ordinary; usual**

► Deadly viruses were commonplace in the Middle Ages.

致命病毒在中古世紀司空見慣。

---

communicative [kəˈmjuː.nə.kə.t̬ɪv]

adj. 暢談的；通訊的

同 **talkative**

反 **reserved**

► I tried to get answers from him. But he wasn't very communicative.

我試圖取得他的回答，可是他不大講話。

---

communism [ˈkɑː.m.jə.nɪ.zəm]

n. 共產主義

反 **capitalism**

► Communism is found in Cuba and China.

古巴和中國實行共產主義。

---

communist [ˈkɑm·jə·nɪst] *adj.* 共產主義的

反 **capitalist**

► Communist leaders rule China.

共產主義的領導人統治中國。

---

commute [kəˈmjuːt] *v.* 通勤

► Jane commutes to her office by taxi.

珍搭計程車通勤上班。

Exercise 15

I. Derivatives

1. I am afraid that I won't be able to attend the conference due to a prior ___________ (commit) but thank you for the invitation.
2. The driver was so lucky to avoid a head-on ___________ (collide) with an oncoming bus.
3. He has dedicated many years to write this novel that is about social upheaval and cultural background under the ___________ (Communism) Party's reign.
4. The value of our business team is to achieve success and make better decisions through ___________ (collect) intelligence.
5. Many elders in Taiwan speak Japanese because they were raised and educated under Japanese ___________ rule.

II. Choices

1. Jason replied an email to his client in an easy ________ style, which made it more friendly and direct to approach them.
   (A) collective (B) colloquial (C) rhetorical (D) oratorical
2. Roger's main job is to provide a running ________ for football games, which is available on radio and TV.
   (A) community (B) communication (C) commentary (D) contemporary
3. One of the issues that President Donald Trump has addressed is that he will take action to ________ human trafficking.
   (A) combine (B) commend (C) combat (D) compare
4. The government has established a ________ to reform the health care system after the presidential election.
   (A) compassion (B) compensation (C) commotion (D) commission
5. The seminar is scheduled to ________ in the middle of December so we still have enough time to prepare.
   (A) commence (B) commend (C) command (D) commerce

Unit 16

commuter [kə'mjuː.t̬ɚ] *n.* 通勤者

▶ The commuters boarded the plane for a short flight.
這些通勤人士登機做短程飛行。

---

compact [kəm'pækt] *adj.* 小的；緊密的

同 **dense**

實用片語與搭配詞

a compact mass of sand 堅實的沙堆

▶ I gave your mother a compact tin of cookies.
我給了你母親一小盒餅乾。

▶ After the 2004 tsunami, people had to clear away the compact mass of sand and debris in search of missing relatives.
在 2004 年的海嘯之後，人們必須清除密實的沙堆以及殘骸，以找尋他們失蹤的家屬。

---

companionship [kəm'pæn.jən.ʃɪp]

n. 友誼；情誼

同 **company; friendship**

▶ They found the companionship they were looking for in each other.
他們在彼此身上找到了所尋求的友誼。

99

comparable ['kɑːm.pɚ.ə.bəl] *adj.* 可比較的

同 **analogous**

反 **incomparable**

▶ The quality of BMW's cars is comparable to those of Mercedes Benz.
寶馬汽車的品質可以媲美賓士汽車。

comparative [kəm'per.ə.t̬ɪv] *adj.* 比較的

反 **absolute**

▶ He mentioned another author as a comparative example.
他提到了另一名作者以作為相互比較的例子。

compass ['kʌm.pəs] *n.* 指南針；羅盤

實用片語與搭配詞

the points of the compass
羅盤上指針的方向

▶ The hikers used their compass to find the trail.
登山客用指南針尋找步道。

▶ The points of a compass are also known as wind directions and there are 32 points including north, east, south and west.
羅盤上的方位，另有風向之稱，上面有 32 個方位，包含了東、西、南、北。

compassion [kəmˈpæʃ.ən] *n.* 憐憫；同情

同 **sympathy**

反 **cruelty**

▶ Marla showed great compassion by feeding the homeless man.
瑪拉提供食物給流浪漢，展現了豐富的同情心。

C

---

compassionate [kəmˈpæʃ.ən.ət]

adj. 有同情心的；憐憫的

同 **sympathetic**

實用片語與搭配詞

deeply compassionate 深具同情心的

▶ The compassionate woman stopped to help the crying child.
很有同情心的婦人停下腳步，來幫那個哭泣的孩子。

▶ Mother Theresa, a nun from Calcutta, was a deeply compassionate person who cared for the sick and dying.
德雷莎修女來自加爾各答，她深具同情心地照料病患與垂死者。

---

compatible [kəmˈpæt̬.ə.bəl]

adj. 能共處的；相容的

同 **well-matched**

反 **incompatible**

實用片語與搭配詞

compatible with sb. / sth.
能共處的 / 相容的

▶ Her friends all got along because they were all very compatible.
他的朋友全都相處融洽，因為他們都很合得來。

▶ I don't think Peter is compatible with his new job in customer care because he does not have enough patience.
我不認為彼德能勝任顧客關懷這份工作，因為他缺乏足夠的耐心。

---

compel [kəmˈpel] *v.* 迫使；使不得不

同 **force**

反 **liberate**

實用片語與搭配詞

compelling story 引人入勝的故事

▶ The court compelled the man to pay his ex-wife.
法院強制這名男子付前妻贍養費。

▶ The sailor told a compelling story of how she stayed alive in the ocean for weeks after her boat sank.
這位船員說了一個引人入勝的故事，關於她在沈船後數週間如何在海上求生。

96

compensate [ˈkɑː.m.pən.seɪt]

v. 彌補；補償；賠償

同 **reimburse**

實用片語與搭配詞

compensate for 彌補

▶ He sat in the front of the boat to compensate the weight difference.
他坐在船首，以彌補重量上的差異。

▶ The student's willingness to learn from others compensates for the fact that he does not have any experience.
這位學生樂於向他人學習的意願，彌補了他經驗不足的事實。

compensation [ˌkɑːm.penˈseɪ.ʃən]

n. 彌補；補償；賠償

同 **recompense**

實用片語與搭配詞

accept / gain / get / obtain / receive some compensation 收到一些補償

- The extra flour added was compensation for the extra water in the recipe.
  多加的麵粉是為了彌補食譜中多加的水。
- Students who do internships must receive some compensation; they cannot be expected to work for free.
  從事實習工作的學生們應當得到一些補償；不能要求他們在無償的情況下工作。

---

competence [ˈkɑːm.pə.t̬əns] *n.* 能力；才幹

同 **capability; ability**

實用片語與搭配詞

lack the competence of 缺乏某種能力

- Her boss frequently asked her questions about this topic because of her competence.
  因為她對這個主題經驗豐富，所以長官常常問她相關的問題。
- Young doctors lack the competence to do complex operations and need to learn from experienced doctors.
  由於年輕的醫師缺乏執行複雜的手術的能力，因此他們必須向經驗豐富的醫師們學習。

---

competent [ˈkɑːm.pə.t̬ənt]

adj. 有能力的；能幹的；稱職的

同 **capable**

反 **incapable**

實用片語與搭配詞

extremely / highly / very competent
非常有能力

- He has worked there 20 years and is very competent at his job.
  他在那裡做了二十年，工作能力很強。
- Julia got the job at the law firm because she is extremely competent.
  因為茱麗雅非常有能力，她得到了一份在法律事務所上班的工作。

---

compile [kəmˈpaɪl] *v.* 彙編

同 **put together; list**

- They compiled all his poems into one book.
  他們把他所有的詩作都彙編成一本書。

---

complement [ˈkɑːm.plə.ment]

① *n.* 使增色之物；補充物；使完善之物

同 **accompaniment; supplement**

② *v.* 為⋯增色；補充；使完善

- The wine was a complement to the meal.
  那酒為這餐飯增色不少。
- The new flowers complimented the rest of her garden.
  新栽種的花和她花園裡的其他植物相得益彰。

complexion [kəmˈplek.ʃən] *n.* 氣色；膚色

同 **skin tone; skin texture**

▶ Sarah wears makeup to brighten her complexion.
莎拉靠化妝來讓膚色更亮麗。

---

complexity [kəmˈplek.sə.t̬i] *n.* 複雜

同 **complication**

反 **simplicity**

▶ The child did not understand the complexity of the issue.
那孩子不了解這個問題有多麼複雜。

---

complication [ˌkɑːm.pləˈkeɪ.ʃən]

n. 使情況複雜化的事物；複雜；併發症

反 **simplification**

▶ Jim created complication at work with his bad attitude.
吉姆惡劣的態度使他在公司製造了麻煩。

---

compliment [ˈkɑːm.plə.mənt]

① *n.* 讚美的話；恭維

同 **flatter; praise**

反 **insult**

② *v.* 讚美；恭維

同 **flatter; praise**

反 **insult**

▶ We paid a nice compliment to the chef after the meal.
我們用完餐後稱讚了主廚。

▶ Simon complimented his wife on her new hairstyle.
賽門讚美了太太的新髮型。

---

component [kəmˈpoʊ.nənt]

① *n.* 成份；構成要素；零件

同 **constituent; ingredient; part**

② *adj.* 組成的；構成的

實用片語與搭配詞

component failure 零件故障

▶ A component of a car is its engine.
引擎是汽車的零件之一。

▶ Finishing early was only a component objective.
提早完成只是一個組成的目標。

▶ The car company will recall thousands of cars due to a component failure that makes their cars explode.
這間汽車公司零件故障的問題造成多起汽車爆炸事件，因此他們將會召回數千輛汽車。

---

compound [ˈkɑːmˈpaʊnd]

① *n.* 化合物；混合物

同 **mix; complex**

實用片語與搭配詞

compound noun 複合名詞

▶ We used a compound of chemicals to make the solution.
我們用了一種化合物來製作溶液。

▶ Compound nouns are words made up of different nouns used together to get a new meaning, like “fireflies.”
複合名詞是由不同的名詞組成，以形成一個新的含義，如「firefly（螢火蟲）」這個字。

② *adj.* 複合的；合成的

③ *v.* 使混合

同 **combine**

- The word "birthplace" is a compound word.
  「birthplace（出生地）」這個英文字是複合字。
- Tin compounded with lead makes pewter.
  錫混和鉛後產生白鑞。

---

comprehend [ˌkɑːm.prəˈhend]

v. 理解；領會

同 **realize; understand**

實用片語與搭配詞

fail to comprehend 不明白 / 無法了解

- The math problem was difficult to comprehend.
  這道數學題目令人難以理解。
- When couples fail to comprehend the importance of talking to each other, their relationship will suffer.
  如果伴侶們無法理解彼此溝通的重要性，他們的感情將會遭遇困難。

---

comprehension [ˌkɑːm.prəˈhen.ʃən]

n. 理解力

同 **intellectual capacity**

實用片語與搭配詞

a lack of comprehension 缺乏了解

- Luke's math comprehension is very advanced.
  路克對數學的理解力很強。
- The kids' puzzled faces showed their lack of comprehension of the difficult math problem.
  孩子們困惑的表情顯示出他們對那道困難的數學題缺乏理解能力。

---

comprehensive [ˌkɑːm.prəˈhen.sɪv]

adj. 包羅萬象的；詳盡的；廣泛的；全面的

反 **incomprehensive**

實用片語與搭配詞

be comprehensively defeated
徹底的失敗了 / 被打敗了

- The museum has a comprehensive showing of works from the 1800s.
  那家博物館展示包羅萬象的十九世紀作品。
- During World War II, Japan was comprehensively defeated after the U.S. bombed Hiroshima and they surrendered.
  二戰期間美國轟炸廣島後，日本徹底被擊敗進而投降。

Exercise 16

I. Choices

1. Many beauty products are appealing to customers who want to look younger and achieve effortless, glowing ________ .
   (A) completion (B) commotion (C) complexion (D) complexity
2. Yvonne considered herself the happiest girl in the world because she already found the one who can ________ her perfectly in their relationship.
   (A) complain (B) complement (C) compliment (D) compare
3. There are some key ________ s that you must have on your resume, which are contact information, educational backgrounds, and work experiences.
   (A) competence (B) comprehension (C) composition (D) component
4. We are assigned to ________ data and project reports for the management meeting that is scheduled in two weeks.
   (A) complete (B) complain (C) compete (D) compile
5. I opt for a ________ digital camera rather than a digital single-lens reflex camera because it's much easier to handle and convenient for light travels.
   (A) compact (B) combat (C) comply (D) complicate

II. Derivatives

1. The keys for a happy marriage lie in the faithful ___________ (companion) and constant communications with each other.
2. It usually will take years to walk steps by steps to get to the particular field that you've chosen and become professionally ___________ (competence).
3. After the bus accident, he has learned how to negotiate a settlement and made a ___________ (compensate) claim for his families who have suffered injuries.
4. This book provides a fairly ___________ (comprehend) overview of what speech and language therapists do and how they change lives.
5. My mom is my rule model who relentlessly encourages me to set high goals for myself, maximize my potential and to love ___________ (compassion).

Unit 17

comprise [kəmˈpraɪz] *v.* 包含；由…組成

同 **consist of; contain**

▶ The sandwich is comprised of two pieces of bread.
這個三明治是由兩片麵包所組成。

---

compromise [ˈkɑːm.prə.maɪz]

① *n.* 妥協；和解

② *v.* 互讓解決；妥協

同 **concede; settle**

▶ The competing companies reached a compromise.
這兩家彼此競爭的公司達成妥協了。

▶ We compromised and decided to share the duties.
我們互讓一步，決定分擔責任。

---

compute [kəmˈpjut] *v.* 計算；估算

同 **calculate; estimate**

▶ Dana computed how much we all owed at dinner.
吃晚餐時，黛娜計算我們所有人要付多少錢。

---

computerize [kəmˈpjuː.t̬ə.raɪz] *v.* 使電腦化

同 **mechanize; automate**

▶ The library is now fully computerized.
這間圖書館現在已經全面電腦化。

---

comrade [ˈkɑːm.ræd]

n. 志同道合的同好；戰友

同 **buddy; companion**

▶ Bryan joined his comrades on the camping trip.
布萊恩跟同好一塊去露營。

---

conceal [kənˈsiːl] *v.* 隱藏；隱瞞

同 **cover up; hide**

反 **disclose; reveal**

實用片語與搭配詞

conceal sth. / sb. from sb.
隱藏某人 / 物不讓某人知道

▶ She concealed the gift behind her back.
她把禮物藏在她背後。

▶ The judge tried to conceal her affair from the public, but news of it became known and she had to resign because of the scandal.
評審嘗試對大眾隱藏她的緋聞，但這新聞爆發後，她仍因此而隱退。

---

concede [kənˈsiːd] *v.* 承認；讓步

同 **admit; confess**

▶ The sister conceded that her little brother was right.
姊姊承認弟弟是對的。

實用片語與搭配詞

be forced to concede 被迫 / 不得不讓步

▶ After Jonathan lost the bet, he was forced to concede defeat and pay for his friend's new car.
在強納生賭輸後，他不得不認輸並且出錢幫朋友買一台新車。

---

conceit [kən'si:t] *n.* 自負；自大

同 conceitedness; snobbery

實用片語與搭配詞

full of conceit 極其自負的

▶ The player was full of conceit after scoring.
那名球員得分之後變得驕傲自大。

▶ The sport star thinks he is better than everyone else; I do not like people who are full of conceit.
那位運動明星認為自己比任何人都厲害；我不欣賞如此自負的人。

---

conceive [kən'si:v] *v.* 懷孕；構想

同 imagine; conceptualize

▶ Anna conceived her first child in Canada.
安娜在加拿大懷了她的第一胎。

---

conception [kən'sep.ʃən]

n. 受孕；懷孕；概念；觀念

同 idea; notion

實用片語與搭配詞

have no conception of sth.
對某事毫無概念

▶ Conception takes place before birth.
出生之前，先有受孕。

▶ Before Jenny saw how hard her father worked, she had no conception where money came from.
在珍妮目睹她的父親是如何賣力地工作之前，她完全沒有概念家中的錢從何處來。

---

concession [kən'seʃ.ən] *n.* 讓步

同 yielding; surrendering

實用片語與搭配詞

make no concessions to sb./sth.
對某人 / 事毫不讓步

▶ The parents made a concession to allow the children to stay up 30 minutes later.
那對父母作出讓步，允許孩子可以晚個半小時睡覺。

▶ I worked hard for my career and I will not make concessions to lazy people who just want an easy life.
我為了我的事業辛勤地工作，而我無法認同那些只想輕鬆過生活的懶人。

---

concise [kən'saɪs]

adj. 簡明扼要的；簡潔的；簡明的

同 brief

反 redundant

▶ He gave the concise answer, "Yes."
他簡明扼要地回答：「好」。

condemn [kən`dem] *v.* 譴責；責難

同 blame

反 forgive

實用片語與搭配詞

condemn sb. for sth. 為了某事責難某人

► The protesters condemned the condition of the prison.

抗議群眾譴責監獄的狀況。

► Don't condemn yourself for the accident. There is nothing you could of done.

不要因為那起意外而譴責自己。即使時光倒流，你也無力挽救。

condense [kən`dens] *v.* 壓縮；縮短；濃縮

同 compress

反 enlarge

實用片語與搭配詞

condense sth. into / to sth.

把某物作成濃縮的某物

► The clothes were condensed in the suitcase.

那些衣服都被壓縮放到手提箱裡了。

► The speaker had to condense his hour-long speech into 20 minutes because the meeting started late.

由於會議延遲開始，那位講者必須把兩小時的演講濃縮成二十分鐘。

conduct [`kɑ:n.dʌkt] *n.* 行為；品性

同 behavior; manner

實用片語與搭配詞

regulate the conduct of sb.

約束某人的行為

► Mac's conduct has never been questioned.

大家都相信麥可的為人。

► The government strictly regulates the conduct of diplomats to avoid international scandals.

政府嚴格規範外交官的舉止，以避免國際醜聞。

conduct [kən`dʌkt] *v.* 引導；指引

同 direct; guide

實用片語與搭配詞

conduct oneself well 行為表現良好

► The police officer conducted cars through the intersection.

員警指引車輛通過十字路口。

► The accused conducted himself well during the hearing and the judge commended him.

被告人在公聽會上行為表現良好，受到了法官的讚揚。

---

confer [kən`fɝ:] *v.* 授予；商議

同 discuss; talk over

實用片語與搭配詞

confer with sb. on / about sth.

向某人請教

► The mayor conferred a medal to the brave boy.

市長授予獎章給那名勇敢的男孩。

► You should confer with your family before going on a working holiday -- they might have some good advice.

在你去打工度假前應該先請教你的父母一他們或許能給你一些不錯的建議。

97

confession [kən'feʃ.ən] *n.* 承認；招供

同 **admission; affirmation**

實用片語與搭配詞

make a confession 認罪

▶ She wrote her confession to the crime in a letter to the police.
她在致警方的信中承認了犯行。

▶ The killer made a confession to his priest.
那位兇手向牧師懺悔。

confidential [ˌkɑːn.fə'den.ʃəl]

adj. 祕密的；機密的

同 **secret; classified**

實用片語與搭配詞

highly confidential 高度機密

▶ I can't tell you about it. It's confidential.
我不能告訴你，那是祕密。

▶ The government gets upset when highly confidential decisions are leaked to the media.
當政府高度機密的文件被洩露給媒體時，他們相當惱火。

---

conform [kən'fɔːrm] *v.* 遵守；遵照

同 **obey the rules; be conventional**

實用片語與搭配詞

in conformity with the rules 依照規則

▶ The student conformed to the master's teachings.
那名學生遵照大師的教導。

▶ If you do not play the game in conformity with the rules, you will be kicked off the team.
如果你不遵循遊戲規則，你將會被踢出此隊。

---

confront [kən'frʌnt] *v.* 對質；遭遇

同 **deal with; face up to**

實用片語與搭配詞

confront sb. with sb. / sth.
使某人面對某人 / 事物

▶ Max confronted the man who stole his wallet.
麥克斯和偷他皮夾的人當面對質。

▶ After the house burned down, police confronted the couple with starting the fire and they admitted guilt.
在這棟房子被焚燬後，警方與那對夫妻當面對質是否縱火一事，而他們認罪了。

104

confrontation [ˌkɑːn.frən'teɪ.ʃən]

n. 對抗；衝突

同 **conflict; argument**

實用片語與搭配詞

bring sb. into confrontation with sb. / sth. 造成某人與某事物相衝突

▶ The mother broke up the brothers' confrontation with each other.
母親化解了兄弟間所發生的衝突。

▶ The animal rights activists were brought into confrontation with the government over the sale of shark fins.
那些動物保育人士在販售鯊魚鰭一事上與政府產生衝突。

congressman / congresswoman

[ˈkɑːŋ.gres.mən / ˈkɑːŋ.gresˌwʊm.ən]

n. 美國國會（男）議員 / 美國國會女議員

同 **representative**

▶ He works in the government as a congressman.
他在政府擔任國會議員。

---

conquest ['kɑːŋ.kwest] *n.* 佔領；征服

反 **surrender**

實用片語與搭配詞

by / through conquest
以征服的手段

▶ The army was successful in its conquest.
軍隊成功達成佔領任務。

▶ The king greatly expanded his kingdom's territory through conquests.
那位國王使用征服的手段，大規模地擴張他的王國領地。

---

conscientious [ˌkɑːn.ʃiˈen.ʃəs]

adj. 憑良心的；認真的

同 **diligent**

反 **careless**

▶ He was a good leader because of his conscientious decisions.
他是一位好領袖，因為他都憑良心作決定。

---

consensus [kənˈsen.səs]

n. 共識；（意見）一致

同 **agreement**

反 **disagreement**

實用片語與搭配詞

have consensus on sth.
對某事達成意見一致的看法

▶ The friends came to a consensus about what to do tomorrow.
那群朋友對明天要作的事已經達成一致共識。

▶ The Syrian government and the rebels have reached a consensus on a peace treaty.
利亞政府和反抗者在和平協定中達成共識。

Exercise 17

I. Derivatives

1. Jason feels extremely frustrated that there is always an inevitable ____________ (confront) between his wife and his mom.
2. One of the good traits I admire about my husband is that he is a ____________ (conscience) man who always earnestly maximizes his potential on what he does.
3. He is full of ____________ (conceited) that he can manage to tackle the complex problem but he doesn't realize how challenging it would be to handle it by himself.
4. After many hours of negotiation, he is not prepared to offer any ____________ (concede) for this settlement on this amount of pay.
5. This premarital counseling course helps them to have some fundamental ____________ (conceive) of joining into a marriage and building a family.

II. Vocabulary Choices

(A) conduct	(B) condemn	(C) conquest	(D) conform
(E) condense	(F) concise	(G) compromise	(H) confidential
(I) comprise	(J) conceal		

1. Before she becomes the official employee of this technology company, she is requested to sign the non-compete agreement that she has to keep customer information _________ and all the business trades in secret.
2. They did try their best to reach a satisfactory _________ in their communication but still ended up in a silent war for several weeks.
3. The celebrity has carefully tried to _________ the fact from the public that he is already married for ten years and has two children.
4. Many humanists have raised an outcry that the British prime minister refused to _________ the policy on refugee restrictions that has led to ripple effects on earth.
5. All the students attending the culinary and pastry arts school are required to _________ to the dress code—wearing chef coats, white aprons, and hats.

Unit 18

consent [kən'sent]

① *v.* 同意；贊成；答應

同 **agree**

反 **deny**

實用片語與搭配詞

consent to sth. 同意某事

② *n.* 同意；贊成；答應

同 **agreement**

反 **disagreement**

實用片語與搭配詞

with / without sb.'s consent
在某人的同意之下

▶ The doctor consented to see me without an appointment.
醫生答應不用預約就幫我看診。

▶ If you want to get married before you are 18, your parents must consent to the marriage.
如果你想在 18 歲前結婚，你的父母必須同意才行。

▶ Terry gave her consent for April to attend the field trip.
泰瑞答應了讓艾波參加戶外教學。

▶ You cannot enter your sister's room without her consent; she will be very angry.
你不能未經你姊姊的允許就進入她的房間；她會非常生氣。

conservation [ˌkɑːn.sɚ'veɪ.ʃən]

n. 保存；（自然環境的）保育

同 **preservation**

實用片語與搭配詞

environmental conservation
環境保育

▶ Put food in the refrigerator for better conservation.
把食物存放在冰箱能保存得更好。

▶ Recycling and using less plastic is one way we can contribute to environmental conservation.
為環境保護盡一分心力的其中一個方法就是落實回收及減少塑膠用量。

conserve [kən'sɝːv] *v.* 保存；保護

同 **guard; save**

實用片語與搭配詞

conserve one's strength 保存體力

▶ It's important to conserve our natural resources.
保護自然資源是很重要的事。

▶ The best way to conserve your strength while hiking is to take short breaks and drink lots of water.
健行時，保存體力的最佳方式就是頻繁休息以及大量飲水。

conserve ['kɑːn.sɝːv] *n.* 果醬；蜜餞

同 **jam; marmalade**

▶ My aunt served a delicious peach conserve.
我阿姨端上了美味的桃子醬。

considerate [kənˈsɪd.ɚ.ət]

adj. 考慮周到的；體貼的

同 **thoughtful**

反 **inconsiderate**

實用片語與搭配詞

considerate towards others
體貼 / 為人著想的

- Be considerate of others when you are in public.
當你身處公共場所時，請為他人著想。
- My friend is very considerate towards others and will always help whenever there is need.
我的朋友非常為別人著想，並且每當他人有困難，他總是提供協助。

---

consolation [ˌkɑːn.səˈleɪ.ʃən] *n.* 安慰

反 **agony; distress**

實用片語與搭配詞

seek consolation 尋求慰藉

- He received many consolations after receiving the bad news.
他接獲壞消息之後，得到了很多人的安慰。
- After her husband passed away, Mary sought consolation from her family and friends.
當瑪麗的丈夫過世後，她向她的親友尋求慰藉。

---

console [kənˈsoʊl] *v.* 安慰；撫慰

同 **comfort**

反 **torment**

實用片語與搭配詞

console sb. with sth.
安慰受到某事影響的某人

- Harry consoled his friend after his dog died.
哈利朋友的狗死了之後，哈利就去安慰他。
- My best friend lost her job and became very depressed, so I tried to console her with some flowers.
我最好的朋友失業了並且極度沮喪，所以我試著送她一些花來安慰她。

console [ˈkɑːn.soʊl] *n.* 控制板；操縱臺

同 **control panel/board**

- Open the console to adjust the stereo's settings.
打開控制板來調整音響的設定。

---

conspiracy [kənˈspɪr.ə.si] *n.* 密謀；陰謀

同 **plot; scheme**

實用片語與搭配詞

be involved in / be part of a conspiracy 涉入某種陰謀

- Ten men were involved in the conspiracy to overthrow the government.
有十個人涉及密謀顛覆政府。
- The president's bodyguards were part of the conspiracy to assassinate him.
在暗殺總統的陰謀之中，總統的貼身保鑣是其中一個部分。

constituent [kən'stɪtʃ.u.ənt]

① *adj.* 構成的；組成的

同 **component; essential**

② *n.* 成份；組成要素

同 **component; ingredient**

► Each student's constituent effort helped to complete the project on time.
每個學生的心力集結起來構成的集體努力，有助於及時完成專案。

► The chef discerned each constituent factor of the meal.
大廚辨別出那餐飯中的每一個組成要素。

---

constitutional [ˌkɑːn.stə'tuː.ʃən.əl]

① *adj.* 憲法的；生來的；本質上的

反 **autocratic**

② *n.* 健身散步

► A constitutional amendment alters a previous law.
一項憲法修正案改變了一條先前的法律。

► The man took a constitutional around the park.
這名男子繞著公園散步健身。

---

consultation [ˌkɑːn.sʌl'teɪ.ʃən]

n. 諮詢；商議

同 **discussion; talk**

實用片語與搭配詞

in consultation with sb. 和某人請教

► She sought her mother's consultation on the matter.
她針對那件事情徵詢媽媽的意見。

► In consultation with her lawyer, Jennifer decided to continue the case against the stalker despite her fear.
在與她的律師諮詢後，儘管珍妮佛心生畏懼，仍決定繼續起訴那位跟蹤狂。

---

consumption [kən'sʌmp.ʃən]

n. 消耗；消費（量）

反 **production**

實用片語與搭配詞

cut down / reduce consumption
減少消費

► They had to refuel many times because the car's gas consumption was high.
因為那輛車很耗油，所以他們必須加油很多次。

► Take shorter showers to reduce your water consumption.
為了減少用水量，不妨縮短淋浴的時間。

---

contagious [kən'teɪ.dʒəs] *adj.* 傳染的

同 **infectious; spreading**

實用片語與搭配詞

highly contagious 傳染性很強

► His illness wasn't contagious, so Matt went back to work.
麥特的病不會傳染，所以他回去上班了。

► Ebola is a highly contagious disease and you can get it by touching a sick person.
伊波拉病毒是傳染性極高的疾病，並且你會因為觸碰患者而染病。

contaminate [kən'tæm.ə.neɪt]

v. 弄髒；污染

同 **pollute; defile**

實用片語與搭配詞

contaminate sth. / sb. with sth.
以某物汙染某人 / 事

- ▶ The chemicals contaminated the river.
  這些化學物質污染了這條河。
- ▶ The raw fish was outside for too long, so we got sick from eating the sashimi that was contaminated with bacteria.
  因為生魚肉置於常溫下過久已被細菌污染，所以我們吃了生魚片後身體不適，

---

contemplate ['kɑ:n.t̬əm.pleɪt]

v. 深思熟慮；凝視；思忖

同 **consider; think**

實用片語與搭配詞

sit and contemplate 坐下來冥想

- ▶ Jean contemplated what to wear to the wedding.
  珍左思右想到底該穿什麼去參加婚禮。
- ▶ Every day after work, I sit down with a cup of tea and contemplate my day; this helps me relax.
  每天下班後，我邊喝茶邊坐下沈思當日點滴；這樣有助於我放鬆。

---

contemplation [ˌkɑ:n.t̬əm'pleɪ.ʃən]

n. 深思熟慮；沉思

同 **reflection; consideration**

實用片語與搭配詞

be deep in contemplation 入神

- ▶ He spent a long time in contemplation before answering.
  他深思熟慮很久之後才回答。
- ▶ Mary was so deep in contemplation that she did not hear or see me when I entered the coffee shop.
  瑪麗深深陷入沈思，以致於當我走進咖啡店時，她完全沒有看到我或聽到我的呼喊。

---

contemporary [kən'tem.pə.rer.i]

① *adj.* 當代的

同 **modern; present-day**

② *n.* 同時代的人或物；現代人

- ▶ Two contemporary sources supported the facts.
  兩項當代的資料來源都佐證了事實。
- ▶ His grandfather was a contemporary of Chiang Kai-Shek.
  他的祖父跟蔣介石是同時代的人。

---

contempt [kən'tempt] *n.* 蔑視；輕視；輕蔑

同 **despise**

反 **respect**

實用片語與搭配詞

contempt for 輕視某人或某物

- ▶ She couldn't hide her contempt for the man that had attacked her.
  她難以隱藏對那個攻擊她的人的蔑視。
- ▶ Peter had such contempt for animal abusers that he blew up the car of a dog-fighting gangster.
  彼得非常鄙視虐待動物者，以致於他還損毀了一群虐狗流氓的車子。

C

contend [kən'tend] *v.* 爭奪；競爭

同 **fight quarrel**

實用片語與搭配詞

contend with / against sb. / sth.
與某人 / 事競爭；必須面對某人 / 某事

▶ The armies contended for control of the region.
各軍隊相互爭奪這個地區的控制權。

▶ Jane did not have enough money for a trip to Thailand, so she had to contend with staying home during the long weekend.
珍沒有足夠的錢去泰國旅行，所以她得面對長假必須待在家的煎熬。

---

contestant [kən'tes.t̬ənt] *n.* 參賽者；角逐者

同 **competitor; challenger**

▶ Three contestants were left for the final round.
最後一回合只剩下三名參賽者角逐。

---

continental ['kɑ:n.t̬ən.ənt] *adj.* 大陸的

反 **insular**

▶ They will limit their trip to within the continental United States.
他們會把旅行的範圍限定在美國大陸內。

---

continuity [ˌkɑ:n.tən'u:.ə.t̬i] *n.* 連續性

同 **persistence; permanence**

▶ There is continuity between season 1 and 2 of this TV series.
這齣電視劇的第一季和第二季節目情節是連續的。

---

contractor ['kɑ:n.træk.tɚ]
n. 承包業者；立契約者

同 **service provider; outworker**

實用片語與搭配詞

independent contractor 獨立承包商

▶ They hired a contractor to finish the job.
他們僱請了承包商來完成那項工作。

▶ The company needed an IT engineer but could not afford to employ one, so they used an independent contractor.
這家公司需要但卻無法雇用一位資訊技術工程師，因此他們找了獨立承包商。

100

contradict [ˌkɑ:n.trə'dɪkt] *v.* 反駁；與…矛盾

同 **oppose**

實用片語與搭配詞

contradict oneself 自相矛盾

▶ The policeman found that their two stories contradicted each other.
警察發現他們兩人的說法相互矛盾。

▶ The court found the suspect guilty after he contradicted himself on where he was on the night of the murder.
法官認為該嫌疑犯有罪，因為他在交代自己案發前晚的行蹤時自相矛盾。

contradiction [ˌkɑːn.trəˈdɪk.ʃən] *n.* 矛盾

實用片語與搭配詞

in direct contradiction with sb. / sth.
與某人或事相矛盾

▶ She noted her husband's contradiction of watching TV instead of exercising like he said.
她注意到自己丈夫很矛盾，嘴上說要運動，可是實際上卻看電視。

▶ Drug smuggling in Malaysia is in direct contradiction with the law and can get you the death penalty.
在馬來西亞，走私毒品是牴觸法律的，並且可以讓你被判死刑。

Exercise 18

I. Choices

1. Mia has been working as a curator in ________ arts field for more than six years, and she is responsible for all the content to support exhibitions.
   (A) conciliatory (B) extemporary (C) contemporary (D) contrary
2. Many people believe that the US government was involved in the ________ to assassinate Dr. Martin Luther King and the Court has found government agencies guilty in the assassination.
   (A) conspiracy (B) consistency (C) contumacy (D) confederacy
3. Tina has been given two options to work as a ________ or a freelancer, and she finally opts for the former because the company can take care of the employment taxes and pay her by the hour.
   (A) consolidator (B) contributor (C) congregator (D) contractor
4. Celina has a personality that can authentically bring much joy and ebullience to everyone around her and her smile is just ________ .
   (A) conscious (B) conspicuous (C) contentious (D) contagious
5. The food company is being investigated by the food safety affair on the use of gutter oil in their products, an element unfit for human ________ .
   (A) convention (B) consumption (C) contamination (D) consternation

II. Derivatives

1. The visit to Africa gives him a quiet time to absorb in ____________ (contemplate) to recognize how far he has come and how far he has to go.
2. If you are interested in getting more detailed discussion, please contact Eddy for a face-to-face ____________ (consult) and he will provide professional advice and guidance to your management on business.
3. I found the pastor's response in fundamental ____________ (contrary) to what he has been preaching on the stage.
4. Ross Sea in Antarctica is the largest marine ____________ (conserve) area in the world, which is designed to protect its diverse and abundant wildlife.
5. After the loss of his wife, his faith was a great ____________ (console) to help him find peace in the time of need.

controversial [ˌkɑːn.trəˈvɝː.ʃəl]

adj. 有爭議的；引起爭論的

同 **contentious; divisive**

實用片語與搭配詞

highly controversial
高度爭議性的

▶ This traditional practice was controversial but still legal.
這項傳統做法雖然有爭議性，卻仍屬合法。

▶ Legalizing abortions in the U.S. is a highly controversial issue and many people fight over it.
在美國，墮胎合法化是一個具高度爭議性的議題，並且許多人與其奮戰。

---

controversy [ˈkɑːn.trə.vɝː.si] *n.* 爭論；爭議

同 **argument; debate**

實用片語與搭配詞

a controversy about / over sth.
關於某事的爭議

▶ The controversy caused her to quit her job.
那起爭議導致她辭職。

▶ There is controversy over whether the country should build another nuclear power plant.
關於該國是否該興建另一座核電廠一事，引起許多爭議。

convert [kənˈvɝːt] *v.* 變換；轉變

同 **change; transform**

實用片語與搭配詞

gain converts for sth. 轉換為某物

▶ The heat converted most of the ice into water.
熱能把大部分的冰化成了水。

▶ In order for you to gain converts for this crazy idea, you will have to be very persuasive.
為了改變這個瘋狂的想法，你必須讓自己非常具有說服力。

---

convict [kənˈvɪkt] *v.* 判… 罪；使認罪

同 **sentence to**

反 **acquit**

實用片語與搭配詞

convicted sb. of sth. 判某人…罪

▶ The jury convicted the man of murder.
陪審團判這名男子謀殺罪成立。

▶ The court convicted the man of murder charges, but after 20 years in jail, he was found innocent.
法官判這位男子謀殺罪，但在獄中 20 年後，他才被發現是清白的。

convict [ˈkɑːn.vɪkt] *n.* 囚犯

同 **prisoner**

▶ The convict was released from prison after serving his term.
這名囚犯刑期屆滿後，自監獄獲釋。

conviction [kən'vɪk.ʃən] *n.* 定罪；證明有罪

反 **acquittal**

▶ The criminal heard her conviction from the judge.
女罪犯從法官口中聽到了她被判有罪。

---

coordinate [koʊ'ɔːr.dən.eɪt]

① *v.* 協調

同 **organize; arrange**

實用片語與搭配詞

have good / poor coordination
善於 / 不善於協調自己的動作

② *adj.* 同等的；對等的

▶ Mom is the one who coordinates the weekend trips.
媽媽負責統籌協調週末的旅行。

▶ People who have poor coordination find it difficult to do exercises with a lot of quick movements.
協調力不佳的人會覺得含有許多快速動作的運動相當困難。

▶ The children have coordinate responsibilities at home.
孩子們各自在家裡負擔著同等的責任。

---

coordinate [koʊ'ɔːr.dən.ət] *n.* 座標

▶ He used the coordinates on the graph to take measurements.
他利用圖表上的座標來進行量測。

---

copyright ['kɑː.pi.raɪt]

① *n.* 版權；著作權

實用片語與搭配詞

breach of copyright 違反著作權

② *v.* 取得版權

▶ The book's copyright expires next year.
這本書的著作權到明年終止。

▶ The book was made into a film without the author's permission, so she sued them for breach of copyright.
這本書在未經作者允許的情況下被翻拍成電影，所以她控告他們違反著作權。

▶ Peter copyrighted his new invention.
彼得為他的新發明申請專利。

---

coral ['kɔːr.əl]

① *n.* 珊瑚

② *adj.* 珊瑚（色）的

▶ Swim out to the coral, and you can see a lot of fish.
游到珊瑚區時，你會看到許許多多的魚。

▶ Alice wore a coral dress to the party.
愛麗絲穿了件珊瑚色的洋裝參加派對。

---

cordial ['kɔːr.dʒəl] *adj.* 熱誠的；友好的

同 **friendly; hospitable**

▶ Father taught us to always be cordial to older guests that came to our home.
爸爸告訴我們，一定要熱誠招待來我們家的年長客人。

實用片語與搭配詞

remain cordial 仍然保持友好的關係

▶ She remained cordial at the party despite the fact that the hostess was her husband's ex-girlfriend.
儘管這場派對的主辦人是她丈夫的前女友，她仍然與主辦人保持友好關係。

---

core [kɔ:r]

① *n.* 核心；果核

同 **center; heart**

② *v.* 挖去…的果核

▶ The core of the earth is very hot and dense.
地心極熱而且密度極大。

▶ Mom cored apples for the pie.
媽媽把蘋果去核，好拿來作派。

---

corporate [ˈkɔ:r.pɚ.ət]

adj. 公司的；全體的

同 **company; friendship**

▶ The corporate office would come to make observations and give a presentation.
那家公司會來考察，並發表簡報。

---

corporation [ˌkɔ:r.pəˈreɪ.ʃən]

n. 股份有限公司；法人

同 **business; company**

▶ The corporation decided to lay off 500 people.
這家公司決定裁員五百人。

---

corps [kɔ:r] *n.* 部隊；團

同 **army; legion**

實用片語與搭配詞

press corps 記者團

▶ He was part of a special corps in the army.
他隸屬於軍中一個特殊部隊。

▶ A large press corps followed the president on his first foreign trip.
一大群隨行記者跟著總統參加他的第一趟外交之旅。

---

corpse [kɔ:rps] *n.* 遺體；屍體

同 **dead body**

▶ Her corpse was buried after the funeral.
葬禮後，她的遺體被埋葬了。

---

correspondence [ˌkɔ:r.əˈspɑ:n.dəns]

n. 一致；符合

同 **match; equivalence**

實用片語與搭配詞

correspondence with sb. 與某人通信

▶ There was no correspondence between what the two men said they saw.
這兩名男子對於看到的事各說各話，並不一致。

▶ Before they met in person, Julia was in correspondence with her husband on Facebook for several years.
在茱麗雅當面見到她的丈夫之前，他們透過臉書通信聯繫已達數年之久。

correspondent [ˌkɔːr.əˈspɑːn.dənt]

n. （特派）記者；通信者

同 **reporter; journalist**

▶ The news correspondent gave a report on the event.
特派記者發佈了有關那個事件的新聞報導。

---

corridor [ˈkɔːr.ə.dɚ] *n.* 走廊；通道

同 **aisle; walkway**

▶ My bedroom is at the end of a long corridor.
我的臥室在一條長廊的盡頭。

---

corrupt [kəˈrʌpt]

① *adj.* 貪汙的；墮落的；腐敗的

同 **crooked; rotten**

② *v.* 使腐敗；使墮落；收買

▶ The corrupt politician accepted bribes.
這名貪污的政客收受賄賂。

▶ The immoral teacher corrupted his students.
這個道德敗壞的老師帶壞了學生。

---

corruption [kəˈrʌp.ʃən] *n.* 貪腐；墮落

同 **degeneracy; depravation**

▶ Unfortunately, corruption prevented any political change.
遺憾的是，貪腐妨礙了政治變革。

---

cosmetic [kɑːzˈmet̬.ɪk]

① *adj.* 化妝品的

同 **decorative; makeup**

② *n.* 化妝品

同 **makeup**

▶ Please hand me that cosmetic cream for my skin.
請遞給我擦皮膚用的美容霜。

▶ Her bathroom is filled with all kinds of cosmetics.
她的浴室裡滿是各式各樣的化妝品。

---

cosmopolitan [ˌkɑːz.məˈpɑː.lɪ.t̬ən]

① *adj.* 國際性的；世界性的

同 **worldwide; international**

② *n.* 見多識廣的人；四海為家的人

▶ The international news covers many cosmopolitan issues.
國際新聞報導很多國際性的議題。

▶ The cosmopolitan told us of his many travels.
那個見識廣博的人告訴我們他的很多旅遊經驗。

---

counsel [ˈkaʊn.səl]

① *n.* 商議；忠告

同 **advice; guidance**

實用片語與搭配詞

give / offer sb. counsel 給建議

▶ We met in counsel before deciding the company's future.
我們彼此商議討論了之後，才決定公司未來該怎麼走。

▶ The lawyer offered counsel to his client to help him prepare for his trial.
這位律師提供客戶法律諮詢服務，以協助他為審判做準備。

② *v.* 商議

同 **advise; confer**

▶ Lynn's teacher counseled her before Lynn applied for college.

在琳恩申請大學前，琳恩的老師為她提供了些建議。

---

counselor [ˈkaʊn·sə·lər]

n. 顧問；指導老師（諮商師）

同 **therapist; psychotherapist**

▶ The school provided a counselor to the grieving students.

學校請了輔導老師來輔導因親人去世而悲痛的學生。

---

counterclockwise [ˌkaʊn.t̬ɚˈklɑːk.waɪz]

① *adv.* 逆時針方向地

反 **clockwise**

② *adj.* 逆時針方向的

反 **clockwise**

▶ We will pass the ball counterclockwise around the circle.

我們將會圍著圈逆時針方向傳球。

▶ The game is played in a counterclockwise formation.

這場比賽以逆時針方向的隊形進行。

---

counterpart [ˈkaʊn.t̬ɚ.pɑːrt]

n. 極相像的人或物；相對應的人事物

同 **corresponding item**

▶ She looked at the name brand and the generic brand counterpart before deciding.

她先看看知名品牌，又看了普通品牌的類似產品，之後才決定要買哪種。

C

Exercise 19

I. Choices

1. Private ________ revelations and office facilities for personal use are not permitted in a workplace.
   (A) independence (B) correspondence (C) condescendence (D) resplendence
2. His experience in international diplomacy makes him a ________ and has also given him a broader perspective on life.
   (A) cosmological (B) cosmogonical (C) cosmochemical (D) cosmopolitan
3. The exciting trip to Singapore has started with the ________ greeting that we received from the tour guide.
   (A) conchoidal (B) colloidal (C) cordial (D) coral
4. To everyone's surprise, Steve quite openly admitted his previous ________ s for drug smuggling.
   (A) conviction (B) convention (C) confirmation (D) consideration
5. Because of the ________ scandal that the South Korean president allowed a friend to be an interloper in state affairs, Park Geun-hye has become the first president to be impeached from office in the country.
   (A) collision (B) corporation (C)corruption (D) cooperation

II. Vocabulary Choices

(A) copyright	(B) cosmetic	(C) coordinate	(D) controversial
(E) core	(F) corridor	(G) counsel	(H) corporation
(I) convert	(J) counterpart		

1. The busy schedules are well ________ d and the entire meeting is successfully organized due to her responsibility and capability.
2. Tammy is a medical student of dermatology and she believes that ________ surgery can improve people's confidence and self-esteem by making difference of people's appearances.
3. Immigration and abortion have been recognized as a highly ________ and sensitive issue over the years.
4. Gender quality issue and women's empowerment has been highlighted around the globe that women should be ensured to be given as many opportunities as their male ________ .
5. Please kindly note that you have to ________ time zones between different locations before you send out the meeting notification to various attendees from all over the world.

Unit 20

coupon [ˈkuː.pɑːn] *n.* 折價券；聯票
同 **voucher**

▶ Joe used a coupon for free popcorn at the movies.
喬伊用折價券在電影院換了免費的爆米花。

---

courtyard [ˈkɔːrt.jɑːrd] *n.* 庭院；天井
同 **patio**

▶ The children played in the courtyard between the homes.
孩子們在房子間的庭院裡玩耍。

100
coverage [ˈkʌv.ɚ.ɪdʒ]
n. 新聞報導；覆蓋（範圍）
同 **reportage; exposure**

▶ The news had wide coverage of the election.
新聞中大幅報導選舉的消息。

---

covet [ˈkʌv.ət] *v.* 覬覦；垂涎；渴望
同 **desire; long for**

實用片語與搭配詞
covet sb.'s position 覬覦某人的職位

▶ Frank's neighbor coveted his new car.
法蘭克的鄰居相當覬覦他的新車。

▶ I have always coveted my friend's traveling job until I realized that she does not see her family much.
直到我發現我朋友無法時常與家人相聚之前，我還一直嚮往著她那可以到處旅行的工作。

---

cowardly [ˈkaʊ.ɚd.li] *adj.* 膽小的；怯懦的
反 **bold; brave**

▶ The town major's cowardly failure to address the problem resulted in bigger problems.
鎮長因懦弱而無法處理這個問題，卻導致了更嚴重的問題。

---

cozy [ˈkoʊ.zi] *adj.* 舒適的
同 **comfortable**

▶ Jan was warm and cozy in her new winter jacket.
珍穿著新的冬季外套，感到溫暖又舒適。

---

cracker [ˈkræk.ɚ] *n.* 薄脆餅乾

▶ We served crackers and cheese before dinner.
我們在晚餐前供應薄脆餅乾和起司。

---

cramp [kræmp]
① *n.* 抽筋；痙攣
同 **spasm**

▶ She had to stop running because she got a cramp.
她必須停止跑步，因為她抽筋了。

② *v.* 抽筋；痙攣

實用片語與搭配詞

cramp one's progress 阻礙某人的進步

▶ His leg cramped during his exercise.
他在運動時腳抽筋了。

▶ If your goal is to be an entrepreneur, then working for a boss can sometimes cramp your progress.
如果你的目標是成為一位創業家，那麼受僱於人可能會阻礙你的成長。

---

crater [ˈkreɪ.t̬ɚ]

① *n.* 火山口

② *v.* 使成坑

▶ The volcano's eruption created several craters in the earth.
這座火山噴發在地表造成了好幾個火山口。

▶ A missile cratered a hole in the desert.
飛彈在這片沙漠上炸出了一個坑洞。

---

creak [kriːk]

① *n.* 嘎吱聲

同 **creaking; squeak**

實用片語與搭配詞

the creak of a floorboard 地板的嘎吱聲

② *v.* 嘎吱作響

同 **squeak**

▶ The old door makes a loud creak when you open it.
這扇老舊的門打開時會發出很大的嘎吱聲。

▶ Benjamin tried to sneak out of the house, but the creak of a floorboard woke up his dad and spoiled his plans.
班杰明試著逃出這棟房子，但是地板的嘎吱聲吵醒了他的父親並且讓他的計劃泡了湯。

▶ The steps creak when you walk on them.
走在這些台階上時，台階會嘎吱作響。

---

credibility [ˌkred.əˈbɪl.ə.t̬i]

n. 可信度；可靠性

同 **trustworthiness; reliability**

實用片語與搭配詞

regain / gain credibility 重新取得信用

▶ Everyone listens to him. He has a lot of credibility among the community.
大家都聽從他。他在社區裡非常受到大家信賴。

▶ The company tried to regain their credibility after the oil scandal, but the damage was too great.
在石油醜聞爆出後，這間公司試著挽回大眾的信任，但其損失已大到無以彌補。

101

credible [ˈkred.ə.bəl] *adj.* 可信的；可靠的

同 **believable**

▶ Don't believe what you hear unless the source is credible.
不該輕信你所聽到的傳言，除非來源可信。

---

creek [kriːk] *n.* 小河；溪

同 **brook**

▶ The boys went swimming in the creek.
男孩們去了那條小溪游泳。

crib [krɪb]

① *n.* 小兒床；糧倉

同 **cot; cribbage**

② *v.* 把…關住；把…放進糧倉

實用片語與搭配詞

crib sth. from / off sb. 抄襲某人的東西

▶ Our baby slept in a crib until she was three years old.
我們的孩子三歲前一直睡在小兒床上。

▶ The dog was cribbed in a cage in the garage.
這條狗被關在車庫的一個籠子裡。

▶ Harry did not study for the Math test, so he had to crib the answers from his friend or fail again.
哈利並未為那個數學考試做準備，所以他必須抄襲朋友的答案，不然他就要再次不及格了。

---

criterion [kraɪˈtɪr.i.ən] *n.* 標準；準則

同 **measure; standard**

▶ The teacher gave them the criterion for the project.
老師給了他們那項專案的相關準則。

---

crocodile [ˈkrɑː.kə.daɪl] *n.* 鱷魚

▶ The fishermen were careful not to go near the sleeping crocodiles.
這名漁夫小心翼翼地跟那隻正在睡覺的鱷魚保持距離。

---

crook [krʊk]

① *n.* 曲柄手杖；彎曲之物

同 **bend; curve**

② *v.* 彎曲

同 **bend; curve**

▶ The shepherd uses a crook for the sheep.
那個牧羊人用曲柄手杖來放羊。

▶ The car hit the pole and crooked it.
那部車撞到柱子，把它撞彎了。

---

crooked [ˈkrʊk.ɪd] *adj.* 歪的；彎曲的

反 **straight**

▶ Please fix the picture on the wall because it's crooked.
請調整牆上掛的那幅畫，因為它歪掉了。

---

crossing [ˈkrɑː.sɪŋ]

n. 橫度海洋的旅程；越過；十字路口

反 **traversing; passover**

▶ Many people died during the crossing of early America.
美國早期有不少人在橫度海洋的旅程中喪生。

---

crouch [kraʊtʃ]

① *v.* 蹲伏；曲膝

同 **cower; cringe**

▶ I crouched down to give the crying child a hug.
我蹲下來抱抱這個哭鬧的小孩。

實用片語與搭配詞

crouched down 蹲伏著

② *n.* 蹲伏

同 **squat; cringe**

▶ The tiger crouched down behind the bush, ready to pounce on the unsuspecting deer.
那隻老虎在灌木叢後蜷伏著，準備好要襲擊那隻毫無戒備的鹿。

▶ His crouch at the plate makes it hard for pitchers to throw strikes.
有他蹲在本壘板上，眾投手難以投出好球。

104

crucial ['kru:.ʃəl]

adj. 決定性的；重要的；至關重大的

同 **critical; decisive**

▶ She was about to have a baby. It was crucial to get her to the hospital.
她即將臨盆了，重要的是該把她送到醫院去。

---

crude [kru:d] *adj.* 天然的；未經加工的

同 **raw**

反 **refined**

▶ They take crude iron from the mine and put it on a train.
他們把從礦坑裡取得生鐵，並運送到火車上。

---

cruise [kru:z]

① *v.* 巡航；航遊

同 **sail**

② *n.* 巡航；航遊

同 **sail**

▶ They cruised around the islands.
他們繞著各個島嶼航行。

▶ My parents went on a cruise this summer.
我爸媽今年夏天搭船旅遊。

---

cruiser ['kru:.zɚ] *n.* 巡洋艦；遊艇

同 **patrol ship; pleasure craft**

實用片語與搭配詞

a round-the-world cruise 環遊世界遊艇

▶ My friend in the navy worked on a cruiser.
我有個朋友是海軍，他在巡洋艦上工作。

▶ I am saving money to go on a round-the-world cruise that will include more than a hundred countries.
為了那趟環遊世界百國以上的郵輪之旅，我正在存錢當中。

---

crumb [krʌm] *n.* 碎屑

反 **crust**

實用片語與搭配詞

crumb of comfort 些許的安慰

▶ All that was left from dinner were crumbs.
晚餐只剩下一點點殘羹剩飯而已。

▶ Harriet lost the beauty competition, but winning the "Best Personality Prize" was a crumb of comfort.
哈里特在那場選美競賽中未獲勝，但是贏得「最佳個性獎」也算些許的安慰。

Exercise 20

I. Choices

1. Party delegates are facing a number of ________ and challenging issues after the presidential election.

   (A) cultural (B) cruel (C) crucial (D) credential

2. Yvonne could barely walk and almost fainted to the ground when she had her menstrual ________ so she was sent to an emergency room.

   (A) cramp (B) camp (C) crampon (D) crump

3. He knows how to create news release for the fundraising event not only on TV but also on social media, which has given it a wide and full media ________ .

   (A) cover-up (B) coverage (C) crusade (D) coverture

4. The lion ________ es in the grasses to stalk its prey for an amount of time before it pounces on the cape buffalo.

   (A) crust (B) crunch (C) crush (D) crouch

5. The door next to my room ________ s when it is opened, which constantly annoys me during my rest.

   (A) creak (B) crook (C) crop (D) creek

II. Derivatives

1. From many entrepreneurs' experiences, the most essential tactic to earn immediate ____________ (credible) for your start-up business is to be upfront and honest about your brand and products.
2. Objective ____________ (criterion) such as skin color, ethnicity, or religion for employment could be seriously considered as discrimination.
3. Before I found out that she was a ____________ (crook) and dishonest lawyer, I was convinced by her professional appearance.
4. The chocolate cake that mom makes is the best on earth because there will be no ____________ s (crumbable) left at all.
5. The bridegroom made a ____________ (coward) decision without saying anything to have cold feet on his wedding day.

Unit 21

crumble ['krʌm.bəl]

① *v.* 粉碎；碎裂

同 **break up; disintegrate**

實用片語與搭配詞

crumble sth. up 把某物弄碎

② *n.* 碎裂之物；破碎之物

- She liked to crumble crackers into the soup.
  她喜歡把餅乾剁碎放進湯裡。
- To make a meat loaf, crumble up the bread, and add ground beef and onion.
  製作肉糕時，必須把麵包壓碎，並且加入碎牛肉及洋蔥。
- I love her berry crumble for dessert.
  我喜歡吃她做的莓果酥派當點心。

---

crunch [krʌntʃ]

① *v.* 嘎吱作響地咬嚼

② *n.* 嘎吱聲；咬嚼聲

同 **crackle; crush**

實用片語與搭配詞

when the crunch comes
當關鍵時刻來臨之時

- Noah crunched on his cereal at breakfast.
  諾亞早餐時嘎吱嘎吱地嚼穀片。
- The crunch of Mark's popcorn was so loud that Mia couldn't hear the movie.
  馬克嘎吱嘎吱地吃爆米花，聲音大到讓米雅聽不到電影的聲音。
- Everybody said Susan would not make a good nurse, but when the crunch came, she out-performed everyone.
  之前大家都說蘇珊無法成為一位稱職的護士，但在關鍵時刻來臨時，她的表現卻優於其他人。

---

crust [krʌst]

① *n.* 麵包皮；派餅皮

反 **crumb**

實用片語與搭配詞

a crisp brown crust 有焦皮的麵包

② *v.* 覆有硬皮

實用片語與搭配詞

crust over 表層變硬

- Do you eat the crust on the pizza?
  你會吃披薩的硬皮嗎？
- I like to eat toast with a crisp brown crust.
  我喜歡吃有脆邊皮的吐司。
- When the wound dried, it crusted.
  傷口乾了之後就結痂了。
- The gold coins were buried under the sea for hundreds of years and were completely crusted over with coral.
  那些金幣幾百年來被埋在海底，表層已被珊瑚包覆而完全硬化。

crystal [ˈkrɪs.təl]

① *n.* 水晶

同 **gemstone**

② *adj.* 清澈透明的；水晶的

實用片語與搭配詞

crystal ball 水晶球

▶ The shiny crystal glimmered in the light.
光亮的水晶在燈光下閃閃發亮。

▶ The crystal clear lake made fishing easy.
這個湖水清澈透明，釣起魚來很省事。

▶ The fortune teller looked into her crystal ball and told Jennifer that she would marry a rich man.
那位算命師凝視著水晶球，並告訴珍妮佛她會嫁給一位富有的男人。

---

cuisine [kwɪˈziːn] *n.* 烹飪；烹調法

實用片語與搭配詞

offer / serve cuisine 供應美食

▶ Mexican cuisine uses a lot of rice and beans.
墨西哥料理使用大量的米和豆子。

▶ The new five-star hotel offers cuisine from all over the world, including Vietnamese and Chinese food.
那間新的五星級飯店供應來自世界各地的美食，包括越南和中華料理。

---

cultivate [ˈkʌl.tə.veɪt] *v.* 耕種；培養

同 **develop; raise**

實用片語與搭配詞

cultivate the mind 陶冶性情

▶ The farmer cultivated the land.
那名農夫耕種土地。

▶ Traveling around the world cultivates the mind and broadens one's horizons.
環遊世界能夠幫助我們陶冶性情並且拓展視野。

---

cumulative [ˈkjuː.mjə.lə.t̬ɪv]

adj. 累積的；漸增的

同 **accumulative**

實用片語與搭配詞

the cumulative effect of 日積月累的

▶ He sold the car because of the cumulative amount of work he spent fixing it.
他把車子賣掉了，因為累積起來已經花了很大的工夫不斷得去修理它。

▶ The cumulative effect of the typhoon and the earthquake happening at the same time caused the disastrous landslide.
颱風與地震經年累月的侵襲造成了嚴重的坍方。

---

curb [kɝːb]

① *n.* 路邊；控制；約束

同 **check; stop**

▶ The car pulled up to the curb and dropped me off.
車靠路邊停了下來，放我下車。

實用片語與搭配詞

put / keep a curb on sth.
抑制 / 控制某種情緒 / 事物

② *v.* 抑制；遏止

同 **control; restrain**

- I am trying to lose weight so I need to put a curb on sweet things and only eat healthy food.
  我正在試著減重，所以我必須節制甜食的攝取並且只吃健康的食物。
- My mom is trying to curb her desire for chocolate.
  我媽正努力克制想吃巧克力的慾望。

currency ['kɝː.ən.si] *n.* 貨幣

同 **cash; money**

實用片語與搭配詞

local currency 當地的貨幣

- We need to exchange our money for the local currency.
  我們需要把錢換成當地貨幣。
- If you travel to another country, it is good to change some of your money into the local currency.
  若你到異國旅遊，最好用現金兌換一些當地貨幣。

---

curriculum [kə'rɪk.jə.ləm]

n. 學校的全部課程

同 **course of study; program**

實用片語與搭配詞

core curriculum 核心課程

- Ron's curriculum this year focuses on business.
  朗恩今年的學校課程著重商業。
- Teaching children to think critically and to solve problems is part of the core curriculum at our school.
  教導孩子們批判性思考以及解決問題是我們學校核心課程的一部分。

---

curry ['kɝː.i] *n.* 咖哩；咖哩粉

實用片語與搭配詞

curry powder 咖哩粉

- Indian dishes often use curry.
  印度菜常常使用咖哩。
- Please buy me a packet of curry powder from the Indian store because I want to make lamb curry.
  請幫我從印度商店買一包咖哩粉，因為我要做羊肉咖哩。

---

customary ['kʌs.tə.mer.i]

adj. 習慣上的；慣常的

同 **accustomed; habitual**

- It's customary to celebrate Christmas on December 25.
  一般習慣在十二月二十五日慶祝聖誕節。

---

customs ['kʌs·təmz] *n.* 關稅

同 **custom duty; impost**

- We paid customs before leaving the airport.
  我們離開機場前付了關稅。

daffodil [ˈdæf.ə.dɪl] *n.* 黃水仙

同 **Narcissus**

▶ She has beautiful daffodils in her garden.
她的花園裡有美麗的黃水仙。

---

dandruff [ˈdæn.drəf] *n.* 頭皮屑

實用片語與搭配詞

cure sb.'s dandruff
治療 / 去除某人的頭皮屑

▶ She uses a special shampoo for her dandruff.
她用特殊的洗髮精來治療頭皮屑。

▶ This special shampoo contains ingredients that will help you cure your dandruff.
這瓶特別的洗髮精含有去除頭皮屑的配方。

---

dart [dɑːrt]

① *n.* 飛鏢

同 **dash; arrow**

② *v.* 狂奔；射鏢

同 **scoot; scurry**

▶ Jim and his friends like to play darts after work.
吉姆和他的朋友喜歡在下班後一起玩射飛鏢。

▶ The cat darted across the room.
這隻貓衝過了房間。

---

daybreak [ˈdeɪ.breɪk] *n.* 黎明；破曉

反 **nightfall**

▶ They left the camp at daybreak.
他們在破曉時分離開營地。

---

dazzle [ˈdæz.əl]

① *v.* 使眼花；使迷惑

同 **flash; astonish**

實用片語與搭配詞

be dazzled by sth. 被某物照的眼花撩亂

② *n.* 耀眼的光；燦爛

同 **amaze; astound**

▶ The sunlight dazzled me when I went outside because it was so bright.
我走到室外，陽光太耀眼，令我眼花。

▶ The first time I went to Disneyland, I was dazzled by the colorful lights and the real-life characters.
我第一次去迪士尼時，那裡的五彩燈光及活生生的卡通人物使我目眩神迷。

▶ Wear sunglasses to protect your eyes from the sunlight's dazzle.
戴太陽眼鏡來保護你的眼睛不受到刺眼的陽光直射。

104

deadly [ˈded.li]

① *adj.* 致命的；有害的

同 **lethal; lifelessly**

② *adv.* 完全的；極端的；像死一般地

▶ This deadly spider should not be touched.
不可以碰觸這隻可能會致命的蜘蛛。

▶ He was deadly serious about going.
他是很認真的，非去不可。

實用片語與搭配詞

deadly serious / boring 非常嚴肅 / 無聊

▶ If you do not come home on time, you will be grounded for a month. Don't test me; I am deadly serious.

如果你不準時回家，你就會被禁足一個月。別想試驗我；我是說認真的。

---

decay [dɪˈkeɪ]

① *v.* 腐壞；蛀蝕

同 **decompose; rot**

② *n.* 腐朽；蛀牙；衰退

同 **decomposition; rot**

▶ The rotting fruit decayed in the hot sun.

這顆壞掉的水果在熾熱的陽光下腐爛了。

▶ After months of decay, the rotting animal smelled terrible.

經過幾個月的腐朽，這隻腐爛的動物散發出惡臭。

---

deceive [dɪˈsiːv]

v. 欺騙；蒙蔽

同 **beguile; betray**

▶ William deceived his parents and lied about his new job.

威廉欺騙了他的父母，新工作的事他說了假話。

---

decent [ˈdiː.sənt]

adj. 相當不錯的；體面的；正派的

同 **adequate; well-mannered**

反 **coarse**

▶ The teacher was liked by everyone because she was a very decent person.

大家都很喜歡那個老師，因為她是個大好人。

---

decisive [dɪˈsaɪ.sɪv]

adj. 果斷的；有決斷力的；決定性的

反 **indecisive**

實用片語與搭配詞

a decisive battle / moment
決定性的戰役 / 時刻

▶ The group needed to be decisive about their choices.

那個團體必須對自己的選擇更果斷一點才行。

▶ The huge fight Mary had with her boyfriend was the decisive moment for her decision to break up with him.

瑪莉與男友的那場大吵是她打算分手的決定性時刻。

---

declaration [ˌdek.ləˈreɪ.ʃən]

n. 聲明；宣佈；宣告

同 **announcement; statement**

實用片語與搭配詞

issue / make a declaration
發表聲明 / 宣言

▶ The mayor's declaration was printed in the newspaper.

市長的聲明刊印在報紙上。

▶ We were all shocked when the company's president made a declaration that he would immediately leave the company.

當公司負責人發表了他將立即離開公司的聲明時，我們都很震驚。

decline [dɪˈklaɪn]

① *v.* 拒絕；下降；減少

同 **refuse**

反 **accept**

② *n.* 下降；減少

同 **descent; fall**

實用片語與搭配詞

fall / go into decline 進入衰退

► She declined the opportunity because she had other interests.
她婉拒了那個機會，因為她對其他的事情感興趣。

► The movie star declined in popularity after that really bad film.
那位電影明星演了那部爛片之後，受歡迎度就下滑了。

► The buildings in the old part of town fell into decline when business moved to the industrial park.
當商業被遷移到工業園區後，舊城鎮裡的建築物日漸衰落。

D

Exercise 21

I. Derivatives

1. The sales director has a deliberate intention to ____________ (deception) the fresh graduate by telling her that there is no full-time job position for her.
2. The increases in house price have given the restaurants and stores in the area challenges and a ____________ (decide) factor in the business's ability to sustain operating.
3. It is ____________ (custom) for my grandma to wrap rice dumplings with bamboo leaves during the Dragon Boat Festival.
4. Some religious leaders from other countries come altogether to sign a ____________ (declare) to combat human trafficking.
5. Ebola virus is a ____________ (dead) disease that is transmitted to people from infected animals to attack the brains through close contact, such as bodily fluids or blood.

II. Vocabulary Choices

(A) cynical	(B) crystal	(C) cumulative	(D) crunch
(E) currency	(F) cultivate	(G) curriculum	(H) curb
(I) decay	(J) decent		

1. Julian, a resource teacher, who has dedicated her life to devise a ________ to fulfill individual children's needs, is going to publish a storybook in the upcoming year.
2. She elaborated on her proposal for this project, giving us a ________ clear idea and a brand-new perspective on the profitable growth of our business.
3. To avoid tooth ________ and to maintain gum health, regular dental checkups and cleanings are essential.
4. As in forex trading, Daniel has been skillfully experienced with buying and selling in major ________ pairs in the world.
5. Colorectal cancer could be caused by the ________ effects of years of high intake of fat, processed meats, alcohol, or smoking.

Unit 22

99
dedicate [ˈded.ə.keɪt] *v.* 以…奉獻
同 **devote; give**

▸ Mother Teresa dedicated her life to helping the poor.
德蕾莎修女畢生奉獻於協助貧民。

102
dedication [ˌded.əˈkeɪ.ʃən] *n.* 奉獻；獻身

實用片語與搭配詞
require / show / need dedication
需要奉獻的精神

▸ We admire John's dedication to his job.
我們都很欣賞約翰全心投入工作的精神。

▸ Success in life requires dedication, hard work and tenacity.
人生的成功需要奉獻的精神、努力以及堅持。

---

deem [diːm] *v.* 認為；視為
同 **consider; think**

▸ The building was deemed unsafe after the fire.
那棟大樓在火災後被認為有安全上的疑慮。

102
defect [ˈdiː.fekt] *n.* 缺陷
同 **deficiency; flaw**

▸ The product didn't work when he bought it because of a defect.
他買到那項產品時，發現無法操作，因為有瑕疵。

defect [dɪˈfekt] *v.* 叛逃；背叛
同 **blemish**

▸ She defected from the United States to Canada.
她叛逃離開美國，去了加拿大。

---

deficiency [dɪˈfɪʃ.ən.si] *n.* 不足
同 **insufficiency; lack**

▸ The deficiencies in her diet lead to health problems.
她飲食中的營養不足導致了健康上的問題。

---

degrade [dɪˈɡreɪd]
v. （品質或品格等）降低；降級
同 **downgrade**

▸ The wood degraded over time and had to be replaced.
時間久了之後，那塊木頭腐朽了，所以必須換掉。

---

delegate [ˈdel.ə.ɡət] *n.* 代表
同 **agent; representative**

▸ The country sent a delegate to represent it at the Olympics.
這個國家派遣了一名代表出席奧運。

delegate [ˈdel.ə.geɪt] *v.* 委派…為代表

同 **appoint; assign**

▶ We need to delegate a person to represent our company at the conference.
我們需要指派人員代表我們公司參加會議。

---

delegation [ˌdel.əˈgeɪ.ʃən] *n.* 分配；委派

同 **commission; deputation**

▶ The CEO will decide on the company's delegation at the meeting.
執行長將在會議上決定公司的職責分配。

---

deliberate [dɪˈlɪb.ɚ.ət]

adj. 深思熟慮的；慎重的；蓄意的；刻意的

同 **considerate**

反 **hasty**

▶ She made a deliberate choice to not participate in the event.
她經過慎重考慮後，決定不去參加那項活動。

deliberate [dɪˈlɪb.ə.reɪt] *v.* 慎重考慮

同 **consider; think over**

▶ She deliberated about what to do next.
她慎重考慮接下來該作什麼。

---

delinquent [dɪˈlɪŋ.kwənt]

① *n.* 不良青少年；少年犯

同 **crook**

② *adj.* 違法的；少年犯的

同 **aberrant; criminal**

▶ Many ignored and avoided the delinquent.
很多人都會忽視並避免和不良青少年接觸。

▶ The delinquent person was put in jail.
那位少年犯被關進牢裡了。

---

democrat [ˈdem.ə.kræt]

n. 民主主義者；民主派人士

▶ Ben Franklin was a true democrat.
班・富蘭克林是實實在在的民主主義者。

---

denial [dɪˈnaɪ.əl] *n.* 拒絕；否定

同 **rejection**

反 **acknowledgment**

▶ The court's denial of bail meant that Jim had to remain in jail.
法院拒絕保釋，意味著吉姆得繼續坐牢。

---

denounce [dɪˈnaʊns] *v.* 指責；譴責

同 **accuse; blame**

▶ The school principle denounced bad behavior.
校長譴責不良行徑。

103

density [ˈden.sə.t̬i] *n.* 稠密（度）；密集（度）

同 **compactness; denseness**

▶ The density of the object was greater than the water, so it sank.
那個物體的密度比水大，因此就沈入水裡。

dental [ˈden.t̬əl] *adj.* 牙齒的

同 **alveolar**

▶ He went to the dentist for dental care.
他去看牙醫護理牙齒。

---

depict [dɪˈpɪkt] *v.* 描述；描繪

同 **describe; illustrate**

▶ The story depicts a boy growing up in a difficult situation.
故事描述一名男孩在困苦的環境中成長。

95

deprive [dɪˈpraɪv] *v.* 剝奪；奪走

同 **take away**

▶ The mother deprived them of dessert because of their bad behavior.
媽媽剝奪了他們吃甜點的權利，因為他們的表現很差。

---

deputy [ˈdep.jə.t̬i] *n.* 代理人

同 **agent; representative**

▶ The deputy officer handled the situation while the sheriff was away.
警長不在時，代理警官替他處理事情。

---

derive [dɪˈraɪv] *v.* 從…中得到；從…中獲得

同 **gain; obtain**

▶ Her happiness was derived from her children.
她的快樂來自於子女。

---

descend [dɪˈsend] *v.* 下降

同 **decline**

反 **ascend**

▶ After reaching the top of the mountain, they descended it slowly.
他們抵達山頂之後，就慢慢下山了。

---

descendant [dɪˈsen.dənt] *n.* 子孫；後裔

同 **offspring**

反 **ancestor**

▶ All her descendants learned to play the piano too.
她所有子孫也都學會彈鋼琴。

---

descent [dɪˈsent] *n.* 下降

反 **ascent**

▶ The descent from the top was slow.
從山頂下山的速度相當緩慢。

---

descriptive [dɪˈskrɪp.tɪv]

adj. 描寫的；記述的

實用片語與搭配詞

purely / entirely descriptive
完全是描述性的

▶ Julian told a descriptive story about his trip to Paris.
朱利安描述了他的巴黎之旅。

▶ When you write an academic paper, you should not just be purely descriptive; you have to be analytical as well.
當撰寫一篇學術論文時，你不該完全用描述性的方式寫作；你也必須善於分析。

designate ['dez.ɪg.neɪt]

① *v.* 指出；指定

同 **appoint; specify**

② *adj.* 指定的；選派的

實用片語與搭配詞

designated as sth. 被定為某事

▶ The boss designated Mike to lead the new project.
老闆指派麥克來領導新專案。

▶ He was the class designate for the task.
他是班上被指派執行那項任務的代表。

▶ The government designated March 27th as a national holiday in honor of indigenous people.
政府指定三月二十七日作為紀念原住民的國定假日。

---

despair [dɪ'sper]

① *n.* 絕望

實用片語與搭配詞

feel despair at sth. / sb.
對某人 / 事感到絕望

② *v.* 使絕望

同 **lose hope**

▶ In an act of despair, Brad cried out to God for help.
布萊德在絕望之下，向上帝大聲求助。

▶ Jennifer felt despair at her inability to get the job she wanted, so she just gave up and stayed home.
珍妮佛因為她無法得到想要的工作而感到絕望，所以她就放棄並待在家中。

▶ Adam despaired that he would never find his lost cat.
亞當已經絕望了，他認為永遠無法找回走失的貓咪。

Exercise 22

I. Choices

1. As Craig sees the pile of work stacking higher and higher with no end, ________ looms upon him.
   (A) detection (B) detention (C) destiny (D) despair
2. The very first painting by Franco ________ s his childhood through the lens of a grown-up.
   (A) depict (B) deficit (C) delegate (D) deposit
3. As the day of her retirement approaches, Jo knew that she had to train her ________ well in order for her business to operate as usual.
   (A) delicacy (B) democracy (C) delivery (D) deputy
4. Being ________ d of water for many days in the desert, John searched for an oasis like a ravaged man.
   (A) define (B) desire (C) deprive (D) derive
5. Being a ________ youth, Peter was finally given a chance to turn over a new leaf and he didn't do drugs anymore.
   (A) delinquent (B) deficient (C) default (D) defendant

II. Derivatives

1. Despite having birth ____________ (defective), Daniel overcame all hardships with hope and went on to become a champion in his industry.
2. Darwin's theory of evolution essentially brings about a framework that all living creatures and humans are ____________ (descend) of the same family.
3. The ____________ (delegate) from Russia is poised to meet the president of the United Nations any moment now.
4. The reason why you cannot mix water and oil together is because of their different ____________ (dense).
5. The recollection of my grandmother's story of the war was so vivid and ____________ (describe) that it felt as if I was there.

Unit 23

despise [dɪˈspaɪz] *v.* 瞧不起；鄙視

同 **loathe**

反 **admire**

▶ Jennifer despises anyone that cheers for the Red Sox.
珍妮佛瞧不起紅襪隊的支持者。

104

destination [ˌdes.təˈneɪ.ʃən]

n. 目的地；終點

同 **end; target**

▶ The pilot announced that we had arrived at our destination.
機長宣布我們已經抵達了目的地。

---

destined [ˈdes.tɪnd] *adj.* 命中注定的

同 **fated; meant**

▶ She was always destined to become a professional singer.
她命中注定要成為專業歌手。

---

destiny [ˈdes.tɪ.ni] *n.* 命運

同 **fate; fortune**

▶ Amanda felt it was her destiny to marry Francis.
雅曼達認為她命中注定要和法蘭西斯結婚。

---

destructive [dɪˈstrʌk.tɪv]

adj. 破壞的；毀滅性的

同 **disparaging**

反 **constructive**

▶ His destructive behavior forced the company to fire him.
他的不良行徑迫使公司開除了他。

---

detach [dɪˈtætʃ] *v.* 分離；分開

同 **separate**

反 **attach**

▶ She detached the key from the chain and gave it to her sister.
她把鎖匙從鎖匙環中取出來，交給她的姊妹。

---

detain [dɪˈteɪn] *v.* 拖延；耽擱

同 **delay**

反 **release**

▶ Fans detained him from leaving after the performance.
表演過後，粉絲群一直拖延著不讓他離開。

---

deter [dɪˈtɝː] *v.* 阻止；阻撓；使不敢做

同 **prevent**

反 **recommend**

▶ She deterred them from going to the restaurant with a bad review.
她用一篇負評阻止他們去那家餐廳。

detergent [dɪˈtɝː.dʒənt]
n. 洗潔劑；洗衣粉；洗衣精
同 **detersive**

▶ Please put laundry detergent in the washing machine.
請把洗衣劑放進洗衣機裡。

---

deteriorate [dɪˈtɪr.i.ə.reɪt] *v.* 惡化
反 **improve**

▶ The weather deteriorated the object over time.
氣候讓那個物品因長時間受氣候影響而腐化。

---

devalue [ˌdiːˈvæl.juː] *v.* 使貶值
同 **depreciate**

▶ The spill devalued the painting.
那幅畫因為被濺到污漬而貶值了。

---

devotion [dɪˈvoʊ.ʃən] *n.* 奉獻；獻身
同 **affection; dedication**

▶ Tanya's devotion to her dying grandmother touched everyone in the hospital.
譚雅對垂死祖母的盡心照顧令醫院每個人感動不已。

---

devour [dɪˈvaʊ.ɚ] *v.* 狼吞虎嚥地吃；吞沒
同 **swallow**

▶ The children devoured the birthday cake.
孩子們狼吞虎嚥地吃下生日蛋糕。

---

diabetes [ˌdaɪ.əˈbiː.t̬əs] *n.* 糖尿病

▶ My grandfather has diabetes.
我祖父有糖尿病。

96

diagnose [ˌdaɪ.əgˈnoʊz] *v.* 診斷
同 **analyze; deduce**

▶ The doctor diagnosed the condition as not serious.
醫師診斷病情並不嚴重。

---

diagnosis [ˌdaɪ.əgˈnoʊ.sɪs] *n.* 診斷（結果）
同 **diagnosing**

▶ The patient asked her questions about the diagnosis.
患者詢問她有關診斷的結果。

---

diagram [ˈdaɪ.ə.græm]
① *n.* 圖表
同 **depict; draw**
② *v.* 圖示
同 **portray; sketch**

▶ Look at the diagram for clarity.
看那張圖表就會更清楚了。

▶ Please diagram your idea on this paper.
請把你的想法以圖示的方式在這張紙上畫出來。

dialect [ˈdaɪ.ə.lekt] *n.* 方言

同 **vernacular**

► Morris couldn't understand the man's dialect of Chinese.
莫理斯聽不懂這個人的華語方言。

---

diameter [daɪˈæm.ə.t̬ɚ] *n.* 直徑

反 **radius**

► Find out the diameter of the wheel in order to buy the right tire.
找出這輪胎的直徑才能買對輪胎。

---

dictate [ˈdɪk.teɪt] *v.* 口述；使聽寫

同 **command; say**

反 **obey**

► She dictated the letter while her secretary took notes.
她口述信的內容，而她的秘書則記錄下來。

---

dictation [dɪkˈteɪ.ʃən] *n.* 口述；聽寫

► He typed out everything from the dictation.
他把口述的內容全都打字出來。

實用片語與搭配詞

give sb. a dictation 給某人聽寫練習

► The author of that book cannot use a computer, so he gives a dictation to his secretary who then types it up.
那位作者無法使用電腦，所以他的秘書邊聽他口述邊打字。

---

dictator [ˈdɪk.teɪ.t̬ɚ] *n.* 獨裁者

同 **authoritarian; tyrant**

► The dictator controls every decision in the country.
獨裁者掌控了那個國家的一切決策。

---

differentiate [ˌdɪf.əˈren.ʃi.eɪt] *v.* 區別；區分

同 **distinguish; separate**

► The tags differentiated what was his and what was hers.
不同的標籤把他和她的物品區分出來。

---

disbelief [ˌdɪs.bɪˈliːf] *n.* 不相信；懷疑

同 **distrust; doubt**

► Harry watched in disbelief as the man stole his car.
哈利不可置信地看著那個人偷他的車。

---

discard [dɪˈskɑːrd]

① *v.* 丟棄；拋棄

同 **cast; dispose of**

► I discarded the empty bottles into the recycling bin.
我把這些空瓶丟進回收桶裡。

實用片語與搭配詞

be completely discarded 完全被拋棄

► Mary's family did not approve of her gangster husband, so they completely discarded her.
瑪莉的家人不認可她的流氓丈夫，所以他們徹底拋棄了她。

② *n.* 被遺棄的人、物；拋棄

▸ Lisa has 4 cats now because she picks up discards from the street.

麗莎現在養了四隻貓，因為她會收養街上被拋棄的流浪動物。

D

Exercise 23

I. Derivatives

1. You'll find it particularly difficult to ____________ (different) between Tom and Mike when they are wearing the similar clothes as they look like peas in a pod.
2. ____________ (dictate) can be used as form of test for students learning new languages as they write down what they have just heard.
3. Just because you know where your ____________ (destine) is in your life doesn't mean you will certainly get there as planned; the other way around, you might be taken somewhere unexpected along this journey.
4. The provisional ____________ (diagnose) and some information that Emma received from the doctor have filled her with anxiety and anguish.
5. The epitome of ____________ (destruct) power can be seen when the atomic bomb was released in World War II.

II. Choices

1. It is heartbreaking and heart wrenching when you see the health of your loved ones ________ day by day.
   (A) determine (B) detect (C) recuperate (D) deteriorate
2. When I am hungry and see a burger, I will definitely run over and ________ it in one big bite!
   (A) devour (B) detour (C) deserve (D) divest
3. The fact that he had been adopted to rise from poverty to the middle class never makes him ________ the poor and the weak but instead uphold and encourage them.
   (A) disagree (B) disguise (C) despise (D) devise
4. When the police opened up the crates and saw the illegal drugs, they proceeded to ________ the crews in question.
   (A) sustain (B) detain (C) disdain (D) maintain
5. Looking at the stack of old clothes that she has, Perry decided to clean up her wardrobe, but instead of ________ ing them to the dump, she chose to donate to a local charity.
   (A)disregard (B) discard (C)safeguard (D) discredit

Unit 24

disciple [dɪˈsaɪ.pəl] *n.* 門徒；追隨者

同 **believer; follower**

▶ Peter was a disciple of Jesus.
彼得是耶穌的門徒。

---

discriminate [dɪˈskrɪm.ə.neɪt]

v. 區別；區分出

同 **distinguish; separate**

▶ The line of chairs will discriminate the two teams from each other.
這一排椅子將可清楚區分出這兩支隊伍。

---

dispense [dɪˈspens] *v.* 分配；分發

同 **distribute; give out**

▶ Mary's aunt dispenses advice about any topic.
瑪麗的阿姨在任何話題上都有意見可提供。

---

dispose [dɪˈspoʊz]

v. 使（某人）對…產生感覺；配置；佈置

同 **arrange; set out**

▶ The audience wasn't disposed to the speaker's ideas.
觀眾對演講者的想法沒什麼感覺。

---

distinction [dɪˈstɪŋk.ʃən] *n.* 區別

同 **differentiation**

反 **similarity**

▶ There is a clear distinction between my role and my supervisor's.
我和上司的角色壁壘分明。

distinctive [dɪˈstɪŋk.tɪv]

adj. 特殊的；有特色的

同 **characteristic; idiosyncratic**

▶ John easily recognized the distinctive sound of his mother's voice.
約翰輕易地就辨識出了她母親特殊的嗓音。

---

distress [dɪˈstres]

① *n.* 悲痛；苦惱

同 **afflict**

反 **consolation**

② *v.* 使心煩；使憂慮

同 **afflict**

反 **comfort**

▶ The distress caused by the accident forced Bo to quit his job.
那起意外導致的悲痛逼得波辭去了工作。

▶ The boss chose to keep the bad news a secret rather than distress the staff.
老闆選擇隱瞞這個壞消息，而不願意讓員工感到難過。

98 96

document [ˈdɑː.kjə.mənt]

① *n.* 文件；公文

同 **article; paper**

② *v.* 提供文件或證據；用文件證明

同 **record; authenticate**

- The legal document required Jane to sign her full name.
這份法律文件需要珍簽全名。
- Please document all your work so the next person can do your job after you leave.
請提供你所有工作的相關文件，以便在你離職之後，讓下一個接任的人能接手你的工作。

---

doorstep [ˈdɔːr.step] *n.* 門階

同 **access way**

- The cat stood on the doorstep waiting to be let into the house.
這隻貓站在門階上，等著被放進家裡去。

---

doorway [ˈdɔːr.weɪ] *n.* 門口；出入口

同 **entrance**

- We stood in the doorway waiting to be invited into the house.
我們站在門口，等人邀請我們進去。

---

dormitory [ˈdɔːr.mə.tɔːr.i] *n.* 宿舍

同 **dorm; student residence**

- Alex slept in the dormitory during his freshman year of college.
艾力克斯大學一年級時住學校宿舍。

---

dough [doʊ] *n.* 麵團

- Ally kneaded the dough before baking the bread.
艾莉烤麵包前先把麵團揉好。

---

downward [ˈdaʊn.wɚd]

① *adj.* 向下的；下降的

同 **descending**

反 **upward**

實用片語與搭配詞

downward toward sth. 向某處傾斜

② *adv.* 向下；日趨沒落地

- The downward trend in sales made the owners think about closing the store.
銷售額下降，使得店主們考慮關店。
- The eagle swooped downward towards the defenceless rabbit at lightning speed.
這隻老鷹用迅雷不及掩耳的速度向毫無反抗能力的兔子俯衝而去。
- We headed downwards to a lower floor of the mall.
我們向下往購物中心的低樓層走去。

---

drape [dreɪp]

① *v.* 覆蓋；垂掛

同 **cover; swathe**

- The soldiers draped the coffin with the American flag.
這群士兵以美國國旗覆蓋棺木。

實用片語與搭配詞

drape sth. around / over sth.
將衣物 / 窗簾掛在某物上

② *n.* 窗簾；幔

▶ A red cloth was draped around the sculpture and nobody was allowed to peek at it until the official unveiling.
一條紅布披裹在雕像上，沒有任何人有權利在官方揭幕儀式前窺視。

▶ Close the drapes to make the room dark.
把窗簾拉上，讓房間變暗。

---

dreadful [ˈdred.fəl] *adj.* 可怕的

同 **awful; terrible**

實用片語與搭配詞

dreadful weather 糟糕的天氣

▶ A dreadful disease killed many of the villagers.
一種可怕的疾病造成了許多村民死亡。

▶ Despite the dreadful weather, we had to continue hiking to reach the camp before nightfall.
儘管天氣惡劣，我們仍須在夜幕低垂前健行至紮營區。

---

dresser [ˈdres.ɚ] *n.* 衣著…的人；梳妝台

▶ Moe is a snappy dresser.
莫爾是個衣著講究的人。

95

dressing [ˈdres.ɪŋ]

n. （包紮傷口的）敷料；沙拉醬汁

同 **bandage; medicine**

▶ The nurse changed the dressing on the man's wound.
護士幫這個男子的傷口更換敷料。

---

driveway [ˈdraɪv.weɪ]

n. 私人車道；馬路；汽車道

▶ Can I park my car in your driveway?
我可以把車停在你的車道上嗎？

---

duration [duːˈreɪ.ʃən] *n.* 持久；持續時間

同 **period; term time**

實用片語與搭配詞

overall duration 大致上的時間

▶ Carrie sat still for the duration of the movie.
整場電影，凱莉一直坐著不動。

▶ The overall duration for a one-way flight to South Africa is about 20 hours.
前往南非的單程飛行時間大致是 20 小時。

---

dusk [dʌsk] *n.* 薄暮；黃昏

同 **twilight**

反 **dawn**

▶ The boys stopped playing baseball at dusk because it was too dark.
黃昏天色太暗，這些男孩停下來不打棒球了。

dwarf [dwɔːrf]

① *n.* 矮子；侏儒

反 **giant**

② *v.* 使矮小；萎縮

實用片語與搭配詞

be dwarfed by sth. 和某物相比顯得很小

▶ Paul is a dwarf and will never grow taller than three feet.
保羅是個侏儒，最多只能長到三英尺高。

▶ The tree was dwarfed from a lack of rain.
由於缺乏雨水，這棵樹長得不高。

▶ Buildings around Taipei 101 are dwarfed by the height of this gigantic architectural structure.
在台北 101 這個巨大建築旁的眾樓房顯得相形見絀。

---

dwell [dwel] *v.* 居住

同 **inhabit; live**

▶ The family dwells in the abandoned building.
這家人住在廢棄的建築裡。

---

dwelling [ˈdwel.ɪŋ] *n.* 住處

同 **abode; habitation**

▶ The city provides dwellings for people released from prison.
這個城市為出獄的人提供住處。

---

eclipse [ɪˈklɪps]

① *n.* 蝕；遮蔽

同 **veil**

② *v.* 蝕；遮蔽

實用片語與搭配詞

be eclipsed by sth. 相形見絀

▶ Albert took pictures of the solar eclipse.
艾伯特照了日蝕的相片。

▶ The moon eclipses the sun only during a new moon.
月亮遮住太陽造成的日蝕只會發生在新月的時候。

▶ The excitement she felt over getting married was eclipsed by the devastation caused by her mother's passing.
她的喪母之痛使她的新婚之喜相較之下黯然失色。

---

eel [iːl] *n.* 鰻魚

▶ The eels swam quickly through the water.
鰻魚群迅速地在水裡游過。

Exercise 24

I. Choices

1. Jane had been in less ____________ since she started to intake the treatment, which helped alleviate the pain throughout the process.

   (A) dismiss (B) discuss (C) distress (D) disperse

2. The phenomenon of solar ____________ occurs when the Moon goes in between the Sun and the Earth.

   (A) estate (B) essence (C) eclipse (D) escape

3. In order to create a relaxed shot, the model proceeded to ____________ the scarf over her shoulder.

   (A) drape (B) drip (C) drag (D) drift

4. Kay has made such a ____________ mistake so that she was asked to leave the company immediately.

   (A) distinctive (B) despiteful (C) ungrateful (D) dreadful

5. One of the differences between the twins is the ____________ mole on John's cheek.

   (A) disaggregated (B) distinctive (C) dispose (D) dedicative

II. Vocabulary Choices

(A) discriminate	(B) dwelling	(C) duration	(D) dispose
(E) disciple	(F) disbelief	(G) distress	(H) dispense
(I) distinction	(J) discretion		

1. The _________ of a person does reflect their personality and preference as shown through the design and layout of the interior.

2. The usage of tear gas is controversial but it does _________ rowdy crowds and the massive wave of riots effectively.

3. When certain policies or processes _________ against a group of people, it can bring reputation loss to the company.

4. When a person _________ s garbage or any poisonous materials into sea, one must know the consequences that it brings to the ecosystem.

5. How well a relationship is maintained between people does not fully depend on the _________ but comprises of various aspects, such as trust, openness and vulnerability.

Unit 25

ego [ˈiː.goʊ] *n.* 自我意識；自我

實用片語與搭配詞

bruise / damage / wound sb.'s ego
傷到某人的自尊心

▶ Psychologists study the effects of depression on the ego.
心理學家研究憂鬱對自我意識造成的影響。

▶ The young man's ego was bruised after the girl of his dreams rejected him.
在他的夢中情人拒絕他以後，這位年輕人感到自尊受挫。

---

101 100

elaborate [iˈlæb.ɚ.ət]

adj. 精心製作的；詳盡的

同 **detail**

反 **plain**

▶ The robbers had an elaborate plan for holding up the bank.
這群搶匪精心策劃了搶劫銀行的計畫。

elaborate [iˈlæb.ə.reɪt]

v. 詳細說明；精心製作；闡述

實用片語與搭配詞

elaborate further 進一步的闡述

▶ During the interview the boss asked me to elaborate on my career plans.
面試時，老闆要我詳細說明我的生涯規劃。

▶ The CEO announced the immediate closure of the company, but he did not elaborate further.
總裁宣布立即關閉公司，但他並未作進一步的說明。

---

elevate [ˈel.ə.veɪt] *v.* 提高；抬起

同 **lift**

反 **degrade**

實用片語與搭配詞

elevate the minds of sb. 提高某人的修養

▶ The doctor told Anna to elevate her injured ankle.
醫生叫安娜把受傷的腳踝抬起。

▶ Traveling and meeting people from other cultures can elevate the mind more than any textbook.
旅遊並且認識來自不同文化的人們能夠提高我們的素養，其作用勝於任何一本教科書。

---

embrace [ɪmˈbreɪs]

① *v.* 擁抱；抓住（機會）

同 **grasp; hold**

▶ The man embraced his daughter before she left for college.
這名男子在女兒離家讀大學前擁抱她。

實用片語與搭配詞

embrace sb. warmly / tightly
溫暖的 / 緊緊的擁抱某人

② *n.* 擁抱

同 **hug**

實用片語與搭配詞

hold sb. in embrace 擁抱著某人

▶ Scientists say hugging or embracing another person tightly once a day can help you fight depression.
科學家表示一天緊緊擁抱一個人一次便可幫助你對抗憂鬱。

▶ Mary held her son in a long embrace after he returned from the army.
瑪麗的兒子退伍回來時，她擁抱了他好一會兒。

▶ The mother held her danghters in a long embrace.
那位母親抱住她的女兒們久久不能放開。

---

endeavor [ɪnˈdev·ər]

① *v.* 努力；竭力

同 **effort; strive**

反 **neglect**

② *n.* 努力

實用片語與搭配詞

make every / best endeavor 盡最大努力

▶ Jordan studied hard and endeavored to be at the top of his class.
喬登用功讀書，努力在班上名列前茅。

▶ After many endeavors to bake a cake, Rachel finally succeeded.
經過多次的努力，瑞秋終於烤好蛋糕了。

▶ After the plane crash, the airline promised to make every endeavor to determine the causes.
飛機失事後，航空公司承諾會盡最大的努力查明空難起因。

---

enroll [ɪnˈroʊl] *v.* 登記；註冊

同 **enlist; sign up**

▶ The students must enroll in their classes by December 15th.
學生必須在十二月十五號前登記課程。

103

enrollment [ɪnˈroʊl·mənt]

n. 註冊；登記；入會；入伍

同 **registration**

▶ The teachers got a raise this year because student enrollment increased dramatically.
因為學生註冊人數遽增，所以今年教師都加薪了。

---

ensure / insure [ɪnˈʃʊr] *v.* 保證；擔保

同 **make sure**

▶ Please ensure that all of the information is correct.
請確保所有資料都正確無誤。

---

enterprise [ˈen.t̬ɚ.praɪz]

n. （有冒險性的）事業；進取心

同 **venture business**

▶ Strong leadership is required to start an enterprise and build a successful company.
想要創業並且建立成功的公司，優秀的領導力是不可或缺的。

實用片語與搭配詞

private enterprise 私人企業

▶ Private enterprises are important to the economy because they create jobs and pay taxes to the government.
私人企業在國家經濟上扮演重要的角色，因為它們創造工作機會並且納稅給政府。

---

enthusiastic [ɪnˌθuː.ziˈæs.tɪk]

adj. 熱忱的；熱心的

同 **eager; interested**

實用片語與搭配詞

highly enthusiastic 高度的熱心

▶ Tim's enthusiastic attitude encouraged his teammates to do their best.
提姆熱忱的態度鼓舞了他的組員全力以赴。

▶ Upon hearing that the top five students would accompany their teacher on a trip, the class became highly enthusiastic.
當學生們得知前五名的學生能夠與老師一同旅遊時，全班變得異常熱衷。

entitle [ɪnˈtaɪ.t̬əl] *v.* 給…頭銜、稱號；給…權力（資格）；為書取名

同 **authorize**

反 **deprive**

實用片語與搭配詞

entitle sb. to sth. 給予某人做某事的權利

▶ Employees are entitled to 2 weeks of paid vacation per year.
員工每年都有權休兩週的有薪假。

▶ Famous people often feel entitled to respect from those they deem to be lower in status.
名人時常覺得自己應當被他們認為身份地位較低的人尊重。

---

equate [ɪˈkweɪt] *v.* 等同；使相等

同 **associate**

實用片語與搭配詞

equate sth. to / with sth.
把某事物和另一事物畫上等號

▶ Even though Jim is the oldest, his parents equated his allowance with the rest of his siblings'.
儘管吉姆是長子，但他的父母給他的零用錢跟他的弟弟妹妹一樣多。

▶ If you equate the effort you put into becoming a movie star to what you get out of it, it is not worth it.
若你把成為電影明星所付出的努力與你所得到的回報相比，這一切並不值得。

---

erect [ɪˈrekt]

① *adj.* 直立的；豎起的

同 **upright; vertical**

② *v.* 建立；使豎直

同 **build**

反 **destroy**

▶ We could see the erect buildings of the city tracing the skyline.
我們可以看到市區聳立的建築物刻畫出天際線。

▶ The city came together to erect a new clock tower after a severe storm.
在劇烈暴風侵襲後，全市民齊心協力建造了一個新的鐘樓。

實用片語與搭配詞

erect a tent 搭起帳篷

▶ Before you go camping, you have to learn how to erect that tent or you will be sleeping outside.
在去露營之前，你必須學會如何搭帳篷，否則你只能露宿戶外了。

E

erupt [ɪˈrʌpt] *v.* 爆發；噴出

同 burst; vomit

實用片語與搭配詞

erupt into violence 發生暴動

▶ The audience erupted with applause when the performer did a back flip.
這名表演者做了後空翻後，觀眾爆出熱烈掌聲。

▶ The protest march by animal activists erupted into violence after police tried to arrest them.
這群動物保護人士的示威遊行在警方試圖逮捕他們時發生暴動。

102

escort [ˈes.kɔːrt] *n.* 護送者；護衛者

實用片語與搭配詞

armed escort 武裝衛隊

▶ Our hotel provided an escort to take us to the airport.
我們住的飯店派專人護送我們去機場。

▶ The gangster was moved to jail under armed escort to prevent him from escaping.
這名歹徒被武裝衛隊護送至監獄以防他逃脫。

escort [esˈkɔːrt] *v.* 護送；陪同

同 accompany; shepherd

實用片語與搭配詞

escort sb. to sth. 護送某人到某處

▶ The police escorted the famous singer away from the screaming crowd.
警方護送這個名歌手遠離尖叫的人群。

▶ When the mayor arrived at the ceremony, I was lucky to escort him to the VIP section.
當市長到達典禮會場時，我很幸運地能護送他至貴賓區。

estate [ɪˈsteɪt] *n.* 地產

同 land; property

實用片語與搭配詞

an heir to an estate 地產繼承人

▶ Johnny's parents left him their estate, business and life savings.
強尼的父母把他們的地產、公司和一生的積蓄都留給了強尼。

▶ The old man had no relatives, so the orphanage where he grew up became heir to his estate.
這名長者沒有親人，所以他長大的孤兒院成為了他遺產的繼承人。

96

esteem [ɪˈsti:m]

① *v.* 尊敬；尊重

同 **respect**

反 **disesteem**

② *n.* 尊敬；尊重

同 **regard; admiration**

實用片語與搭配詞

be held in great / high esteem by sb.
受到某人的尊重 / 尊敬

- Sally highly esteemed her older sister and wanted to do everything like her.
  莎莉極為尊敬她的姊姊，什麼事都要效法她。
- There has been a big drop in people's esteem for teachers in recent years.
  近年來，民眾對於教師的尊敬已大不如前。
- After saving the lives of thousands of people during the war, the soldier was held in high esteem by his country.
  這位士兵在戰爭中救了上千條人命，因此他受到國家的敬重。

---

eternal [ɪˈtɝ:.nəl] *adj.* 永恆的；無窮的

同 **endless; everlasting**

實用片語與搭配詞

eternal life 永生

- Homework may feel like an eternal task, but you'll graduate eventually.
  回家功課也許像是永無止盡的任務，但是你終究會畢業的。
- Many people have tried to find the secret to eternal life, but they have not found it.
  至今有許多人在尋找永生的秘密，但他們未有任何發現。

---

ethic(s) [ˈeθ.ɪk(s)] *n.* 倫理學；道德標準

同 **moral principles**

- Mark has a strong work ethic and always gives his best effort.
  馬克非常重視職場倫理，總是盡其所能。

---

evergreen [ˈev.ɚ.gri:n]

① *adj.* 長青的；常綠的

② *n.* 常綠植物；長青樹

- The evergreen tree requires very little water and always looks healthy.
  那棵長青樹幾乎不需要澆水，而且看起來總是生氣勃勃。
- From our window, we could see the snow had completely covered the evergreens.
  從我們的窗戶望出去，可以看到雪已經完全覆蓋住那些常綠植物了。

---

exaggeration [ɪɡˌzædʒ.əˈreɪ.ʃən]

n. 誇張；誇大

反 **understatement**

- Billy's exaggeration of every situation made it difficult to take him seriously.
  比利凡事喜歡誇大，讓我們很難把他的話當真。

97

exceed [ɪkˈsiːd] *v.* 超過；勝過

同 **go beyond; go over**

實用片語與搭配詞

exceeded all expectations 超出預料之外

▶ We couldn't get into the concert because the crowd exceeded the number of seats.
我們進不了音樂會，因為觀眾人數超過了座位數量。

▶ The large amount of money people donated for children in Africa exceeded all expectations.
人們捐獻給非洲孩童的金額遠遠超出所有人的預期。

---

excel [ɪkˈsel] *v.* 勝過；優於

同 **stand out**

實用片語與搭配詞

excel in / at sth. 擅長某事物

▶ After countless hours of studying, Jordan excelled in her math class and received an A.
經過長時間的用功學習，喬丹在數學課上表現優異，獲得了甲等。

▶ Jenny might not be good at sport or math, but she excels in speaking seven languages.
珍妮也許在體育跟數學方面並不突出，但她擅長說七種語言。

99

exceptional [ɪkˈsep.ʃən.əl]

adj. 優異的；例外的

同 **outstanding**

反 **ordinary**

實用片語與搭配詞

exceptional talent / ability
罕見的天分 / 能力

▶ Shelly set new records with her exceptional running skills.
雪麗憑著優異的跑步技巧，創造了新紀錄。

▶ Milly has an exceptional talent for music and could already compose her own music by age four.
米莉有過人的音樂天份，而且她四歲時便能作曲。

---

excess [ɪkˈses]

① *n.* 過剩；過量；過度

同 **surplus**

反 **shortage**

實用片語與搭配詞

an excess of ... dollars 超出…元

② *adj.* 過量的；額外的

同 **extra**

▶ Go ahead and make extra food; any excess can be saved for dinner tonight.
儘管多準備些菜吧；吃不完的可以留到今天晚餐。

▶ After returning from our overseas holiday, we had an excess of U.S. currency.
從海外度假返國後，我們持有過多的美金。

▶ The cafeteria encouraged smaller portions to avoid wasting excess food.
學校自助餐廳提倡縮減菜量，以免吃不完浪費。

實用片語與搭配詞

excess baggage / luggage 超重的行李

▸ The airport clerk told me I would have to pay extra for my excess luggage.
機場的地勤人員告訴我必須為超重的行李額外付費。

Exercise 25

I. Choices

1. Danny pulled up his sock and ___________ to strive even harder to make ends meet for the whole family to sustain.
   (A) endorsement (B) exaggeration (C) endeavor (D) exasperation
2. On Equal Pay Day, feminists across the globe rise up together to advocate on the issue regarding gender pay gap as men's salaries ___________ women's for the same jobs, and this strikes a cord with many people around the world.
   (A) examine (B) exceed (C) succeed (D) exploit
3. This pass will ___________ you and your chosen guest to access not only our exclusive rides but also skip queues for rides.
   (A) explode (B) express (C) explore (D) entitle
4. Providing an ___________ customer service can increase customer loyalty.
   (A) external (B) educational (C) exceptional (D) experimental
5. Whenever the minister leaves the parliament, you will almost always sight at least one ___________ within 100 meters of him.
   (A) escort (B) erupt (C) evaluate (D) eschew

II. Vocabulary Choices

(A) enterprise	(B) eternal	(C) erupt	(D) enroll
(E) esteem	(F) elaborate	(G) excel	(H) ensure
(I) equate	(J) evergreen		

1. Fabian has always been held in high ________ by his daughter as he treats her absolutely like a princess.
2. The ________ flame in Washington, D.C. is a tribute to soldiers who have sacrificed their lives to defend their country.
3. Gary is at the pinnacle of his sporting career, and he is unparalleled in his field as the hunger to ________ never ceases to die off.
4. Within a country, specific approaches taken to ________ national security, such as economic power, diplomacy, or political system, protect the people from internal and external threats.
5. Two wrongs do not ________ to a right, and once a person realized that they are going down the wrong way, they need to turn back and head toward the right way.

Unit 26

exclaim [ɪkˈskleɪm] *v.* 呼喊；驚叫

同 **cry out; shout**

▶ The winning team waved their hands in the air and exclaimed, "We are the champions!"
這支獲勝的隊伍揮手呼喊：「我們是冠軍！」

95

exclude [ɪkˈsklu:d] *v.* 把…排除

同 **forbid; keep out**

反 **include**

實用片語與搭配詞

exclude sb. / sth. from sth.
把某人 / 物排除在某事 / 物外

▶ Cheryl was very careful not to exclude anyone from her party; everyone was invited.
雪瑞很仔細，不願漏請任何人參加她的派對，所以大家都受邀了。

▶ We decided to exclude Mary from our trip to Japan because she is always complaining.
我們決定要把瑪麗排除在我們的日本行之外，因為她總是愛抱怨。

---

execute [ˈek.sə.kju:t] *v.* 執行；實行

同 **accomplish; carry out**

▶ Albert was determined to execute everything on his to-do list before 5:00 p.m.
艾伯特決心在下午五點以前，把所有待辦事項都執行完畢。

---

executive [ɪgˈzek.jə.t̬ɪv]

① *n.* 領導階層；高階主管；行政部門

同 **administrative; supervisory**

② *adj.* 管理的；決策的

實用片語與搭配詞

chief executive officer 執行長

▶ Our company's executive created a new policy that will go into effect next month.
我們公司的領導階層制定了一項新政策，並且將在下個月實施。

▶ While his boss is away, Charles will make the executive decisions at work.
查爾斯的老闆不在時，由他負責公司的管理決策。

▶ The company's chief executive officer received a huge annual bonus for good performance.
這間公司的執行長因為其優秀的業績而獲得巨額年終獎金。

---

exile [ˈek.saɪl]

① *n.* 流亡；離鄉背井

同 **refugee; outcast**

▶ After years of being in exile, the prisoner was allowed to return home.
過了數年的流亡生活，這名犯人獲准返鄉。

實用片語與搭配詞

send sb. into exile 流放某人

② *v.* 流放；放逐

同 **banish; cast out**

實用片語與搭配詞

be exiled from sth. 從某個國家被逐出

▶ In ancient times, some criminals were sent into exile and were never allowed to return to their country.
在古代，一些罪犯會被流放邊疆並且再也不能返回他們的祖國。

▶ The criminals were forced to leave their homes and families and exiled to another country.
這群罪犯被迫離開家鄉和家人，被流放到另一個國家。

▶ The king was exiled from his kingdom by his jealous brother who wanted the throne.
這位國王的弟弟因嫉妒他的王位而將他逐出王國。

---

98 95

extension [ɪkˈsten.ʃən] *n.* 延長；擴大

同 **addition; expansion**

實用片語與搭配詞

apply for extension 申請延期

▶ The new road extension now allows more traffic flow.
這條新的延伸路段現在可容納更多車流量。

▶ She could not finish her project on time, so she applied for an extension.
她無法如期完成她的專案，因此她申請延期。

96

extensive [ɪkˈsten.sɪv]

adj. 廣泛的；遼闊的；大規模的

同 **wide**

反 **intensive**

實用片語與搭配詞

extensive knowledge 學識淵博

▶ After extensive research, the doctoral student had enough information for his research paper.
經過廣泛探究，這名博士生獲得了足夠的資料來進行他的研究報告。

▶ Before qualifying as a doctor, you must have extensive knowledge of diseases and how to treat them.
在取得醫師資格前，你必須具備關於疾病與其療法的淵博知識。

---

exterior [ɪkˈstɪr.i.ɚ]

① *adj.* 外部的；外用的

同 **external**

反 **center**

② *n.* 外表；外部

同 **outside**

反 **interior**

▶ Make sure you dust the exterior surfaces of all the furniture before the guests arrive.
賓客抵達以前，請務必把所有家具表面的灰塵撣除。

▶ We painted the exterior of the house, but the inside still needs a fresh coat.
我們油漆了房子外部，但是屋裡還需要塗一層新漆。

external [ɪkˈstɝː.nəl]

① *adj.* 外部的；外面的

同 **exterior**

反 **internal**

② *n.* 外觀

實用片語與搭配詞

judge people by externals alone
以貌取人；以外在條件論斷他人

▶ The external parts of the car were damaged, but everyone inside remained unharmed.
這輛車的外部受損了，但是車內的每個人都毫髮無傷。

▶ The inside of the house looked smaller than the external.
這棟房子的內部看起來比外觀小。

▶ It is dangerous to judge people by there externals alone without considering their inner beauty.
無視一個人內心之美，只憑外在條件評斷他人是很冒險的。

96

extinct [ɪkˈstɪŋkt]

adj. 絕種的；熄滅的；破滅了的

同 **died out; vanished**

實用片語與搭配詞

an extinct species 已滅絕的物種

▶ The team found the bones of many animals that are now extinct.
這個小組發現了許多目前已絕種的動物的骨骸。

▶ Dinosaurs are an extinct species. They have been extinct for millions of years.
恐龍是一個已滅絕的物種。牠們已絕種了上百萬年。

95

extraordinary [ɪkˈstrɔːr.dən.er.i]

adj. 非凡的；特別的

同 **exceptional; remarkable**

▶ Oliver's extraordinary singing talent instantly captivated the judge's attention.
奧利佛非凡的歌唱天分立刻獲得裁判關注。

---

eyelash/lash [ˈaɪˌlæʃ / læʃ] *n.* 睫毛

▶ Kristen's eyelashes are so long they touch the lenses of her glasses.
克麗絲汀的睫毛長到連她眼鏡的鏡片都碰得到。

---

eyelid [ˈaɪˌlɪd] *n.* 眼皮

▶ As she stared out the window, Kate's eyelids became heavy and she drifted off to sleep.
凱特望著窗外時，眼皮變得沈重，然後打起瞌睡來了。

100

fabric [ˈfæb.rɪk] *n.* 布料；紡織品

同 **cloth; textile**

▶ We chose the fabric for our new couches based on comfort, not color.
我們替新沙發選擇的布料是以舒適為考量，而非顏色。

fad [fæd] *n.* 潮流；流行

同 **fashion; craze**

▶ Lily continually buys new shoes to keep up with the latest fads.
莉莉不停買新鞋，好跟上最新潮流。

Fahrenheit [ˈfer.ən.haɪt] *n.* 華氏度

▶ We started to sweat as the temperature outside approached 80 degrees Fahrenheit.
室外的氣溫來到華氏八十度時，我們開始流汗了。

---

falter [ˈfɑːl.tɚ]

v. 動搖；躊躇；搖晃；結巴地說

同 **hesitate; waver**

實用片語與搭配詞

voice falter 聲音顫抖

▶ Evelyn never faltered in her desire to attend university, even though she was very poor.
儘管愛芙琳經濟拮据，卻從沒動搖過上大學的決心。

▶ In her Oscar acceptance speech the actress was overcome by emotion and her voice faltered to a mere whisper.
這位女演員在奧斯卡授獎演說情緒激動且聲音顫抖到只能發出低語。

fascinate [ˈfæs.ən.eɪt]

v. 迷住；使神魂顛倒

同 **charm; attract**

▶ The biology teacher's lesson on the different parts of the brain fascinated the students.
那名生物老師的大腦構造課程讓學生上得津津有味。

---

fatigue [fəˈtiːg]

① *n.* 疲勞

同 **exhaustion; tiredness**

實用片語與搭配詞

reduce fatigue 減輕疲勞

② *v.* 使疲勞

同 **exhaust; wear out**

▶ You may experience fatigue if you haven't gotten enough sleep.
如果你沒有充足的睡眠，可能會感到疲勞。

▶ If you take a nap at lunch time, it could reduce fatigue by 70 percent.
如果你在午飯時間小睡，便能夠降低 70% 的疲勞。

▶ Ruth fatigues easily and must get 10 hours of sleep each night.
茹絲很容易疲勞，每晚需要十個小時的睡眠。

---

federal [ˈfed.ɚ.əl] *adj.* 聯邦的；國家的

同 **central**

反 **confederate**

▶ Many teachers hope that the government will increase federal funding for public schools.
許多老師都希望政府能增加公立學校的聯邦經費。

feeble [ˈfiː.bəl] *adj.* 虛弱的

同 **weak**

反 **strong**

▶ After being ill for several days, Trent was very feeble and had difficulty walking.

病了好幾天後，川特全身虛弱，行走困難。

---

feminine [ˈfem.ə.nɪn]

① *adj.* 女性的；女性化的

反 **masculine**

② *n.* 陰性

反 **masculine; virile**

▶ My boyfriend patiently shopped at many feminine stores looking for just the right perfume for me.

我男朋友很有耐心地逛了許多女性用品店，尋找最適合我的香水。

▶ The feminine of the Spanish word "alta" is tall in English.

西班牙文中的陰性詞「alta」在英文裡是「高」的意思。

---

fertilizer [ˈfɝː.t̬əl.aɪ.zɚ] *n.* 肥料

▶ The grass turned a bright shade of green when Mr. Jones tried a new fertilizer.

瓊斯先生試了新的肥料後，草地變得綠油油的。

---

fiance / fiancee [ˌfiː.ɑːnˈseɪ]

n. 未婚夫 / 未婚妻

▶ John and his fiancee met in high school and will get married next year.

約翰和他的未婚妻在高中就認識了，兩人明年要結婚了。

---

fiber [ˈfaɪ.bɚ] *n.* 纖維

同 **thread; twine**

▶ If you need more fiber in your diet, try eating fruit with the skin on it.

如果你的飲食需要更多纖維，試試看吃水果時連皮一起吃。

Exercise 26

I. Choices

1. In the face of increasing financial threats and fraud, the remitted must be vigilant and ensure that the details are correct before they ___________ the payment instruction.
   (A) locate (B) persecute (C) exemplify (D) execute
2. Stonehenge has ___________ d me since young age, and I have always marveled over how these stones were arranged in such a precise, organized way with a mystical feel to it.
   (A) jade (B) irritate (C) alienate (D) fascinate
3. Terry ___________ ed loudly once he noticed there were extra funds in his bank account when he was only expecting his usual salary amount.
   (A) reclaim (B) declaim (C) exclaim (D) proclaim
4. It is ___________ to see how normal people in daily life rise up to the occasion as observed from Desmond T. Doss in World War II, who singly saved 75 men in Okinawa.
   (A) outrageous (B) extraordinary (C) extensive (D) exorbitant
5. This room could use a bit of ___________ touch as it is too masculine and dull in its arrangement and color.
   (A) feminine (B) famine (C)frame (D) fame

II. Vocabulary Choices

(A) fertilizer	(B) fatigue	(C) extension	(D) exclude
(E) external	(F) extinct	(G) feeble	(H) exile
(I) exterior	(J) federal		

1. Whenever there are due dates approaching, students will always ask for _________ s to their submission deadline to touch up on their reports.
2. One of the reasons why _________ is an important ingredient to the growth of plants is because it provides macronutrients to the plant.
3. How dinosaurs became _________ has always been a debate for decades, and more theories of their disappearance have been proposed in the recent times.
4. Reducing worker _________ can save companies money as it will reduce rates of human risk and increase the happiness of the staff.
5. James modeled the _________ of his house based on the White House as the idea of staying in the White House fascinated him ever since he watched a documentary on US presidents.

Unit 27

fiddle ['fɪd.əl]

① *n.* 小提琴
同 **violin**

② *v.* 拉小提琴

▶ Everyone tapped their toes as Mary's fingers danced on the strings of her fiddle.
瑪麗的手指像跳舞般撥弄小提琴時，大家的腳都跟著打拍子。

▶ Mark fiddled along with the other people in the band.
馬克在樂團裡和其他人一起拉小提琴。

---

filter ['fɪl.tɚ]

① *n.* 過濾器；淨水器
同 **cleanse; drain**

② *v.* 過濾；濾除
同 **sort out**

實用片語與搭配詞
filter into people's minds 漸入人心

▶ To keep the fish tank clean, we replace the water filter once a month.
為了常保魚缸清潔，我們每個月更換一次過濾器。

▶ This new invention can filter the salt out of ocean water, making it drinkable.
這項新發明可以把海水的鹽分過濾出來，讓海水變成飲用水。

▶ To change traditions, you need to let new ideas slowly filter into people's minds.
為了改變習俗，你需要慢慢將新觀念植入人心。

---

fin [fɪn] *n.* 鰭；鰭狀物

▶ Even with a damaged fin, the fish could still glide through the water.
儘管這條魚的一片鰭已經受傷，但還是能夠在水裡悠游。

---

fishery ['fɪʃ.ɚ.i] *n.* 漁業；漁場

同 **piscary**

▶ Many people in the seaside town work in the fishery.
在這座濱海的鎮上，很多人都從事漁業。

---

flake [fleɪk]

① *n.* 小薄片
同 **shaving**

② *v.* 成片剝落；向雪片似的降落
同 **peel; crumble**

▶ Tiny flakes of snow came down from the thick clouds.
細小的雪片從厚厚的雲層降下來。

▶ Bark began to flake off the tree due to the disease.
因為這種疾病，樹皮開始剝落。

實用片語與搭配詞

flake out 癱倒 / 入睡

▶ After a long day at work, Emily came home and flaked out on the sofa.
在工作了一整天後，艾蜜莉一回家就攤倒在沙發上。

---

flap [flæp]

① *v.* 拍打；上下拍動；振翅

同 **flutter**

② *n.* （信封的）蓋口；拍動；拍打聲

實用片語與搭配詞

be in / get in a flap 內心忐忑不安

▶ The injured little bird flapped its wings but couldn't fly.
這隻受傷的小鳥拍打雙翅，卻飛不起來。

▶ You need to lift the flap of the envelope to get the letter out.
你需要打開信封的蓋口才能把信拿出來。

▶ There is no need to get in a flap over your exam results; I am sure you will do well as usual.
不需要為了考試結果而忐忑不安；我保證你的成績會跟往常一樣優秀。

---

flaw [flɑː]

① *n.* 瑕疵；裂縫

同 **crack; error**

實用片語與搭配詞

a flawless performance 完美的表演

② *v.* 生裂縫；使有缺陷

同 **blemish; defect**

▶ I noticed several flaws in this script, so we need to fix them.
我注意到這個劇本有幾個小錯誤，我們得修改過來。

▶ The opera troupe delivered a flawless performance and it was worth the expensive ticket.
這個歌劇巡演團呈現了一場完美無瑕的演出，儘管票價昂貴但非常值得。

▶ When Frank pulled a loose string, it flawed his new shirt.
法蘭克拔掉了新襯衫上一條鬆脫的線，結果把襯衫弄破了。

---

flick [flɪk]

① *n.* 輕彈；輕彈聲

同 **tap; flip**

② *v.* 輕彈

同 **tap; flip**

實用片語與搭配詞

flick B at A; flick A with B 以 B 輕打 A

▶ Joey successfully annoyed his older sister with several flicks on her back.
喬伊在姊姊背後彈了好幾下，稱心如意地把姊姊惹煩了。

▶ Lisa quickly flicked the mosquito off of her arm.
麗莎快速地把手臂上的蚊子彈開。

▶ Jennifer flicked a piece of eraser at John's head to try and catch his attention.
珍妮佛用一塊橡皮擦輕打約翰的頭，試著要引起他的注意。

flip [flɪp]

① *v.* 輕拋；輕彈

同 **tap; flick**

實用片語與搭配詞

flip sth. over 快速的翻轉某物

② *n.* 空翻；輕彈

同 **tap; flick**

實用片語與搭配詞

a flip comment 輕率的評論

- The chef flipped her pancakes, so they were perfectly cooked on both sides.
  這名主廚輕拋鬆餅，好讓兩面充分煎熟。
- During the typhoon, a big wave flipped over the fishing boat, but all the fishermen survived.
  颱風期間，一陣大浪將漁船翻覆，但全數漁民均倖存。
- The gymnast added several flips to her routine, making it a major success.
  這名體操運動員在她的固定動作裡增加了幾個空翻，令表演大獲成功。
- The boy made a flip comment about the man in the wheelchair and his mom became very angry at his rudeness.
  男孩對輪椅上的男人做出輕率的評論，他的母親因為他的無禮而感到憤怒。

---

flourish [ˈflɝː.ɪʃ]

① *v.* 茂盛；繁榮

同 **thrive**

反 **deteriorate**

② *n.* 炫耀性的動作；揮舞

實用片語與搭配詞

with a flourish 瀟灑的 / 誇張的動作

- With the right amount of water and sunshine, these flowers should flourish and bloom.
  給予適當的水分和陽光，這些花應該會綻放得很茂盛。
- The audience was amazed by the dancer's flourish of fancy footwork.
  這名舞者的花俏舞步精彩絕倫，讓觀眾看得大為驚嘆。
- Judy walked into the room with a flourish, as if she had the world at her feet.
  茱蒂動作誇張地走進房間，好似全世界都拜倒在她的石榴裙下。

---

fluency [ˈfluː.ən.si] *n.* 流暢

- Rita delivered her speech with great confidence and fluency.
  瑞塔自信滿滿而且流暢無礙地發表了演說。

---

foe [foʊ] *n.* 敵人；仇敵

同 **opponent**

反 **friend**

- Cameron and the other players showed great teamwork and defeated their foes.
  卡麥隆和其他隊員同心協力，擊敗了對手。

實用片語與搭配詞

vanquish foes 擊敗對手

▶ Alexander the Great vanquished all his foes to become one of the greatest soldiers of all time.
亞歷山大大帝擊敗了所有對手，成為了有史以來最偉大的戰士之一。

---

foil [fɔɪl] *n.* 挫敗；阻撓；箔

同 **frustrate; prevent**

實用片語與搭配詞

cover / wrap sth. with / in foil
以錫箔紙包裹

▶ We would have arrived earlier, but there were many foils in our schedule.
我們本來可以早一點到的，但是有太多事妨礙了我們的行程。

▶ When baking meat in the oven, it is a good idea to wrap it in foil to keep it moist.
以烤箱烤肉時，用錫箔紙包裹肉品是讓其保持水份的好方法。

F

---

folklore [ˈfoʊk.lɔːr] *n.* 民間傳說；民俗

同 **myths; legends**

▶ For years, people believed giants used to live here, but it was only folklore.
多年來，民眾相信巨人族以前就住在這裡，但這不過是個民間傳說而已。

---

forgetful [fɚˈget.fəl] *adj.* 健忘的

反 **remindful**

▶ I have been so forgetful lately; I left my keys in the refrigerator.
我最近非常健忘；竟然把鑰匙放在冰箱裡了。

102

format [ˈfɔːr.mæt]

① *n.* 版式；編排；形式

同 **arrangement; layout**

② *v.* 以特別的形式規劃或安排；（電腦）格式化

同 **arrange; configure**

▶ The work schedule's new format has greatly increased our efficiency.
這個工作排程的新版本，大大提升了我們的效率。

▶ The teacher formatted the test by arranging the questions from the easiest to the hardest.
這名老師編排這項考試的方法是把題目從最簡單的排到最難的。

---

foul [faʊl]

① *adj.* 惡臭的；骯髒的

同 **stinking; unclean**

實用片語與搭配詞

a foul day 糟糕的一天

▶ The smell of rotten eggs was so foul that we had to open all the windows.
這些腐敗的雞蛋散發惡臭，我們把所有窗戶都打開了才行。

▶ I had such a foul day at work that I just want to go home and relax and forget about everything.
今天這個上班日是如此糟糕，以致於我只想回家放鬆，忘卻所有煩心的事。

② *n.* （比賽）犯規

同 **offensive**

▶ Tim committed a foul during the game and had to sit out for 10 minutes.

提姆比賽時犯了規，因此必須在場邊暫停比賽十分鐘。

③ *adv.* 違反規則地

▶ Jim's nature occasionally makes him play foul, so people don't like to play with him.

吉姆的個性偶爾會讓他犯規，所以大家都不喜歡跟他一起玩。

④ *v.* 弄髒；污染

同 **pollute; contaminate**

反 **clean**

▶ The mud fouled my clothes, so I had to do laundry.

爛泥巴弄髒了我的衣服，我只好把衣服洗一洗。

實用片語與搭配詞

foul sth. up 弄髒某物 / 使某物纏結

▶ The contractor fouled up the project so we had to fire him and start everything from scratch.

這位承辦人將這個案子搞砸了，因此我們必須解僱他並且從零開始。

---

fowl [faʊl] *n.* 禽類

同 **bird poultry**

▶ Sarah spotted doves, crows and other fowl on the nature trail.

莎拉在這條自然步道上看到了鴿子、烏鴉和其他鳥禽。

---

fraction [ˈfræk.ʃən] *n.* 分數；小部分；片段

同 **portion; segment**

反 **integer**

▶ I need more time to finish the fractions on this math test!

我需要更多時間來做完這個數學測驗裡的分數題目！

---

framework [ˈfreɪm.wɝːk] *n.* 架構；骨架

同 **structure; scaffold**

▶ Steve laid down the bricks to start the framework for his house.

史提夫砌下磚塊，開始築起他房子的架構。

---

frantic [ˈfræn.t̬ɪk] *adj.* 發狂似的

同 **delirious; frenzied**

▶ Katie was frantic when she remembered she had a science test.

凱蒂想起要考自然科學時，幾乎快抓狂了。

---

freight [freɪt]

① *n.* 貨物；運費

同 **cargo; goods**

▶ The freight on this cargo ship is mostly canned food.

這艘貨船上的貨物大部分都是罐頭食品。

② *v.* 運送；裝貨於…；用貨運運輸

同 **load; shipment**

▶ The train freighted supplies into the area affected by the storm.

火車把物資載運至暴風受災區。

實用片語與搭配詞

freight sth. with sth. 裝貨於某物

▶ Nicholas' boss freighted him with a huge load of work just before he went home, so he will probably work until very late.

尼古拉斯的老闆在他準備下班回家前交付了大量的工作給他，所以他可能會工作到很晚。

---

frontier [frʌnˈtɪr] *n.* 邊界；邊境

同 **border; outskirts**

▶ The explorer left on a journey to find a new frontier.

這名探險家踏上了旅程去尋找新疆界。

---

fume [fjuːm]

① *n.* （有害、濃烈的）煙；氣

同 **smoke; vapor**

② *v.* 薰；冒煙；發怒

同 **burn; smoke**

實用片語與搭配詞

fume at sb. / sth. 發大火

▶ The fumes from the chemicals caused everyone to start coughing.

這些化學物產生的煙霧導致大家開始咳嗽。

▶ We fumed our house with bug spray to get rid of the mosquitos.

我們用殺蟲劑薰一薰房子，好消滅蚊子。

▶ The motorist fumed at the car driver for cutting him off.

這位駕駛因為被另一位汽車駕駛超車而火冒三丈。

---

fury [ˈfjʊr.i] *n.* 狂怒

同 **anger; rage**

▶ After hearing his mother's calming words, Chris controlled his fury.

克里斯聽到媽媽安撫的話語之後，就控制了自己的怒氣。

Exercise 27

I. Choices

1. For avoidance of doubt, the ________ of this football tournament will be done in knockout instead of round robin.

   (A) format (B) formula (C) force (D) forecast

2. A ________ of the middle class families is unhappy with the new policies that did not address their needs as the sandwich class.

   (A) fracas (B) fraction (C) fracture (D) factuality

3. The ________ of any nation is a highly sensitive and important issue as it tackles and deals with the sovereignty of a nation as seen in the dispute between South Korea and Japan over Dokdo/Takeshima.

   (A) frontier (B) frontlet (C) frontal (D) frontage

4. This lake is full of life and creates a gorgeous backdrop for plants and trees planted around it to ________ beautifully.

   (A) flounder (B) dwindle (C) flourish (D) flush

5. Emails can be managed easier as you can sort them out according to their dates and ________ them to the sender.

   (A) file (B) filiation (C) filial (D) filter

II. Vocabulary Choices

(A) flaw	(B) flake	(C) flick	(D) flap
(E) flip	(F) foul	(G) fluency	(H) freight
(I) framework	(J) fume		

1. As globalization spreads in a rapid speed in the past decade, the need for ________ in various languages arises in order to secure more business deals.
2. The ________ of a man can often be seen when intense stress is applied in a difficult situation that demands decision-making.
3. The industry of sea ________ companies is facing bigger threats to their cargoes and profits since the resurgence of the Somalian pirates.
4. Providing a ________ to employees will guide them in the direction on how the organization should be run.
5. Once the detectives arrived at the crime scene, they investigated the dead body and suspected a ________ play.

fuse [fju:z]

① v. 熔合；熔接

同 blend; combine

② n. 引線；保險絲；熔線

▶ Using intense heat, Melvin fused the pieces of metal together.
馬文用了極高的溫度把金屬片焊接在一起。

▶ We prepared for a loud explosion once Brandon lit the fuse on the firework.
布蘭登點燃鞭炮的引線時，我們已經做好準備迎接一聲巨響。

---

fuss [fʌs]

① n. 無謂的緊張；大驚小怪

同 worry

反 calm

② v. 小題大作

同 worry

反 calm

▶ All of these deadlines are causing a big fuss among my coworkers.
這些截止期限搞得我的同事個個緊張不安。

▶ Don't fuss about every little thing.
不要凡事都小題大做。

---

garment [ˈgɑːr.mənt] n.（一件）衣服

同 item of clothing

▶ This garment of clothing is too big for me.
這件衣服對我來說太大了。

---

gasp [gæsp]

① v. （因驚奇、痛苦或震驚等）倒抽一口氣；喘氣

同 choke; pant

實用片語與搭配詞

gasp for air 大口吸氣

② n. 引申為嘩然

同 choke; pant

實用片語與搭配詞

gasps of horror 嚇的喘氣

▶ I gasped as the child fell to the floor.
那孩子跌倒在地時，我嚇得倒抽了一口氣。

▶ The diver ran out of oxygen underwater and was gasping for air once he reached the surface.
這位潛水者在水底已將氧氣使用殆盡，所以一浮至水面便大口吸著空氣。

▶ There was a loud gasp when the wife stood up in court.
那位太太在法庭上站起來時，現場一片嘩然。

▶ Gasps of horror filled the theatre where the new zombie movie was showing.
新上映的殭屍電影讓驚悚的氣氛充滿整個影廳。

gathering [ˈgæð.ɚ.ɪŋ] *n.* 集會；聚集

同 **congregation; assemble**

▶ There's a gathering at the church this Sunday.
本週日在教會有聚會。

---

gay [geɪ]

① *adj.* 同性戀的；鮮豔的；快樂的

同 **homosexual; happy**

② *n.* 同性戀者

同 **homosexual**

▶ Patrick is a gay man.
派翠克是男同性戀者。

▶ Gays want the same freedom of choice as other citizens.
同性戀者想享有和其他公民一樣的選擇自由。

---

gender [ˈdʒen.dɚ] *n.* 性別

同 **sexuality**

實用片語與搭配詞

gender differences 性別差異

▶ What is the gender of the baby? Girl or boy?
嬰兒的性別是什麼？是女孩還是男孩？

▶ Gender differences does not mean companies should pay women less than men for the same jobs.
性別差異並不代表公司應該要付更多的薪水給男性，勝於同工的女性。

---

geographical [ˌdʒi.əˈgræf.ɪ.kəl] *adj.* 地理的

同 **geographic**

▶ The United States covers a large geographical area of North America.
美國在北美洲佔了很大的地理面積。

---

geometry [dʒiˈɑː.mə.tri] *n.* 幾何學

▶ I learned geometry in math class.
我在數學課中學到了幾何學。

---

glacier [ˈgleɪ.si.ɚ] *n.* 冰河

同 **iceberg**

▶ Many glaciers in Alaska are melting.
阿拉斯加州有很多冰河正在融化中。

---

glare [gler]

① *v.* 怒目注視

同 **glower; frown**

實用片語與搭配詞

glare at sb. / sth. 怒目而視

② *n.* 怒視；瞪眼；刺眼的強光

同 **stare; fierce look**

▶ Lisa glared at Brandon after he laughed at her.
布蘭登嘲笑麗莎之後，她就氣得瞪他一眼。

▶ Benjamin came home after his curfew to find his mother sitting on the sofa, angrily glaring at him.
班杰明超過了門禁時間才到家，發現媽媽坐在沙發上怒瞪著他。

▶ Rebecca's angry glare immediately warned Peter to be careful.
蕾貝加氣憤的目光立即提醒了彼得要小心點。

gleam [gliːm]

① *n.* 微光；一線（希望）

同 **beam; ray**

實用片語與搭配詞

a gleam of hope 一線希望

② *v.* 發微光；閃爍

同 **glimmer; twinkle**

實用片語與搭配詞

gleam with sth. 眼睛流露著某種情感

- I saw a gleam of light shine through the clouds.
  我看見穿透雲層的一絲陽光。
- There was a gleam of hope following the destructive earthquake when the government promised financial help.
  在這起可怕的地震災害後，政府承諾提供經濟援助，給了災民一線希望。
- The marble roof gleamed under the moonlight.
  那個大理石屋頂在月光下微微發光。
- Katie's parents gleamed with pride after she was accepted to an Ivy League university.
  在凱蒂申請上常春藤名校後，她的父母滿心驕傲。

---

glee [gliː] *n.* 快樂；歡欣

同 **delight**

反 **grief**

實用片語與搭配詞

be glee at sth. 欣喜若狂

- The children were filled with glee as they entered the amusement park.
  孩子們進入遊樂園裡時，開心得不得了。
- The students were reacting with glee at the news that their class won the basketball competition.
  這些學生們得知他們班贏得籃球比賽的消息後欣喜若狂。

---

glitter [ˋglɪtɚ]

① *v.* 閃爍；光彩奪目

同 **glimmer; sparkle**

② *n.* （裝飾用）小發光物；閃光；閃耀

同 **gleam; sparkle**

- The sparkles glittered in the sun.
  亮片在陽光中閃爍。
- You can put glitter on the card to make it shinier.
  你可以在卡片上撒亮片來讓它變得更閃亮。

---

gloom [gluːm]

① *n.* 黑暗；幽暗

同 **gloominess**

實用片語與搭配詞

a deep gloom 愁雲慘霧

- Tom turned on the light to banish the gloom of the windowless room.
  湯姆開燈，掃除了這個沒有窗戶的房間中的幽暗。
- A deep gloom fell over the country when news broke of the president's assassination.
  當新聞播報總統遇刺的消息後，全國被愁雲慘霧籠罩著。

② *v.* 變暗；使陰暗

▶ As the storm came in, the sky gloomed.
暴風雨一來，天空就變暗了。

---

gnaw [nɑː] *v.* 啃；咬

同 **chew; gnash**

實用片語與搭配詞

gnaw at sth. 啃咬某物 / 使受折磨

▶ The dog gnawed away at the bone all night.
那隻狗整晚都在啃那塊骨頭。

▶ Guilt gnawed away at the criminal's conscience until he confessed to stealing the money.
直到這名罪犯坦承偷錢之前，罪惡感折磨著他的良心。

---

gobble [ˈgɑː.bəl] *v.* 狼吞虎嚥

同 **guzzle; devour**

實用片語與搭配詞

gobble sth. up 吞沒某物

▶ The hungry child gobbled the food before him.
那餓腸轆轆的孩子狼吞虎嚥地吃面前的食物。

▶ The holiday at the expensive resort gobbled up our money quickly, so we had to return home earlier.
我們在這昂貴的度假勝地花了很多錢，因此我們必須提早返家。

---

gorge [gɔːrdʒ]

① *n.* 峽谷

同 **valley**

② *v.* 暴食；大吃

同 **gobble; gulp**

實用片語與搭配詞

gorge oneself on / with sth.
大吃某種東西

▶ Toroko Gorge is a beautiful landmark in Hualian.
太魯閣峽谷是花蓮的美麗地標。

▶ The man gorged himself with food after exercising.
那名男子在運動後暴飲暴食。

▶ Peter gorged himself on the delicious food at the wedding, and got a terrible stomach ache.
彼得在婚宴上狼吞虎嚥弟吃著美食，便感到劇烈的腹痛。

---

gorgeous [ˈgɔːr.dʒəs]

adj. 極漂亮的；華麗的

同 **beautiful; stunning**

▶ The decorations for the party were gorgeous.
那場派對的裝飾漂亮極了。

---

gorilla [gəˈrɪl.ə] *n.* 大猩猩

▶ The big gorilla reached for a banana in the tree.
那隻大猩猩伸手去拔樹上的香蕉。

gospel [ˈgɑː.spəl] *n.* 福音

同 **evangel**

實用片語與搭配詞

gospel truth 完全可信的事實

▶ Christians share the gospel all around the world.
基督徒在全球各地傳福音。

▶ If you don't want to make your parents angry, you had better tell them the gospel truth about going to the party.
如果你不想讓你的父母生氣，你最好全盤托出你要去派對的事實。

G

grant [grænt]

① *v.* 准予；同意；給予

同 **permit; consent**

實用片語與搭配詞

grand someone permission to do sth. 允許某人做某事

② *n.* 輔助金；獎學金

同 **award; scholarship**

實用片語與搭配詞

take sb. / sth. for granted
把某人 / 事物當成理所當然的

▶ The boss granted me permission to go home early.
老闆准許我提早回家。

▶ Your parents did not grant you permission to go to that party, so you might get in trouble.
你的父母並不允許你參加派對，所以你也許會惹上麻煩。

▶ The university applied for a grant from the government.
那所大學向政府申請輔助金。

▶ Never take your good luck for granted because everything might change in the blink of an eye.
千萬不要把你的好運視為理所當然，因為萬事在一眨眼間便可能翻轉。

---

gravity [ˈgræv.ə.t̬i] *n.* 重力；地心引力

同 **seriousness**

▶ The apple fell on Isaac's head because of gravity!
那顆蘋果之所以會掉在艾薩頭上，是出於地心引力！

---

graze [greɪz] *v.* 吃草；放牧

同 **browse; nibble**

實用片語與搭配詞

graze A in / on B 在 B 放牧 A

▶ The sheep graze the fields on the hill every day.
每天羊群都在山坡的原野上吃草。

▶ The shepherd grazes sheep on his field.
那個牧羊人在自己的田地裡牧羊。

---

grease [griːs]

① *n.* 油脂；動物脂

同 **fat; lubrication**

▶ Wash the pan! There is so much grease on it.
請清洗那個平底鍋！上面好油。

實用片語與搭配詞

grease-proof paper 烘烤食物的耐油紙

▶ It is a good idea to use grease-proof paper to prevent food from sticking to the pot.

為了避免食物沾黏到鍋子上，使用耐油紙是一個好主意。

② *v.* 給…加潤滑油；塗油脂於…

同 **lubricate; smear**

▶ Before you ride your bike, grease the chain.

你騎腳踏車前，請替鏈子上潤滑油。

Exercise 28

I. Choices

1. Once Peter laid his eyes on his beloved fried chicken, he ran to the table in an instant to ___________ it up.
   (A) gaggle (B) goggle (C) gobble (D) google
2. Once Jane heard of a new breakthrough in a cure for her terminal disease, you can see the ___________ of hope in her eyes.
   (A) glide (B) gleam (C) glitch (D) grip
3. An angry ___________ from your spouse is probably more terrifying than any horror movie in this world.
   (A) glare (B) glee (C) glimpse (D) glance
4. ___________ inequality has been an issue focused on worldwide, but can we truly eradicate this in our generation to put men and women on equal footing?
   (A) Gander (B) Gender (C) Genre (D) Gene
5. With a shadow right behind her, Sally felt a pair of hands grip her neck, and she ___________ for air.
   (A) grid (B) gain (C) gasp (D) gap

II. Vocabulary Choices

(A) glitter	(B) gorgeous	(C) gravity	(D) gloom
(E) glee	(F) fuss	(G) glacier	(H) grant
(I) gnaw	(J) fuse		

1. I _________ you the full authority to make wholesale changes in our company and to hire anyone you deem fit for the job.
2. Today Annabelle is wearing a _________ grown designed by her close friend, and it is making heads turn as it brings out the charm from within her.
3. You can see the _________ in every dog's eyes once you tell them they are going for a walk.
4. With major events and uncertainties with policies of nations, this year might just be a year of _________ for our economy.
5. The trend to _________ water with fruits is on the roll as it is a healthier substitute for soft drinks and provides benefits for the body.

Unit 29

greed [gri:d] *n.* 貪心；貪婪

同 **avarice; voracity**

▶ The greed of some people can hurt a lot of other people.
某些人的貪心可能會傷害很多人。

---

grim [grɪm] *adj.* 令人擔憂的；令人沮喪的

同 **bleak**

反 **cheerful**

▶ His condition is very grim. I don't know if he'll survive.
他的情況相當令人擔憂，我不知道他能不能存活。

---

grip [grɪp]

① *v.* 握緊；掌握

同 **clasp**

反 **loosen**

② *n.* 緊握；理解；掌握

同 **clasp; grasp**

實用片語與搭配詞

get / keep / take a grip on oneself
振作起來

▶ The child tightly gripped his father's hand.
那個孩子緊握住爸爸的手。

▶ Mark's grip on the rock began to slip as it rained harder.
雨下得越來越大，馬克緊抓岩石的手開始鬆脫了。

▶ Maggie got a grip on herself very quickly after losing her job, and started her own business.
梅姬在失業後很快就振作起來並且開始創業。

---

groan [groʊn]

① *v.* 哀號；呻吟

同 **howl; moan**

實用片語與搭配詞

groan at sb. / sth. 對某人／事物發出嘆息

② *n.* 哀號聲；呻吟聲

同 **howl; moan**

實用片語與搭配詞

a groan of pain 痛苦的呻吟

▶ The students all groaned as the teacher announced the homework assignment.
老師宣佈家庭作業時，學生們一片哀號。

▶ The fitness instructor told Jenny to do 10 more push-ups, but she just groaned at him.
健身教練要珍妮再做十下伏地挺身，但她只對著他嘆息。

▶ I heard a groan as I tried to wake Jane.
我試圖叫醒珍時，聽到了一聲哀號。

▶ After falling down the stairs, the student held her broken ankle and gave a groan of pain.
在跌下樓梯後，這名學生抱著她斷掉的腳踝，發出一聲痛苦的呻吟。

gross [groʊs]

① *adj.* 總的

同 **whole**

反 **little**

▶ What is your gross income?
你的總收入是多少？

② *v.* 總收入為；總共賺到

同 **earn; receive**

▶ The company grossed over 1 million dollars a year.
那家公司一年的總收入超過一百萬美元。

實用片語與搭配詞

sb.'s gross income 某人的總收入

▶ It is a disgrace that the CEO's gross income per year is more than that of all the employees put together.
執行長每年的總收入比全體員工的薪水加總還要多，這實在太不像話了。

③ *n.* 總收入；總額

同 **whole**

反 **little**

▶ His gross included his commission.
他的總收入中包含了佣金。

實用片語與搭配詞

a gross person 過胖的人

▶ John's friends think he is a gross person because he likes to eat fried insects and sheep intestines.
約翰的朋友認為他是一個臃腫的人，因為他喜歡吃炸昆蟲以及羊腸。

---

growl [graʊl]

① *v.* （狗）低吼；咆哮

同 **snarl; rumble**

▶ The dog growled at me as I walked by.
那條狗在我經過時對我低吼。

實用片語與搭配詞

growl at sb. / sth. 發出低沉的怒吼

▶ My mom just growled at me when I asked her for the tenth time if I could go to the school party.
當我問我媽媽第十次我可否參加學校派對時，她就發出了低沈的怒吼。

② *n.* 低吼聲；咆哮

同 **complain; grumble**

▶ The tiger's growl scared the children.
那隻老虎的低吼聲嚇壞了孩子們。

---

grumble [ˋgrʌm.bəl] *v.* 埋怨；對…表示不滿

同 **complain; mutter**

▶ The employees grumbled under their breath as the manager complained about their work.
經理抱怨那些員工的工作表現時，他們都低聲埋怨著。

實用片語與搭配詞

grumble at / to sb. about / at / over sth 向某人抱怨某事

▶ My brother always grumbles at me when I remind him to do his chores before mom comes home.
當我提醒我弟弟必須在媽媽回家前完成例行工作時，他總是向我抱怨。

grumble [ˋgrʌm.blɚ] *n.* 埋怨；牢騷

同 **complain; mutter**

▶ The grumble of the crowd could be heard miles away.
群眾怨聲載道，好幾里外都能聽到。

G

實用片語與搭配詞

full of grumbles
滿腹牢騷

- The students were full of grumbles over the large amount of holiday homework they were given.
  學生們在假期間被指派了大量的回家作業，他們因此滿腹牢騷。

---

guideline ['gaɪd.laɪn]

n. 指導原則；指導方針

同 **teaching; principle**

- The guidelines for the game are very clear.
  那場比賽的規則與指導原則非常清楚明確。

---

gulp [gʌlp]

① *v.* 大口地喝；狼吞虎嚥地吃

同 **swig**

反 **sip**

實用片語與搭配詞

gulp sth. down 狼吞虎嚥地吃東西

② *n.* 一（大）口；吞

同 **mouthful; swallow**

實用片語與搭配詞

a gulp of sth. 一大口液體 / 飲料

- Drink the soda, don't gulp it!
  請喝汽水，可是別大口猛灌！
- It is unhealthy to gulp down so much soda; drink more water or green tea.
  灌下這麼多汽水是不健康的；多喝一點水或綠茶吧。
- I had one gulp of juice at lunch.
  午餐時，我喝了一大口的果汁。
- When a big wave unexpectedly washed over Tommy, he swallowed several gulps of salt water.
  當一陣大浪無預警地沖刷過湯米，他喝了好幾口海水。

---

gust [gʌst]

① *n.* 一陣狂風；一陣強風

同 **burst; explosion**

實用片語與搭配詞

a gust of temper 大發脾氣

② *v.* 猛吹

同 **blast**

- A strong gust of wind blew the tree down.
  一陣狂風把那棵樹吹倒了。
- The woman released a gust of temper at the man who pushed in front of her at the cashier line.
  這位女人對那位在結帳隊伍前推擠的男人大發脾氣。
- The wind gusted up a lot of dirt.
  那陣風吹起了許多塵土。

---

gut [gʌt]

① *v.* 取出內臟；摧毀內部裝設

② *n.* 腸子

同 **bowel; intestine**

- The fisherman gutted the fish on the boat.
  那名漁夫在船上取出魚的內臟。
- I don't like seeing guts and gore of horror movies.
  我不喜歡看肚破腸流、血淋淋的恐怖片。

gypsy [ˈdʒɪp.si] *n.* 吉普賽人

同 **nomad**

▶ Gypsies often move from place to place, country to country.
吉普賽人常常遷徙到不同的地區和國家。

104

hail [heɪl]

① *n.* 冰雹

同 **frozen rain; sleet**

② *v.* 下冰雹

同 **flag down; shout for**

實用片語與搭配詞

hail sth. down on sb. 某物落在某人上

▶ I have never seen so much hail.
我從來沒見過那麼多的冰雹。

▶ All of a sudden, it started to hail.
突然間就下冰雹了。

▶ The teacher hailed down praise on the student for achieving the highest math grade in the country.
老師大大稱讚這位全國數學分數最高的學生。

---

hairstyle / hairdo [ˈher.staɪl / ˈher.duː]

n. 髮型

同 **hairdo**

▶ The short hair is the trendy new hairstyle these days.
現在短髮是最新流行的髮型。

---

handicap [ˈhæn.dɪ.kæp]

① *n.* （使弱者略佔優勢的）讓步賽；殘障

同 **disadvantage; hindrance**

② *v.* 妨礙；使不利

同 **burden**

▶ In certain sports, handicaps are normal so that players have an equal chance to win.
在某些運動中，讓步賽是很正常的，這能讓每個選手都有同等的獲勝機會。

▶ The stairs handicap those who have difficulty walking up and down.
樓梯妨礙了行動不便者上下行動。

---

handicraft [ˈhæn.di.kræft] *n.* 手工藝（品）

同 **craft**

▶ Jessie is great at making all sorts of handicrafts.
潔西擅長製作各種手工藝品。

---

hardy [ˈhɑːr.di]

adj. 能吃苦耐勞的；耐寒的；勇敢的

同 **resilient; tough**

▶ Sailors must be hardy people in order to deal with rough conditions at sea.
船員必須能吃苦耐勞才足以應付海上的惡劣環境。

---

harness [ˈhɑːr.nəs]

① *n.* 輓具；馬具

同 **saddle; yoke**

② *v.* 套（馬）；上挽具

同 **saddle; yoke**

▶ The farmer strapped the harness around the ox and tied it to the plow.
農夫把輓具繫在牛身上，然後再綁在犁上。

▶ The cowboy harnessed the horse with a long piece of rope.
那名牛仔用很長的繩索套住馬。

haul [hɑːl]

① *v.* 拖；拉；搬運

同 **drag; tug**

實用片語與搭配詞

haul sb. up 把某人帶上法庭審問

② *n.* 〈用力〉拖；拉；搬運

同 **drag; tug**

▶ The child hauled his backpack on the floor.
那個孩子把背包拖在地板上。

▶ Following the bullying incident at school, the teacher hauled Paul up to the principle's office where his angry parents were already waiting.
在學校發生霸凌事件之後，老師將保羅拖到校長室，他生氣的父母早已在那等待。

▶ The movers sweated over the haul of the heavy load.
搬家工人用力拖重物時，汗流浹背。

---

haunt [hɑːnt]

① *v.* （鬼魂）出沒於…

同 **hang around**

② *n.* 常去的地方

實用片語與搭配詞

a haunted house 鬧鬼的房子

▶ In the novel A Christmas Carol, Scrooge is haunted by three ghosts.
在小氣財神一書中，史古基被三個鬼糾纏。

▶ Starbucks is one of Evelyn's favorite haunts.
星巴克是艾福琳最喜歡去的地方之一。

▶ During Halloween, many students like to visit the haunted house at the amusement park.
在萬聖節期間，許多學生喜歡造訪主題樂園裏的鬼屋。

---

hearty [ˈhɑːr.t̬i] *adj.* 熱情的；精力充沛的

同 **vigorous; energetic**

▶ The visitor received a hearty welcome.
那名訪客獲得了熱情的歡迎。

---

heavenly [ˈhev.ən.li] *adj.* 極好的；天堂的

反 **earthly; mundane**

▶ The heavenly voices of little children singing are so nice.
幼童們美妙的歌聲很好聽。

---

hedge [hedʒ]

① *n.* 籬笆

同 **border; boundary**

② *v.* 用籬笆圍住；圍住

同 **limit**

▶ James's property extends from that hedge to the fence in the backyard.
詹姆斯的房地產範圍是從那個籬笆一直延伸到後院圍籬。

▶ The man hedged his property so the children could not run out of the yard.
那名男子用籬笆圍住自己的地產，這樣孩子就無法跑到院子外面了。

實用片語與搭配詞

hedge sb. / sth. against sth. with sth.
以某物限制某人 / 物不准作某事物

▶ To hedge yourself against financial losses, you should get expert opinion on investing.
為了避免財務損失，你應當諮詢專家的投資意見。

---

heed [hi:d]

① *v.* 聽從；留心

同 **follow; mind**

② *n.* 聽從；留心；注意

實用片語與搭配詞

take heed of sth. 聽從某事

▶ Please heed the police's advice not to speed.
請聽從警察所說不要超速的規勸。

▶ He paid no heed to his mother's advice and wasted all his money.
他不聽從母親的規勸，而把所有錢都揮霍光了。

▶ Anne did not take heed of her mom's warning about studying hard and now she cannot find a good job.
安當初並沒有聽取媽媽的警告好好念書，因此現在她無法找到一份好工作。

---

heighten [ˈhaɪ.t̬ən] *v.* 增高；增強

反 **lower**

▶ The child's scream heightened her mother's anxiety.
孩子的尖叫讓她的母親更加焦慮了。

Exercise 29

I. Choices

1. The skill of ________ is often preserved and retained through the passing down of skills from one generation to another.

   (A) handicraft (B) handkerchief (C) handicap (D) handcuff

2. Investors often ________ their securities against other derivatives as it can minimize losses from unforeseen circumstances.

   (A) ledge (B) hedge (C) cadge (D) fledge

3. ________ is different from snow as it is larger in general and formed under different conditions.

   (A) Hell (B) Hail (C) Hall (D) Hale

4. ________ provides a safety zone for the participants and gives true freedom as it grants them protection.

   (A) Pipeline (B) Borderline (C) Guideline (D) Deadline

5. Ariel's stomach ________ s as she thinks about all the delicious food in the world after a long day of work with no meals in between.

   (A) grumble (B) stumble (C) mumble (D) tumble

II. Vocabulary Choices

(A) graze	(B) gust	(C) groan	(D) haul
(E) hearty	(F) greed	(G) hardy	(H) haunt
(I) heavenly	(J) harness		

1. Despite their looks, plants are really ________ as they are able to adjust to weather conditions and survive.
2. The ________ of wind beats vehemently against the windows as a thunderstorm draws near.
3. The ________ of human is insatiable, and hence getting more no longer remains a solution.
4. As Tim ________ s the basket up the slope, he reminds himself the purpose of getting herbs to prepare medicine for his sick mother.
5. Throughout human history, one of the greatest quest is to find the ________ places or the ________ One who created the whole universe.

Unit 30

heir [er] *n.* 繼承人；嗣子

反 **heiress**

實用片語與搭配詞

heir to sth. 繼承某物

▶ The Prince of Wales is the heir to the British throne.
威爾斯王儲是英國王位繼承人。

▶ Mike is the sole heir to his family's wealth, but he will only get everything once he turns 30.
邁克是他家族財產的唯一繼承人，但是他必須年滿 30 歲才能獲得所有財產。

---

hence [hens] *adv.* 因此；從此

同 **accordingly; consequently**

▶ Danny is the baby of the family and hence his immaturity.
丹尼是家中年紀最小的一個，因此顯得不成熟。

---

herald [ˈher.əld]

① *n.* 傳令官；通報者

② *v.* 宣布

同 **announce; proclaim**

實用片語與搭配詞

herald in sb. / sth. 宣布某人 / 事來臨

▶ The herald announced the royal baby's birth.
傳令官宣佈皇室新生兒誕生的消息。

▶ The CEO heralded that the company was entering a new era.
公司執行長宣佈公司邁入了新的時期。

▶ The invention of the compass heralded in an era of seafaring and the discovery of the new world.
羅盤的發明宣告航海與探索新世界時代的來臨。

---

herb [ɝːb] *n.* 香草；草本植物

▶ Oregano is my favorite herb to cook with.
牛至是我烹飪時最愛用的香草。

101

hermit [ˈhɝː.mɪt] *n.* 隱士

同 **recluse; solitary person**

▶ An old hermit lived in the mountains.
一位年邁的隱士住在山林間。

---

heroic [hɪˈroʊ.ɪk]

① *adj.* 英雄的；英勇的

同 **brave; courageous**

▶ Brandon's attempt to save the dog was very heroic.
布蘭登企圖拯救那隻狗的行為相當英勇。

實用片語與搭配詞

heroic deeds 英勇事跡

- The fire-fighter was awarded a medal for his heroic deeds in saving three kids from a burning house.
  這位消防員從著火的房子裡救出三名孩童，他因為這起英勇事蹟而被授予獎牌。

② (n.pl.) 英勇行為

- Gordon's heroics helped to save the little girl.
  葛登的英勇行為拯救了那名小女孩。

實用片語與搭配詞

in such heroics 如此的誇張

- The fisherman told the tale of losing his big catch in such heroics that no-one really believed him.
  漁夫如此誇張地說了一個他差點抓到一尾大魚的故事，以致於沒人真的相信他。

---

heterosexual [ˌhet̬.ə.roʊˈsek.ʃu.əl]

① adj. 異性戀的

- Heterosexual men like women.
  異性戀男人喜歡女人。

同 **straight person**

② n. 異性戀的人

- Heterosexuals make up the majority of societies.
  異性戀者佔了社會上的大多數。

---

hi-fi / high fidelity [ˈhaɪ.faɪ / ˌhaɪ fɪˈdel.ə.t̬i]

n. 高傳真；高傳真的音響裝置

- This is a hi-fi stereo soundtrack.
  這是一台高傳真音響。

---

hijack [ˈhaɪ.dʒæk]

① v. 劫持；搶奪

- Don't hijack my project!
  不要搶走我的專案！

同 **take control**

實用片語與搭配詞

instance of hijacking 劫持交通工具之事件

- Recent instances of extremists hijacking planes have led to much stricter security at airports all over the world.
  最近一連串極端份子的劫機事件促使全世界的機場都加強保安。

② n. 劫持事件

- The hijack of the plane made headline news.
  被劫持的飛機登上了頭條新聞。

同 **takeover**

---

hiss [hɪs]

① v. 發出嘶吼聲；發出嘶嘶聲

- The cat hissed at his owner.
  貓向主人發出嘶吼聲。

實用片語與搭配詞

hiss at sb. / sth. 向某人 / 某事發出噓聲

- The kitten was hungry and scared, but she still hissed at the rescuers.
  這隻小貓既飢餓又害怕，但她仍然對著救援者發出生氣的嘶嘶聲。

② *n.* 嘶嘶聲；嘶吼聲

▶ Do you hear that hiss? Is it coming from the pipe?
你有沒有聽到嘶嘶聲？是從水管裡傳出來的嗎？

---

hoarse [hɔːrs] *adj.* 沙啞的；粗啞的

同 **gruff; harsh**

▶ My voice is very hoarse.
我的聲音非常沙啞。

---

hockey [ˈhɑː.ki] *n.* 曲棍球

▶ Countries in cold climates like to play hockey.
寒帶氣候的國家喜歡打曲棍球。

---

homosexual [ˌhoʊ.moʊˈsek.ʃu.əl]

① *adj.* 同性戀的

同 **gay**

② *n.* 同性戀者

同 **gay**

▶ Many countries are starting to discuss homosexual rights.
很多國家都開始商議同性戀的權益。

▶ In many countries, homosexuals would like to get married.
在很多國家裡，同性戀者都想結婚。

---

honk [hɑːŋk]

① *n.* 汽車喇叭聲；鳴叫聲

同 **hoot; beep**

② *v.* 按喇叭

同 **beep; hoot**

實用片語與搭配詞

honk at sb. / sth. 對某人 / 物按喇叭

▶ The rush hour air is filled with sounds of many honks.
尖峰時刻，空中充斥著很多喇叭聲。

▶ Don't honk your horn near the tunnel.
在隧道附近不要按喇叭。

▶ I know it is rude to honk at other drivers, but I can't help myself if they drive carelessly.
我知道對其他駕駛按喇叭是沒禮貌的，但當他們隨意行駛時我就無法控制自己了。

---

hood [hʊd]

① *n.* 兜帽；頭巾

同 **cover; top**

② *v.* 戴上兜帽

▶ I want to buy a jacket with a hood to cover my head.
我想買有兜帽的外套，好蓋住我的頭部。

▶ The mother hooded the child to shield him from the rain.
媽媽為孩子戴上兜帽避雨。

---

hoof [huːf] *n.* 蹄

▶ The trainer put a horseshoe on the horse's hoof.
訓練師為馬蹄裝上馬蹄鐵。

horizontal [ˌhɔːr.ɪˈzɑːn.t̬əl]

① *adj.* 地平線的

反 **vertical**

② *n.* 水平的東西；水平線；水平面

同 **flat; plane**

▸ Jeff likes to take horizontal photos where the sea meets the sky.
傑夫喜歡照海天一線之隔的地平線照片。

▸ The artist prefers horizontal to vertical.
那位藝術家偏好水平勝於垂直的東西。

---

hostage [ˈhɑː.stɪdʒ] *n.* 人質

同 **surety**

實用片語與搭配詞

seize / keep sb. as a hostage
脅持某人作為人質

▸ The police helped free the hostages.
警方協助讓人質獲釋。

▸ During war women and children are often kept as hostages to prevent enemy attacks.
戰爭期間，女人與孩童時常被作為人質以防止敵方攻擊。

hostile [ˈhɑː.stəl] *adj.* 不友善的；敵對的

同 **antagonistic**

反 **amiable**

▸ Don't upset the raccoon. It is a hostile animal.
別激怒那隻浣熊，牠不是一隻友善的動物。

---

hound [haʊnd]

① *n.* 獵犬

② *v.* 緊追；追逼

同 **chase**

實用片語與搭配詞

hound sb. / sth. 窮追某人某物

▸ Hounds can help hunters find prey when they are hunting.
狩獵時，獵犬能協助獵人找到獵物。

▸ The reporters hounded the President with questions.
記者窮追不捨地向總統發問。

▸ The king swore to avenge his father and hound his murderer to the ends of the earth.
國王誓言為了他的父親報仇，並且窮追殺父兇手直到世界盡頭。

---

housing [ˈhaʊ.zɪŋ] *n.* 住宿；住房

同 **accommodations; dwelling**

▸ Does the university provide students with housing on campus?
那所大學有提供學生在校園內的住宿嗎？

hover [ˈhɑː.vɚ]

① *v.* 盤旋；徘徊

同 **float; drift**

▸ The seagulls hovered over the water looking for fish to eat.
海鷗盤旋在水面上，找尋魚類果腹。

實用片語與搭配詞

hover above / over 在上盤旋

② *n.* 盤旋；徘徊

▶ Hummingbirds are the only birds who can hover above a flower in one place to drink its nectar.
蜂鳥是唯一能夠盤旋在花朵上方以吸取花蜜的鳥類。

▶ The pilot told the student to keep the helicopter in hover.
那名駕駛員要學員保持直升機盤旋。

---

howl [haʊl]

① *n.* 嚎叫；怒吼；嚎啕大哭

同 **bawl; wail**

▶ The injured dog's howl was sad and despondent.
受傷的狗的嚎叫聲既悲傷又消沈。

② *v.* 嗥叫；怒吼；大喊

同 **yowl; wail**

▶ Wolves howl at night.
狼群在夜間嚎叫。

實用片語與搭配詞

howl with laughter 高聲大笑

▶ The stand-up comedian at the new bar downtown had us howling with laughter at his jokes.
在市中心一家新酒吧裡，單口相聲表演者的笑話讓我們放聲大笑。

---

hurl [hɝːl]

① *v.* 猛力投擲

同 **fling; throw**

▶ The pitcher hurled the baseball at home plate.
棒球投手朝本壘板猛力投球。

實用片語與搭配詞

hurl stone at sb. 對某人丟石頭

▶ It is quite common for student protesters to hurl stones and other objects at police during demonstrations.
當學生在示威抗議時，對員警投擲石頭或其他物品是相當常見的事。

② *n.* 猛力投擲

▶ His hurl was so strong that the ball flew over the fence.
他猛力投球的力道很大，以致於球飛出籬笆外了。

---

hymn [hɪm]

① *n.* 詩歌；聖歌

同 **psalm; chant**

▶ We sang a hymn in church.
我們在教會裡唱了一首詩歌。

② *v.* 唱詩歌；唱聖歌

▶ Can we hymn some songs on Sunday morning?
我們能不能在週日早上唱幾首詩歌？

H

Exercise 30

I. Choices

1. The experiment ended in a failure, and ________ we need to make adjustments to it for our next experiment to achieve better results.
   (A) henceforth (B) hence (C) furthermore (D) moreover
2. The whole gist of the debate on homosexuality is whether ________ activity is immoral or moral.
   (A) homogeneous (B) heterosexual (C) homosexual (D) hassle
3. The chances of getting a dog being ________ to you is higher when you are standing up than when you are at eye level or even lower.
   (A) gentile (B) versatile (C) hustle (D) hostile
4. The ________ of the Singapore Airline in 1991 by four militants was remarkable as the hostages were all unhurt, and the rescue operation was completed in thirty seconds.
   (A) hibernate (B) highlight (C) hijack (D) hiccough
5. The US soldiers were held ________ for a few months in Afghanistan before a rescue squad was sent.
   (A) hostage (B) heritage (C) heritance (D) hermitage

II. Derivatives

1. ____________ (house) is one of the main concerns for governments as Maslow's hierarchy of needs states that shelter is one of the basic needs of humans.
2. The ____________ (horizon) of the plane is beautiful with the lush of grass and mountains as the backdrop.
3. Should the ____________ (heir) to the throne be dependent on family ties or on ability as the future on the nation rests on the next king?
4. The ____________ (hero) deed of her brave father saving her from two kidnappers spread to the surrounding towns.
5. The angry man ____________ (hurl) his phone across the room when he found out he was fired.

Unit 31

idiot [ˈɪd.i.ət] *n.* 白癡；傻瓜

同 **fool**

反 **genius**

▶ Don't be an idiot and spend all of your money in one place.
別當個傻瓜，把所有錢都花到同一處。

---

immense [ɪˈmens] *adj.* 巨大的；廣大的

同 **enormous; vast**

▶ Simon is under immense pressure to increase the company's profit margin.
賽門肩負著莫大的壓力，為了要努力提高公司的獲利率。

---

imperial [ɪmˈpɪr.i.əl] *adj.* 皇帝的；帝國的

同 **regal**

▶ South Korea has several imperial palaces open to tourists.
南韓有幾個皇宮宮殿是開放給遊客參觀的。

104

impose [ɪmˈpoʊz] *v.* 推行；強制實行

同 **force**

反 **liberate**

實用片語與搭配詞

impose on / upon sb. / sth.
強行做某事；占某人便宜；贏取某人歡心

▶ Don't try to impose too many new rules at once.
不要試圖一次推行太多新規定。

▶ Mary apologised for imposing on the meeting, but said she had an urgent message for her boss.
瑪莉為了自己硬是舉行此會議而道歉，但她表示她有緊急的消息要讓老闆知道。

---

impulse [ˈɪm.pʌls] *n.* 衝動；驅使人的力量

同 **compulsion; urge**

▶ Laura followed her impulse and ran for class president.
蘿拉忠於自己的衝動而競選班長。

---

incense [ˈɪn.sens] *n.* 香；香味

同 **aroma; fragrance**

▶ Some religions require you to burn incense.
有些宗教會要信徒焚香。

incense [ɪnˈsens] *v.* 激怒；焚香

同 **anger; exasperate**

▶ I am incensed at how rude the receptionist was towards my mother.
接待員粗魯地對待我媽媽，把我激怒了。

---

index [ˈɪn.deks]

① *n.* 索引

▶ Look through the index to find Vickie's phone number.
你從索引裡找維琪的電話。

I

實用片語與搭配詞

living index 生活費用指數

② *v.* 編索引；表明

實用片語與搭配詞

index sth. in sth. 將某事物編入索引

▶ According to a recent cost of living index, Tokyo and Hong Kong were the most expensive cities in the world to live in.
根據最近的零售物價指數，東京與香港是世界上兩個物價最高的城市。

▶ Can you index these papers in alphabetical order?
你能不能以字母先後順序來為這些報告編個索引？

▶ The company hired an assistant to index all their client files in the computer system.
這間公司雇用了一位助理將所有的客戶資料編入電腦系統中的索引。

103

indifference [ɪnˈdɪf.ɚ.əns]

n. 漠不關心；冷淡；不感興趣

同 **unconcern**

反 **concern**

▶ Tiffany's attitude towards winning or losing was one of indifference.
蒂凡妮對輸贏所抱持的態度是漠不關心。

99

indifferent [ɪnˈdɪf.ɚ.ənt]

adj. 不關心的；冷淡的

同 **disinterested**

反 **concerned**

實用片語與搭配詞

indifferent to sb. / sth.
漠不關心；毫不在乎

▶ I'm indifferent as to which car you want to buy.
你想買哪輛車，我一點也不在乎。

▶ People used to be indifferent to the plight of the poor in Africa, but social media has changed that.
人們以前總對非洲窮苦人民的困境冷眼看待，但社群媒體已經改變了這種狀況。

---

indignant [ɪnˈdɪg.nənt]

adj. 憤怒的；義憤填膺的

同 **angry**

實用片語與搭配詞

indignant with sb. at / over / about sth. 因某事對某人大為惱火

▶ Anna was indignant after someone insulted her parents.
有人侮辱了安娜的父母，使她憤怒不已。

▶ The lawyer became very indignant with the judge for suggesting that she was lying.
法官暗示律師在說謊，這件事讓這位律師變得極為惱火。

indispensable [ˌɪn.dɪˈspen.sə.bəl]

adj. 不可缺少的；必須的

同 **crucial**

反 **dispensable**

▶ Stephanie is an indispensable part of the organization.
史蒂芬妮是機構裡不可或缺的成員。

---

induce [ɪnˈduːs] *v.* 導致；引誘

同 **elicit**

反 **deduce**

▶ The road blocks induced many drivers to take the detour.
路障導致許多駕駛都繞路而行。

---

indulge [ɪnˈdʌldʒ] *v.* 放縱；沉迷

同 **spoil; pamper**

實用片語與搭配詞

indulge oneself / sb. with sth.
放縱某人做某事

▶ I indulged in an extra piece of chocolate cake.
我縱容自己又吃了一片巧克力蛋糕。

▶ Once in a while, after a really bad day, I indulge myself with a good cup of coffee and some cake.
我偶爾會在糟糕的一天結束後放縱自己喝杯好咖啡並吃些蛋糕。

---

infinite [ˈɪn.fə.nət] *adj.* 無限的；無邊的

同 **limitless**

反 **finite**

實用片語與搭配詞

infinite space 無限的空間

▶ There are infinite possibilities for the future!
未來有無限的可能性！

▶ Scientists have tried, but have so far failed, to measure the infinite space of the universe.
科學家們不停嘗試測量宇宙中無限大的空間，但至今都未成功。

---

inherit [ɪnˈher.ɪt] *v.* 繼承

同 **come into; become heir to**

實用片語與搭配詞

inherit from sb. 從某人那獲得遺產

▶ I inherited my grandmother's old car.
我繼承了祖母的舊車。

▶ I was heartbroken when I lost the antique ring I inherited from my grandmother.
當我遺失祖母贈予我的古董戒指時，我簡直心碎了。

---

initiate [ɪˈnɪʃ.i.eɪt] *v.* 開始

同 **begin; launch**

▶ I initiated a discussion with the class about the effects of bullying.
我針對霸凌的影響在班上發起討論。

實用片語與搭配詞

initiate sb. into sth.
介紹某人加入某組織 / 團體

▶ It is customary for seniors to initiate freshmen into a university's culture and traditions.
由學長姐介紹大學的文化與傳統給大一新鮮人，這是一種傳統。

initiate [ɪˈnɪʃ.i.ət]

① *n.* 新成員；新入會的人

② *adj.* 新加入的；新入會的

▶ The club welcomed its new initiates.
那個社團對新加入的成員表示歡迎。

▶ The initiated members were each given a gift.
每個新加入的成員都收到了一份禮物。

---

inland [ˈɪn.lənd]

① *adj.* 內陸的

同 **domestic**

反 **foreign**

② *n.* 內陸

③ *adv.* 在內陸

▶ Is your house right on the beach or more inland?
你的房子就位在海灘上，還是比較靠近內陸？

▶ The inland of this country is very flat.
這個國家的內陸地區非常平坦。

▶ If you live inland, you have to travel far to go to the beach.
如果你住在內陸，就得長途旅行才能到達海邊。

---

innumerable [ɪˈnuː.mɚ.ə.bəl]

adj. 無數的；數不清的

同 **countless; numerous**

▶ The amount of migrants in the world is innumerable.
全球移民人數是數不清的。

---

inquire [ɪnˈkwaɪr] *v.* 詢問；調查

同 **ask question**

反 **reply**

實用片語與搭配詞

inquire into sth. 調查 / 查問 / 究問某事

▶ Angela inquired with the dealership about buying the car.
安琪拉詢問經銷商有關購買那輛車的事情。

▶ If you want to study abroad, it is useful to first inquire into different possibilities in different countries.
如果你想要出國唸書，先查明各國有什麼樣不同的機會是很有幫助的。

---

institute [ˈɪn.stə.tuːt]

① *n.* 機構；學院；研究院

同 **organization; foundation**

② *v.* 制定；著手；創立

同 **establishment; set up**

▶ Universities are institutes of education.
大學是教育機構。

▶ Did the president institute the new attendance policy?
新的出席率政策是校長制定的嗎？

實用片語與搭配詞

institute inquiries into sth.
對某事展開調查

▶ Following the fatal accident in which the engineer died, the company instituted inquiries into the cause of the accident.
工程師於致命車禍中喪生後，公司對這起車禍的起因展開調查。

---

insure [ɪnˈʃʊr] *v.* 確保；為…投保

同 **assure**

反 **risk**

實用片語與搭配詞

insure sb. / sth. against sth.
對某人 / 事投保預防某事發生的保險

▶ My car insurances insures that I have coverage in case of an accident.
我的汽車保險確保我在車禍事故中能獲得理賠。

▶ Most companies will insure workers against injury, especially if they perform dangerous jobs.
大部分的公司會幫員工投保意外傷害險，尤其是從事危險工作的員工。

---

intent [ɪnˈtent]

① *n.* 目的；意圖

同 **aim; purpose**

② *adj.* 執意要做的；熱切的

同 **absorbed; focussed**

▶ What is your intent for taking this class?
你修這堂課的目的是什麼？

▶ The CEO was intent on giving all of his workers better wages.
執行長執意要給所有員工更高的薪資。

---

interference [ˌɪn.t̬ɚˈfɪr.əns]

n. （電波等的）干擾；干預

同 **meddling**

▶ I can't hear you because there is too much interference.
我聽不清楚你說的話，因為有太多干擾了。

---

interior [ɪnˈtɪr.i.ɚ]

① *adj.* 內部的

同 **inside**

反 **exterior**

② *n.* 內部；內陸

同 **domestic**

反 **foreign**

▶ The house's interior walls are painted in different colors.
那間房子的內牆漆著不同的顏色。

▶ Are you renovating the interior or exterior of your house?
你是在裝潢你家的內部還是外部？

95

interpretation [ɪnˌtɝː.prəˈteɪ.ʃən]

n. 解釋；口譯

同 **understanding; explanation**

▶ What is your interpretation of the poem?
你怎麼詮釋那首詩？

Exercise 31

I. Derivatives

1. The stars are ____________ (numerable) as the galaxy is expanding at a great speed with each passing second.
2. Everyone is valuable but not ____________ (dispensable) especially with the adaptability and creative minds of people to navigate and resolve problems.
3. ____________ (indifferent) not only can be poisonous to a relationship but can also cause harm to the person as it builds up walls in his life.
4. To ____________ (indulgent) oneself with ice cream in front of a television might be a great way to end the day for some people.
5. ____________ (Interfere) with investigation in crime is not to be taken lightly and can be considered quite a serious matter.

II. Choices

1. It is not difficult to _________ a conversation as long as you are willing to communicate and take interest in the other person.
   (A) inflict (B) initiate (C) innovate (D) innominate
2. To _________ oneself in an experience is not touching the surface but bringing yourself to experience in totality, body, soul and spirit.
   (A) immense (B) immerse (C) impress (D) imprison
3. _________ shopping might be more evident during sales period such as Black Friday or Christmas as people buy because of the slash in prices rather than the need of it.
   (A) Implementation (B) Implication (C) Impulse (D) Impose
4. The possibilities to science and medicine are _________ as we have yet to explore the whole earth, especially in the deep waters.
   (A) inadequate (B) measurable (C) circumscribed (D) infinite
5. When parents _________ rules on their children without giving them reasons, a counter effect could take place.
   (A) impose (B) impair (C) imply (D) impede

Unit 32

interpreter [ɪn'tɝː.prə.t̬ɚ] *n.* 口譯員

同 **spokesperson; real-time translator**

實用片語與搭配詞

speak through an interpreter
透過口譯員說話

▸ We need an interpreter to help the audience understand what the speaker is saying.
我們需要口譯員來協助聽眾理解演講者所說的內容。

▸ The Russian actress we interviewed could not speak English, so we had to speak through an interpreter.
我們訪問的俄國女演員無法說英文，所以我們必須透過口譯員跟她溝通。

---

intuition [ˌɪn.tuː'ɪʃ.ən] *n.* 直覺；敏銳的洞察力

同 **instinct; insight**

實用片語與搭配詞

intuition about sth. / that...
對某事的感覺

▸ Listen to your gut intuition!
要聽從你自己的直覺！

▸ My aunt has a sixth sense and her intuition about people has never been wrong.
我的阿姨第六感很準，而且她看人的直覺從未有誤。

---

inward ['ɪn.wɚd] *adv.* 向內；內心裡

反 **outward**

▸ Please move inward, not outward.
請向內移動，不要往外走。

---

isle [aɪl] *n.* 島；小島

同 **islet**

▸ Jeremy and his family live on the British Isles.
傑若米和他的家人住在不列顛群島上。

issue ['ɪʃ.uː]

① *n.* 問題

同 **matter; problem**

實用片語與搭配詞

take issue with sb. about / on / over sth. 就某事向某人提出異議或爭論

② *v.* 發佈；出版

同 **publish; release**

▸ I don't have any issues with this matter.
我對這個議題沒有任何問題。

▸ I took issue with my best friend about her gossiping because I think it is a bad habit.
我非常不贊同我摯友愛說閒話的壞習慣。

▸ Did you issue another update of the email?
你有沒有再發佈那封電子郵件的更新訊息？

實用片語與搭配詞

issue sth. to sb. / sth. 將某物發 / 分配給

▶ My brother was issued with a summons to appear in court as a witness in a crime.
我哥哥被傳喚至法庭，作為這起犯罪事件的目擊證人。

---

ivy [ˈaɪ.vi] *n.* 常春藤

▶ Ivy is a plant that can grow on buildings.
常春藤是一種能夠攀爬於建築上生長的植物。

---

jack [dʒæk]

① *n.* 普通人；起重機

② *v.* 用起重機舉起

▶ Louis is no superman, he is just an ordinary jack.
路易斯不是超人，他只是一個平凡的普通人。

▶ A mechanic must jack up the car in order to check its brakes.
機工必須用起重機抬起那輛車，才能檢查車子的煞車。

---

jade [dʒeɪd] *n.* 玉；玉製品

同 **emerald**

▶ Jade is a very valuable commodity in Asia.
玉石在亞洲是非常貴重的商品。

---

janitor [ˈdʒæn.ə.t̬ɚ] *n.* 工友；管理員

同 **gatekeeper; doorkeeper**

▶ Can you call the janitor to clean up this mess?
你能不能叫工友來清掃這處髒亂？

---

jasmine [ˈdʒæz.mɪn] *n.* 茉莉

▶ I love the smell of jasmine tea.
我很喜歡茉莉花茶的香味。

---

jaywalk [ˈdʒeɪ.wɑːk]

v. 不遵守交通規則亂過馬路

▶ It's dangerous to jaywalk. Just wait for the light to turn green.
不遵守交通規則亂過馬路是很危險的行為，等轉綠燈再過。

---

jeer [dʒɪr]

① *v.* 嘲笑；嘲弄

同 **mock**

反 **respect**

實用片語與搭配詞

jeer at sb. / sth. 嘲笑 / 嘲弄某人 / 事物

▶ The crowd jeered at the comedian's bad joke.
群眾嘲笑那名諧星的冷笑話。

▶ The spectators jeered at the opposition team when they took the lead shortly after the game started.
敵隊在比賽開始不久便領先，觀眾們便嘲弄他們。

② *n.* 嘲笑；嘲弄

▶ The jeers of his classmates caused the student to cry.
同學的嘲笑害那名學生哭了。

---

jewelry [ˈdʒu·əl·ri] *n.* （英國）珠寶；首飾

▶ My older sister often wears jewelry outside the house.
我姊姊出門往往會戴珠寶。

---

jingle [ˈdʒɪŋ.gəl]

① *n.* 叮噹聲

同 **ring; tinkle**

② *v.* 發出叮噹聲

同 **ring; tinkle**

▶ I heard the jingle of her keys from across the room.
我從房間的另一頭就聽到她鎖匙發出的叮噹聲。

▶ The dog's collar jingled as it walked along the grass.
那隻狗在草地上走時，頸圈發出了叮噹聲。

---

jolly [ˈdʒɑː.li]

① *adj.* 開心的；興高采烈的

同 **cheerful**

反 **gloomy**

② *adv.* 非常；很

同 **cheerfully**

反 **gloomily**

③ *v.* 使開心；使人高興

同 **cheer; please**

實用片語與搭配詞

jolly sth. up 使某物看上去鮮豔奪目 / 有生氣

④ *n.* 歡樂時光

▶ Santa Claus is a very happy and jolly man.
聖誕老人是個很快樂又開心的人。

▶ The fans had a jolly good time watching their team win.
粉絲們觀賞著支持的隊伍獲得勝利，度過了極為開心的時光。

▶ His job was to jolly the party.
他的任務是炒熱派對的開心氣氛。

▶ My friend's hospital room was so gloomy that I had to jolly it up with some colorful balloons.
我朋友的病房如此幽暗，以致於我必須用五彩的氣球點綴，讓它更有生氣。

▶ The evening was full of jolly.
那個傍晚是段非常歡樂的時光。

---

journalism [ˈdʒɝː.nə.lɪ.zəm] *n.* 新聞業

同 **newspaper reporting / writing**

▶ I'm very interested in learning about war journalism.
我對學習有關戰地新聞的知識相當感興趣。

---

journalist [ˈdʒɝː.nə.lɪst]

n. 新聞工作者；新聞記者

同 **newspaper writer**

▶ Naomi is a newspaper journalist.
拿俄米是報社新聞工作者。

jug [dʒʌg]

① *n.* 水罐、壺；甕

同 **pitcher**

② *v.* （用罐）煮；燉

- Put this jug of water on the counter please.
  請把這罐水放到櫃台上。
- The hunter jugged the rabbit for dinner.
  那名獵人燉兔子當晚餐。

---

jury [ˈdʒʊr.i] *n.* 陪審團

同 **adjudicator**

- The jury sat in the courtroom listening to the evidence of the case.
  陪審團坐在法庭內聆聽案件的證據。

102

justify [ˈdʒʌs.tə.faɪ]

v. 證明…正當的；為…辯護

反 **condemn**

實用片語與搭配詞

justify for sth. / doing sth.
做某事的正當理由

- How can you justify spending all this money when you don't have a job?
  你沒有工作，如何能證明花那麼多錢是應該的？
- The police justified using violence at the protest by claiming they were in danger.
  警方聲稱自身陷入危險，便將他們對抗議人士的暴力行為合理化。

---

juvenile [ˈdʒuː.və.nəl]

① *adj.* 少年的

同 **youthful**

反 **adult**

② *n.* 青少年；孩子

同 **young**

反 **adult**

- This store sells a lot of juvenile clothes.
  這家商店賣好多青少年的衣服！
- The juvenile was sent home to his parents after being arrested by the police.
  那名青少年遭到警方逮捕之後，被送回家給他的父母。

---

kin [kɪn]

① *n.* 親戚；家族；同類

同 **family**

② *adj.* 有親戚關係的；同類的

同 **relative**

- My mother's kin live in Asia.
  我媽媽的親戚住在亞洲。
- She was kin to our neighbor.
  她和我們的鄰居有親戚關係。

---

kindle [ˈkɪn.dəl] *v.* 點燃；激起

同 **arouse**

反 **extinguish**

實用片語與搭配詞

kindle with passion 激起熱情

- The new movie kindled an interest for justice in the people.
  那部新片激起民眾對於公平正義的興趣。
- Every person must kindle with passion the things they want to achieve in life.
  每個人必須點燃對於人生成就的熱情。

knowledgeable [ˈnɑː.lɪ.dʒə.bəl]

adj. 有知識的；博學的

同 **well-educated; intellectual**

▶ Stephanie is very knowledgeable about health-related matters.
史蒂芬妮對健康相關議題知識豐富。

---

lad [læd] *n.* 男孩；小伙子

同 **boy**

反 **lass**

▶ Andy is not a lady; he is a lad!
安迪不是位小姐，他是個男孩子！

K

Exercise 32

I. Choices

1. If we can find ways on how to ________ billings to our customer, we will receive lesser queries and be able to focus on other areas of growth.
   (A) irritate (B) isolate (C) issue (D) investigate
2. The president doesn't speak Spanish, so her ________ accompanied her to Spain.
   (A) interpreter (B) intervention (C) interaction (D) interjection
3. ________ can be convenient and time saving but the jaywalker will face more risk by approaching traffic or unforeseen circumstances.
   (A) Jolt (B) Jargon (C) Jaywalk (D) Jurisdiction
4. To ________ the means with the end might make it work but that does not mean that it is the right thing to do.
   (A) juggle (B) justify (C) judge (D) joint
5. ________ a fireplace and it can bring light to fill the darkness, but more than that, it brings warmth and security to those around it.
   (A) Spindle (B) Kindle (C) Quench (D) Douse

II. Vocabulary Choices

(A) jolly	(B) kin	(C) janitor	(D) jewelry
(E) jeer	(F) journalism	(G) jingle	(H) juvenile
(I) jug	(J) jury		

1. War ________ is a risky job as one can get caught in the action and come in harm's way, but the news it brings is extremely valuable.
2. A ________ is often a person under the age of eighteen and will require consent from a guardian for certain activities.
3. With good companions and food, we are going to rock the house and have a ________ good time together.
4. The ________ is having a difficult time in finalizing their decision, as there are spilt opinions over this unique case.
5. To ________ at people might seem fun when you are younger, but this very same act can be immature as it brings about no positive changes.

Unit 33

lame [leɪm]

① *adj.* 瘸的；跛的

同 **crippled; gimpy**

② *v.* 使跛腳

同 **cripple**

▶ Zachary has a lame leg. He is unable to walk.
柴克瑞有隻腿瘸了，沒辦法走路。

▶ After his motorcycle accident, Mark was lamed.
馬克發生機車事故之後，就瘸了腿。

---

landlady [ˈlændˌleɪ.di] *n.* 女房東；女地主

反 **landlord**

▶ I pay rent to my landlady on the first of every month.
我每個月一號會付房租給女房東。

---

landlord [ˈlænd.lɔːrd] *n.* 房東；地主

▶ Can you call the landlord to fix the faucet in the bathroom?
你能不能叫房東來修浴室的水龍頭？

---

laser [ˈleɪ.zɚ] *n.* 雷射

同 **optical maser**

▶ The doctor used a powerful laser to remove the blemish from her skin.
那位醫師用強力雷射來去除她皮膚上的斑點。

---

latitude [ˈlæt̬.ə.tuːd] *n.* 緯度

反 **longitude**

▶ What is Spain's latitude on the map?
地圖上西班牙的緯度是多少？

---

lawmaker [ˈlɑːˌmeɪ.kɚ] *n.* 立法者

同 **legislator**

▶ Senators are important lawmakers in the United States.
參議員在美國是重要的立法者。

---

layer [ˈleɪ.ɚ]

① *n.* 層；階層；地層

同 **level; straum**

② *v.* 把…堆積成層

實用片語與搭配詞

be covered with a layer of sth.
覆蓋一層某物

▶ There are three different layers in the cake.
那個蛋糕有三層。

▶ Layer the blankets by thickness.
依照厚度來堆疊那些毯子。

▶ The furniture in the old house were covered with a layer of dust and cobwebs were hanging from the roof.
老屋裡的傢俱都蒙上一層灰，並且有許多蜘蛛網從在天花板上垂下。

L

league [liːg]

① *n.* 聯盟

同 **alliance; group**

② *v.* 使結盟；使聯合

同 **alliance; associate**

實用片語與搭配詞

in league with sb. 共謀 / 聯合

► I play in a baseball league.
我在棒球聯盟中打球。

► Let's league together and protest against smoking.
讓我們聯合起來一起進行反菸抗議。

► My mother was in league with my friends to organize a surprise birthday party for me.
我媽媽跟我的朋友們串通好，為我舉辦一場驚喜生日派對。

---

legislation [ˌledʒ.əˈsleɪ.ʃən] *n.* 法律；立法

同 **enactment; lawmaking**

► Legislation must be approved by lawmakers before they come into effect.
法律在生效之前，必須先經過立法者的核准通過。

legitimate [ləˈdʒɪṭ.ə.mət] *adj.* 合法的

同 **legal**

反 **illegal**

實用片語與搭配詞

the legitimate heir 法定繼承人

► Shirley runs a legitimate money lending agency.
雪莉經營一家合法的放款機構。

► The man had no legitimate heir to his business empire, so he chose one of his nieces to take over.
這位男人沒有法定繼承人接手他的企業帝國，所以他挑選他其中一位外甥女繼承。

legitimate [ləˈdʒɪt.ə.meɪt] *v.* 使合法

反 **illegitimate**

► The country legitimated the president's rule by reelecting him to another term.
那個國家藉由讓總統再連任一期而使他能繼續合法統治。

---

lengthy [ˈleŋ.θi] *adj.* 冗長的

同 **prolonged; protracted**

實用片語與搭配詞

lengthy speeches 冗長的演講

► Tim suffered from a lengthy illness but is doing better now.
提姆深受長期慢性病所苦，但現在好多了。

► There is nothing as boring as lengthy speeches, especially during wedding ceremonies.
世上沒有比冗長的演講還無趣的事了，特別是在婚宴中的演講。

lessen ['les.ən] *v.* 減少；變小；減輕

反 **increase; raise**

實用片語與搭配詞

lessen the impact of sth.
減少某事物的影響

▸ Losing weight will lessen the overall physical damage to your knees in your lifetime.
減重能降低一生中膝蓋所遭受的整體生理損害。

▸ During times of disaster, governments try to lessen the impact of losses by giving financial aid.
在災害期間，政府嘗試用金援減緩衝擊。

102

lest [lest] *conj.* 惟恐；以免

▸ Patrick practiced his violin daily lest he perform and do poorly.
派翠克每天都會練習小提琴，以免在表演時錯誤百出。

---

liable ['laɪ.ə.bəl] *adj.* 負有（法律）責任的；容易…的；很可能會發生的

同 **accountable; responsible**

▸ The judge found the woman liable for the accident, so she had to pay a fine.
法官發現那名婦女對那宗意外事故負有法律責任，因此她必須繳罰款。

103

liberate ['lɪb.ə.reɪt] *v.* 使自由

反 **restrain; restrict**

實用片語與搭配詞

liberate sb. / sth. from sth.
解放某人 / 物的自由

▸ Carla wants to liberate the local people from poverty.
卡拉想解救當地民眾脫離貧窮。

▸ She was liberated from her fear of the dark after seeing a psychologist for treatment.
在與一位心理醫師諮商過後，她從怕黑的恐懼中被解放出來。

---

liberation [ˌlɪb.ə'reɪ.ʃən] *n.* 解放

同 **freeing; release**

▸ The liberation of slaves in the country was a slow process.
解救該國奴隸是個緩慢漸進的過程。

---

lieutenant [luː'ten.ənt] *n.* 中尉；海軍上尉

▸ The lieutenant ordered the foot soldiers to walk towards the barracks.
中尉下令步兵朝軍營邁進。

---

lifelong ['laɪf.lɑːŋ] *adj.* 一輩子的；終身的

同 **enduring; lifetime**

▸ Evelyn and Cathy are lifelong friends.
艾福琳和凱西是一輩子的朋友。

100

likelihood [ˈlaɪ.kli.hʊd] *n.* 可能；可能性

同 **probability**

▶ The likelihood of me winning the lottery is not very high.
我中樂透彩券的可能性並不高。

100

likewise [ˈlaɪk͵waɪz] *adv.* 同樣地

同 **also; similarly**

▶ Ben enjoys playing sports and likewise enjoys going to the gym.
班喜歡從事體育活動，同樣也很喜歡上健身房運動。

---

lime [laɪm]

① *n.* 萊姆

② *v.* 灑石灰於…；用石灰水塗刷

▶ I love adding lemons and limes to my water.
我喜歡在水裡加檸檬和萊姆。

▶ Plans have been made to lime the water.
在水裡加石灰的計畫已經制定好了。

---

limousine / limo [͵lɪm.əˈziːn / ˈlɪm.oə]

n. 豪華轎車

▶ Diane rented a limousine for her wedding.
黛安為自己的婚禮租了一輛豪華轎車。

---

limp [lɪmp]

① *v.* 跛行

同 **hobble; shuffle**

② *n.* 跛行

同 **hobble**

反 **stiff**

▶ The dog limped his way across the street.
那隻狗一跛一跛地過街。

▶ Joe's limp looked very painful.
喬跛腳走路看起來很痛。

---

liner [ˈlaɪ.nɚ] *n.* 郵輪

▶ My parents are taking a cruise on an ocean liner this summer.
我爸媽今年夏天要搭郵輪航行。

---

linger [ˈlɪŋ.gɚ] *v.* 繼續逗留；徘徊

同 **dawdle; stay**

▶ Please don't linger by the doorway to the store.
請不要在店門口逗留。

Exercise 33

I. Derivatives

1. The fall of Berlin Wall was the day of ______________ (liberate) as finally Germany can be unified once again.
2. ______________ (Less) the burden of your friend rather than making it worse, as a little kindness goes a long way rather than selfish ambition.
3. A ______________ (length) explanation or essay does not necessarily mean it is better than a short one, but rather it is the ability to drive the point to the audience that matters.
4. When prices are too good to be true, the goods might not be ______________ (legitimize) and the quality might not be the best.
5. In order to build a strong foundation, there is no shortcut, and things get rougher as you ______________ (layer) one building block on top of another, and that requires patience and time.

II. Vocabulary Choices

(A) latitude	(B) limp	(C) lawmaker	(D) lame
(E) league	(F) likelihood	(G) liable	(H) lifelong
(I) likewise	(J) lest		

1. The _________ of man getting pregnant is like a pig flying to the moon as it is medically impossible for a naturally born male to do so.
2. _________ up with likeminded people and learn from each other, because, indeed, iron sharpens iron.
3. When the borrowers are unable to fulfill their obligations to repay the loan, the guarantor will be _________ for this amount and thus have to repay it.
4. Learning is a _________ journey and does not stop once you have graduated from school as the possibilities are infinite.
5. John walks with a _________ . This could be due to a rollerblading accident he had a few years ago.

Unit 34

linguist [ˈlɪŋ.gwɪst] *n.* 語言學家

▶ Kathryn is a linguist and spends her time studying languages.
凱特琳是語言學家，把時間都花在研究語言上。

---

liter [ˈliː.t̬ɚ] *n.* 公升

▶ Mark brought five liters of soda to the party.
馬克為派對買了五公升的汽水。

---

literacy [ˈlɪt̬.ɚ.ə.si] *n.* 識字；讀寫能力
反 **illiteracy**

▶ The teacher focuses on literacy by helping her students learn to read and write.
那名老師著重讀寫能力，她幫助學生學習閱讀和寫字。

---

literal [ˈlɪt̬.ɚ.əl] *adj.* 字面的；逐字的
同 **factual**
反 **figurative**

▶ Marcy uses the literal meaning of words to express her ideas. She doesn't joke.
瑪西用字面上的意義來傳達她的理念，她不開玩笑。

實用片語與搭配詞
translate sth. literally 照字面翻譯某語言

▶ When you translate literally from one language into another, you come up with some funny phrases.
當你將一個語言逐字翻成另一語言，就會發現其中有一些奇怪的詞彙。

---

literate [ˈlɪt̬.ɚ.ət]

① *adj.* 識字的；能讀寫的
同 **cultured; educated**

▶ The literate girl learned to read and write when she was five years old.
那名識字的女孩五歲時就學會了讀寫。

② *n.* 有文化素養的人；有讀寫能力的人

▶ The literate will meet to discuss education policies for the town.
那些具有文化素養的人將會面討論鎮上的教育政策。

---

livestock [ˈlaɪv.stɑːk] *n.* 家畜
同 **cattle**

▶ The farmer has many different types of livestock.
那名農夫養了很多種家畜。

---

lizard [ˈlɪz.ɚd] *n.* 蜥蜴；蜥蜴類之爬行動物

▶ The green lizard crawled around in the grass.
那隻綠色的蜥蜴在草叢中爬來爬去。

locomotive [ˌloʊ.kəˈmoʊ.t̬ɪv]

① *n.* 火車頭

② *adj.* 有移動力的；活動的；火車頭的

▶ The locomotive departed from the station at exactly three o'clock.
火車頭在三點半整駛出火車站。

▶ The new high speed train has great locomotive strength.
新的高速鐵路有很強的移動力。

---

locust [ˈloʊ.kəst] *v.* 蝗蟲

▶ Farmers dislike locusts because they can destroy great volumes of crops.
農民討厭蝗蟲，因為牠們會破壞大量農作物。

---

lodge [lɑːdʒ]

① *n.* 旅舍；看守人的小屋

同 **babin; cottage**

② *v.* 住宿；暫住

同 **stay; live**

實用片語與搭配詞

lodge at 租住某處

▶ The ski lodge is at the bottom of the mountain.
那家滑雪旅社位於山腳下。

▶ Are we lodging in a cabin or hotel?
我們要住宿在小木屋，還是飯店裡？

▶ During our stay in the national park, we lodged at a beautiful campsite with great views.
在我們停留在國家公園的期間，我們租住在一個有美景相伴的紮營區。

---

lofty [ˈlɑːf.ti] *adj.* 崇高的；極高的

同 **dignified**

反 **humble**

實用片語與搭配詞

in a lofty manner 態度傲慢

▶ Johnny's lofty goal is to become CEO of Apple.
強尼崇高的目標是要當上蘋果公司的執行長。

▶ Soldiers often like to tell stories of their conquests in a lofty manner, but no one really believes them.
軍人們時常喜歡用自負的態度訴說征戰的故事，但沒有人真的會相信他們。

---

logo [ˈloʊ.goʊ] *n.* 商標；標幟

▶ Studio Classroom's logo is an owl.
空中英語教室的商標是一隻貓頭鷹。

---

lonesome [ˈloʊn.səm] *adj.* 孤獨的；寂寞的

同 **sole; solitary**

▶ Jay doesn't have many friends. He is a lonesome individual.
傑的朋友不多，他是個孤獨的人。

---

longevity [lɑːnˈdʒev.ə.t̬i] *n.* 長壽

▶ John's longevity was due to a healthy lifestyle and positive attitude.
約翰的長壽歸功於健康的生活方式和正面積極的態度。

L

longitude [ˈlɑːn.dʒə.tuːd] *n.* 經度

反 **latitude**

▶ What is Brazil's longitude coordinate?
巴西的經度座標是多少？

---

lottery [ˈlɑː.t̬ɚ.i] *n.* 彩券；摸彩；抽籤

同 **drawing; raffle**

▶ I want to win a lot of money playing the lottery!
我希望玩樂透彩券贏得大筆金錢。

---

lotus [ˈloʊ.t̬əs] *n.* 蓮花；荷花

▶ Lotus flowers grow on the surface of the water.
蓮花在水面上生長。

---

lounge [laʊndʒ]

① *v.* 閒蕩；混時間

同 **laze; sprawl**

▶ Sophie's mom told her to do her homework and stop lounging on the couch.
蘇菲的媽媽叫她去作功課，不要坐在沙發上混時間。

② *n.* 休息廳；休息室

▶ Victor relaxed in the hotel lounge while waiting for his wife to arrive.
維克多在飯店休息廳裡休息，等候他太太。

實用片語與搭配詞

the departure lounge 候機室

▶ Once you have checked in for your flight, you can go to the departure lounge to wait for the boarding call.
你一旦辦理完登機手續，就可以去候機室等候登機通知。

---

lumber [ˈlʌm.bɚ]

① *n.* 木材；木料

同 **timber wood**

▶ The lumber in this yard came from the rain forest.
院子裡的木材來自雨林。

② *v.* 伐木；採伐林木

▶ Lumbering trees is a very lucrative business.
伐木是非常賺錢的行業。

實用片語與搭配詞

lumber sth. up with sth.
在某處零亂堆滿某物

▶ After Sunday lunch, I usually get lumbered up with doing the dishes while the rest of the family can relax.
週日午餐後，當其他的家人在放鬆時，我通常在碗盤堆中洗碗。

---

lump [lʌmp]

① *n.* 腫塊；團

同 **bump; swelling**

▶ After hitting his head on the table, there was a lump on Albert's forehead.
艾伯特的頭撞到桌子之後，額頭腫起了一塊。

實用片語與搭配詞

a lump of 一塊

- In England, tea is usually served with milk and one or two lumps of sugar.
  在英格蘭，茶通常與牛奶以及一或兩塊方糖一起被供應上桌。

② *v.* 把…併到一起；把…弄成一團

同 **combine; amass**

- The teacher lumped all the Asian students together during class.
  老師在課堂上把所有亞洲學生都併成一組。

實用片語與搭配詞

lump sb. / sth. together
將人或物併在一起 / 視為一類

- I don't like summer camps because you always get lumped together with a bunch of strangers.
  我不喜歡夏令營，因為你總是得與一大群陌生人為伍。

---

lunatic [ˈluː.nə.tɪk]

① *n.* 瘋子

- People thought the man was a lunatic when he told them his crazy plan.
  那名男子告訴大家他的瘋狂計畫時，大家都認為那人是瘋子。

② *adj.* 瘋的

同 **outrageous**

反 **sane**

- The lunatic woman continued to yell at strangers for several hours.
  那個女瘋子持續好幾個小時一直向陌生人大喊大叫。

---

lure [lʊr]

① *v.* 引誘

同 **seduce; tempt**

- The fisherman lured many fish to his boat with special bait.
  那名漁夫用特殊的釣餌引誘很多魚到他的船邊。

實用片語與搭配詞

lure sb. into a trap 引誘某人掉入圈套

- Police lured the drug dealer into a trap by pretending they wanted to buy drugs from him.
  警方假裝要跟毒梟買毒品，以讓他落入圈套。

② *n.* 誘惑物

同 **bay**

- The lure of fresh baked cookies caused Trina to forget about her diet.
  剛烤好的餅乾的誘惑，讓提娜忘記自己還在減肥了。

---

lush [lʌʃ] *adj.* 青翠繁茂的；多汁的

- The lush forest floor was covered in small, green plants.
  那青翠繁茂森林的地上，佈滿了小型綠色植物。

---

lyric [ˈlɪr.ɪk]

① *adj.* 抒情的

反 **epic**

- Richard enjoys writing lyric poems for his wife.
  里察很喜歡寫抒情詩送給太太。

L

② *n.* 抒情作品；歌詞

反 **epic**

▶ The English class is studying a lyric written by a famous poet.
那堂英文課在研究一位著名詩人的抒情詩。

---

magnify [ˈmæg.nə.faɪ] *v.* 放大；擴大

同 **enlarge; expand**

反 **diminish**

▶ The doctor magnified the image to have a better look.
醫師把影像放大以便看得更清楚。

Exercise 34

I. Choices

1. One of the criteria to be the candidate of this job is that the person must be a certified ________ engineer with at least five years of experience in transportation departments.
   (A) locative (B) lubricative (C) locomotive (D) proactive
2. ________ is more important than the speed to reach the top as it shows your true character and perseverance to stay at the top.
   (A) Longchamp (B) Longstop (C) Longitude (D) Longevity
3. A ________ ambition is respectable, but the verdict is out there to see if it is impossible to achieve or just not practical to apply in the real world.
   (A) lofty (B) humble (C) degraded (D) debased
4. The ________ of a nation lies fundamentally in the educational system and create the right environment to reinforce the values of reading.
   (A) inveteracy (B) literacy (C) itinerancy (D) accuracy
5. As globalization takes place at a rapid speed, the need for ________ increases, and companies are willing to pay more to obtain this valuable skill.
   (A) ultraists (B) linguists (C) pharmacists (D) archaists

II. Vocabulary Choices

(A) lump	(B) lumber	(C) lure	(D) lodge
(E) lonesome	(F) linger	(G) longitude	(H) lunacy
(I) lottery	(J) lounge		

1. The carpenter sawed the logs into smaller pieces and then used the ________ to build this cabin.
2. In order to ________ a complaint, kindly provide the relevant details with supporting documents for us to investigate further.
3. There is a good reason why you do not ________ good apples with bad apples as the bad ones will affect the good ones, and all that is left will only be bad apples.
4. A ________ chair will be perfect at this spot as one can rest here and see the scenic view of the forest right before them.
5. It will be ________ for Jill to take up this job offer as the job scope is the same but all other remuneration is worse than before and with longer hours.

Unit 35

magnitude [ˈmæg.nə.tuːd]

n. 震級；強度；巨大

▶ The magnitude of the earthquake was 7.9 on the Richter Scale.
地震強度芮氏規模 7.9。

maiden [ˈmeɪ.dən]

① *n.* 少女

② *adj.* 未婚的；少女的

反 **experienced**

▶ Many Disney princesses are delicate, fair maidens.
很多迪士尼公主都是嬌貴又美麗的少女。

▶ All maiden women at a wedding can participate in the bouquet toss.
在婚禮上，所有未婚女性都可以參與拋捧花的儀式。

mainland [ˈmen͵lænd] *n.* 大陸；本土

▶ Many tourists around the world are now from the mainland.
現在世界各地很多遊客都是來自大陸。

mainstream [ˈmeɪn.striːm] *n.* 主流

同 **conventional; majority**

▶ Learning a new language has now become very mainstream.
如今學習新語言蔚為主流。

maintenance [ˈmeɪn.tən.əns] *n.* 維修；保養

反 **abandonment**

▶ All electronics and gadgets will need some maintenance.
所有電子產品和裝置都會需要某種程度的維修。

majestic [məˈdʒes.tɪk]

adj. 雄偉的；威嚴的；崇高的

同 **regal; royal**

▶ The majestic sound of the trumpets could be heard on the city wall.
在城牆上可以聽到喇叭的雄偉音色。

majesty [ˈmædʒ.ə.sti] *n.* 雄偉；壯麗；威嚴

同 **loftiness; magnificence**

▶ The majesty of the mountains is impossible to describe.
山脈的雄偉難以用言語形容。

103

malaria [məˈler.i.ə] *n.* 瘧疾

▶ Malaria is a disease spread by mosquitoes.
瘧疾是由蚊子傳播的疾病。

mammal [ˈmæm.əl] *n.* 哺乳動物

同 **mammalian**

▶ Whales are large mammals.
鯨是大型哺乳類動物。

---

manifest [ˈmæn.ə.fest]

① *v.* 顯示；表明

同 **display; reveal**

實用片語與搭配詞

manifest itself / themselves 顯露自身

② *adj.* 顯而易見的；明顯的

同 **apparent; obvious**

實用片語與搭配詞

a manifest truth / fact 明顯的事實

▶ Small problems can manifest themselves into big problems.
小問題可能會外顯為大問題。

▶ Stress can manifest itself in many different ways, including headaches, stomach aches and depression.
壓力能以許多不同的方式顯現出來，包含頭痛、肚子痛以及憂鬱。

▶ Lisa's manifest beauty helped her to gain many fans.
麗莎顯而易見的美貌為她吸引很多粉絲。

▶ Many scientists believe global warming is a manifest truth that cannot be denied.
許多科學家們相信全球暖化是一個顯而易見的事實，是無法被否認的。

102

manipulate [məˈnɪp.jə.leɪt] *v.* 操作；操控

同 **control; operate**

實用片語與搭配詞

attempt / try to manipulate sb. / sth.
企圖操控某人 / 物

▶ The politician manipulated the media.
那政客操弄了媒體。

▶ All attempts to manipulate my parents into letting me go to the party failed.
我所有企圖操控我父母讓我參加派對的手段都失敗了。

---

mansion [ˈmæn.ʃən] *n.* 豪宅；大廈

同 **manor**

▶ The wealthy millionaire lives in a mansion.
那位富裕的百萬富翁住在豪宅裡。

---

manuscript [ˈmæn.jə.skrɪpt] *n.* 手稿

同 **composition; draft**

▶ Jeff found a manuscript written by his grandfather.
傑夫發現祖父親手寫的手稿。

---

maple [ˈmeɪ.pəl] *n.* 楓樹

▶ Canada makes many things from maple including maple syrup.
加拿大人用楓樹製造很多產品，其中包括了楓糖漿。

mar [mɑːr] *v.* 毀損

同 **damage; ruin**

▶ The new car was marred by a falling rock and has a large dent in it.
那部新車被落石砸毀了，上面有一個大凹痕。

---

marginal [ˈmɑːr.dʒɪ.nəl] *adj.* 微小的；邊緣的

同 **trivial; minor**

▶ Candice's improvement has only been marginal. She has not improved a lot.
坎蒂絲的進步非常微小。她其實沒有改善多少。

---

marine [məˈriːn]

① *adj.* 海洋的；海生的

同 **maritime; nautical**

② *n.* 海軍陸戰隊隊員；海運業

▶ You can visit the aquarium to see marine animals.
你可以造訪水族館，欣賞海洋生物。

▶ Bobby has always lived by the sea as his parents are marines.
巴比一直住在海邊，因為他的父母是海軍陸戰隊的軍人。

---

marshal [ˈmɑːr.ʃəl] *n.* 元帥；高級將官

▶ The marshal is a very important person in the military.
那位元帥是軍中非常重要的人物。

---

martial [ˈmɑːr.ʃəl]

adj. 戒嚴的；軍事的；軍隊的

同 **belligerent**

反 **civil**

實用片語與搭配詞

martial law 軍事管制

▶ Countries with military leaders as heads of state are often under martial law.
以軍事領袖為元首的國家往往施行戒嚴法。

▶ When the war started, the president declared martial law to give police power to do anything.
戰爭開打時，總統宣布實施戒嚴，並給警方執行任何事的權力。

---

marvel [ˈmɑːr.vəl]

① *n.* 奇蹟；令人驚奇的事或人

同 **wonder**

實用片語與搭配詞

a marvel of sth. 出奇地好的人 / 事物

② *v.* 感到歎為觀止；感到驚奇

同 **be in awe**

▶ Taipei 101 is a marvel of modern architecture.
台北 101 是現代建築的奇蹟。

▶ The marvel of how the pyramids were built is still puzzling people today.
金字塔不可思議的建造方式至今仍使人們感到困惑。

▶ I marveled at the grandeur of the building.
我對那棟建築的雄偉感到歎為觀止。

實用片語與搭配詞

marvel at sth. 大為驚訝

▶ I still marvel at how much my life has changed for the better since I changed jobs.
自從換工作後，我仍對於自己的人生漸入佳境感到非常驚奇。

---

masculine [ˈmæs.kjə.lɪn]

① *adj.* 男性的；男子氣慨的
同 **manly**
反 **feminine**
② *n.* 男性
同 **man**
反 **female**

▶ Stephen is a very masculine name.
史帝芬是很男性化的名字。

▶ There are two genders: masculine and feminine.
性別有兩種：男性和女性。

---

mash [mæʃ] *v.* 搗成糊狀；壓碎

同 **crumble; crush**

實用片語與搭配詞

mash sth. up 將某物搗成泥

▶ Mash all the ingredients together until they are soft.
把所有材料一起搗成糊狀，直到質地變軟為止。

▶ The bus was completely mashed up after it collided with the high speed train.
這輛巴士在與高速列車相撞後完全被嚴重毀損。

---

massacre [ˈmæs.ə.kɚ]

① *n.* 大屠殺
同 **butchery; slaughter**
② *v.* 殘殺
同 **butcher; slaughter**

▶ The battle turned into a massacre when one group of fighters ran out of bullets.
其中一群戰士子彈用盡之後，那場戰爭變成一場大屠殺。

▶ The Nazis massacred millions of Jews during World War II.
在二次世界大戰期間，納粹黨羽屠殺了數以百萬計的猶太人。

---

massage [məˈsɑːʒ]

① *n.* 按摩（術）；推拿（法）
② *v.* 按摩；推拿
同 **knead; rub**

▶ My back is sore. I need a massage.
我背好痛，我需要按摩。

▶ Derek massaged his mother's feet on Mother's Day.
德瑞克在母親節幫媽媽按摩腳。

---

massive [ˈmæs.ɪv] *adj.* 巨大的；大量的

同 **huge; enormous**

▶ The child has a massive bruise on his knee.
那孩子膝蓋上有很大一塊瘀傷。

Exercise 35

I. Choices

1. ________ pop culture will always change and what you know as pop culture while you are youth might become a classical when you are older.
   (A) unconventional (B) peripheral (C) mainstream (D) fringe
2. When you ________ someone to achieve your goal, it may seem beneficial now, but the true question remains as to whether it will come back to haunt you.
   (A) assibilate (B) depopulate (C) manipulate (D) stipulate
3. The difference between these two chairs is ________ , being only in the materials used.
   (A) marginal (B) cardinal (C) imaginal (D) vicinal
4. A man who is ________ might not have manhood, as one cannot mistake one for another.
   (A) timid (B) effeminate (C) feminine (D) masculine
5. It is good ideat to ________ food up for young children so that they will have an easier time swallowing food and not choking on it.
   (A) mass (B) dash (C) crush (D) mash

II. Vocabulary Choices

(A) mar	(B) manuscript	(C) majestic	(D) mainland
(E) marshal	(F) mansion	(G) marine	(H) massacre
(I) marvel	(J) maintenance		

1. The ________ of servers is not an easy job as it faces internal and external threats that will overload the server.
2. ________ is a rare beauty as the whole document is handwritten rather than made by the quick and easy method of printing.
3. ________ Telio is pacing up and down the command room as he ponders upon his next move for this great war.
4. The eagles are ________ , free and wise, as when storms come, they will soar above the clouds to avoid the thunderstorms and enter into the clear blue skies.
5. One of the most frightening events in history is the Holocaust as six million Jews were killed during the ________ ordered by Adolf Hitler.

Unit 36

masterpiece [ˈmæs.tɚ.piːs] *n.* 傑作；名作

同 **work of art**

▶ The artist's painting was a masterpiece.
那位藝術家的畫作是傑作。

---

mastery [ˈmæs.tɚ.i] *n.* 熟練；統治

同 **command; control**

實用片語與搭配詞

gain mastery over sb. / sth.
獲得控制權 / 佔上風

▶ The artist has a mastery of oil paint and watercolor techniques.
那名藝術家的油畫和水彩技巧都很熟練。

▶ Following years of depression, Michael finally gained mastery over his disorder with the help of his doctor.
在好幾年的抑鬱後，麥克終於在醫生的幫助之下，克服了他的失調症狀。

material [məˈtɪr.i.əl] *n.* 質地；物質

反 **spiritual**

▶ The material for this dress is very soft.
這件洋裝的質地很柔軟。

---

materialism [məˈtɪr.i.ə.lɪ.zəm]
n. 物質主義；唯物論

反 **idealism**

▶ Karla is a strong believer in materialism and has a physical explanation for everything.
卡拉是堅信物質主義的人，對一切事物都以物質的角度來詮釋。

---

mattress [ˈmæt.rəs] *n.* 床墊

▶ Steven wants to buy a more comfortable mattress to sleep on.
史帝芬想買張更舒服的床墊以供睡眠之用。

---

mayonnaise [ˈmeɪ.ə.neɪz]
美乃滋；蛋黃醬

▶ Can you put some mayonnaise on my sandwich?
你可以幫我在三明治上塗美乃滋嗎？

---

meantime [ˈmiːn.taɪm]

① *adv.* 同時；期間

同 **meanwhile**

實用片語與搭配詞

in the meantime 同時

▶ He is between jobs. Meantime, he is helping his wife watch the kids.
他正在找工作，在此同時，他也幫太太帶孩子。

▶ I need a moment to finish my work, but help yourself to a coffee in the meantime.
我需要一點時間完成我的工作，但是同時你也可以幫自己沖一杯咖啡。

M

② *n.* 期間

同 **interim; meanwhile**

▶ The bill is not due until next month. In the meantime, I must still pay other bills.

那個帳單下個月才到期要支付。在此期間，我仍然必須付掉其他的帳單。

---

mechanics [məˈkæn·ɪks]

n. 運作方式；機械學

同 **technicalities**

▶ I don't understand the mechanics of this machine.

我不了解這台機器的運作方式。

---

mechanism [ˈmek.ə.nɪ.zəm]

n. 機械裝置；機制

同 **device**

▶ The mechanic used a special mechanism to lift the car into the air.

那名機械工匠利用特殊的機械裝置，將那輛車吊高。

100

mediate [ˈmiː.di.eɪt] *v.* 調解；斡旋

同 **arbitrate; intercede**

▶ The man helped to mediate the volatile situation.

那名男子協助調解一觸即發的緊張局勢。

99

medication [ˌmed.əˈkeɪ.ʃən] 藥物

▶ The doctor gave her some medication for her cold.

那位醫生開了一些藥來治療她的感冒。

---

medieval [ˌmed.iˈiː.vəl] *adj.* 中世紀的

反 **ancient; modern**

▶ The historian wrote a book about medieval sports and competitions.

那位歷史學家寫了一本有關中世紀運動和競賽的書。

---

meditate [ˈmed.ə.teɪt] *v.* 靜坐；冥想；沉思

同 **contemplate; reflect**

實用片語與搭配詞

meditate on / upon sth. 沉思／冥想

▶ Gloria meditated to clear her mind of stressful thoughts.

葛羅麗雅透過靜坐來清除腦中充滿壓力的思緒。

▶ Kevin finally agreed to accept the new job after meditating on his possibilities for weeks.

經過長時間的深思熟慮，凱文終於願意接受這份工作。

---

meditation [ˌmed.əˈteɪ.ʃən]

n. 靜坐；冥想；沉思

同 **speculation**

▶ Meditation can help people relax.

靜坐可以幫助人們放鬆。

melancholy ['mel.əŋ.kɑː.li]

① *n.* 憂鬱

同 **gloomy**

反 **happy**

② *adj.* 憂鬱的

同 **gloomy**

反 **delightful**

► His melancholy was obvious from the sad look on his face.
從他臉上憂傷的表情，可以明顯看出他很憂鬱。

► Her melancholy voice made people feel sad when they talked to her.
她憂鬱的聲調，讓人光是和她說話就會感到憂傷。

---

mellow ['mel.oʊ]

① *adj.* 成熟的

同 **full-grown; mature**

② *v.* 使成熟

同 **mature**

► This mellow fruit is sweet and juicy.
這顆成熟的果實非常甜而多汁。

► Jack waited for the mango to mellow before eating it.
傑克要先等那顆芒果熟透了才吃。

---

menace ['men.əs]

① *n.* 威脅；有危害性的人、物

同 **threat**

② *v.* 威脅；恐嚇

同 **threat**

► Rodents are a real menace for homeowners.
嚙齒動物對屋主構成真正的威脅。

► Don't menace the neighbors, they are very nice people.
別威脅鄰居，他們都是好人。

---

mentality [men'tæl.ə.t̬i] *n.* 心態；智力

同 **intelligence; mind-set**

► Sherry has a positive mentality and looks at the good in every situation.
雪麗有積極正向的心態，她都能看出每個情況中好的一面。

---

merchandise ['mɝː.tʃən.daɪs]

① *n.* 商品

同 **goods**

② *v.* 買賣；經營

同 **trade; buy and sell**

實用片語與搭配詞

a range of merchandise 一系列的商品

► The store receives new merchandise every two weeks.
那間商店每兩週就會收到新商品。

► The shop merchandises new and used clothing.
那間商店經營新衣和二手衣的買賣。

► Online shopping has become popular because of the wide range of merchandise offered.
線上購物因為提供一系列的商品而變得受歡迎。

merge [mɝːdʒ] *v.* 合併

同 **blend; combine**

實用片語與搭配詞

merge with / into sth. 合併成某事／物

▶ The two small businesses merged into one large company.
那兩家小公司合併成一家大公司了。

▶ Jenny decided to merge her company with her husband's to make it financially stronger.
珍妮決定將她的公司與她丈夫的公司合併，讓公司財務更加穩固。

---

mermaid [ˈmɝː.meɪd] *n.* 美人魚

▶ The man searched his whole life for mermaids in the sea.
那名男子一生都在尋找海中的美人魚。

metaphor [ˈmet̬.ə.fɔːr] *n.* 隱喻

同 **allegory**

▶ The singer used a metaphor to describe love.
那位歌手用了一個隱喻來描述愛情。

---

metropolitan [ˌmet.rəˈpɑː.lə.tən]

① *adj.* 都會的；大都市的

同 **city; municipal**

② *n.* 都會人

▶ This newspaper reports on metropolitan news happening in the city.
這家報紙報導市區內發生的都會新聞。

▶ Stan is a true metropolitan and loves living in the city.
史丹是貨真價實的都會人，他很喜歡住在都市裡。

---

midst [mɪdst]

① *prep.* 在…之中

② *n.* 正當…的時候；在…之中；中間；當中

同 **middle; center**

▶ Are you standing in the midst of the crowd?
你是站在人群中間嗎？

▶ I'm in the midst of finishing my writing assignment.
我正在完成我的寫作功課。

---

migrant [ˈmaɪ.grənt]

① *adj.* 流動的；遷徙的

同 **immigrant; emigrant**

② *n.* 遷徙的動物

▶ Many migrant workers around the world work in very poor conditions.
世界各地有很多流動工人都在很惡劣的環境中工作。

▶ Migrants such as zebras move around in Africa each year.
像斑馬這樣的遷徙動物，每年在非洲四處遷移。

Exercise 36

I. Derivatives

1. The ______________ (mental) of the coach affects the players' performance and the goal they are pursing during the game.
2. The way to get out of ______________ (material) is actually giving; as one gives, the giver starts to realize that there is more satisfaction to it.
3. Living a life of ______________ (meditate) can be beneficial, but it should not take hold in your life as the master.
4. To learn a new skill is easy but to gain ______________ (master) in it is hard work, as Malcolm Gladwell said, "Ten thousand hours is the number of greatness."
5. The ______________ (mechanic) of a watch is profound, and the more accurate a watch is over a period of time, the most expensive it will be.

II. Choices

1. ________ on the good things in life and not the bad as life becomes enjoyable when you appreciate the goodness in every single person.
   (A) Medicate (B) Mediate (C) Meditate (D) Mitigate
2. Jane has been feeling ________ over a period of time, and we as friends must help her tide through and overcome her grief.
   (A) blithe (B) jolly (C) joyous (D) melancholy
3. A ________ city is full of life and interesting things to do, but some people prefer the beauty of quietness in the countryside.
   (A) metropolitan (B) merchandise (C) migrant (D) habitant
4. The words spoken by Dan were full of ________ , and his colleagues started to become wary of him to get out of harm's way.
   (A) maintenance (B) menace (C) mischance (D) misalliance
5. It is pretty common to see political parties ________ their chosen spokesman tn order to put up a figurehead and gather more votes.
   (A) subsidizing (B) merchandising (C) supervising (D) marginalizing

Unit 37

migrate [ˈmaɪ.greɪt] *v.* 搬遷；遷徙
反 **remain; stay**

▶ Jenny's family migrated to the southern part of the country last year.
珍妮全家去年搬遷到國內的南部了。

---

migration [maɪˈgreɪ·ʃən] *n.* 遷徙

▶ The annual bird migration is a good time to take photos of birds.
每年鳥類大遷徙是拍攝鳥類照片的大好機會。

---

mileage [ˈmaɪ.lɪdʒ] *n.* 總英哩數；行駛哩數

▶ What is the mileage on the car's odometer?
那輛車里程表上的行駛里數是多少？

---

milestone [ˈmaɪl.stoʊn] *n.* 里程碑
同 **landmark; highlight**

▶ Walking is an important milestone for little kids.
對幼兒來說，學會走路是重大的里程碑。

---

militant [ˈmɪl.ə.tənt]
① *adj.* 好戰的
同 **confrontational; combative**
② *n.* 好戰份子；激進份子
同 **aggressive; belligerent**

▶ The militant government started wars with the neighboring countries.
軍政府發動與鄰國之間的戰爭。

▶ The militants were defeated by the army.
那些好戰份子被軍隊打敗了。

---

miller [ˈmɪl.ɚ] *n.* 磨坊主人

▶ Ron is a successful miller and owns three grain mills.
朗恩是成功的磨坊主人，擁有三座穀物磨坊。

---

mimic [ˈmɪm.ɪk]
① *v.* 模仿
同 **copy; imitate**
② *n.* 善於模仿的人
同 **copycat; imitator**

▶ Susie likes to mimic her sister by repeating everything she says.
蘇西喜歡模仿她的姊妹，會重複她說的每句話。

▶ The actor is a skilled mimic and often copies the behaviors of famous people.
那位演員擅長模仿，常常模仿名人的行為舉止。

102

mingle [ˈmɪŋ.gəl] *v.* 相往來；相交往
同 **associate; socialize**

▶ It is important to mingle with people at parties.
在派對中與人打成一片是很重要的。

實用片語與搭配詞

mingle with sth. 與某物混合

▶ At a party, it is a good idea to try and mingle with other people and make new friends.
在派對上試著跟其他人交際並交些新朋友是一個不錯的主意。

---

miniature [ˈmɪn.i.ə.tʃɚ]

① *adj.* 小型的

同 **small; tiny**

② *n.* 縮小物

▶ Patty has several miniature horses at her farm.
派蒂的農場上有幾隻迷你馬。

▶ The museum is full of models, including an Eiffel Tower miniature.
這座博物館充滿了模型，其中包括艾菲爾鐵塔的迷你模型。

---

minimal [ˈmɪn.ə.məl] *adj.* 最少的；最小的

反 **maximal**

▶ The minimum wage in New York is $8.75.
紐約州最低工資是（每小時）8.75 美元。

---

minimize [ˈmɪn.ə.maɪz] *v.* 使減到最少

反 **maximize**

▶ Tracy minimized the amount of time she spent driving by moving closer to the office.
崔西搬到離公司更近的地方，以便節省開車上下班的時間。

---

mint [mɪnt] *n.* 薄荷

▶ I love drinking tea with mint.
我很喜歡喝薄荷茶。

---

miraculous [məˈræk.jə.ləs]

adj. 奇蹟的；神奇的

同 **amazing; astounding**

▶ God's love for us is miraculous.
上帝對人的愛非常奇妙。

---

mischievous [ˈmɪs.tʃə.vəs] *adj.* 淘氣的

同 **naughty; playful**

▶ The children's mischievous behavior caused many problems for their teachers.
孩子淘氣的行為替老師們惹來很多麻煩。

---

miser [ˈmaɪ.zɚ] *n.* 小氣鬼；守財奴

同 **money-grubber**

▶ Be generous. Don't be a miser!
大方點，別當小氣鬼！

M

missionary [ˈmɪʃ.er.i]

① *adj.* 宣教的

② *n.* 宣教士

同 **missioner**

▶ Gladys is doing missionary work in Kenya.
葛萊蒂斯在肯亞做宣教的工作。

▶ Brett wants to be a missionary in South America.
布雷特想到南美當宣教士。

---

mistress [ˈmɪs.trəs] *n.* 情婦；女主人

反 **master**

▶ The man's relationship with his mistress destroyed his marriage.
那名男子和情婦交往而毀了他的婚姻。

---

moan [moʊn]

① *n.* 哀號聲；呻吟聲

② *v.* 哀號；呻吟；嗚咽

同 **rumble; groan**

實用片語與搭配詞

moan about sth 抱怨；發牢騷

▶ The crowd's collective moan could be heard throughout the arena as the player missed the goal.
那名選手踢球不進，便聽到全體觀眾的哀號聲迴盪在體育場中。

▶ Jerry moaned in pain after his accident.
傑瑞發生意外事故之後，痛苦地哀號著。

▶ My mother told me to stop moaning about my homework because it wouldn't change anything.
我媽媽要我停止因為功課而發牢騷，因為這樣做一點幫助也沒有。

---

mobile phone [ˌmoʊ.bəl ˈfoʊn] *n.* 行動電話

▶ Paul used his mobile phone to call us from the train.
保羅用手機從火車上打給了我們。

mobilize [ˈmoʊ.bə.laɪz] *v.* 動員

同 **rally; muster**

▶ The general mobilized his soldiers for battle.
那將軍動員戰士準備作戰。

---

mock [mɑːk]

① *v.* 嘲弄；模仿

同 **ridicule; taunt**

實用片語與搭配詞

mock at sb. / sth. 模仿嘲弄某人

▶ Everyone mocked the disgraced politician as he stepped off the platform.
那位顏面盡失的政客走下講台之際，大家都嘲弄他。

▶ The children mocked at their teacher and called him names for being so eccentric.
這些孩子嘲笑他們的老師並古怪地叫著他的名字。

② *n.* 嘲弄；笑柄

▶ You should not make a mock of things you do not understand.
你不應該嘲笑那些你自己不了解的事情。

---

mocking [ˈmɑː.kɪŋ] *adj.* 假裝的；仿製的

同 **mimic**

▶ The soldiers stage a mock battle every year.
士兵每年演習模擬戰事。

---

mode [moʊd] *n.* 方式；方法

同 **manner; method**

▶ What mode of transportation do you prefer?
你比較喜歡哪種交通方式？

---

modernization [ˌmɒdərnəˈzeɪʃən] *n.* 現代化

▶ The modernization of the historic house took several years.
那棟具有歷史意義的建築翻修得更現代化的過程，花了好幾年。

---

modernize [ˈmɑː.dɚ.naɪz] *v.* 使現代化

▶ It is important to update and modernize one's thinking and not to live in the past.
重要的是，人應該把自己的思考模式更新，使它更現代化，而不要活在過去。

Exercise 37

I. Derivatives

1. The core of ___________ (mock) others to boost self-confidence is essentially bullying as it degrades the person, and this can take place in various forms such as in person, messages or even over the internet.
2. The ___________ (miracle) recovery of Garry after fracturing his wrist and winning the trophy after two weeks is a story to be told in years to come.
3. Bird ___________ (migrate) takes place when they need to change location in order to find more food and a more suitable environment.
4. The ___________ (minimize) qualification for this entry-level job is a bachelor diploma; therefore no previous experience is required.
5. Linda made a big decision to go in the ___________ (mission) work to engage in ecumenical ministries outside of her country of origin.

II. Choices

1. This book provides some helpful strategies for those people who are being single parents on how to handle children's wild and ________ behavior in a positive way.
   (A) impervious (B) envious (C) previous (D) mischievous
2. The tip of cooking a beef stew is to give everything a good stir and leave it overnight to ________ the flavors together.
   (A) mingle (B) mangle (C) multiply (D) maintain
3. This car has clocked a lot of ________ , but yet it is still in tip top shape and can be used for a few more years.
   (A) Implementation (B) mileage (C) miscarriage (D) bandage
4. One of the most popular ways to display talent is to ________ a celebrity's way of speech.
   (A) misconduct (B) moisturize (C) mistake (D) mimic
5. This year is a significant ________ for the company as we managed to beat off many competitors and secure the biggest project we have ever undertaken.
   (A) milestone (B) motion (C) motivation (D) movement

Unit 38

98

modify [ˈmɑː.də.faɪ] *v.* 修改

同 **adjust; revise**

▶ My father renovated and modified the layout of our house.
我爸爸整修了我家，而且還修改了房子的格局。

---

mold [moʊld]

① *n.* 模型

同 **form; cast**

② *v.* 塑造；鑄造

同 **shape; sculpt**

③ *n.* 黴菌；黴

▶ The artist put the soft clay into the cat-shaped mold to make a clay cat.
藝術家把柔軟的黏土塞進貓形狀的模型裡，要做一隻黏土貓。

▶ The potter molded the clay into a beautiful tea pot.
陶匠把黏土塑造成美麗的茶壺。

▶ There is mold growing in the wall.
牆上長了黴菌。

---

molecule [ˈmɑː.lɪ.kjuːl] *n.* 分子

同 **corpuscle; particle**

▶ How many molecules are there in water?
水含有多少分子？

---

momentum [məˈmen.t̬əm] *n.* 動量；衝力

同 **force; impetus**

▶ The math teacher taught her students how to find the momentum of a basketball.
數學老師教學生如何找出籃球的動量。

---

monarch [ˈmɑː.nɚk] *n.* 君主

同 **emperor; ruler**

▶ The monarch of the British royal family is Queen Elizabeth.
英國王室的君主是伊莉莎白女王。

---

monopoly [məˈnɑː.pəl.i] *n.* 壟斷

同 **domination; corner**

▶ The monopoly in the electronics market ended when more companies started to sell similar products.
電子產品市場不再有被壟斷的情況了，因為有更多公司開始販售類似的產品。

---

monotonous [məˈnɑː.t̬ən.əs] *adj.* 單調的

同 **dull**

反 **various**

▶ The speaker's monotonous voice caused the audience to fall asleep.
講員單調的聲音導致聽眾都睡著了。

monotony [məˈnɑː.t̬ən.i] *n.* 單調

反 **variety**

▶ Many people complained about the monotony of the speech.

很多人都抱怨那場演講的單調乏味。

---

monstrous [ˈmɑːn.strəs]

adj. 巨大的；駭人聽聞的

同 **dreadful; hideous**

▶ The surfers travel to that beach to surf the monstrous waves.

衝浪者旅行到那個海灘，為了衝大浪。

---

morale [məˈrɑːl] *n.* 士氣

同 **enthusiasm; spirit**

▶ The students' morale increased when their teachers announced there would be no homework.

老師宣佈沒有回家作業之後，學生的士氣暴增。

---

morality [məˈræl.ə.t̬i] *n.* 道德

同 **ethics**

▶ His parents taught him the importance of morality, so he knows what's right and what's wrong.

他的父母教過他道德的重要性，所以他懂得分辨是非對錯。

mortal [ˈmɔːr.t̬əl]

① *adj.* 會死的；致命的

同 **fatal; lethal**

② *n.* 凡人；人

同 **human; individual**

▶ Humans are mortal beings.

凡是人必有一死。

▶ He is a mortal. He is not a god.

他只是凡人，不是神。

---

mortgage [ˈmɔːr.gɪdʒ] *n.* 抵押借款；房貸

實用片語與搭配詞

mortgage (v.) sth. to sb. for sth.

把某些東西抵押給某人以換取某物

▶ I finally paid off the mortgage on my house!

我終於繳完了房貸！

▶ Hank lost his job and had to mortgage his house to the bank to buy food for his family.

漢克失業了且必須抵押他的房子給銀行，才能買食物給他的家人。

---

moss [mɑːs]

① *n.* 苔蘚；地衣

② *v.* 使長滿苔蘚

▶ There is moss growing all over the buildings in Harvard Square.

哈佛廣場上的建築都長滿了苔蘚。

▶ The roof, which was mossed, looked terrible.

長滿苔蘚的屋頂看起來好可怕。

motherhood [ˈmʌð.ɚ.hʊd] *n.* 母職

反 **fatherhood**

▶ Motherhood is a very busy but important job.
母職是很忙碌卻很重要的工作。

---

motive [ˈmoʊ.t̬ɪv] *n.* 動機；主旨；目的

同 **cause; purpose**

▶ What is your motive for wanting to buy a new car?
你想買新車的動機是什麼？

101

motto [ˈmɑː.t̬oʊ] *n.* 座右銘

同 **dictum; aphorism**

▶ Julie wants to think of a good motto to express her company's values.
茱麗希望能想出一個好的座右銘，好傳達出她公司的價值觀。

---

mound [maʊnd]

① *n.* 土石堆

同 **heap; pile**

② *v.* 堆起

同 **stack; heap**

▶ Don't climb on that mound of rocks!
別爬到那處岩石堆上！

▶ The gardener mounded the soil around the new plant.
園丁在那株新種的植物四周堆土。

---

mount [maʊnt]

① *v.* 騎上；登上

同 **get on**

反 **dismount**

② *n.* 可乘騎的東西；底座

▶ Hazel mounted the pony before the trail ride.
在去小徑漫騎之前，黑澤兒先騎上那匹小馬。

▶ Before riding a horse, be sure to strap on a mount.
騎馬之前，一定要繫好座騎。

---

mourn [mɔːrn] *v.* 哀痛；哀悼

同 **grieve; lament**

實用片語與搭配詞

mourn for / over sb. / sth.
為喪失某人 / 事物表示哀悼

▶ The city mourned the fireman after the big accident.
發生重大意外事故後，全城都哀悼那位消防員。

▶ Humans will one day mourn for the loss of polar bears once they become extinct.
人們終有一天會為了北極熊的絕種而哀痛。

---

mournful [ˈmɔːrn.fəl]

adj. 令人悲痛的；憂傷的

同 **doleful; plaintive**

▶ The man let out a mournful cry when he found out his dog died.
那個人發現自己的狗死了之後，發出了悲痛的哭聲。

M

mouthpiece [ˈmaʊθ.piːs]

① *n.* （樂器的）吹口

② *n.* 發言人；喉舌

▶ Melanie adjusted the mouthpiece on her flute as she put the instrument together.
梅蘭尼調整笛子的吹口，她正在組合這個樂器。

▶ Robert is a political mouthpiece for one of the presidential candidates.
羅伯是一位總統候選人的政治發言人。

---

mower [ˈmoʊ.ɚ] *n.* 割草機

▶ The boy trimmed the front lawn with his brand new mower.
那名男孩用全新的割草機修剪前院的草。

mumble [ˈmʌm.bəl]

① *v.* 咕噥著說；含糊地說

同 **mutter; grumble**

實用片語與搭配詞

mumble about sth. 咕噥著說著某事

② *n.* 咕噥；含糊的話

同 **mutter; grumble**

▶ I heard Vanessa mumble under her breath.
我聽到維娜莎輕聲咕噥著。

▶ My sister is always mumbling about her chores because she is too lazy to do anything.
我的妹妹懶到什麼都不想做，因此總是在咕噥著不想做家庭雜務。

▶ I heard Simon's mumble as I walked by.
我走過賽門身邊時，聽到他在咕噥著。

---

municipal [mjuːˈnɪs.ə.pəl] *adj.* 市（政）的

同 **civic; metropolitan**

▶ The municipal buildings are located downtown.
市政建築座落在鬧區。

Exercise 38

I. Choices

1. Jenny feels no motivation in the work she is doing due to the tedious and ________ job scope to the point that it drains her and affects her sleeping and eating habits.
   (A) multifarious (B) monstrous (C) meticulous (D) monotonous
2. The outcome of this case is simple in that, though the offenders were able to escape death sentence through an interpretation of the law, the judge gave the most severe punishment possible due to ________ .
   (A) modesty (B) minority (C) mobility (D) morality
3. As a result of a ________ or a merger between the companies, most of the small business at that time was impelled to implement a shutdown of production.
   (A) monochrome (B) monopoly (C) monolog (D) monograph
4. Joan and her husband are thinking to take out a ________ and also coming up with some strategies to pay it off ahead of schedule.
   (A) moratorium (B) mortgage (C) movement (D) motion
5. The ________ of a man lies not in his appearance but in his heart, for the heart affects his whole being.
   (A) motive (B) motion (C) mote (D) move

II. Vocabulary Choices

(A) mound	(B) morale	(C) mournful	(D) modify
(E) mount	(F) mortal	(G) mouthpiece	(H) momentum
(I) mower	(J) motive		

1. When the heart is sick and longing for the beloved one, ________ expressions can be seen from the eyes because they are windows to the soul.
2. Unanimously they decided to have John to be the ________ of this campaign to drive the point of AIDS awareness.
3. We can only do this as all of us are ________ , but the future lies on the sovereignty of the one who created us all.
4. A small object thrown down from above can be fatal and dangerous to passersby due to the ________ of the object, and this can be termed as killer litters.
5. After we ________ some parts here and decorate nicely, this place is ready to be the main set for the upcoming blockbuster movie.

Unit 39

muscular ['mʌs.kjə.lɚ]

adj. 肌肉發達的；肌肉的

同 **brawny; hefty**

▶ Jimmy goes to the gym everyday; his arms are very muscular.
吉米每天都會上健身房，他的手臂肌肉很發達。

---

muse [mju:z] *n.* 深思；冥想

同 **deliberate; contemplate**

▶ I don't care about your muses. I want to see you start working.
我不在乎你沉思默想，可是我希望能看到你開始工作。

---

mustard ['mʌs.tɚd] *n.* 芥末醬；芥末

▶ I put mustard on my hot dog.
我在熱狗上加芥末醬。

---

mute [mju:t]

① *adj.* 沉默的

同 **dumb**

反 **talkative**

② *n.* 啞巴

③ *v.* 消除聲音

同 **silence**

▶ The mute suspect refused to answer the police officer's questions.
沉默的嫌犯拒絕回答警方的任何問題。

▶ Christina is a mute, so she uses sign language to communicate.
克麗絲汀是啞巴，所以她用手語來跟人溝通。

▶ Justin used his hand to mute the sound of his trumpet and make it quieter.
賈斯汀用手來摀住小喇叭發出聲音，想藉此讓聲音變得小一點。

---

mutter ['mʌt̬.ɚ]

① *v.* 低聲嘀咕；低聲含糊地說

同 **grumble; mumble**

實用片語與搭配詞

mutter sth. to sb.
對某人咕噥著

② *n.* 抱怨；嘀咕

同 **grumble; complaint**

▶ Jamie muttered under his breath as the teacher walked away.
老師走過傑米身邊時，他輕聲嘀咕著。

▶ My teacher muttered something to my mother so I couldn't hear and now I am very worried.
我的老師對著我母親低聲嘀咕，我因為聽不到而非常擔憂。

▶ The politician has heard the mutter of discontent from the people.
那名政治家聽到了民眾不滿的抱怨之聲。

mutton [ˈmʌt̬.ən] *n.* 羊肉

▶ In some countries, mutton is a delicacy.
在有些國家裡，羊肉是佳餚

---

myth [mɪθ]
n. 虛構的故事；虛構的人或事物；神話
同 **fable; fiction**

▶ That story is not real; it is a myth.
那個故事不是真的，那是虛構的故事。

---

mythology [mɪˈθɑː.lə.dʒi] *n.* 神話
同 **legends; folklore**

▶ Students in the class studied the mythology of African tribes to learn about their beliefs.
那堂課的學生研究非洲部落的神話，以便了解他們的信仰。

---

nag [næg]
① *v.* 嘮叨；糾纏不休
同 **badger; bother**

實用片語與搭配詞
nag at sb. 不斷挑剔 / 批評某人

② *n.* 好嘮叨的人

▶ His mother nagged him everyday to take out the garbage.
他母親每天都會嘮叨要他倒垃圾。

▶ Tom nagged at his mother to let him go on the class trip until she finally said yes.
湯姆在他媽媽答應讓他參加校外教學之前，不停地對她嘮叨著。

▶ Never call your wife a nag! She will definitely get angry.
永遠都不要說你太太是嘮叨的人！她一定會生氣的。

104

naive [naɪˈiːv] *adj.* 天真的；幼稚的
同 **inexperienced; innocent**

▶ Joanne is so naive. She believes everything.
瓊安好天真，她什麼事都相信。

---

narrate [nəˈreɪt] *v.* 敘述
同 **describe**

▶ The witness narrated his story in front of the judge.
目擊者在法官面前描述他所看到的情形。

---

narrative [ˈner.ə.t̬ɪv]
① *n.* 故事；記敘文
同 **story; tale**
② *adj.* 敘事的

▶ The writer's narrative describes the life of a young girl growing up in New York.
作家的故事描述在紐約長大的年輕女孩的人生。

▶ Writing narrative poetry is a unique way to tell a story.
撰寫敘事詩是相當獨特的說故事方式。

narrator [ˈner.eɪ.t̬ɚ] *n.* 敘述者

同 **storyteller; reporter**

▶ The narrator described the events of the play while the actors were on stage.
演員在台上時，還有一位敘述者描述著這齣劇中發生的事件。

---

nasty [ˈnæs.ti]

adj. 令人作嘔的；非常惡劣的；下流的

同 **disgusting; filthy**

▶ There's a nasty smell coming from the bathroom.
有種噁心的味道從浴室傳出來。

---

nationalism [ˈnæʃ.ən.əl.ɪ.zəm] *n.* 民族主義

▶ Leo's nationalism was obvious from his speeches, which praised the country.
里歐的民族主義可以從他的演講中明顯看出，他的演講總是讚美祖國。

---

naturalist [ˈnætʃ.ɚ.əl.ɪst]

n. 自然學家；博物學家

▶ The naturalist carefully observed the animals in the jungle.
這位博物學家仔細觀察叢林裡的動物。

---

naval [ˈneɪ.vəl]

① *adj.* 海軍的

反 **military**

② *n.* 肚臍

▶ Soldiers will experience six weeks of naval training.
軍人將歷經六個星期的海軍訓練。

▶ Indian women often wear saris which reveal their navels.
印度婦女往往穿著會暴露出肚臍的莎麗服飾。

98

navigate [ˈnæv.ə.geɪt]

v. 航行於…；飛行於…

同 **cruise; sail**

▶ Can you navigate this boat from this harbor to the next city?
你能把這艘船從這個港口航行到下個城市嗎？

---

navigation [ˌnæv.əˈgeɪ.ʃən] *n.* 航海；航空

同 **steering**

▶ Sailors need to study navigation if they hope to become captain of their own ship.
船員如果想要當上自己的船的船長，就必須學習航行。

---

negotiation [nəˌgoʊ.ʃiˈeɪ.ʃən] *n.* 協商

同 **compromise; concession**

▶ Negotiations between the two companies will begin next week.
兩家公司將從下週開始進行協商。

neon [ˈniː.ɑːn] *n.* 氖；霓虹燈

▶ Neon is used in electric lamps.
氖氣被用在一些電燈裡。

---

neutral [ˈnuː.trəl]

① *adj.* 中立的

同 **impartial; independent**

② *n.* 中立國；中立者

▶ The governments asked a neutral person to arrange the peace talks.
政府請一位中立的人士來居中安排和平談判。

▶ The surrounding nations were neutrals and refused to join the war.
周遭的國家都是中立國，都拒絕加入那場戰爭。

---

newlywed [ˈnuː.li.wed] *n.* 新婚者

▶ Newlyweds look forward to having a romantic honeymoon.
新婚夫妻期待能度過浪漫的蜜月。

---

newscast [ˈnuːz.kæst]

n. 新聞報導；新聞廣播

同 **broadcast**

▶ I watch the evening newscast every day.
我每天都看傍晚的新聞報導。

---

newscaster [ˈnuːzˌkæs.tɚ]

n. 新聞播報員（男女通用）

同 **broadcaster**

▶ Newscasters must know a lot about current events to deliver the news accurately.
新聞播報員必須了解很多時事，才能正確播報新聞。

N

Exercise 39

I. Choices

1. Communication is simply the art of ________ and getting to bring one's point to another while understanding the other party to bring to a conclusion.
   (A) indication (B) exaggeration (C) conurbation (D) negotiation
2. Mia has more than 10 years of experiences in social work that one of her jobs is to help those people who have suffered in trauma to formulate a coherent ________ .
   (A) narcissism (B) narrative (C) native (D) nature
3. I saw Paul ________ ing to himself and pulling a long face while he walked out from the manager's office.
   (A) mind (B) master (C) mutter (D) shutter
4. The Star Wars fiction has been inspired by various concepts and sources such as Greek and Roman history, ________ , and philosophy.
   (A) mythology (B) biology (C) phycology (D) philology
5. The ________ of the Loch Ness Monster has always intrigued people throughout ages, and rumor has it that it inhabits in the Scottish highlands.
   (A) mystic (B) myth (C) mythology (D) myriad

II. Vocabulary Choices

(A) neutral	(B) newlywed	(C) narrator	(D) naive
(E) nag	(F) mumble	(G) navigate	(H) mute
(I) muse	(J) naturalist		

1. On the wedding day, the ________ s stand in front of the public to exchange vows to promise to faithfully stay in their marriage and make it stronger and stronger.
2. He was born in an atheist family and doesn't support any organized religion; therefore, he always takes a religious ________ position.
3. Don't be too ________ and don't just take his words for it, he is a pathological liar.
4. After a long day at work, he took off the shoes and sat down on the couch, starting to ________ about where his life is heading.
5. We always want to ________ life easily but as we grow up, you will realize that it is not about how easy it is but how well you can maneuver through it wisely.

Unit 40

nibble [ˈnɪb.l]

① *v.* 小口咬；一點點地吃

同 **chew; munch**

實用片語與搭配詞

nibble at sth. 輕咬

② *n.* 細咬；啃

同 **bite; chew**

▶ I wasn't that hungry, so I only nibbled at my lunch.
我不太餓，所以午餐只吃了幾口。

▶ My sister never eats a proper meal, but she is always nibbling at some snacks.
我姐姐從沒好好吃正餐，總是吃著零食。

▶ Can I have a nibble of your cookie?
你的餅乾可不可以給我吃一口？

---

nickel [ˈnɪk.əl]

① *n.* 五美分硬幣；鎳

② *v.* 鍍鎳於…

▶ I paid a nickel for a stick of gum.
我付了五美分硬幣買了一條口香糖。

▶ These wires have been nickeled and bronzed.
這些金屬絲已經鍍了鎳和銅。

---

nightingale [ˈnaɪ.t̬ɪŋ.geɪl] *n.* 夜鶯

▶ The nightingale's beautiful song put me to sleep.
夜鶯的美妙鳴叫聲帶我進入夢鄉。

---

nominate [ˈnɑː.mə.neɪt] *v.* 提名

實用片語與搭配詞

nominate sb. for / as sth.
為某職位 / 職務提名某人

▶ Eric nominated Isaac for class president.
艾瑞克提名艾薩克當班代。

▶ Fred nominated his best friend as class leader and everyone accepted his nomination.
弗列德提名他最好的朋友擔任班長，所有人都沒有異議。

---

nomination [ˌnɑː.məˈneɪ.ʃən] *n.* 提名

同 **appointment; designation**

▶ Everyone was excited to watch the presidential nomination.
每個人都興奮地觀看著總統提名的過程。

---

nominee [ˌnɑː.məˈniː] *n.* 被提名者

同 **campaigner; candidate**

▶ Larry is the Democratic nominee for mayor.
拉瑞是民主黨提名的市長候選人。

N

nonetheless [ˌnʌn.ðəˈles]

adv. 不過；但是；儘管

同 **however; nevertheless**

► I don't like cats; nonetheless, I will watch your cat while you're on vacation.

我不喜歡貓，儘管如此我可以在你渡假的期間幫你照顧你的貓。

---

nonviolent [nɑnˈvaɪ·ə·lənt] *adj.* 非暴力的

同 **peaceful**

► We are holding a nonviolent protest in front of city hall.

我們在市政廳前舉行非暴力的抗議活動。

---

norm [nɔːrm] *n.* 常態；標準；規範

同 **standard; average**

► Studying two languages was the norm at Betty's school.

在貝蒂的學校，學生學兩種語言是常態。

---

nostril [ˈnɑː.strəl] *n.* 鼻孔

► Gorillas have big nostrils.

大猩猩鼻孔很大。

---

notable [ˈnoʊ.t̬ə.bəl]

① *adj.* 明顯的；顯著的

同 **distinguished; prominent**

② *n.* 名人；顯要人物

同 **celebrity**

► There was a notable difference in the twins' personalities.

那對雙胞胎的個性有明顯的不同。

► Many notables attended the charity event last night.

很多名人參與昨晚的慈善活動。

103

noticeable [ˈnoʊ.t̬ɪ.sə.bəl]

adj. 顯而易見的；明顯的

同 **obvious; conspicuous**

► The shift in the group dynamic when he left was very noticeable.

他離開後，原有團隊動能的轉變顯而易見。

97

notify [ˈnoʊ.t̬ə.faɪ] *v.* 通知；報告

同 **inform; tell**

實用片語與搭配詞

notify sb. of sth. 通知某人某事

► Notify the fire department that there is a fire on First Street.

請通知消防隊，第一街發生火災了。

► My supervisor asked me to notify him of any changes to the contract.

我的主管要求我通知他任何合約上的修改。

---

notion [ˈnoʊ.ʃən] *v.* 概念；想法

同 **idea; conception**

► The notion of lining up is foreign in certain cultures.

在有些文化中，排隊是很陌生的概念。

notorious [noʊˈtɔːr.i.əs] *adj.* 惡名昭彰的

同 **infamous**

反 **famous**

▶ The notorious thief still hasn't been arrested.
惡名昭彰的竊賊還沒有被抓到。

---

nourish [ˈnɝː.ɪʃ] *v.* 增添營養；滋養

同 **feed; nurture**

▶ Martha nourishes her children with fresh fruits and vegetables.
瑪莎用新鮮水果和蔬菜來為孩子增添營養。

---

nourishment [ˈnɝː.ɪʃ.mənt]

n. 含有營養的食物；食物；養分

同 **food; diet**

▶ After running a long race, Tim needed nourishment.
提姆長跑過後，需要攝取營養的食物。

---

novice [ˈnɑː.vɪs] *n.* 新手；初學者

同 **beginner; freshman**

▶ I'm a novice tennis player. I haven't played for very long.
我是網球新手，打網球的時間還不太久。

---

nowhere [ˈnoʊ.wer]

① *adv.* 任何地方都不

反 **everywhere**

② *pron.* 不知名的地方

▶ She is nowhere to be found.
所有地方都找不到她。

▶ I'm in the middle of nowhere.
我置身在一處鳥不生蛋的地方。

---

nucleus [ˈnuː.kli.əs] *n.* 核心；細胞核

同 **core; center**

▶ My mother is the nucleus of the family.
我媽媽是全家的核心。

---

nude [nuːd]

① *adj.* 裸的；與生俱有的

同 **bare; naked**

② *n.* 裸體

▶ The nude model posed for an art class at the university.
那名裸體模特兒為大學藝術課擺姿勢。

▶ The artist drew many nudes during his career.
這位藝術家在他的藝術生涯中，畫了很多裸體畫。

---

nuisance [ˈnuː.səns] *n.* 令人討厭的人或事物

同 **annoyance; irritation**

▶ The long wait times for the rides were a big nuisance.
要等很久才能搭乘遊樂設施，是最討厭的事。

nurture [ˈnɝː.tʃɚ]

① *n.* 養育；培養

② *v.* 養育；培養

同 **bring up; foster**

▸ The nurture of a child often affects the child for the rest of its life.
養育孩子的方式，常會影響到這孩子往後的一生。

▸ Christopher nurtured his son with love and care.
克里斯多福以愛心和呵護來養育他的兒子。

---

nutrient [ˈnuː.tri.ənt]

① *n.* 營養素；養分

② *adj.* 營養的

▸ There aren't many nutrients in instant noodles.
速食麵裡的營養素不夠多。

▸ This smoothie has a lot of nutrient vitamins in it.
這個思慕昔裡面含有大量營養的維生素。

Exercise 40

I. Derivatives

1. This system will ___________ (notification) you via your hand phone when there is an approaching typhoon or tsunami within the next three hours.
2. Although peaceful in nature, ___________ (violent) protests are essentially still leading protests that can disrupt the nation's growth, as tourist will in general avoid these countries.
3. The plant gets its ___________ (nourish) from the ground through its root, and it teaches a valuable lesson that one should stay rooted to grow big.
4. After going through rounds of counseling with the psychiatrist for his depression, John's change has been ___________ (notice) and remarkable as it is helping him.
5. The ___________ (nominate) of Don as the new team leader is well-supported, and chances of him being appointed are very high.

II. Vocabulary Choices

(A) nickel	(B) newscaster	(C) novice	(D) nonetheless
(E) notorious	(F) nostril	(G) nude	(H) norm
(I) nibble	(J) notable		

1. A master at one stage of his life was a ________ , and hence one should never belittle their small beginnings.
2. James is a ________ scientist as his thesis and works have brought about much benefit to the medical field.
3. This work seems difficult to achieve, but ________ at your word, I will strive and give my best to fulfill it.
4. Now it is a social ________ to associate boys with blue and girls with pink, but in the early 1900's, it was the other way round.
5. Billy was so ________ and infamous that his name and reputation went beyond his school to the next region.

Unit 41

nutrition [nuː'trɪʃ.ən] *n.* 營養

實用片語與搭配詞

adequate nutrition 適當的營養

▶ Having good nutrition is an important part of staying healthy.
攝取良好的營養，是保持健康的重要因素。

▶ In order for your body to be healthy, you need adequate nutrition and regular exercise.
為了讓身體健康，你需要適當的營養和規律的運動。

100

nutritious [nuː'trɪʃ.əs] *adj.* 有營養的

▶ Jasmine ate a nutritious breakfast to give her energy for the day.
賈絲敏吃了營養的早餐，以便讓她整天都能活力充沛。

---

oar [ɔːr] *n.* 槳；櫓

▶ Does that boat have any oars?
那條船有槳嗎？

---

oasis [oʊ'eɪ.sɪs] *n.* 綠洲

▶ In the dry desert heat, the nomads searched for an oasis.
在這乾燥沙漠的炙熱中，遊牧民族尋找綠洲。

---

oath [oʊθ] *n.* 誓言；誓約

同 **pledge; vow**

▶ The president of the United States takes an oath of office.
美國總統宣誓就職。

---

oatmeal ['oʊt.miːl] *n.* 燕麥片

同 **oats**

▶ I eat oatmeal in the morning for breakfast.
我早上吃燕麥片當早餐。

---

obligation [ˌɑː.blə'geɪ.ʃən] *n.* 義務

同 **duty; responsibility**

實用片語與搭配詞

comply with obligation 盡義務

▶ Jimmy had an obligation to complete the contract he signed with the company.
吉米有義務去履行他和公司簽的合約內容。

▶ Miriam complied with her obligation to take care of her sick father, but she had to give up her dreams.
米利暗盡了她照顧生病父親的義務，但是她必須放棄她的夢想。

oblige [əˈblaɪdʒ] *v.* 使不得不做⋯

- ▶ Alexa was obliged to go home early due to her illness.
  艾麗莎因為生病而不得不提早回家。

實用片語與搭配詞

oblige sb. with sth. / by doing sth.
強迫 / 要求某人做某事物

- ▶ Please oblige me by giving me a ride to the nearest bus stop because I am already late.
  麻煩你把我載到最近的公車站牌，因為我已經遲到了。

---

oblong [ˈɑː.blɑːŋ]

① *adj.* 橢圓形的；矩形的

- ▶ This hairstyle is suitable for faces that are oblong.
  這種髮型適合橢圓形的臉。

實用片語與搭配詞

an oblong table 長方桌

- ▶ An oblong table can fit more people than a square or round table and would be perfect for parties.
  比起正方桌或圓桌，長桌能容納更多人並且適合在派對上使用。

② *n.* 矩形；橢圓形

- ▶ I want you to draw an oblong on the board.
  我要你在板子上畫橢圓形。

---

obscure [əbˈskjʊr]

① *adj.* 陰暗的

同 **dim**

反 **clear**

- ▶ During his adventures, the explorer had a hard time seeing inside the obscure caves.
  那個探險家在探險的過程中，在陰暗的墓穴裡面一直看不清楚。

② *v.* 使變暗

同 **darken**

- ▶ The man's face was obscured by the poor light.
  黯淡的燈光讓那個人的臉變暗了。

---

observer [əbˈzɝː.vɚ] *n.* 觀察者

同 **beholder; commentator**

- ▶ I'm not a participant. I'm only an observer.
  我不是參加者，只是觀察者。

---

obstinate [ˈɑːb.stə.nət] *adj.* 固執的；頑固的

同 **stubborn**

反 **docile**

- ▶ The obstinate child refused to listen to his parents.
  那個固執的孩子拒絕聽從父母的話。

---

occurrence [əˈkɝː.əns] *n.* 發生；發生的事

- ▶ A shooting star is a rare occurrence.
  流星是很少發生的現象。

N O

實用片語與搭配詞

everyday occurrence 日常事件

▶ Seeing people eat at street vendors in Asia is an everyday occurrence and part of the culture.
在亞洲，吃路邊攤是稀鬆平常的事，也是文化的一部分。

---

octopus [ˈɑːk.tə.pəs] *n.* 章魚

▶ An octopus has eight legs.
章魚有八隻腳。

---

odds [ɑːdz] *n.* 機率；可能性

同 **probability; chances**

▶ The odds of me winning the contest are pretty low.
我贏得比賽的機率很低。

---

odor [ˈoʊ·dər] *n.* 氣味；香氣；臭氣

同 **fragrance; scent**

▶ There is a really bad odor coming from the bathroom.
從浴室傳來很難聞的臭味。

---

offering [ˈɑː.fɚ.ɪŋ]

n. 提出（工作、機會等）；祭品；禮物

▶ The company's job offerings sound very exciting.
那家公司提出的職缺看來真的很棒。

---

offspring [ˈɑːf.sprɪŋ] *n.* 子孫

同 **descendant; child**

▶ Dana hopes all of her offspring will attend college.
丹娜希望她所有子孫都能上大學。

---

olive [ˈɑː.lɪv]

① *n.* 橄欖

② *adj.* 橄欖的

▶ There are too many olives on this pizza!
這塊披薩上的橄欖太多了！

▶ Jason's favorite color is olive green.
傑森最喜歡的顏色是橄欖綠。

---

operational [ˌɑː.pəˈreɪ.ʃən.əl]

adj. 可運轉的；操作的

同 **functional**

實用片語與搭配詞

remain operational 保持運作

▶ The factory is fully operational and ready to begin production.
這家工廠完全可運轉，已經準備就緒可以開始生產了。

▶ The subway system remained operational during the typhoon.
地鐵系統在颱風期間保持運行。

---

opponent [əˈpoʊ.nənt] *n.* 對手；反對者

同 **adversary; rival**

反 **ally**

▶ Linda's opponent is Rebecca.
琳達的對手是蕾貝加。

103 102 96

opposition [ˌɑː.pəˈzɪʃ.ən] *n.* 反對

同 **enemy; foe**

▶ Opposition to the new law can be made through a vote next week.

可以透過下個星期的投票來對那條新的法規表示反對。

---

oppress [əˈpres] *v.* 壓迫

同 **crush; suppress**

▶ The slaves were oppressed and longed for freedom.

奴隸備受壓迫，渴望自由。

---

oppression [əˈpreʃ.ən] *n.* 壓迫

實用片語與搭配詞

political / racial / sexual oppression

政治 / 種族 / 性向壓迫

▶ The oppression of religious groups has become a major problem.

宗教團體遭到壓迫已經成為很嚴重的問題。

▶ Martha is a women's rights activist and she fights against sexual oppression in many countries.

瑪莎是女權主義份子，她反對許多國家的性別壓迫。

---

optimism [ˈɑːp.tə.mɪ.zəm] *n.* 樂觀；樂觀主義

反 **pessimism**

▶ Josh's optimism is infectious.

喬許的樂觀具有感染力。

O

Exercise 41

I. Derivatives

1. Since traffic accidents are an everyday ______________ (occur), monitors have been widely set up at intersections to facilitate the investigation of causes afterwards.
2. Education is considered a civil right and an ______________ (oblige) for everyone in this country, which compels the parents to enroll their children in school when they are of age.
3. A ______________ (nutrition) diet is necessary for a patient after surgery since the wounds require adequate supply of nutrients to heal.
4. Political ______________ (oppress) seems to be a concept found only in history; yet, it is quite common in countries with totalitarian regimes, such as North Korea.
5. The criminal attempted to ______________ (obscurity) the truth by giving false testament, involving innocent yet related people into the case under investigation.

II. Vocabulary Choices

(A) optimism	(B) nutrition	(C) obstinate	(D) oatmeal
(E) offering	(F) oar	(G) odds	(H) opposition
(I) oath	(J) odor		

1. To show the emperor his loyalty, the knight took a(n) ________ , swearing he would protect the country and his lord at the cost of his life.
2. With a firm belief in mind that she knew marketing more than anyone else in her section, Janet remained ________ toward all suggestions for adjustments in her proposal of sale strategy for the next season.
3. There are heavy ________ against people winning lottery, but still many believed otherwise since the press released news story only about those who won.
4. Despite the obvious depression shown in the patient who'd been amputated, the doctor still tried to purvey a message of ________ , hoping to replenish him with enthusiasm to move on in life.
5. The organizer of the singing contest announced and guaranteed a great ________ to the winner in the hope of attracting as many participants as possible.

Unit 42

102

option [ˈɑːp.ʃən] *n.* 選擇

同 **alternative; choice**

實用片語與搭配詞

keep / leave your options open
保持 / 放棄開放的選擇

▶ Tammy chose the option of becoming a doctor instead of a scientist.
潭米選擇當醫生而非科學家。

▶ If I were you, I would keep my options open and wait before rejecting that job.
如果我是你，在拒絕那家公司之前，我會持開放的態度並等待其他公司的回應。

103

optional [ˈɑːp.ʃən.əl]

adj. 自由選擇的；選修的；非必需的

同 **voluntary**

反 **compulsory**

▶ Attending the speech is optional for students.
學生可以自由選擇要不要聽那場演講。

---

orchard [ˈɔːr.tʃɚd] *n.* 果園；果樹林

▶ The farmer checks his orchard on a daily basis.
那名農夫每天都會巡查他的果園。

---

ordeal [ɔːrˈdɪəl]

n. 煎熬；磨難；苦難；嚴峻考驗

同 **test; trial**

實用片語與搭配詞

endure / go through / suffer ordeal
忍受 / 經歷 / 遭受考驗

▶ Recovering from the car accident was a major ordeal for Tony.
發生車禍後的復原過程，對東尼來說是相當大的煎熬。

▶ Teresa had to go through the ordeal of physical theraphy after her car accident.
在車禍之後，德瑞莎必須經歷物理治療的痛苦。

---

orderly [ˈɔːr.dɚ.li]

① *adj.* 整齊的；井然有序的

同 **consistent; regulated**

② *n.* 護理員；雜役工

同 **hospital; attendant**

▶ Sasha has a very orderly desk. She's very organized.
莎夏的桌面整齊有序，她凡事都井井有條。

▶ The patient asked the orderly to bring her some water.
患者請護理員幫她拿點水。

O

103

organism [ˈɔːr.gən.ɪ.zəm] *n.* 微生物；有機體

同 **being; life form**

▶ Using a microscope, the scientist looked at the tiny organisms.
科學家用顯微鏡來觀察微生物。

---

organizer [ˈɔːr.gən.aɪ.zɚ] *n.* 籌辦人；組織者

▶ Johnny is the organizer of the graduation party.
強尼是畢業慶祝會的籌辦人。

104

orient [ˈɔːr.i.ənt]

① *n.* （大寫）東方；優質珍珠

同 **Asian; Far East**

② *v.* 定方位；使朝東

▶ Japan, China and Korea are all countries of the Orient.
日本、中國和韓國全都是東方國家。

▶ Orient the table towards the door.
把桌子朝向門擺放。

---

oriental [ˌɔːr.iˈen.t̬əl]

① *adj.* （大寫）東方的；亞洲的

同 **Asian; Far East**

② *n* （大寫）東方人；亞洲人

▶ Janet wore an oriental dress to the show.
珍娜穿著亞洲風格的洋裝去參加那場秀。

▶ It is rude to ask someone if they are Oriental.
問別人是不是東方人，是很無禮的行為。

---

originality [əˌrɪdʒ.ənˈæl.ə.t̬i] *n.* 原創性

同 **innovation; novelty**

實用片語與搭配詞

originality in sth. 對於某事的原創性

▶ The writer's originality made her stories very popular with people who wanted something new.
那名作家的原創性，使她的故事在求新求變的人士當中大受歡迎。

▶ The advertising company has won many awards for its originality in creating innovative ads.
這間廣告公司至今贏得許多獎項，因為它製作的創新廣告具有高度原創性。

103

originate [əˈrɪdʒ.ən.eɪt] *v.* 來自；源自

實用片語與搭配詞

originate from / with sb. 始自某人

▶ The idea for the new business originated from a discussion with my father.
開創新事業的點子來自於我和我爸爸的一次討論。

▶ The family tradition of going to the cabin by the lake for Thanksgiving originated with my grandfather.
我們家在感恩節都會去湖邊木屋度假，這個傳統是由我的祖父開創的。

103

ornament ['ɔːr.nə.mənt]

① *n.* 裝飾品

同 **decoration; embellishment**

② *v.* 裝飾；美化

實用片語與搭配詞

ornament sth. with sth. 裝飾點綴某物

▶ I put a new ornament on the Christmas tree.
我在聖誕樹上放了一個新的裝飾品。

▶ Lisa ornamented the coffee shop's window with tinsel and lights.
麗莎用閃亮的箔紙和燈來裝飾咖啡店的窗子。

▶ It is always a good idea to ornament your home with beautiful things you like.
用你喜歡的物品裝飾點綴你家是一個很棒的主意。

---

orphanage ['ɔːr.fən.ɪdʒ]

n. 孤兒院；孤兒（總稱）

▶ Can you volunteer at the orphanage this weekend?
這個週末你能不能來孤兒院當志工？

---

ostrich ['ɑː.strɪtʃ] *n.* 鴕鳥

▶ Some ostriches live at the zoo.
有幾隻鴕鳥住在動物園裡。

---

ounce [aʊns] *n.* 盎司

同 **oz.**

▶ The receipe asks for two ounces of meat.
食譜上寫要兩盎司的肉。

---

outbreak ['aʊt.breɪk] *n.* 爆發

同 **eruption; outburst**

實用片語與搭配詞

lead to an outbreak of sth.
導致某事的爆發

▶ There was a sudden outbreak of measles that caused many children to become sick.
突然爆發痲疹疫情，導致很多孩子都染上了。

▶ The flood led to an outbreak of malaria.
洪水導致了瘧疾的爆發。

---

outdo [ˌaʊt'duː] *v.* 勝過；超越

同 **beat; defeat**

▶ Siblings often compete and try to outdo each other.
兄弟姊妹常常相互競爭，而且試圖勝過彼此。

---

outfit ['aʊt.fɪt]

① *n.* 裝束；全套裝備

實用片語與搭配詞

wedding outfit 婚禮套裝

▶ Dan put on his plumber's outfit before going to help a customer.
丹出去幫客戶修理之前，先穿上了水電工的裝束。

▶ My sister is getting married this Saturday and I still have not chosen a wedding outfit to wear.
我姐姐這週六就要結婚了，然而我還未挑選到適合的婚禮套裝。

② *v.* 為…提供配備或服裝；裝備；配備

同 **equip; prepare**

▸ This store outfits campers with everything they need for a great camping trip.

這家店為露營者提供的配備，能讓他們擁有絕佳露營之旅所需的一切。

96

outgoing [ˈaʊt.goʊ.ɪŋ]

adj. 外向的；向外出去的；出發的

實用片語與搭配詞

outgoing personality 外向的個性

▸ Rebecca has a very outgoing personality.

蕾貝加的個性非常外向。

▸ Mary makes friends easily because of her outgoing personality.

瑪莉外向的個性使她很容易交到朋友。

---

outing [ˈaʊ.t̬ɪŋ] *n.* 郊遊

同 **excursion; trip**

▸ The couple went on an outing to the lake to relax.

這對夫妻去湖邊郊遊，好放鬆身心。

---

outlaw [ˈaʊt.lɑː]

① *n.* 歹徒

同 **criminal**

實用片語與搭配詞

declare sb. an outlaw 宣佈某人為逃犯

② *v.* 宣佈…為不合法

同 **convict**

▸ The outlaw has been hiding from the police for three weeks.

那個歹徒三週來一直躲避警察的追緝。

▸ The rebel leader was declared an outlaw by the government, and he fled into the jungle.

叛亂領袖被政府宣布為逃犯，而他已經逃入叢林之中。

▸ This year the state outlawed the sale of fireworks.

今年該州禁止販售煙火。

---

outlet [ˈaʊt.let] *n.* 出口；出路

反 **inlet**

▸ The rat ran through an outlet into the street to escape from the cat.

那隻老鼠為了躲避那隻貓，就從一個出口逃到街上了。

---

outlook [ˈaʊt.lʊk] *n.* 觀點；展望

同 **view**

實用片語與搭配詞

outlook onto / over sth. 某處的景致

▸ Katie has a positive outlook on life and always thinks of the good things she has.

凱蒂對生活有著積極正面的觀點，而且總是不忘記自己所擁有的美好事物。

▸ We have a house by the coast that has an outlook over the sea and a beautiful beach.

我們有棟海岸邊的房子，能看到海洋以及美麗海灘的景致。

outnumber [ˌaʊtˈnʌm.bɚ] *v.* 數量超過…

同 **exceed**

▶ The students outnumbered the teachers with only one teacher for every 50 students.

學生們人數超過老師，每五十個學生就只有一位老師而已。

---

output [ˈaʊt.pʊt]

① *n.* 產出；產量

實用片語與搭配詞

steady output 穩定的輸出

② *v.* 輸出；生產

同 **production; yield**

▶ Did your output meet the minimum work requirement?

你的工作產出有沒有達到最低工作要求？

▶ The water pump has a steady output of 1000 liters of clean water every hour.

抽水機每個小時能穩定輸出 1000 公升的淨水。

▶ Did the printer output your document?

印表機有沒有輸出你的文件？

O

Exercise 42

I. Derivatives

1. In this department, Freshmen English, Linguistics, and Language Analysis are compulsory for English majors, but other courses are ___________ (option), which means students can decide for themselves according to their interests.
2. The employees were demanded to arrange all the products in the shop in an ___________ (orderly) fashion so as to leave great impressions on the customers.
3. The fiction that Ariel composed was particularly praised by critics on its ___________ (originality), which it deserved since Ariel worked on the plot without reference to any other classics.
4. The troops were ___________ (outfit) with the latest radar-tracking device which enabled them to keep track of the enemy without being detected and targeted.
5. The Personal Information Protection Act has ___________ (outlaw) any public display of data concerning individuals and even the names of the applicants who got admission to any organization cannot be exposed in complete form.

II. Vocabulary Choices

(A) oriented	(B) orphanage	(C) ostrich	(D) ordeal
(E) oriental	(F) originated	(G) organism	(H) outnumbered
(I) outdo	(J) outbreak		

1. After being trapped deep into the mountain for a week, the hikers' ________ finally came to an end when the rescue team found them.
2. In The Transformers series, all the robots that could freely transform from vehicles were living ________ from outer space, not simply lifeless machines as human would normally think they were.
3. Mr. Wayne, who used to be an orphan and now a billionaire, sponsored the ________ , providing everything required for raising and educating the orphans.
4. Delia was of an ambitious and competitive disposition and always attempted to ________ every colleague in her section; she simply wanted to be the best.
5. In this class, female students far ________ the male students, and every boy was responsible for any labor-intensive work.

Unit 43

outrage ['aʊt.reɪdʒ]

① *n.* 惡行

同 **assault**

實用片語與搭配詞

feel / express / voice outrage 表達憤怒

② *v.* 激怒

同 **infuriate**

實用片語與搭配詞

be outraged by sth. 被某事觸怒

▸ People couldn't believe the outrages the company committed against its employees.
人們無法相信那家公司對員工所犯下的惡行。

▸ After the team lost the baseball game, they voiced outrage over the unfairness of the referee.
在那支籃球隊輸掉球賽之後，他們對裁判不公平的判決表達憤怒。

▸ Tina was outraged when she found out her car was stolen.
提娜發現貓被偷了之後，變得勃然大怒。

▸ The residents were outraged by the students who broke into the mall to play computer games.
闖入購物中心玩電腦遊戲的學生們觸怒了居民。

95

outrageous [ˌaʊtˈreɪ.dʒəs]

adj. 無法無天的；可憎的

同 **absurd; disgraceful**

▸ The man's outrageous behavior led to him being arrested.
那男子無法無天的行為導致他遭到逮捕。

---

outright [ˌaʊtˈraɪt]

① *adv.* 毫無保留地；完全地；當場

同 **completely; absolutely**

② *adj.* 無保留的；直率的；完全的

同 **complete; absolute**

▸ The bold little girl stated her opinions outright.
那個大膽的小女孩毫無保留地說出自己的意見。

▸ In an outright statement, the man admitted to his crimes.
那男子在聲明中毫無保留地坦承自己犯下的罪行。

---

outset ['aʊt.set] *n.* 最初；開端

同 **beginning; start**

實用片語與搭配詞

at / from the outset of sth. 一開始的時候

▸ From the outset, Charlene could tell that Paul liked her.
打從一開始查琳就可以看出保羅喜歡她。

▸ From the outset of summer, we realized that it was going to be extremely hot.
夏季一開始，我們就明白天氣即將變得非常炎熱。

O

outsider [ˌaʊtˈsaɪ.dɚ] *n.* 門外漢；局外人

反 **insider**

▶ Jack is an outsider. He doesn't belong to our group.
傑克是外人，他不屬於我們的團體。

---

outskirts [ˈaʊt.skɝːts] *n.* 郊外；郊區

▶ I live on the outskirts of town.
我住在城鎮的郊區。

---

outward [ˈaʊt.wɚd]

① *adj.* 外面的；向外的

反 **inward**

② *adv.* 向外；朝外

▶ The outward appearance of the car looks decent.
那輛車的外觀相當不錯。

▶ Move all the chairs outward towards the aisle.
把所有椅子都向外朝走道搬。

---

overall [ˌoʊ.vɚˈɑːl]

① *adj.* 全面的；整體的

同 **total; entire**

② *adv.* 從頭到尾；大體上

同 **totally; entirely**

③ *n.* 背帶工作褲

▶ The overall length of the show is four hours.
這場秀的全長是四小時。

▶ Overall, everyone is happy and healthy.
整體而言，大家都很快樂而健康。

▶ I wore jean overalls to the farm.
我穿牛仔背帶工作褲去農場。

---

overdo [ˌoʊ.vɚˈduː]

v. 做得過頭；表演過火；使過於疲勞

同 **exceed; carry too far**

▶ Be careful. Don't overdo it.
小心點，別做得太過火了。

---

overeat [ˌoʊ.vɚˈiːt] *v.* 吃得過多

同 **overindulge**

▶ Don't overeat before dinner!
晚餐前別吃太多了！

99

overflow [ˌoʊ.vɚˈfloʊ]

① *v.* 擠滿；氾濫；滿得溢出

同 **flood; spill over**

實用片語與搭配詞

overflow into sth. 溢到某範圍去

② *n.* 溢出；氾濫；過剩

▶ The emergency room is overflowing with patients waiting to see the doctor.
急診室擠滿了等候看診的患者。

▶ Once the dam filled up because of the rain, it overflowed into the river and flooded the valley.
當水庫集滿了雨水，它便會外溢到河流中並且使河谷淹水。

▶ The overflow from the tub spilled onto the floor.
浴缸的水溢出，流到地上了。

overhead [ˈoʊ.vɚ.hed]

① *adv.* 在頭頂上地；高架地

② *adj.* 在頭頂上的；高架的

同 **above; aloft**

③ *n.* 經常費用

▸ There is a plane flying overhead.
有一架飛機飛過頭頂上。

▸ Our room is nice and cool thanks to our overhead air conditioner.
拜高架的冷氣機所賜，我們房間很舒適又涼爽。

▸ The company has a large overhead because their rent is quite high.
公司的經常性開支很高，因為租金非常貴。

---

overhear [ˌoʊ.vɚˈhɪr] *v.* 無意中聽到；偷聽

▸ I overheard Jessie talking about Vicky.
我無意中聽到潔西講了有關維琪的話。

---

overlap [ˌoʊ.vɚˈlæp]

① *v.* 部分重疊

實用片語與搭配詞

partially / partly / slightly overlap
部分／輕微重疊

② *n.* 重疊

▸ Overlap the blankets on the bed so you will be warmer when you sleep.
可以把床上的毯子疊起來，這樣你睡覺時就會更暖和。

▸ Our jobs slightly overlap, so we need to communicate with each other.
我們的職務內容稍有重疊，所以我們需要與彼此溝通。

▸ Due to the document overlap, Carrie couldn't see what was written on the bottom paper.
由於文件疊起來了，所以卡麗看不到紙張背面寫了些什麼。

---

oversleep [ˌoʊ.vɚˈsliːp] *v.* 睡過頭

▸ Don't oversleep tomorrow. It's your wedding day!
明天不要睡過頭了，那是你結婚大喜的日子！

---

overturn [ˌoʊ.vɚˈtɝːn]

① *v.* 使翻轉；使傾覆

同 **reverse**

實用片語與搭配詞

seek / try to overturn sth.
企圖翻轉／逆轉某事物

② *n.* 推翻；傾覆

同 **reversal**

▸ The strong winds overturned the chairs in the yard.
強風把院子裡的椅子都吹翻了。

▸ The company tried to overturn its bad sales record of the past year.
這間公司嘗試翻轉去年慘澹的銷售紀錄。

▸ The company's overturn of employee benefits resulted in several people quitting.
公司推翻了員工福利的計畫，導致幾名員工辭職了。

overwelm [ˌoʊ.vɚˈwelm]

v. 使難以承受；使不知所措

實用片語與搭配詞

be overwhelmed with grief
陷入悲傷中

- I'm overwhelmed by the situation.
  這個處境令我難以承受。
- Mary-Anne was overwhelmed with grief after her father's death.
  在瑪莉安娜的父親過世後，她陷入悲傷之中。

---

overwork [ˌoʊ.vɚˈwɝːk]

① *v.* （使）工作過度；使過勞

同 **burn the midnight oil; burn the candle at both ends**

② *n.* 工作過度；過勞

實用片語與搭配詞

ill through overwork 積勞成疾

- Remember to take breaks. Don't overwork yourself.
  要記得休息。不要工作過度了。
- Justin is exhausted from overwork.
  賈斯汀因為工作過度而筋疲力盡。
- Science has proved that it is possible to get ill through overwork, and to work oneself to death.
  科學證實工作太操勞可能患病，並且可能導致過勞死。

---

oyster [ˈɔɪ.stɚ] *n.* 牡蠣；蠔

- Is there a pearl in this oyster?
  這個牡蠣裡面有珍珠嗎？

---

ozone [ˈoʊ.zoʊn] *n.* 臭氧

- The ozone layer is an important part of our atmosphere.
  臭氧層是大氣層裡很重要的一個部份。

---

pacific [pəˈsɪf.ɪk]

① *adj.* 愛好和平的；溫和的；（大寫）太平洋的

② *n.* （大寫）太平洋

- The government's pacific gesture surprised the media.
  政府求和的態度讓媒體大感意外。
- The ships of Magellan sailed across the Pacific.
  麥哲倫的船隻航行渡過太平洋。

---

packet [ˈpæk.ɪt] *n.* 小包（裹）

同 **package; bundle**

- There are five individual packets of cookies in that bag.
  那袋裡裝了五小包餅乾。

---

pact [pækt] *n.* 契約；協定

同 **agreement; treaty**

- The United States made a trade pact with Canada to formalize their trade agreements.
  美國和中國訂定了貿易協定，讓雙方之間的貿易協議正式化。

paddle [ˈpæd.əl]

① *n.* 槳

實用片語與搭配詞

paddling pool 兒童戲水池

② *v.* 用槳划、行進

同 **scull; row**

▶ Use the paddle to row the boat.
用槳來划船。

▶ Summer is coming and it is time to blow up the paddling pool for the kids to cool off in.
夏天將至，是時候將兒童戲水池充氣，讓孩子們消暑一下。

▶ Paddle your canoe to the other side of the lake.
用槳把獨木舟划到湖對岸。

---

pamphlet [ˈpæm.flət] *n.* 小冊子

同 **booklet; brochure**

▶ Serena handed out pamphlets promoting a new church to people passing by.
莎琳娜向路過的民眾發放小冊子，宣傳一間新建的教堂。

P

Exercise 43

I. Derivatives

1. What the director in this section is responsible for is not the work on details, but rather, an ____________ (overall)overall doesn't have any derivatives coordination of each employee and the supervision on the progress of the projects.
2. After learning that the government had yet again failed the promise to monitor the contractor in urban renewal, the local residents felt ____________ (outrage).
3. The riverbanks around this region are not very high, and the river always ____________ (overflow) whenever a typhoon strikes.
4. In Taiwan, many employees are assigned a lot of tasks within a relatively short period of time, which compels them to ____________ (overwork) constantly.
5. Due to the fact that the rental in downtown area is unreasonably high, quite many businesses are moving to the suburban districts in order to cut down on the ____________ (overhead).

II. Vocabulary Choices

(A) overdo (B) pact (C) outset (D) overhear
(E) oysters (F) pamphlets (G) overlap (H) overturn
(I) overeat (J) overwhelmed

1. It is wise to avoid sensitive topics for conversation in the workplace, for people tend to _________ gossip and spread it around.
2. After the pastry chef sliced the fancy cake, he asked the interns to partially _________ them with one on top of another, creating a terraced pattern.
3. Two of John's colleagues left the company recently, so John has to do the work of three people. He feels _________ by his work.
4. All the people who were willing to take part in this experiment would need to sign a _________ stipulating their rights of pension and obligation of keeping every detail secret.
5. In most famous scenic spots where there are tourist centers or traffic stations, tourists usually have free access to _________ containing useful traveling information.

Unit 44

pane [peɪn] *n.* （窗）玻璃

同 **window**

▶ Be careful not to break the window pane.
小心不要打破窗子上的玻璃。

---

paradox [ˈper.ə.dɑːks]

n. 似非而是的論點；自相矛盾的人或事

▶ That is a strange paradox. I don't' know the answer.
那真是很奇怪的矛盾問題，我不知道答案是什麼。

---

parallel [ˈper.ə.lel]

① *adj.* 平行的

實用片語與搭配詞

parallel line 平行線

② *n.* 相似處；平行線；平行面

實用片語與搭配詞

draw a parallel between A and B
B 把 A 和 B 相比較

③ *v.* 與…平行；比較

▶ The tabletop is parallel with the floor.
桌面和地板平行。

▶ These two streets run next to each other in a parallel line.
這兩條街道以平行的方式比鄰著。

▶ There's an incredible parallel between the fashion of the 80's and today!
一九八〇年代和今日流行時尚的相似處，簡直令人難以置信！

▶ The essay draws parallels between the lives of the two german composers.
這篇短文比較了兩位德裔作曲家的生平。

▶ The highway parallels the service road.
那條高速公路和支線道路平行。

---

paralyze [ˈper.əl.aɪz] *v.* 使麻痺；使癱瘓

同 **cripple; disable**

▶ Tommy's right arm was paralyzed after his car accident.
湯米的右手臂在車禍後癱瘓了。

---

parliament [ˈpɑːr.lə.mənt] *n.* 國會；議會

▶ Parliament will vote on the new law this week.
國會本週將針對新法案投票表決。

---

parlor [ˈpɑːr.lɚ] *n.* 客廳

同 **living room**

▶ The family sat together in the parlor.
那家人一起坐在客廳裡。

102 97

participant [pɑːrˈtɪs.ə.pənt]

n. 參加者；參與者

▶ Jenny is a participant in the local singing competition.

珍妮是當地歌唱比賽的參加者。

100

particle [ˈpɑːr.t̬ə.kəl] *n.* 微粒

同 **atom; molecule**

▶ The dust particles in the air often give people allergies.

空氣中的灰塵微粒往往會使人起過敏反應。

---

partly [ˈpɑːrt.li] *adv.* 部份地；不完全地

反 **wholly**

▶ You can only partly see the moon tonight.

你今晚只能看到部分的月亮。

---

103 95

passionate [ˈpæʃ.ən.ət] *adj.* 熱情的；熱烈的

實用片語與搭配詞

passionate support 熱情的支持

▶ Stephanie is very passionate about music.

史蒂芬妮非常熱愛音樂。

▶ The president's campaign received a lot of passionate support.

這場總統候選人造勢活動得到許多熱情的支持。

---

pastime [ˈpæs.taɪm] *n.* 消遣；娛樂

同 **amusement; recreation**

▶ My favorite pastime is watching old movies.

我最喜歡的消遣是看老電影。

---

pastry [ˈpeɪ.stri] *n.* 酥皮糕點

同 **dough**

▶ Let's go to the bakery and buy some pastries.

我們去麵包店買一些糕點吧。

---

patch [pætʃ]

① *n.* 補釘；貼片

② *v.* 修補

同 **mend**

▶ The patch on my raincoat leaks.

我雨衣上的補釘漏水了。

▶ My mom patched up my ripped jeans.

我媽媽把我破了的牛仔褲補起來了。

---

patent [ˈpæt.ənt]

① *n.* 專利（權）

實用片語與搭配詞

obtain a patent for sth. 取得某物的專利

▶ Simon has many patents on his inventions.

賽門為自己的發明申請了很多專利。

▶ James must obtain a patent for his new invention, or someone else might copy it.

詹姆士必須取得他新發明的專利，否則其他人可能會加以抄襲。

② *adj.* 獲得專利的；有專利權的

③ *v.* 取得專利權；給予專利權

▶ The company made a lot of money over its patented product.
這間公司因其享有專利的產品，賺了很多錢。

▶ Patenting something can be a very complicated process.
為某樣東西取得專利可能會是相當複雜的過程。

---

pathetic [pə'θeţ.ɪk] *adj.* 可憐的；可悲的

同 **miserable; pitiful**

▶ Sara saw the pathetic puppy and decided to adopt it.
莎拉看到那隻可憐的小狗，就決定收留牠。

104

patriot ['peɪ.tri.ɑːt] *n.* 愛國者

反 **traitor**

▶ Love and be loyal to your country. Be a patriot!
要盡忠愛國，做個愛國的人！

---

patriotic [ˌpeɪ.tri'ɑː.ţɪk] *adj.* 愛國的

同 **nationalistic**

反 **traitorous**

▶ John loved his country and wrote many patriotic songs.
約翰熱愛他的國家，寫了很多愛國歌曲。

---

patrol [pə'troʊl]

① *n.* 巡邏；巡邏兵、艦隊

實用片語與搭配詞

on patrol 巡邏

② *v.* 巡邏；偵查

▶ The community requested more patrols in the neighborhood.
社區要求在這處街坊派出更多巡邏員。

▶ Every night members of our community go out on patrol to protect our homes against criminals.
我們社區的成員們每晚都會巡邏，以防範罪犯入侵。

▶ Police officers patrol this neighborhood every night.
每天晚上警察都會巡邏這個街坊。

---

patron ['peɪ.trən] *n.* 贊助者；資助人

同 **sponsor; supporter**

▶ Nina is an important patron of the museum.
妮娜是這個博物館的重要贊助人。

---

peacock ['piː.kɑːk] *n.* 孔雀

反 **peahen**

▶ A peacock's feathers are amazingly beautiful.
孔雀的羽毛美得驚人。

P

peasant [ˈpez.ənt] *n.* 農夫

同 **farmer**

▶ The peasant spent hours working in the field.
那名農夫在田裡工作了好幾個小時。

---

peck [pek]

① *v.* 啄食；啄穿

同 **beak**

實用片語與搭配詞

peck at sth. 啄食

② *n.* 啄出的洞；啄

▶ The bird pecked away at the tree for hours.
那隻鳥在樹上啄了好幾個小時。

▶ No wonder she is so slim; she is always pecking at her food and never eats a proper meal.
難怪她這麼瘦；她總是小口小口地吃東西並且從未吃過正常份量的一餐。

▶ The bird gave the tree branch a peck and flew away.
那隻鳥在樹枝上啄了一個洞，然後就飛走了。

---

peddle [ˈped.əl] *v.* 兜售；叫賣

同 **vend**

實用片語與搭配詞

peddle sth. 沿街兜售某物

▶ The merchant peddled his goods to people on the street.
這商人向街上民眾兜售商品。

▶ In the old days vendors would come around to your home to peddle their goods, from tea to cloth.
往日的小販會來到你家附近兜售物品，從茶葉到布料均有販售。

---

peddler [ˈped.lɚ] *n.* 小販

▶ The street peddler tried to sell me a fake Rolex!
街上的小販試圖賣給我一只假勞力士錶！

---

pedestrian [pəˈdes.tri.ən]

① *n.* 行人

同 **walker**

② *adj.* 行人的；步行的

實用片語與搭配詞

pretty pedestrian 相當沉悶的

▶ When you drive, be sure to watch for pedestrians crossing the road.
你開車時，一定要注意過馬路的行人。

▶ To avoid cars, be sure to take the pedestrian bridge when you walk to the store.
為了避開車潮，走路到那家店時務必走行人天橋。

▶ The new edition of the computer game is pretty pedestrian and I got bored easily.
新版的電腦遊戲相當乏味，我很快就感到無聊了。

Exercise 44

I. Derivatives

1. Tourists who wish to take a walk on the streets in this ancient town are advised to bring enough cash, since there are a lot of ___________ (peddle) selling goods and snacks of all kinds.
2. Due to the uprising rate of robbery in this neighborhood, ten shifts of police force are set on ___________ (patrolling) a day.
3. Having devoted many years of hard work and resources on developing the genetic code identification, the scientist filed a ___________ (patented) on it before the releasing date.
4. With the tension between China and South Korea uplifted, many Chinese felt it was their ___________ (patriot) duty to boycott all Korean products.
5. While minor quarrels can be appeased in a relatively short time, serious ones may result in broken relationships that require much longer time for the couples to ___________ (patched) up.

II. Vocabulary Choices

(A) parlor	(B) participant	(C) pastime	(D) patron
(E) paralyzed	(F) pathetic	(G) parliament	(H) particle
(I) peasant	(J) passionate		

1. A strong earthquake struck the coastal area, causing a huge tide wave that surged over the land and ________ the city.
2. The organizer of this contest lay particular emphasis on the outfit and required every ________ to wear formal suits.
3. Though appearing lukewarm and sometimes even indifferent, Mr. Dent is actually a ________ host who always welcomes his friends to visit.
4. Mason was so ________ he always failed to keep his promises to the people around him, gradually ending up alienated by all his friends.
5. Professional photography will require much energy, time, money and devotion, which is why for most people who do not make a living by it, they do it as a ________ .

Unit 45

peek [piːk]

① *v.* 瞄；偷看；窺看

實用片語與搭配詞

peek at sth. 偷瞄某物

② *n.* 瞄；偷偷一看；一瞥

同 **glimpse; peep**

- Can I peek at the seating chart?
  能不能讓我瞄一下座位表？
- Every Christmas we search the house to have a peek at our presents, but Mom hides them too well.
  每年聖誕，我們找遍全家想要偷瞧瞧我們禮物，但是媽媽總是把它們藏得很好。
- Mark took a peek at Lisa's wedding dress.
  馬克瞄了麗莎的新娘禮服一眼。

---

peg [peg]

① *n.* 掛衣鉤；釘；栓

同 **hook; hanger**

② *v.* 用木釘釘牢

實用片語與搭配詞

peg sb. down 迫使表態

- I hung my jacket on the peg.
  我把夾克掛在掛衣鉤上。
- The worker tried to peg the two panels together.
  那名工人試圖把兩塊板子釘在一起。
- John does not like any commitment, so it is almost impossible to peg him down for something serious.
  約翰不喜歡給承諾，所以要迫使他對正經事表態，幾乎是不可能的事情。

penetrate [ˈpen.ə.treɪt] *v.* 刺入；穿過；滲透

實用片語與搭配詞

penetrate into / through sth.

深入穿過某物

- A sharp knife can penetrate through frozen fruit.
  銳利的刀子能刺入冰凍的水果。
- The rain was welcome in this drought, but it was not enough to penetrate deep into the ground.
  久旱逢甘霖，但雨量不夠大到能滲入地底深處。

---

peninsula [pəˈnɪn.sə.lə] *n.* 半島

- Lois spent her vacation on a tropical peninsula with beautiful ocean views on three sides.
  路易絲在一座熱帶半島上渡假，那裡三面環海，擁有優美的海景。

pension [ˈpen.ʃən]

① *n.* 退休金

同 **retirement; fund**

② *v.* 發給退休金

實用片語與搭配詞

pension sb. off
准予 / 迫使某人退休並給退休金

▶ Even though he is retired, Rob still receives a pension every month from his former employer.
雖然羅伯已經退休了，但每個月仍然會收到前雇主所發的退休金。

▶ Lily took the job because she would be pensioned after leaving the company.
麗莉接下這個工作，因為離開公司之後會收到退休金。

▶ The company needed to scale down, so it pensioned off all employees over 50 years.
這間公司必須要縮減員工數量，所以所有年資超過 50 年的員工都被遣散。

perceive [pɚˈsiːv] *v.* 察覺；感知

同 **recognize**

實用片語與搭配詞

perceive sth. as sth.
把某物視為另外一物

▶ I started to perceive the beauty of nature around me.
我開始覺察到周遭的大自然之美。

▶ Most people in western countries perceive crows as bringing bad luck.
大部分的西方人將烏鴉視為帶來厄運的象徵。

---

perception [pɚˈsep.ʃən]

n. 感覺；理解力；覺察

▶ Greg had the perception of a faint smell beginning to fill the room.
葛瑞格感覺有種微弱的味道正開始充滿房間。

---

perch [pɝːtʃ]

① *n.* 棲息處；高處

同 **rest; settle**

② *v.* 棲息；停留在（較高處）

實用片語與搭配詞

perch on sth. （鳥類）棲息在（枝上）；停留，靠坐（人） 在某處

▶ Each bird found their own perch to rest on.
每隻鳥都找到讓自己休息的棲息處。

▶ The eagle perched himself on a tree after a long flight.
長程飛翔之後，那隻老鷹棲息在一棵樹上。

▶ The movie was scary. It had Milly perched on the edge of her seat the whole time.
這部電影很可怕，蜜莉因此全場都坐在座位的邊緣。

---

performer [pɚˈfɔːr.mɚ] *n.* 表演者；執行者

同 **performing; artist**

▶ The performer of the procedure was very experienced.
執行手術的人經驗老道。

peril ['per.əl]

① *n.* 極大的危險

同 **danger**

反 **safety**

實用片語與搭配詞

at sb.'s peril 後果堪慮

② *v.* 使陷入危險；使有危險

- ▶ I saw the peril of crossing the street and turned back.
  我發現跨越那條街很危險，於是就回頭了。
- ▶ If you travel to that war-torn country on your own, you do so at your own peril because it is not safe.
  如果你隻身造訪戰地，你將會身陷危險，因為那很不安全。
- ▶ We were periled the moment we stepped onto the boat.
  我們踏上船的那一刻，就身陷險境了。

perish ['per.ɪʃ] *v.* 毀滅；喪生

同 **decay**

反 **survive**

- ▶ All of our belongings perished in the burning fire.
  我們所有的財產都在熊熊烈火中付之一炬。

permissible [pɚ'mɪs.ə.bəl] *adj.* 可允許的

同 **allowable**

- ▶ Running in the hallway is not permissible.
  在走廊上跑是不允許的。

perseverance [ˌpɝː.sə'vɪr.əns] *n.* 堅持不懈

同 **persistence; insistence**

- ▶ Carrie's perseverance helped her overcome the challenges and reach her goal.
  卡莉的堅持不懈幫助她克服挑戰，達成目標。

persevere [ˌpɝː.sə'vɪr] *v.* 堅持不懈

同 **persist**

實用片語與搭配詞

persevere with sb. 不畏堅難的做某事

- ▶ The basketball team persevered through difficult training, which helped them win many games this year.
  那個籃球隊堅持不懈地通過困難的訓練，訓練幫助他們今年贏得多場比賽。
- ▶ Doctors persevered through the night with Mandy's operation and by morning she was stable.
  醫生們整晚不畏艱辛地為曼蒂進行手術，早上時她的狀況已穩定。

101

persist [pɚ'sɪst] *v.* 堅持不懈；堅持

同 **persevere**

反 **desist**

實用片語與搭配詞

persist in (doing) sth. 執意 / 堅持做某事

- ▶ I will try to persist through my hardships!
  我會堅持不懈地度過難關！
- ▶ If you want to go to an Ivy-league university, you need to persist in studying hard.
  如果你想要進常春藤名校，你必須繼續努力用功。

persistence [pɚˈsɪs.təns] *n.* 堅持

同 **perseverance**

▶ Heather's persistence to get a kitten paid off, and her parents adopted one for her.

希瑟對養隻小貓的堅持終於有了收穫，她爸媽讓她養貓了。

101

persistent [pɚˈsɪs.tənt] *adj.* 堅持的

同 **relentless**

實用片語與搭配詞

extraordinarily / incredibly / extremely persistent

格外地 / 不可思議的固執 / 堅持

▶ Marco's persistent attitude helps him succeed when other people might quit.

馬可堅持不屈的態度幫助他成功，要是其他人可能就會放棄了。

▶ My boss can be extremely persistent in making you do what he wants you to do, even work overtime.

我的老闆格外堅持你照他所說的話做，即使是加班。

---

personal digital assistant (PDA)

[ˈpɝː.sən.əl ˈdɪdʒ.ə.t̬əl əˈsɪs.tənt] *n.* 個人數位助理

▶ Marley's PDA helps her keep track of her appointments.

瑪蕾的個人數位助理幫助她掌握她的約會安排。

---

personnel [ˌpɝː.sənˈel]

n. 職員；全體人員；員工

同 **staff; worker**

▶ She was a personnel of a well-known company.

她是一家知名公司的職員。

---

perspective [pɚˈspek.tɪv]

① *n.* 觀點；角度

同 **viewpoint; standpoint**

② *adj.* 透視的；展望

實用片語與搭配詞

view / put / see sth. in its true / proper perspective

從實際的 / 適當的角度觀察 / 看待某事物

▶ From Tom's perspective, his wife's actions caused their divorce.

在湯姆看來，是他妻子的行為導致了兩人離婚。

▶ This perspective drawing helps us see through the eyes of the artist.

這幅透視畫能讓我們透過畫家的角度來觀看。

▶ It will take some time for you to see the benefits of this new system in the proper perspective, but you will.

你還需要一些時間才能夠以適當的角度看待這個新系統的優點，但你終究會明白的。

---

pessimism [ˈpes.ə.mɪ.zəm]

n. 悲觀（情緒）；悲觀主義

反 **optimism**

▶ His pessimism was causing others to become depressed.

他的悲觀情緒導致其他人也跟著變沮喪了。

P

pesticide [ˈpes.tə.saɪd] *n.* 殺蟲劑

▶ Mom sprayed pesticide on the plants to kill the bugs.
我媽媽在植物上噴殺蟲劑來殺死蟲子。

---

petroleum [pəˈtroʊ.li.əm] *n.* 石油

同 **crude oil; fossil**

▶ Like most vehicles, this car runs on fuel made from petroleum.
這輛車和大多數車種一樣，也是靠石油所萃取出的燃料來運轉。

---

petty [ˈpet̬.i] *adj.* 小的；不重要的

同 **little; insignificant**

反 **great**

▶ The two girls had a petty argument over who would sit in the front seat of the car.
兩個女孩為了誰能坐在車的前座而起了小爭執。

---

pharmacist [ˈfɑːr.mə.sɪst] *n.* 藥劑師

同 **druggist; chemist**

▶ Pharmacists must be careful to give patients the right amount of medicine.
藥劑師必須小心謹慎，開給患者的劑量必須正確。

Exercise 45

I. Derivatives

1. The newly legislated regulation makes it more difficult for one to be ___________ (pension) off unless he/she is quite advanced in years.
2. The key to success lies in intelligence, not so much as ___________ (persevere), and yet most people undervalue the importance of going on despite frustration.
3. The media can be regarded as the sole influential factor that determines people's ___________ (perceive).
4. The doctor indicated that if ___________ (persist) of fever shows, the patient must be sent to the hospital immediately.
5. The editorial in this newspaper offers a brand new ___________ (perspective) on social events independent of political inclinations.

II. Vocabulary Choices

(A) pessimism	(B) performer	(C) penetrate	(D) pesticide
(E) pharmacist	(F) petty	(G) personnel	(H) peninsula
(I) peril	(J) permissible		

1. This chemical, once dispersed into the air on a massive scale, would come back down on earth with the help of rain and ________ the soil, affecting plantation.
2. This path in the mountain is sealed for after the typhoon; it is fraught with ________ since trees were tumbled and scattered everywhere.
3. In Taiwan, the motorcycles have to be examined to ensure the vehicle exhaust emissions are within the ________ level.
4. Due to the writer's miserable childhood, his novels were permeated with a sense of ________ and are thus not advisable for youngsters.
5. Employees in this company often complained about the manager's over-emphasis on ________ details of paper work, such as the margin, layout, or fonts, rather than the content.

Unit 46

98

pharmacy [ˈfɑːr.mə.si] *n.* 藥房

同 **chemist's shop; drugstore**

▶ Gary went to the pharmacy to pick up his medicine.
蓋瑞去藥房拿藥。

---

phase [feɪz]

① *n.* 階段

同 **stage**

實用片語與搭配詞

passing phase 過渡期

② *v.* 分階段實行

實用片語與搭配詞

phase sth. in / out
逐步或分段引進 / 撤出某事物

▶ The country's economic plan is now entering its second phase.
該國的經濟方案現在已經進入第二階段了。

▶ Teenagers usually become very moody during their adolescence. Don't worry. It's a passing phase.
在青春期的青少年情緒通常非常多變。別擔心，這是必經的階段。

▶ The company is phasing the policy changes over the next ten months.
公司將在接下來的十個月內分階段執行政策上的變更。

▶ In trying to modernize, the company phased out old equipment and replaced it with new technology.
這間公司試圖實行現代化，他們逐步淘汰舊的設備並且以新的科技取代。

---

photographic [ˌfoʊ.t̬əˈɡræf.ɪk] *adj.* 攝影的

▶ Photographic equipment is often expensive.
攝影器材相當昂貴。

---

picturesque [ˌpɪk.tʃərˈesk]
adj. 美麗的；風景如畫的

▶ The picturesque sunset was so beautiful that I had to take a photo.
風景如畫的日落景致好美，我一定要拍張照。

---

pier [pɪr] *n.* 碼頭；防波堤

同 **dock; wharf**

▶ Let us go fish by the pier at the beach!
我們一起去海邊那處碼頭旁釣魚吧！

---

pierce [pɪrs] *v.* 刺穿

同 **penetrate; puncture**

▶ Sara pierced her ears yesterday.
莎拉昨天去穿耳洞。

實用片語與搭配詞

pierce through sth. 尖物刺入 / 透某物

▶ The woman's screams pierced through the quiet night, waking up everyone in the house.
那女人的尖叫劃破寂靜，將屋裡的每個人都吵醒了。

---

piety [ˈpaɪə.t̬i] *n.* 虔敬

▶ Piety is an important part of the Catholic priest's daily life.
天主教神父日常生活中重要的一環就是敬虔。

---

pilgrim [ˈpɪl.grɪm] *n.* 朝聖者

▶ We saw a pilgrim walk towards the nearby temple.
我們看到一名朝聖者向附近寺院走過去。

---

pillar [ˈpɪl.ɚ] *n.* 柱子；棟梁

同 **column**

▶ There were four pillars supporting the platform.
舞台有四個柱子支撐。

---

pimple [ˈpɪm.pəl] *n.* 面皰；青春痘

▶ I found a pimple on my face when I looked into the mirror.
我照鏡子時，看到臉上有個面皰。

---

pinch [pɪntʃ]

① *v.* 捏；擰

同 **squeeze; tweak**

▶ He waited for a chance to pinch her on the cheek.
他等待機會好捏她的臉頰。

實用片語與搭配詞

pinch sth. off / out 掐掉某物

▶ Pinch off the buds of the lower branches of the rose bush. The flowers on top will bloom.
將玫瑰花叢下方樹枝上的花苞掐掉。這樣頂部的花朵才能綻放。

② *n.* 捏；擰

▶ The pinch she gave me on my arm caused much pain.
她把我手臂捏得好痛。

實用片語與搭配詞

give sb. a pinch 擰了某人一把

▶ My mother gave my brother a pinch to stop speaking in church, and he started crying very loudly.
我媽媽為了阻止我弟弟在教堂裡講話而擰了他一把，他便開始放聲大哭。

---

pious [ˈpaɪ.əs] *adj.* 虔誠的

同 **devout**

反 **impious**

▶ Maria is a pious nun who works hard to obey God's commands.
瑪麗亞是敬虔的修女，她努力遵守神所定的誡命。

pipeline [ˈpaɪp.laɪn] *n.* 管道；管線

▶ The water pipeline was damaged during the earthquake.
水管在地震中被震壞了。

---

piss [pɪs]

① *v.* 撒尿；小便

實用片語與搭配詞

piss sb. about / around 對某人故意搗亂

② *n.* 小便；尿

▶ The dog pissed on the tree in the park.
那隻狗對著公園裡的樹撒尿。

▶ Amy told her boss to stop pissing her about because she deserved better treatment, so he fired her.
艾咪叫她的老闆停止擾亂她，因為她值得更好的待遇，所以他解雇了她。

▶ Don't step in the piss on the floor of the bathroom.
別踏到浴室地板上的尿。

---

pistol [ˈpɪs.təl]

① *n.* 手槍

同 **firearm; gun**

② *v.* 用手槍射擊

同 **fire; shoot**

▶ This antique pistol is as old as my great grandfather.
這只古董手槍和我曾祖父一樣老。

▶ The marksman skillfully pistoled down his target.
那位神射手嫻熟地用手槍射中了靶。

---

pitcher [ˈpɪtʃ.ɚ] *n.* 投手；水壺

反 **catcher**

▶ The pitcher threw the ball toward the other player.
投手把球投向另一個球員。

---

plague [pleɪg] *n.* 瘟疫

同 **epidemic; pestilence**

▶ It was too difficult to stop the plague from spreading.
要防止瘟疫蔓延實在太困難了。

---

plantation [plænˈteɪ.ʃən] *n.* 農園；大農場

▶ We grow all sorts of crops and trees on our plantation.
我們在自己的農園裡種植了各式各樣的作物和樹木。

---

playwright [ˈpleɪ.raɪt] *n.* 劇作家

同 **dramatist**

▶ Our playwright wrote the entire script for our musical.
我們的劇作家為我們的音樂劇撰寫了整部劇本。

---

plea [pliː] *n.* 請求；懇請；抗辯

同 **appeal; petition**

▶ His plea to the nations was for peace and unity.
他懇請各國維護和平與團結。

plead [pli:d] *v.* 懇求；懇請

實用片語與搭配詞

plead with sb. 懇求某人

▶ My friend tried to plead for a second chance.
我朋友試圖懇求給他第二次機會。

▶ Tom's mother pleaded with his teacher to give him another chance.
湯姆的媽媽懇求他的老師再給他一次機會。

---

pledge [pledʒ]

① *n.* 誓言；保證

同 **guarantee; oath**

② *v.* 發誓；保證

同 **guarantee; promise**

實用片語與搭配詞

pledge sth. to sb. / sth. 承諾把某物給某人

▶ All the students said a pledge at school every morning.
全體學生每天早上都要在學校念一次誓言。

▶ I will pledge allegiance to my home country!
我將宣誓對我的祖國效忠！

▶ When you become president, you pledge your loyalty to your country and its people.
當你當上總統後，你要對你的國家以及人民效忠。

---

plight [plaɪt] *n.* 困境；（困難的）處境

同 **difficulty; troubles**

▶ Josh's family worried about their plight when their business failed.
喬許家的事業垮掉之後，他的家人都很擔心他們所處的困境。

---

plow [plaʊ]

① *n.* 犁

② *v.* 犁；耕

同 **cultivate**

▶ Every farmer will keep a plow in their tool shed.
每個農夫都會在工具間裡放一個犁。

▶ We must plow the soil before planting the seeds.
播種之前，我們必須先犁土。

---

pluck [plʌk]

① *n.* 拔；摘

同 **pick; pull**

實用片語與搭配詞

pluck sth. off / out 拔或摘除某物

② *n.* 拔

▶ It is my job to pluck the weeds from the garden.
我的職責是拔庭園裡的草。

▶ Brian plucked the spider off Jane's shoulder before she noticed because he knew she would go crazy.
布萊恩在珍發現她肩上有蜘蛛前，就先摘除了牠，因為他知道她會抓狂。

▶ She looked different after she gave her eyebrows a pluck.
她修了眉毛後，看起來很不一樣。

Exercise 46

I. Derivatives

1. With the prevalence of smart phones and the built-in photo taking function, most people are not aware of how complicated and difficult professional ___________ (photography) skills are.
2. The religious ___________ (pious) can be observed in this aboriginal tribe, where the people do everything for their God.
3. In summer, the children in kindergarten often chased one another with a water ___________ (pistoling) at hand, soaking everyone in sight.
4. The parents of the hostages appeared on television, ___________ (plea) with the terrorists for the release of their family.
5. The farmers wake up early, get devices and fertilizer prepared, and head for the ___________ (plant) early, starting a day of work.

II. Vocabulary Choices

(A) pilgrims	(B) plight	(C) plow	(D) plague
(E) picturesque	(F) pinch	(G) pious	(H) playwright
(I) pimple	(J) pillar		

1. Jean was such a _________ follower of the faith, sticking to the regulations, preaching to people around her, and never missing her prayers.
2. This region was of a heavy religious orientation, and there used to be many hostels established to house _________ that came from everywhere.
3. For people who lead a peaceful life in advanced countries, the _________ of the refugees from Muslim-majority countries since 2015 seems unimaginable.
4. In history, there is no shortage of examples in which millions of people died of _________ in periods when medication was not well-developed.
5. The scenery in this countryside is _________ ; the photos taken here resemble paintings of wonderlands that exist only in fairytales.

Unit 47

plunge [plʌndʒ]

① *v.* 跳入；投入

同 **throw**

② *n.* 跳入；猛跌

▶ Everybody at the pool party plunged into the pool.
泳池派對的所有參加者都跳入泳池中。

▶ The diver's plunge created a huge splash of water.
那位跳水者跳入水中時，濺起了很多水花。

---

pneumonia [nuːˈmoʊ.njə] *n.* 肺炎

▶ Mel's lungs were damaged after having a severe case of pneumonia.
梅爾罹患嚴重肺炎之後，他的肺嚴重受損了。

---

poach [poʊtʃ] *v.* 水煮；非法偷獵

▶ Chad loves to poach eggs and eat them for breakfast.
查德喜歡水煮蛋，在早餐時吃。

---

poacher [ˈpoʊ.tʃɚ] *n.* 盜獵者

▶ Poachers have killed thousands of elephants in Africa.
盜獵者在非洲殺死了數以千計的大象。

---

pocketbook [ˈpɑː.kɪt.bʊk] *n.* 筆記本

▶ She often keeps a pocketbook inside of her bag.
她常常在包包裡帶一個筆記本。

---

poetic [poʊˈeţ.ɪk] *adj.* 詩的；詩意的

反 **prosaic**

▶ I enjoy reading poetic books when I have free time.
閒暇時，我喜歡讀詩集。

---

poke [poʊk]

① *v.* 戳

實用片語與搭配詞

poke sb. / sth. with sth. 以某物捅／戳某人

② *n.* 戳；刺

▶ My mom often pokes my dad to get his attention.
我媽媽常常戳我爸爸來引起他的注意。

▶ Anna poked her friend in the ribs with her elbow when the handsome boy walked past.
當那個英俊的男孩經過時，安娜用手肘頂了頂她朋友的肋骨。

▶ The poke on my shoulder was quite painful.
我肩膀上被戳的地方真的好痛。

polar [ˈpoʊ.lɚ] *adj.* 南北極的；極地的

實用片語與搭配詞

polar opposites 截然不同；對立的

▶ Some scientists travel to the polar ice caps to do research.
有些科學家遠赴極地冰帽去進行研究。

▶ Tammy and Sam are polar opposites. Tammy likes to attend parties, while Sam prefers to stay at home.
譚美和山姆的個性截然不同，譚美喜歡參加派對，但山姆喜歡待在家裡。

---

pollutant [pəˈluː.t̬ənt] *n.* 污染物

實用片語與搭配詞

emission of pollutants
汙染排放量

▶ The factory released many pollutants into the air, which made people sick.
工廠排放出很多污染物到空氣中，導致民眾生病了。

▶ One cause of global warming is the emission of pollutants like CO2 into the air.
全球暖化的其中一個起因是污染氣體的排放，例如二氧化碳。

---

ponder [ˈpɑːn.dɚ] *v.* 仔細考量；衡量

同 **consider; contemplate**

實用片語與搭配詞

ponder on / over sth.
長時間仔細思考某事物

▶ Charles pondered what goals he should have for the next five years.
查爾斯仔細考量未來五年應該設定哪些目標。

▶ Jane pondered over whether she should move to Canada for many months.
珍為了她是否該搬到加拿大思量了數個月。

---

populate [ˈpɑː.pjə.leɪt] *v.* 居住在…

▶ The government encouraged people to populate the area.
政府鼓勵民眾居住在那個地區。

---

porch [pɔːrtʃ] *n.* 門廊

實用片語與搭配詞

church porch 教堂的門廊

▶ We will sit on the porch as we watch the sunrise.
我們會坐在門廊上欣賞日出。

▶ Before the wedding, the family greeted all the guests in the church porch before they entered.
婚禮開始前，家族成員會在教堂門廊處招呼欲入席的賓客。

posture [ˈpɑːs.tʃɚ]

① *n.* 姿態

同 **bearing; stance**

② *v.* 擺出姿態；故做姿態

▶ Nancy has very good posture and always sits up straight.
南西姿勢很正確，她坐下時背部都很挺直。

▶ The dancer postured on the stage before beginning his performance.
那名舞者在開始表演之前，先在舞台上擺出姿勢。

---

103 99 97 96

potential [poʊˈten.ʃəl]

① *adj.* 潛在的；可能的

同 **possible; probable**

② *n.* 可能性；潛力

同 **possibility; probability**

▶ Her habit of always being late was a potential problem.
她老是遲到的習慣是潛在的問題。

▶ His potential to be a great actor was very clear.
他成為傑出演員的潛力相當明顯可見

---

poultry [ˈpoʊl.tri] *n.* 家禽

▶ That farm specifically raised poultry to produce eggs.
那座農場專門飼養家禽來生產蛋。

---

prairie [ˈprer.i] *n.* 大草原；牧場

實用片語與搭配詞

across the prairie 橫跨大草原

▶ The prairie stretched to the horizon for many miles.
那處大草原一直延伸到地平線，綿延好幾英里。

▶ Many of the first settlers in America built homes across the prairie because of its open space and fertile land.
許多首批美國的定居者看中大草原的開放空間以及肥沃土地，而在其上建造房子。

---

preach [priːtʃ] *v.* 講道；佈道

同 **lecture; sermonize**

實用片語與搭配詞

preach at / to sb. 說教

▶ Every Sunday, our pastor will preach during the service.
每個星期天，我們的牧師都會在主日崇拜中講道。

▶ Do not preach at someone about doing something wrong, when you are doing it yourself.
當你自己五十步笑百步時，不要針對他人做不好之處說教。

---

precaution [prɪˈkɑː.ʃən]

n. 預防；警惕；謹慎

同 **forewarning; notification**

▶ As a precaution, motorcycle riders must wear a helmet.
機車騎士必須頭戴安全帽作為預防措施。

P

104

precede [priː'siːd] *v.* 處在…之前

反 **follow**

▶ There will be a short film preceding the discussion to introduce the topic.
討論之前，會先播放短片來介紹主題。

---

precedent ['pres.ə.dent] *n.* 先例；前例

同 **forerun**

反 **following**

▶ Jessie set a precedent for her siblings after convincing her parents to let her stay up late.
潔西說服爸媽讓她熬夜，為兄弟姊妹開了先例。

---

precision [prə'sɪʒ.ən] *n.* 精準；準確（性）

同 **preciseness**

▶ The artist's precision allows her to create very detailed paintings.
這位畫家的精準度讓她能創造出鉅細靡遺的畫作。

---

predecessor ['pred.ə.ses.ɚ] *n.* 前輩；前任

同 **forerunner**

反 **successor**

▶ Janet's predecessor was very skilled, so she will have to work hard to impress her boss.
珍娜的前任工作技能非常好，所以她必須很努力才能讓老闆刮目相看。

102

prediction [prɪ'dɪk.ʃən] *n.* 預言

同 **anticipation; forecasting**

▶ Tony made a prediction that his team will win the game tomorrow.
東尼預言他的隊伍明天會贏得比賽。

---

preface ['pref.ɪs]

① *n.* 序言

同 **introduction; preliminary**

② *v.* 為…加前言；為…加序言

▶ Christine is currently writing the preface to her new book.
克麗絲汀目前正在撰寫她新書的序言。

▶ The essay was prefaced with a short introduction on the writer's main points.
這篇文章的前言是介紹作者主要論點的簡介。

98

preference ['pref.ər.əns] *n.* 偏好；偏袒

同 **orientation; taste**

▶ I have a preference for water over sugared drinks.
我比較喜歡喝白開水，多過於含糖飲料。

Exercise 47

I. Derivatives

1. Despite the laws and the constant cruises of the police, traces of ___________ (poach) can still be found in this reservation, which means the protected wild animals are still in danger.
2. After the murderer of the child was sentenced to a mere five-year imprisonment, public concern had been widely aroused, fearing that it would set a dangerous ___________ (precede).
3. This region near the mountain, with fertile soil, perfect humidity, and an abundant water supply from nearby creeks, certainly has enormous ___________ (potentially) for agricultural development.
4. The first lesson for those who want to be a drummer is to hold the drumsticks properly so as to prevent accidental risks like ___________ (poke) others in the eye.
5. The coal-fired power stations release several ___________ (pollute) into the air, one of which is sulphur dioxide.

II. Vocabulary Choices

(A) prairies	(B) precaution	(C) poultry	(D) porches
(E) predecessor	(F) predictions	(G) preach	(H) populate
(I) precision	(J) preferences		

1. With the housing price soaring in the city, people began to move out and came to ________ the suburban areas.
2. Having no idea how to avoid different strains of avian influenza, people put on surgical masks as a general ________ .
3. When bird flu gets out of control, the government intervention would be a ban on the ________ market, requesting a temporary halt of the business for check-ups and extermination, if necessary.
4. The latest model of this car, though still a prototype, is faster, steadier, and thus more comfortable for the driver than its ________ .
5. Much like the human fortune-teller, some animals, like the famous octopus, "Paul," are capable of making shockingly precise ________ about the outcome of football games.

Unit 48

prehistoric [ˌpriː.hɪˈstɔːr.ɪk]

adj. 史前的；非常古老的

► That museum holds a collection of prehistoric fossils.
那座博物館收藏了一批史前化石。

prejudice [ˈpredʒ.ə.dɪs]

① *n.* 偏見

同 **bias; preconception**

② *v.* 使抱偏見

實用片語與搭配詞

prejudice against / towards sth. / sb.
對某事物 / 人存有偏見

► The man's prejudice led him to believe he couldn't trust foreigners.
那個人的偏見導致他認為不能相信外國人。

► Newspaper reports of the athlete's bad behavior prejudiced the public against him.
有關那位運動員的偏差行為的新聞報導使得大眾對他抱持偏見了。

► It is difficult for most people to get rid of their prejudice against people who have been in prison.
對大部分的人來說，屏除對更生人的成見並非易事。

preliminary [prɪˈlɪm.ə.ner.i]

① *adj.* 初步的

同 **preceding; prior**

② *n.* 預賽；初步；開端

► The preliminary introductions were made before we began discussing business matters.
在我們開始討論業務議題前，先進行了初步的簡介。

► Kyle won the preliminary and advanced to the final round of the competition.
凱爾贏得了預賽，晉級到比賽的決賽。

premature [ˌpriː.məˈtʊr] *adj.* 過早的

同 **early; hasty**

► The runner made a premature start during the race and had to quit the competition.
那名跑者在賽跑時起跑過早，導致不能繼續比賽。

premier [prɪˈmɪr]

① *n.* 總理；首相

同 **prime minister**

② *adj.* 首要的

► The country's premier will hold talks with neighboring countries next week.
該國總理下週將與鄰國舉行會談。

► Sony's premier engineer is coming for an interview tomorrow.
索尼首要的工程師明天將來面談。

96

prescribe [prɪˈskraɪb]

v. 開藥方；規定；指定

實用片語與搭配詞

prescribe sth. for sb. 為某人開藥方 / 指示

▶ The doctor prescribed drugs for Peter's flu.
醫師為彼得的感冒開了藥方。

▶ The doctor prescribed some medicine for my dad for high blood pressure.
醫生針對我爸爸的高血壓開了一些藥方。

prescription [prɪˈskrɪp.ʃən] *n.* 處方；藥方

同 **medicine**

▶ My doctor gave me a prescription for my viral infection.
我的醫生開了治療我病毒感染的處方。

---

preside [prɪˈzaɪd] *v.* 主持

同 **administer; direct**

實用片語與搭配詞

preside over sth. 掌管 / 領導某事物

▶ John's manager presided over the meeting yesterday.
昨天約翰的經理主持會議。

▶ I was chosen to preside over the award ceremony and to make sure everything was organized well.
我被任命主持頒獎典禮並且確保一切事物都籌劃得當。

---

presidency [ˈprez.ɪ.dən.si]

n. 總統、公司總裁、大學校長或會長等職位

同 **presidential**

▶ During his presidency, many new laws were passed.
在他總統任期內，通過了很多新法案。

---

presidential [ˌprez.ɪˈden.ʃəl] *adj.* 總統的

▶ I can see the presidential mansion from my office.
我從我的辦公室可以看到總統官邸。

---

prestige [presˈtiːʒ] *n.* 聲譽；聲望

同 **status; esteem**

▶ Lisa earned a lot of prestige after winning the marathon.
麗莎在馬拉松賽獲勝之後，贏得了很高的聲譽。

---

presume [prɪˈzuːm] *v.* 以為；假定；推定

同 **suppose**

▶ Theo presumed his wife would be hungry, but he didn't know she ate a snack earlier.
泰歐以為他太太會很餓，但他不知道她之前已經吃了點心。

---

prevail [prɪˈveɪl] *v.* 戰勝；盛行；普遍

同 **succeed; overcome**

▶ We shall prevail over our hardships and obstacles!
我們將能夠戰勝所遭遇的苦難和阻礙！

實用片語與搭配詞

prevail against / over sb. / sth.
戰勝 / 擊敗某人 / 事物

- Humans over the ages have prevailed against harsh environmental changes.
  隨著時間的推移，人類已具備了戰勝環境變遷的能力。

preventive [prɪˈven.t̬ɪv]

① *adj.* 預防的

實用片語與搭配詞

preventive medicine 預防醫學

② *n.* 預防措施

- Sarah took preventive measures to keep cockroaches out of her house.
  莎拉採取了預防措施，讓家裡不會有蟑螂。
- During flu season, it is important to take preventive medicine such as flu shots.
  在流感期間接受預防醫療措施是很重要的，例如施打流感疫苗。
- Vaccines are preventives against many diseases.
  疫苗能預防很多種疾病。

---

preview [ˈpriː.vjuː]

① *n.* 試映；預先看

同 **prevue；trailer**

實用片語與搭配詞

a preview of sth. 舉行某事物的預展 / 演

② *v.* 預先看；試映；預先審查

- He attended a special preview of the new movie.
  他參加了那部新片的特映會。
- The preview of the new movie is very good; I can't wait to see the actual movie.
  新電影的預告很引人入勝；我等不及要看完整的電影了。
- I allowed my friend to preview my work-in-progress.
  我讓我朋友先看看我未完成的作品。

---

prey [preɪ]

① *n.* 被捕食的動物

實用片語與搭配詞

be / fall prey to sth. 被…欺騙

② *v.* 捕食；劫掠

實用片語與搭配詞

prey on sb's mind 煩擾某人

- The cat ran across the room to catch her prey.
  那隻貓跑過房間去捕捉牠的獵物。
- The elderly often fall prey to unscrupulous scammers who want to steal their money.
  老年人時常落入不道德的詐騙人士的圈套，因而被竊取存款。
- The hungry lion preyed on the unsuspecting victim.
  饑腸轆轆的獅子捕食了毫無戒心的受害獵物。
- I was rude to my friend the other day and it has been preying on my mind, so I had to apologize.
  我前幾天對我的朋友很無禮，這件事使我耿耿於懷，所以我必須道歉。

priceless [ˈpraɪs.ləs] *adj.* 無價的；貴重的

同 **invaluable; precious**

▶ The good times I spent with my friends are priceless.
我和朋友所度過的美好時光是無價的。

---

prick [prɪk]

① *v.* 刺；戳

實用片語與搭配詞

prick sth. with sth. 以某物刺（穿）某物

② *n.* 刺；扎；刺痛

▶ She accidentally pricked her hand on the rose thorn.
她不小心被玫瑰刺刺到手。

▶ I pricked the blister on my foot with a needle.
我用一根針刺破了腳上的水泡。

▶ I could not feel the prick on my finger at all!
我根本就感覺不到手指被刺到的地方！

---

prior [praɪr]

① *adj.* 在先的；在前的；優先的

同 **previous**

反 **posterior**

② *adv.* 在前；居先

③ *n.* 小修道院院長

▶ She refused the invitation because she had a prior engagement.
她回絕了邀請，因為她事先已經有其他的約定。

▶ The email came prior to the arrival of the package.
在包裹送來之前就收到了那封電子郵件。

▶ The prior watched over everything in the monastery.
修道院院長負責管理修道院一切大小事。

100

priority [praɪˈɔːr.ə.t̬i]

n. 優先考量的事；優先權

同 **precedence**

▶ It became my priority to do well with my school studies.
把學校課業學好變成我的首要之務。

---

procession [prəˈseʃ.ən] *n.* 隊伍；行列

同 **march; parade**

▶ The parade procession moved in perfect unison.
遊行隊伍整齊劃一地行進。

---

productivity [ˌproʊ.dəkˈtɪv.ə.t̬i] *n.* 生產力

▶ Productivity is an important part of Diane's life, so she measures how much she does each day.
產能是黛安生活中的重要一環，所以她會計算自己每天的工作成果。

實用片語與搭配詞

a level of productivity 一定程度的生產力

- The company's new factory in Mexico reached a level of productivity unparalleled by those in other countries.
  這間在墨西哥的新工廠已達一定程度的生產力，已非其他國家的工廠可比擬。

---

proficiency [prəˈfɪʃənsi] *n.* 熟練；精通

實用片語與搭配詞

a high level of proficiency
高度熟練 / 精通

- Paul maintains his proficiency as a speaker by giving speeches every week.
  保羅透過每週都演講的方式，讓自己持續成為很熟練的講員。
- In order to study at a university in America, you need to have a high level of English proficiency.
  為了在美國念大學，你必須精通英文。

---

profile [ˈproʊ.faɪl]

① *n.* 側面；輪廓

實用片語與搭配詞

low / high profile 低 / 高調

② *v.* 畫側面像；描出…的輪廓

- After studying the man, I went on to draw his profile.
  在端詳研究過那名男子之後，我就接著畫他的側面像。
- The famous athlete likes to keep a low profile, so she does not like to go where people know her.
  這位知名的運動員喜歡保持低調，所以她不喜歡前往有人知曉她的地方。
- I had to profile many different people in my art class.
  在藝術課中，我必須畫出很多人的側面像。

---

profound [prəˈfaʊnd]

adj. 有深度洞察力的；深度的；深刻的

同 **deep**

反 **shallow**

- Everyone regards Albert as a profound thinker and values his ideas.
  大家都視亞伯特為有深度洞察力的思想家，都很重視他的想法。

Exercise 48

I. Derivatives

1. Regulations against sexual ___________ (prejudicial) must be strictly enacted in the student organization so as to bestow them with the concept of gender equality.
2. Though the result of the experiment was promising, it was still in the ___________ (preliminarily) stage, and further examinations were required.
3. With the doctor's ___________ (prescribe), Janet went to the nearby pharmacy to get her medicine for her symptoms.
4. The ___________ (president) is not a fixed position as that of an emperor in ancient times; it can still be removed by the constitutional court.
5. More often than not, some high school students fail to strike a balance between the schoolwork and extracurricular activities not because of impotence but misplaced ___________ .(prior)

II. Vocabulary Choices

(A) profound (B) pricked (C) procession (D) premier
(E) presumed (F) preyed (G) prestige (H) preview
(I) proficiency (J) productivity

1. Since the host did not receive the reply from some of the guests to whom he sent the invitation, he ________ that they were not coming.
2. Due to the wonderful ________ that the company has built over the years, there are tens of thousands of applicants who came to compete for the recent job openings.
3. The candidate of the president was waving to the people from the center of a huge ________ of police force arranged to protect him.
4. The newcomer in this section was highly praised by the director for his extraordinarily high ________ , nearly twice as much as the experienced employees.
5. The wise elders in this village were often sought after for their counsel since they had ________ knowledge and life experience.

Unit 49

101

progressive [prəˈgres.ɪv]

① *adj.* 漸進的；進步的

反 **conservative**

② *n.* 改革派人士；革新主義者

▶ The lion made progressive moves toward its prey.
獅子漸漸走向獵物。

▶ That politician is a progressive and is always trying to pass new policies.
那位從政者是改革派人士，總是想通過新的政策。

---

prohibit [prəˈhɪb.ɪt] *v.* 禁止

同 **ban**

反 **allow**

▶ Cellphone use is prohibited during the performance.
在表演期間禁止使用手機。

---

prohibition [ˌproʊ.ɪˈbɪʃ.ən / ˌproʊ.hɪˈbɪʃ.ən]

n. 禁止

同 **forbiddance**

▶ The mayor announced a prohibition on selling alcohol to people under 18 years old.
市長宣佈禁止販賣酒精類飲品給十八歲以下的人。

---

projection [prəˈdʒek.ʃən] *n.* 投影；投射

▶ Allie put a projection of her design on the conference room's screen.
艾麗把她的設計投影到會議室的螢幕上。

---

prolong [prəˈlɑːŋ] *v.* 延長；拖延

同 **lengthen**

反 **shorten**

▶ Please do not prolong the meeting longer than needed.
請勿不必要地延長這場會議。

---

prone [proʊn]

adj. 趴著的；容易…的；有…傾向的

同 **prostrate**

反 **supine**

▶ Paula is prone to forgetting the appointments she made.
寶拉很容易忘記她之前已經訂好的約定。

---

prop [prɑːp]

① *n.* 支撐物；道具

同 **support**

② *v.* 支撐；架起

同 **brace**

▶ A prop was placed under the chair to keep it from shaking.
椅子下面放了一個支撐物好讓它不至於搖晃。

▶ We need to prop up the table with a wooden plank.
我們需要用木板來撐起桌子。

實用片語與搭配詞

prop sb. / sth. against sth.
使某人 / 物倚靠在某物上

▶ Steve was so tired after the race that he propped himself against the wall because he could not stand up.
史蒂夫在競賽後非常疲累，以致因無法站立而靠在牆上。

---

propaganda [ˌprɑː.pəˈgæn.də] *n.* 宣傳

▶ Leaders try to spread their propaganda by making it a part of people's daily lives.
領袖往往試圖散播他們的宣傳思想，方式是讓這些宣傳成為人民日常生活的一部份。

---

propel [prəˈpel] *v.* 推動

同 **drive; push**

▶ The soccer player propelled the ball along the ground with his foot.
這位足球員用腳推球在地上滾。

---

propeller [prəˈpel.ɚ] *n.* 推進器、螺旋槳

▶ The boat's propeller isn't working, so it can't move forward.
船的螺旋槳故障了，所以無法往前航行。

---

prophet [ˈprɑː.fɪt] *n.* 先知；傳達神旨意的人

同 **oracle; prophesier**

▶ A crowd of people gathered to hear the prophet speak.
群眾聚集起來聆聽先知說話。

---

proportion [prəˈpɔːr.ʃən]

① *n.* 比例

同 **percentage; ratio**

▶ Is this the right proportion of flour for this recipe?
按照這份食譜，這麵粉的比例對嗎？

實用片語與搭配詞

in / out of proportion to sth.
與某物成 / 不成比例

▶ The child drew an out of proportion picture of a dog with a big head and small body.
這孩子畫了一隻不成比例的狗，牠的頭很大但身體很小。

② *v.* 使成比例

▶ I try to proportion my salt and sugar intake every day.
我試著讓自己每天的鹽分和糖分攝取量成比例。

---

prose [proʊz] *n.* 散文

反 **poetry**

▶ Michelle usually writes prose on her website, but sometimes she writes poetry.
米雪通常在自己的網站上寫散文，但有時也會寫詩。

prosecute [ˈprɑː.sə.kjuːt] *v.* 起訴

實用片語與搭配詞

prosecute sb. for sth. / doing sth.
對某人提起公訴

▶ Oliver is being prosecuted for theft.
奧利佛被以竊盜的罪名起訴。

▶ The young man was prosecuted for trying to sell drugs on the university campus.
這位青年因為試圖在校園中販毒而被起訴。

---

prosecution [ˌprɑː.səˈkjuː.ʃən] *n.* 起訴

反 **defense**

▶ During the court prosecution, the witness started to cry.
在法院訴訟的過程中，目擊證人開始哭了起來。

prospect [ˈprɑː.spekt]

① *n.* 可能性；前景

實用片語與搭配詞

a prospect of v-ing
某事的可能性 / 前景 / 情勢

② *v.* 探勘；勘察

實用片語與搭配詞

prospect for sth. 探勘某物

▶ The prospect of him passing the basketball first was high.
他先傳出籃球的可能性相當高。

▶ After working for weeks on this project, there is finally a prospect of finishing it.
這個專案在數週的策劃後，終於有了告一段落的可能性。

▶ Local miners prospected the underground caves for gold.
當地礦工探勘地下洞穴找尋金礦。

▶ Many people moved to California in the 1850s to prospect for gold.
在 1850 年代，許多人為了探勘金礦而遷移至加州。

---

prospective [prəˈspek.tɪv]

adj. 預期的；潛在的

同 **forthcoming; approaching**

▶ The prospective forecast says it will rain tomorrow.
天氣預報表示，明天會下雨。

---

province [ˈprɑː.vɪns] *n.* 省；州

同 **region; state**

▶ There were multiple farming provinces in the country.
那個國家裡有很多務農的省分。

---

provincial [prəˈvɪn.ʃəl]

① *adj.* 省的

② *n.* 鄉下人

▶ The provincial government is working on a solution to the voting issue.
省政府正努力解決投票的問題。

▶ After interviewing 100 people, the reporter felt she understood the provincials living in the area.
那名記者採訪了一百人之後，就覺得已經很了解居住在當地的鄉下人的情況。

provoke [prəˈvoʊk] *v.* 對…挑釁；激怒

實用片語與搭配詞

provoke sb. to do / into doing sth.
刺激 / 激怒某人去做某事

▶ Don't provoke the bear, or it might attack you.
不要激怒那隻熊，不然牠可能會攻擊你。

▶ The naughty boys provoked the teacher to cry.
那些淘氣的男孩們把老師惹哭了。

---

prowl [praʊl]

① *v.* 悄悄遊走（覓食）；徘徊；（為覓食而）潛行

同 **creep**

② *n.* 來回尋覓；潛行

▶ The tiger prowled through the jungle looking for food.
這隻老虎在叢林裡遊走，尋找可吃的食物。

▶ My sister took a prowl through the mall to look for a new dress.
我的姊妹在購物商城來回尋覓，想找一件新洋裝。

---

prune [pruːn]

① *n.* 西梅乾；洋李乾

② *v.* 修剪；修整；刪除

同 **crop; trim**

實用片語與搭配詞

prune sth. out of sth. 從某物剪除某物

▶ I sometimes eat prunes to help my digestive system.
我有時會吃西梅乾來改善消化系統。

▶ My grandfather used to prune the trees in the backyard.
我祖父從前會修剪後院的樹木。

▶ After the mistakes were pruned out of the president's speech, the speech sounded good.
將總統演講稿中的錯誤刪改後，整篇演講聽起來很流暢。

---

publicize [ˈpʌb.lə.saɪz] *v.* 宣傳；公佈

▶ We spread posters all around town to publicize the event.
我們在鎮上各地張貼海報來宣傳那項活動。

---

puff [pʌf]

① *n.* 一縷（煙霧、氣體等）；泡芙

同 **blow**

② *v.* 吹；吸

實用片語與搭配詞

puff out / up sth. 使某物充氣 / 膨脹

▶ A puff of smoke rose from the chimney of my house.
我家煙囪升起了一縷煙。

▶ The children ran around and puffed the bubbles away.
孩子們跑來跑去，把泡泡吹走。

▶ Jimmy puffed out his cheeks to blow a balloon.
吉米鼓起他的雙頰吹著氣球。

pulse [pʌls]

① *n.* 脈搏

同 **beat**

② *v.* 搏動；跳動

實用片語與搭配詞

pulse through sb.'s vein 使某人熱血沸騰

▶ I checked for my pulse during my health check-up.

我在健康檢查期間，檢查了自己的脈搏。

▶ My hand was pulsing with pain after jamming it against the wall.

我的手被緊壓在牆上後，就隨著脈搏陣陣抽痛。

▶ My friend, Paul, is not afraid of anything and I sometimes think he has steel pulsing through his veins.

我朋友保羅天不怕地不怕，而我有時覺得他沸騰的血液中彷彿有鋼鐵一般。

Exercise 49

I. Derivatives

1. With the newly enacted law, there is a complete ____________ (prohibit) of smoking cigarettes within buildings, enclosures, or some public places.
2. As the hero in the movie fell from the plane, the audience let out a sigh of horror only to find him clinging to the ____________ (propel) of the plane - a sight of great relief.
3. The security guards who failed to recognize the robbers in disguise and thus let out the information of the vault were likely to be held liable to ____________ (prosecute).
4. With the new route of MRT currently under construction, it is expected that ____________ (prospect) customers of the real estate will be on the increase.
5. A lot of young professionals in this big city were from ____________ (province) towns, and as they were employed in urban areas, they moved there.

II. Vocabulary Choices

(A) provoked	(B) prospect	(C) projection	(D) prolonged
(E) propaganda	(F) prone	(G) prophet	(H) prop
(I) progressive	(J) publicized		

1. Linguistic competence is accumulated in a _________ way; there is no instant access to a great command of language capabilities.
2. Japan is an island country, and it is _________ to tsunamis following earthquakes that occur as a result of the tectonic movements
3. With a firm resolution to win the election, the candidate devoted a lot of resources on _________ and campaigns aimed to increase his exposure.
4. The new president of the United States is of a bold personality, and there is little _________ of him being modest in dealing with other countries.
5. The neighbor's dog was quite submissive mostly, but it was _________ one day by some kids throwing stones at it.

Unit 50

punctual [ˈpʌŋk.tʃu.əl] *adj.* 準時的

同 **exact; precise**

▶ Gustav is very punctual and arrives exactly when he says he will.
葛斯塔夫非常準時，說幾點到就會準時抵達。

103

purchase [ˈpɝː.tʃəs]

① *v.* 購買

實用片語與搭配詞

purchase sth. for sb. with sth.
以某物為某人購買某物

② *n.* 購買之物；購買

同 **buy**

反 **sell**

▶ I would like to purchase some clothes at the market.
我想到市場買衣服。

▶ Melanie purchased a new house for her family with the money she inherited from her grandmother.
梅蘭妮用她祖母遺留給她的財產買了一棟新房子給她的家人。

▶ The purchase I made from the app store was worth it.
我在應用程式商店買的東西相當值回票價。

---

purify [ˈpjʊr.ə.faɪ] *v.* 使純淨；淨化

實用片語與搭配詞

purify sth. 淨化某物

▶ You should purify the water before you drink it.
你在喝那水之前，應該先淨化它。

▶ Scientists have found a way to purify salt water and it could solve the world's water problems.
科學家們找到淨化鹽水的方式，如此便能解決世界上的水資源問題。

---

purity [ˈpjʊr.ə.t̬i] *n.* 純淨

反 **impurity**

▶ Sandy is proud of the purity of the oils she sells.
珊蒂對她販售的油的純淨度感到相當自豪。

---

pyramid [ˈpɪr.ə.mɪd] *n.* 角錐；金字塔

▶ She created a pyramid by using some plastic cups.
她用幾個塑膠杯製作了一個角錐形。

---

quack [kwæk]

① *n.* 鴨叫聲；嘎嘎聲

② *v.* （鴨子）呱呱叫；嘎嘎叫

▶ We heard a quack coming from the far side of the lake.
我們聽到湖對岸傳來了鴨叫聲。

▶ The ducks were quacking as they went out to the pond.
那些鴨子去池塘的路上一直呱呱叫。

qualification [ˌkwɑː.lə.fəˈkeɪ.ʃən]

n. 取得資格；資格

▶ Qualification for the chess competition is very challenging.
取得參加西洋棋競賽的資格，難度相當高。

98

qualify [ˈkwɑː.lə.faɪ] *v.* 取得資格；使合格

實用片語與搭配詞

qualify sb. for / as sth.
使某人具有某種資格

▶ His college degree will qualify him to be an engineer.
他的大學學位將會讓他取得工程師的資格。

▶ In order to qualify as a teacher, you need to study four years and get a teaching license.
為了得到教師資格，你需要研讀四年並且考取教師執照。

---

quarrelsome [ˈkwɔːr.əl.səm] *adj.* 愛爭吵的

同 **argumentative**

▶ The quarrelsome man argued with everyone he met.
那個愛爭吵的男子遇到任何人都會和對方吵起來。

---

quart [kwɔːrt] *n.* 夸脫（容量）

▶ I am carrying three quarts of water inside my bag.
我袋子裡帶了三夸脫的水。

---

quench [kwentʃ] *v.* 熄滅；壓制；平息；解（渴）

同 **extinguish; put out**

▶ The firefighter quenched the flames with water.
消防員用水熄滅了火焰。

---

query [ˈkwɪr.i]

① *n.* 詢問

同 **ask; inquire**

② *v.* 詢問

實用片語與搭配詞

query sb. about sth. 向某人提出問題

▶ Dave hopes his manager will answer his query by the end of the week.
大偉希望他的經理能在本週末之前回答他的問題。

▶ Cindy queried why her sister needed to borrow money.
辛蒂詢問她姐姐想借錢的理由。

▶ The police queried the man about his whereabouts on the night of the crime.
警方質問男子在案發前晚的行蹤。

---

quest [kwest] *n.* 尋求；探索；追求

▶ My quest to meet Oscar Owl in person is almost over.
我想親眼見到貓頭鷹奧斯卡的探索之旅幾乎快要結束了。

實用片語與搭配詞

a quest for sth. 尋求 / 尋找某物

▶ After working on their project all night, the college students went on a quest for pizza.
在連夜趕工完成專題後，這些大學生們外出找披薩吃。

---

questionnaire [ˌkwes.tʃəˈner] *n.* 問卷

實用片語與搭配詞

design / draw up questionnaire
設計問卷

▶ Please fill out the questionnaire, so we can better understand the needs of the community.
請填完這份問卷，好讓我們更加了解社區的需求。

▶ The researcher drew up a questionnaire on study habits and distributed it among the students to complete.
研究人員設計了一份關於讀書習慣的問卷並且發放給學生們填寫。

---

quiver [ˈkwɪv.ɚ]

① *v.* 抖動；顫抖
同 **shake; shiver**

② *n.* 顫抖；抖動；顫聲

▶ The line of clothes hanging outside quivered in the wind.
掛在外面的那排衣服在風中抖動著。

▶ Jamie felt a quiver of fear as she walked through the dark forest.
傑咪穿越陰暗的森林時，發現自己因為害怕而顫抖。

---

racism [ˈreɪ.sɪ.zəm] *n.* 種族主義

同 **discrimination; racialism**

▶ Tiffany refused to let racism prevent her from achieving her dreams.
蒂凡妮拒絕任由種族主義阻礙她完成夢想。

---

rack [ræk]

① *n.* 架子
同 **framework; shelf**

② *v.* 使痛苦；折磨；摧毀

實用片語與搭配詞

be racked by guilt / remorse / doubt
深受內疚 / 悔恨 / 懷疑之苦

▶ You can leave your shoes on the rack by the door.
你可以把鞋子放在門邊的架子上。

▶ My body was racked with pain after running the long marathon.
跑完長程馬拉松之後，我全身都很痛。

▶ Benjamin was racked by guilt following the car accident in which his friend got hurt.
班傑明的朋友在車禍中受傷，這使他深受內疚之苦。

radiant [ˈreɪ.di.ənt]

① *adj.* 光芒四射的；發光的；發熱的

同 **luminous**

反 **dim**

② *n.* 發光（或發熱）物

▶ Tom was attracted to Susie because of her radiant smile.
湯姆深受蘇西燦爛的微笑所吸引。

▶ Don't touch the radiant on the heater or you might get burned.
別碰電暖氣的發熱體，否則你會被燙傷。

radiate [ˈreɪ.di.eɪt]

① *v.* 散發；流露出

實用片語與搭配詞

radiate confidence 散發自信

② *adj.* 輻射狀的；有輻射線的

同 **diversify**

▶ The camera's flash radiated the light around the room.
相機的閃光燈散發出光芒照亮了室內。

▶ My sister got the job after an interview in which she radiated confidence about her abilities.
我妹妹卓越的能力使她在面試中散發自信，因此馬上被雇用了。

▶ This flower has beautiful, radiate petals.
這朵花有排成輻射狀的美麗花瓣。

---

radiation [ˌreɪ.diˈeɪ.ʃən]

n. 散發（光或熱）；輻射

▶ Did you hear the news about the nuclear plant's radiation leak?
你有沒有聽到核能廠輻射外漏的新聞？

---

radiator [ˈreɪ.di.eɪ.t̬ɚ] *n.* 暖氣裝置

▶ Ben's dorm room is heated with an old metal radiator.
班的宿舍房間有老舊的金屬電暖器來保暖。

R

---

radical [ˈræd.ɪ.kəl]

① *adj.* 根本的；激進的

同 **extreme**

反 **conservative**

② *n.* 激進份子；基礎；基本原理

▶ Radical differences between the children were obvious. Their basic personalities were different.
兩個孩子間的差異相當明顯，他們基本的個性不同。

▶ The students were labeled as radicals after they tried to overthrow the government.
那些學生試圖推翻政府之後，被貼上了激進份子的標籤。

---

radish [ˈræd.ɪʃ] *n.* 櫻桃蘿蔔；小蘿蔔

▶ I like to cook radishes and put them in my soup.
我喜歡煮櫻桃蘿蔔，然後把它們放進湯裡。

radius [ˈreɪ.di.əs] *n.* 半徑；半徑範圍

▶ The radius of that circle is measured to be very large.

測量出那個圓圈的半徑很大。

Exercise 50

I. Derivatives

1. One important rite that different religions throughout the world share in common is to ____________ (pure) one's mind, freeing it of evil thoughts.
2. One ____________ (qualify) that is particularly emphasized in applying for this work in this section is the applicant's former working experience.
3. Visitors to this museum, when they finished viewing the exhibition, were politely requested to fill out a ____________ (question) for the organizers' reference.
4. Many veterans who retired from World War II suffered ____________ (radiate) sickness that resulted from the atomic bombs back at that time.
5. The protest went out of control, turning into such a desperate situation that ____________ (radicalness) measures had to be taken in order to suppress the violence.

II. Vocabulary Choices

(A) radiant	(B) punctual	(C) purchase	(D) pyramid
(E) quarrelsome	(F) qualify	(G) quench	(H) quiver
(I) query	(J) racism		

1. Being _________ for the appointment no matter whom the meeting is arranged with is one essential manner that respects others' schedule.
2. The veterans think that simply because they've worked here for so long, their experiences _________ them to boss us around.
3. The doctor has the obligation to tell the patients what's wrong with their bodies, and thus if you have any questions, don't forget to make a _________ .
4. The heartbroken boy let out a _________ smile when he heard that his ex-girlfriend would come back to him.
5. Even in an age that stresses zero-discrimination against people from different races, _________ can still be heard from different corners in this society.

Unit 51

raft [ræft]

① *n.* 木筏

② *v.* 用筏子運送

實用片語與搭配詞

raft sb. across / over a river
把某人運過河

▶ Christy built a raft out of wood and used it to float down the river.
克莉絲蒂用木材建造了一艘木筏，而且用它來順河而下。

▶ Let's go rafting on the river this weekend.
週末我們去乘筏遊河吧。

▶ The typhoon destroyed the bridge, so villagers had to be rafted across the river to safety.
颱風摧毀了橋樑，因此村民們必須乘筏子渡河以求安全。

---

ragged [ˈræg.ɪd] *adj.* 破舊的；邋遢的

▶ We'll buy some new shirts to replace your ragged ones.
我們會買幾件新襯衫來替換你那些破舊的襯衫。

---

raid [reɪd]

① *n.* 突擊

同 **assault; attack**

② *v.* 突擊

實用片語與搭配詞

a raid on sb. / sth. 對某人 / 事物突襲

▶ The military conducted a raid on the enemy camp.
軍方對敵人的營地發動了突襲。

▶ Police officers raided the house to search for drugs.
警察突擊檢查那棟房子，以便搜尋毒品。

▶ Police carried out a raid on the newspaper offices to try and find the source of their information.
警方突襲了報社辦公室，試圖找尋資訊的來源。

---

rail [reɪl] *n.* 欄杆；扶手；鐵軌

同 **bar; handrail**

▶ The rails of the iron fence separated the two areas.
鐵圍籬的欄杆區隔了兩個區域。

---

rally [ˈræl.i]

① *n.* 集會；群眾大會

同 **meeting; gathering**

② *v.* 集合；召集

▶ Everyone is excited to go to the rally at school!
大家都對參加學校的集會感到興奮不已！

▶ It is the student leader's job to rally the class together.
集合全班同學是班長的責任。

實用片語與搭配詞

rally around sb. / sth. 集結在某人 / 物邊

▶ Fans rallied around the basketball team after they lost the game because of an unfair referee.
這支球隊因為不公的仲裁而輸掉比賽後，球迷們便集結在球隊四周。

---

ranch [ræntʃ]

① *n.* 大牧場；大農場

同 **cattle farm**

② *v.* 經營牧場；在牧場工作

▶ You will normally see lots of farm animals at a ranch.
你通常會在大牧場看到很多家畜。

▶ I grew up ranching in the countryside with my family.
我是和家人在鄉下經營牧場長大的。

---

random [ˈræn.dəm] *adj.* 隨機的；任意的

同 **casual**

反 **deliberate**

▶ Stephen likes to make random decisions, so we never know what or why he will do something.
史蒂芬喜歡隨機做決定，所以我們永遠都不知道他要做什麼或為何這樣做。

---

ransom [ˈræn.səm]

① *n.* 贖金

同 **redeem**

② *v.* 贖回

實用片語與搭配詞

hold sb. for / to ransom
綁架某人以要求贖金

▶ The kidnappers demanded a ransom of one million dollars.
綁匪要求百萬贖金。

▶ The officers ransomed the prisoner by paying the criminals.
官員付錢給那些歹徒而贖回被囚禁的人。

▶ The gang held the wealthy man's son for ransom until the police found the boy.
歹徒綁架這位富有男士的兒子以要求贖金，直到警方尋獲男孩才告終。

---

rascal [ˈræs.kəl] *n.* 流氓；無賴

同 **rogue; mischief**

▶ A little rascal started pulling at my jacket for no reason.
有個小流氓毫無緣由就開始扯我的夾克。

---

rash [ræʃ]

① *n.* 疹子

② *adj.* 輕率的

同 **impetuous**

反 **calculating**

▶ Joana got a rash after using her new makeup.
喬安娜用了新的化妝品之後長疹子了。

▶ Darren made the rash decision to propose to a woman on their first date.
達倫輕率地在第一次約會就向一名女子求婚。

ratio [ˈreɪ.ʃi.oʊ] *n.* 比例；比率

同 **percentage; proportion**

▶ In the cooking class, what's the ratio of girls to boys?
在烹飪課中，男孩和女孩的比例是多少？

---

rational [ˈræʃ.ən.əl] *adj.* 理性的

同 **logical**

反 **absurd**

▶ After much discussion, the group made a rational decision to solve the problem.
那群人討論了很久之後，就理性地決定要解決問題。

---

rattle [ˈræt̬.əl]

① *v.* 發出嘎嘎聲；喋喋不休地說

實用片語與搭配詞

rattle along / off / past sth.
沿著某物移動並發出雜音

② *n.* 嘎嘎聲；喋喋不休

同 **clatter**

▶ Here, rattle these two sticks together and see if you can scare the dog away.
來，把這兩根棍子互敲發出嘎嘎聲，看看這樣能不能把那條狗嚇跑。

▶ The old car rattled along on the gravel road and we were not sure if we would ever reach our destination.
這輛老車在石子路上沿路發出嘎嘎的聲響，我們不確定能否抵達目的地。

▶ How can anyone sleep with all that rattle coming from the neighbor's house?
隔壁鄰居家一直發出嘎嘎的吵雜聲，怎麼可能有人能睡著？

---

ravage [ˈræv.ɪdʒ]

① *v.* 毀壞

同 **damage**

反 **preserve**

② *n.* 劫掠；毀壞

實用片語與搭配詞

ravage of sth. 某事物造成的破壞

▶ The typhoon ravaged the coastal towns.
颱風肆虐毀壞了濱海的城鎮。

▶ After the ravage of several homes in her neighborhood, Sophie bought a home alarm system.
蘇菲家附近幾戶人家被洗劫之後，她就買了居家警報系統。

▶ The ancient buildings have withstood the ravages of war and have been restored to their former glory.
這些古老建築抵擋了戰爭的摧殘，在被修復後重現往日的風采。

---

realism [ˈriː.ə.lɪ.zəm]

n. 務實作風；現實（作風）；寫實主義

同 **pragmatism**

▶ Donald uses realism to run his life, so his decisions are very practical.
唐諾以務實作風來過生活，所以他的決定都很實際。

realization [ˌriː.ə.ləˈzeɪ.ʃən]

n. 意識到；明白；理解到

▶ Suzy was struck by the realization that she forgot her keys.
蘇西突然意識到她忘記帶鎖匙了。

---

realm [relm] *n.* 領域；王國

同 **domain; province**

▶ Ladies and gentlemen, in tonight's drama, we take you to the realm of the unknown!
各位女士和先生，我們在今晚的戲劇中，將引領大家進入未知的領域！

---

reap [riːp] *v.* 收穫；收割（莊稼）

同 **gain**

反 **sow**

▶ You know what they say, "You reap what you sow."
你一定有聽過這句俗話：「怎麼種，就怎麼收」。

---

rear [rɪr]

① *n.* 後面；背後

同 **back**

反 **front**

② *adj.* 後面的；後方的

▶ I like going to this restaurant because there's always plenty of parking in the rear.
我很喜歡上這家餐廳，因為後面總是有很多停車位。

▶ Sorry, you can't go out through the front, but the rear door is unlocked.
很抱歉，你不能從前門出去，但後門沒鎖可以走。

98

rebellion [rɪˈbel.i.ən] *n.* 叛亂；反叛

反 **support**

▶ The rebellion against the government lasted several years.
反政府的叛亂行徑持續了好幾年。

98

recession [rɪˈseʃ.ən] *n.* 經濟衰退

同 **recess**

▶ The country is still in recession.
國家仍處於經濟衰退中。

---

recipient [rɪˈsɪp.i.ənt]

① *n.* 領受者；接受者

同 **receiver**

② *adj.* 接受的

▶ All of the award recipients smiled during the ceremony.
所有獎項的領獎人在典禮期間都面露微笑。

▶ Carl had a recipient role at the party and accepted gifts to be given to the host later.
卡爾在派對中負責接受禮物，以便之後再交給派對主人。

R

reckless [ˈrek.ləs] *adj.* 魯莽的；不顧後果的

同 **careless; impetuous**

反 **careful**

▶ Driving while texting is a reckless thing to do.
開車時傳簡訊是很魯莽的行為。

---

reckon [ˈrek.ən] *v.* 認為；覺得

實用片語與搭配詞

reckon with sb / sth
面對解決（棘手的事）；應付（有權力的人）

▶ Look at all the dark clouds rolling in. I reckon we're going to get some rain.
看看那席捲而來的烏雲，我認為快要下雨了。

▶ If you hit him, you'll have to reckon with his older brother.
你若是打他，你將要面對的是他的哥哥。

recommend [ˌrek.əˈmend] *v.* 推薦；建議

實用片語與搭配詞

recommend sb. for / as sth.
向某人推薦某人 / 事物擔任某職務

▶ If you're not sure of what to eat, I can recommend something.
如果你不確定該吃什麼，我可以給你一點建議。

▶ The company needed a builder, so I recommended a friend of mine for the job.
這間公司需要一位建築商，因此我將這份工作推薦給我的一位朋友。

Exercise 51

I. Derivatives

1. With ample evidence at hand, the police got the warrant to search the property of the business, and without delay they ____________ (raid) the mansion.
2. In 2009, Typhoon Morakot caused catastrophic floods throughout southern Taiwan, ____________ (ravage) Siaolin Village and claiming a great number of villagers' lives.
3. The reputation and future of this long-standing company were ____________ (reckless) sacrificed to satisfy the immoderate desire of the newly appointed chief executive officer.
4. Our neighbor's dog was not used to staying quietly in captivity and was therefore put into a cage, which he ____________ (rattle) so hard to show his irritation.
5. Despite Miranda's age, she's still a force to be ____________ (reckon) with in the fashion field and is worshiped by a big crowd of young people of the same profession.

II. Vocabulary Choices

(A) radiator	(B) rational	(C) rascal	(D) realm
(E) realization	(F) ravaged	(G) recession	(H) recommended
(I) reckless	(J) random		

1. After a thorough investigation into the bombing attack, the police concluded that it was a _________ act of violence rather than a pre-planned one.
2. Judging from the fact that you got fired the other day and that today your beloved girl decided to leave, I don't think you can make _________ decisions at this moment.
3. After the strong earthquake, a tsunami surged over to the village along the shore, and the buildings, streets, anything you could see were all _________ by the tidal waves.
4. After so many years of hard work, Jean could finally witness the _________ of her dream, becoming the boss of her own enterprise.
5. During the _________ after the war, which consumed too much social resource, many small businesses couldn't survive the poor economy and went bankrupt.

Unit 52

recommendation [ˌrek.ə.menˈdeɪ.ʃən]
n. 推薦
同 **suggestion; advice**

▶ Can you give me a recommendation for a good Italian restaurant?
你可以推薦我一家不錯的義大利餐廳嗎？

---

reconcile [ˈrek.ən.saɪl] 調解；使和好

實用片語與搭配詞
reconcile sb. with sb. 使人重新和好

▶ The parents worked to reconcile their arguing children and restore peace.
那對父母努力調解爭執的孩子，讓他們恢復和睦。

▶ After 40 years of not talking to one another, my sister was finally reconciled with my father.
我姐姐與我爸爸 40 年未曾交談，但她終於跟他重新和好了。

---

recreational [rek.riˌeɪ.ʃən.əl]
娛樂的；消遣的

▶ Anna enjoys recreational running, but she doesn't like to compete in races.
安娜喜歡以跑步作為消遣活動，但她不喜歡參加賽跑。

recruit [rɪˈkruːt]
① *n.* 新兵；新手
同 **enlist; enroll**
② *v.* 徵募

實用片語與搭配詞
recruit to sth. from sth.
從某處招募新人 / 兵至某處

▶ The new army recruits endured harsh training.
陸軍招募到的新兵撐過了嚴酷的訓練。

▶ The navy is trying to recruit new members.
海軍正試圖招募新成員。

▶ Forty police officers were recruited to the new child-care unit from different units over the country.
四十位警員自全國各地不同的單位被招募至新成立的兒童照管單位。

---

recur [rɪˈkɝː] *v.* 重現；再發生
同 **repeat; reappear**

▶ The pain in her leg recurred after running.
她跑步之後，腳又開始痛了。

---

redundant [rɪˈdʌn.dənt] *adj.* 多餘的
同 **excess; extra**

▶ His comments were redundant and added nothing to the discussion.
他的意見相當多餘，對討論無濟於事。

reef [riːf] *n.* 礁；沙洲

▶ The pollution in the water is slowly killing the colorful reef.
水污染正緩緩破壞彩色的礁石。

---

reel [rɪəl]

① *n.* 捲軸

同 **roll**

② *v.* 捲；旋轉

實用片語與搭配詞

reel sth. in / out 在卷軸 / 盤上纏繞某物

▶ I need to get a new reel. This one is broken.
我需要新的捲軸，這個已經壞掉了。

▶ That's a huge fish! Hurry and reel it in!
釣到大魚了！快捲線把牠拉過來！

▶ The clerk knew he had convinced the customer; he just needed to reel her in for the final sale.
那位店員明白自己已說服了顧客；他只需要使顧客慢慢上鉤，最後掏錢購買。

---

referee [ˌref.əˈriː]

① *n.* （籃球，足球）裁判員

同 **judge**

② *v.* 為…擔任裁判；調停

▶ The referee's terrible call allowed the other team to win the game.
那位裁判可怕的判決，讓另一隊贏得比賽。

▶ Since Mr. Wylie is sick, who's going to referee our game?
既然韋利先生生病了，誰會來擔任我們比賽的裁判？

---

refine [rɪˈfaɪn] *v.* 使優美；使變優雅；精煉

▶ Jacob's job is to refine gold to its purest state.
傑克伯的工作是把金子精煉到純淨的狀態。

---

refinement [rɪˈfaɪn.mənt]

n. 精煉；改善；精巧

反 **vulgarity**

▶ Refinement of the metal is a long and difficult process.
精煉金屬是漫長又困難的過程。

---

reflective [rɪˈflek.tɪv] *adj.* 反映的；反射的

同 **thoughtful**

▶ The reflective image in the mirror made Carmen look taller than she really was.
鏡子裡反映出的影像，讓卡門看起來比本人更高。

---

refreshment [rɪˈfreʃ.mənt] *n.* 茶點

▶ Refreshments will be served outside after the ceremony.
典禮之後將在外面供應茶點。

104

refuge [ˈref.juːdʒ] *n.* 收容所；避難處

同 **shelter; sanctuary**

▶ Jane volunteers every Saturday morning at the animal refuge.
珍每個星期六早上都會到動物收容中心擔任義工。

---

refund [ˈriː.fʌnd]

① *v.* 退還

實用片語與搭配詞

refund sth. to sb.

退還所收的錢 / 保證金給某人

② *n.* 退還

同 **pay back; reimburse**

▶ The store refunded the customer's money.
那家店退還了顧客付的錢。

▶ Most online stores will refund money to their customers if they are not happy with a product.
顧客若對商品不滿意，大部分的線上購物商店都能提供退費服務。

▶ Your tax refund will be sent by mail next month.
你將會在下個月收到郵寄的退稅。

---

refute [rɪˈfjuːt] *v.* 駁斥；反駁

同 **dispute**

▶ I found an old picture that helped me refute what Simon said was true.
我找到了一張老照片，有助於讓我用來駁斥賽門口中自稱的事實。

---

regardless [rɪˈɡɑːrd.ləs]

① *adj.* 不管；不注意的；不關心的

同 **despite**

② *adv.* 不管怎樣；無論如何

同 **notwithstanding**

▶ Regardless of the warnings, Mike decided to hike up the snowy mountain.
麥克不顧警告，逕自決定攀登下雪的高山。

▶ Employees must complete their work regardless of how long it takes.
員工必須完成自己的任務，無論要花多久的時間。

---

regime [reɪˈʒiːm] *n.* 政權

同 **authorities**

▶ The regime did not allow its citizens to vote.
那個政權不讓人民享有投票權。

---

rehearsal [rəˈhɝː.səl] *n.* 排練

▶ Rehearsal for the play will be for three hours every Saturday.
那齣戲每週六都會排練三小時。

---

rehearse [rəˈhɝːs] *v.* 排練

同 **practice**

▶ Elizabeth rehearsed her speech in front of the mirror.
伊莉莎白在鏡子前面為演講做排練。

reign [reɪn]

① *v.* 統治；支配

同 **rule**

② *n.* 在位期間；統治

▶ The king reigned for forty years.
那位國王統治了四十年之久。

▶ The king's reign was marked by peace and prosperity.
那位國王在位期間以和平與繁榮著稱。

---

rein [reɪn]

① *n.* 韁繩

實用片語與搭配詞

draw in the rein 收緊韁繩

② *v.* （用韁繩）勒住

▶ Jack used the reins to tell his horse to slow down.
傑克用韁繩來指示馬把速度放慢。

▶ My parents used to be flexible, but after I got arrested at a party, they decided to draw in the reins.
我父母以前在管教上給我很大的空間，但當我在派對上被逮捕後，他們便決定對我嚴加管束。

▶ Joey reined in his horse before he lost control.
喬伊在他的馬失控前，就先勒住那匹馬。

95

reinforce [ˌriːɪnˈfɔːrs] *v.* 增強；加強

同 **intensify; strengthen**

▶ Her faith was reinforced after witnessing a miracle.
她親眼見證神蹟之後，她的信心增強了。

---

rejoice [rɪˈdʒɔɪs] *v.* 高興；欣喜

實用片語與搭配詞

rejoice at / over sth. 為某事物而感到高興

▶ Sarah rejoiced after she found out she passed her exams.
莎拉發現自己通過考試後，高興得不得了。

▶ Jonathan rejoiced over winning the writing competition and the large amount of prize money.
喬納森因為贏得了寫作比賽且獲得鉅額獎金而感到欣喜。

---

relay [ˈriːˌleɪ] *n.* 輪班；接替（的人或動物）

▶ Sam decided that his employees should work in relays in order to finish the huge project on time.
山姆決定讓員工輪班工作，以便及時完成那個大型專案。

relay [ˌrɪˈleɪ / ˈriːˌleɪ] *v.* 轉告；傳達

實用片語與搭配詞

relay sth. to sb. / sth.
收到某訊息並傳給某人／物

▶ The secretary relayed the message to her coworker.
秘書把訊息轉告同事。

▶ I heard the news and relayed it to my colleagues.
我將聽到的消息傳達給同事。

R

Exercise 52

I. Derivatives

1. At a time when the tension between the two nations obviously kept growing, even young teenage males were ____________ (recruit) into the army.
2. Due to the fact that the race was not a pre-planned one and no professional judge was invited, the players had to ask one senior veteran to ____________ (refereeing) the match.
3. The crude oil cannot be used as the fuel for vehicles; it has to undergo the process of ____________ (refine) before it can be put to use.
4. The actors and actresses of the recently-composed drama complained that they got the script so late that they didn't have sufficient time for ____________ (rehearse).
5. Joyce's poor memory could only afford the names of the famous rulers in history, such as Queen Victoria, but as to where she ____________ (reign) over or when, she had no clear idea.

II. Vocabulary Choices

(A) reconciled	(B) regime	(C) recreational	(D) rejoice
(E) recur	(F) refute	(G) reinforced	(H) redundant
(I) relay	(J) refunded		

1. Students often fill their writings with _________ words, like the latter part of this sentence, "Jay was an estranged father whose wife did not live with him," which bears the same meaning with the adjective, "estranged."
2. This famous director successfully instilled the theme of his movie, hope, into the audience's minds by making it _________ many times throughout the whole plot.
3. Having been oppressed for so many years, the people waged a war of revolutionary to overthrow the _________ .
4. The opposing teams in a debate were racking their brains trying to spot any weaknesses in the process in order to successfully _________ the arguments.
5. The security of the whole building was further _________ by adding many monitors after the robbery.

Unit 53

relevant [ˈrel.ə.vənt] *adj.* 相關的；切題的

同 **connected**

反 **inappropriate**

▶ This book is relevant to Jim's research. He should read it.

這本書和吉姆的研究相關。他應該讀一讀。

---

reliance [rɪˈlaɪ.əns] *v.* 依賴；信賴；信任

同 **trust**

▶ Macy's reliance on her parents is understandable since she is still a student.

梅希對父母的依賴不難理解，因為她還是個學生。

---

relic [ˈrel.ɪk] *n.* 遺物；遺風

同 **remnant**

▶ Check out this relic I found in grandma's cellar. Do you think it's worth anything?

看看我從祖母的地窖裡找到的遺物，你覺得它是否值錢？

---

relish [ˈrel.ɪʃ]

① *n.* 津津有味；樂趣

同 **enjoy**

反 **loathe**

實用片語與搭配詞

have a relish for sth. 對某物有興緻

② *v.* 享受；喜歡

▶ Olivia spoke with relish about her fun trip to Europe.

奧莉維雅津津有味地說著她快樂的歐洲之旅。

▶ My best friend has a relish for watching horror movies and she always makes me go along.

我摯友的樂趣之一是看恐怖電影，而她總是愛找我陪她一起看。

▶ Amy and Frank relished every minute of their honeymoon.

艾美和法蘭克享受著他們蜜月旅行的每分每秒。

---

remainder [rɪˈmeɪn.dɚ] *n.* 剩餘物

▶ The remainder of the food should be put in the fridge rather than the garbage.

剩下的食物應該放到冰箱裡，而非扔到垃圾桶。

---

reminder [rɪˈmaɪn.dɚ]

n. 提醒者；令人回憶的東西

同 **prompt**

▶ The expensive necklace was a reminder of just how much Jack loved his wife.

那條昂貴的項鍊代表了傑克深愛妻子的回憶。

removal [rɪˈmuːvəl] *n.* 除去；遷移

同 **elimination**

▶ Garbage removal is done once a week in many places.
很多地區都是每週倒一次垃圾。

---

renaissance [ˈren.ə.sɑːns] *n.* （文藝）復興

▶ The promotional event provided a renaissance for the artist's work.
行銷推廣活動讓那位藝術家的作品再度興起一波熱潮。

---

render [ˈren.dɚ] *v.* 給予；表達；使成為

同 **give**

實用片語與搭配詞

render sth. to / for sth. 提供某物

▶ Sally rendered her opinion on which shoes she liked more.
針對她比較喜歡哪雙鞋，莎莉已經給了意見。

▶ They rendered assistence to the typhoon victims.
他們提供援助給颱風的受災戶。

---

renowned [rɪˈnaʊnd] *adj.* 著名的

同 **famous; notable**

▶ This renowned scientist will present his research at the conference.
這位知名的科學家將在會議中發表他的研究。

---

rental [ˈren.t̬əl] *n.* 租金

同 **payment; fee**

▶ The monthly rental for this apartment is a good price.
這棟公寓每個月的租金相當划算。

---

repay [rɪˈpeɪ] *v.* 報答；償還

實用片語與搭配詞

repay sth. to sb. 付還錢 / 償還某物

▶ You've been so helpful. How can I ever repay you?
你幫了很大的忙，我該怎樣才能報答你呢？

▶ My friend stood by my side during a crisis; I don't think I can ever repay the debt I to her.
我的朋友一路陪我度過危機；我覺得我永遠無法報答她的恩情。

---

repress [rɪˈpres] *v.* 抑制；壓抑

實用片語與搭配詞

repress sb.'s feeling 壓抑某人的情感

▶ Josh repressed a laugh, even though he found the conversation funny.
喬許抑制住想笑的衝動，即使他覺得當時的談話真的很好笑。

▶ It is not healthy to repress your feelings, especially when you are angry; it can lead to depression.
壓抑你的情感是不健康的，尤其是你感到憤怒的時候；如此可能會導致憂鬱症。

reproduce [ˌriː.prəˈduːs]

v. 繁殖；生殖；複製

▶ In the movie, dinosaurs were reproduced in a laboratory and then placed in a park.
在那部片中，恐龍是在實驗室裡被繁殖出來，然後被送到公園裡。

---

reptile [ˈrep.taɪl]

① *n.* 爬蟲類

② *adj.* 爬行（動物）的；卑下的

▶ The snake is a reptile. It is not a mammal.
蛇是爬蟲類，不是哺乳類。

▶ Eve's husband bought her a reptile purse in Thailand.
伊芙的先生在泰國買了一個爬蟲動物的皮做的皮包給她。

---

republican [rəˈpʌb.lɪ.kən]

① *adj.* 共和政體的；共和國的

② *n.* 擁護共和政體者

▶ The U.S. has a republican form of government.
美國採用共和政體。

▶ My grandfather, like most of his family, is a typical, conservative republican.
我祖父就和他大多數家人一樣，也是典型保守的共和黨人。

---

resemblance [rɪˈzem.bləns] *n.* 相似

同 **sameness; similarity**

▶ There is little resemblance between the girls, even though they are sisters.
那些女孩之間沒有什麼相似處，即使她們是姊妹。

---

resent [rɪˈzent] *v.* 生氣；憎恨

反 **submit**

▶ Jane resented her sister's good looks.
珍痛恨她姊妹的漂亮臉蛋。

---

resentment [rɪˈzent.mənt] *n.* 氣憤；憎恨

同 **anger; bitterness**

▶ Sandy has a lot of resentment because her boss overlooked her for the promotion.
珊蒂因為老闆決定升遷人選時忽略了她，而感到忿忿不平。

---

reservoir [ˈrez.ɚ.vwɑːr] *n.* 水庫

▶ The water in the reservoir is quite low. Hopefully it will rain soon.
水庫裡的水位很低，希望很快就能下雨。

R

reside [rɪˈzaɪd] *v.* 居住；住在

實用片語與搭配詞

reside in / at 定居於某處

▶ Lori moved. She now resides on East Lake Avenue.

羅莉搬家了，她現在住在東湖大道。

▶ Herman's family has resided at this address for more than 100 years, but the house is still beautiful.

赫爾曼的家族定居在此處已超過百年，但是他們的房子依然美麗如初。

residence [ˈrez.ə.dəns] *n.* 住宅；定居

▶ Robert worked as a butler at the Lowry residence for almost twenty years.

羅伯在羅瑞家當管家近二十年了。

---

resident [ˈrez.ə.dənt]

① *n.* 居民

② *adj.* 定居的；住校的

反 **migratory**

▶ State residents get a discount if they go to a state university.

本州居民如果就讀州立大學可以有折扣的減免。

▶ Hi everyone, please say hello to Susan, our new resident nurse.

嗨，大家請向蘇珊打個招呼，她是新來的住院護士。

---

residential [ˌrez.əˈden.ʃəl]

adj. 居住的；住宅的

▶ This is considered a residential area because the majority of buildings are houses.

這裡被視為住宅區，因為大多數建築都是住宅。

resistant [rɪˈzɪs.tənt] *adj.* 抵抗的

同 **immune**

▶ Clothing that is resistant to stains is great for children who play outside.

能夠抗污漬的衣服非常適合常在戶外玩的孩子。

Exercise 53

I. Derivatives

1. As an adventurous type of person, Judy always ___________ (relish) challenges rather than boring routine, whether in her career or private life.
2. For the new immigrants, if they want to have a work permit in the local community, they must satisfy the ___________ (resident) qualifications, one of which is to live there longer than six months.
3. This miserable girl harbored a deep ___________ (resent) toward her foster parents, who had been abusing her since adoption.
4. As people nowadays seek fashion and uniqueness, there seems to be a trend of keeping ___________ (reptilian) as pets, such as lizards.
5. After Gareth satisfied all the requirements to legally become an immigrant citizen with nationality, he took up ___________ (reside) in Japan.

II. Vocabulary Choices

(A) renders	(B) remainder	(C) repaid	(D) republican
(E) relevant	(F) resemblance	(G) relic	(H) resistant
(I) renowned	(J) repressed		

1. The lawyer for the defense interrupted the witness, for what he said was not objective and thus not ________ to the case.
2. Our trip to Japan was mostly fantastic, with the first day traveling in rain, but the ________ of the trip was basking in radiant sunshine.
3. The rapid development of smart phones often ________ a new one obsolete within less than an year, and consumers have to keep emptying their pocket to keep up with the trend.
4. The pyramids in Egypt are ________ for its magnificent scale, view, and its unsolved mystery of how the construction was carried out.
5. It's not difficult to tell that these four boys are brothers since they bear a clear family ________ in their appearances; they all look alike.

Unit 54

resolute [ˈrez.ə.luːt] *adj.* 堅決的

同 **determined**

反 **irresolute**

▸ They made a resolute decision to sell the house, so they will be moving soon.
他們堅決想賣掉房子，所以很快就會搬家了。

resort [rɪˈzɔːrt]

① *n.* 度假中心；名勝；訴諸

② *v.* 訴諸；憑藉

實用片語與搭配詞

resort to sth. 訴諸某事物

▸ The newly married couple went to a beach resort for their honeymoon.
那對新婚夫妻去一處海灘度假村度蜜月。

▸ When the thief didn't get what he wanted, he resorted to violence.
那名竊賊沒有得逞時，就訴諸暴力。

▸ Resorting to violence if you do not get what you want is the worst thing you can do.
當你無法得到想要的事物時，訴諸暴力是最差勁的作法。

respective [rɪˈspek.tɪv] *adj.* 各別的；各自的

同 **individual; particular**

▸ While they aren't interested in the same things, they are successful in their respective fields.
雖然他們感興趣的事物不同，但倒是都在自己各別的領域相當有成就。

restoration [ˌres.təˈreɪ.ʃən] *n.* 修復；恢復

同 **refurbishment; renovation**

▸ Restoration of the painting will take several years.
修復那幅畫作要花好多年的時間。

restrain [rɪˈstreɪn] *v.* 抑制；約束

實用片語與搭配詞

restrain sb. / sth. 抑制 / 遏制某人 / 事物

▸ When anyone comes over to the house, it's a little difficult to restrain my dog Jingle.
任何人來到我家時，我都不大能約束好我的狗金格。

▸ Police had to restrain the drunk man who was fighting and kicking wildly.
警方必須遏制那位酒醉後便亂打亂踢的男人。

restraint [rɪˈstreɪnt] *n.* 約束；抑制；克制

反 **incitement**

▸ The parents' restraint of their son prevented him from eating too many cookies.
父母對兒子的約束促使他不再吃過多餅乾。

resume [rɪˈzuːm] *v.* 重新開始；繼續

同 **continue**

實用片語與搭配詞

resume sb.'s work 重新繼續工作

▶ OK everyone, let's resume this meeting tomorrow morning.
大家注意，明天早上再繼續開會。

▶ The author passed away before he finished his book, but his son will resume his work.
那位作者尚未完成他的著作便辭世了，然而他的兒子會繼續執筆完成。

resume [ˈrez.ə.meɪ] *n.* 履歷表

▶ Before you look for a new job, be sure to update your resume.
你找新工作之前，一定要先更新履歷。

retail [ˈriː.teɪl]

① *n.* 零售

反 **wholesale**

② *adj.* 零售的

③ *adv.* 以零售方式

④ *v.* 零售

實用片語與搭配詞

retail sth. at / for sth. 以某價格零售某物

▶ Sharon has worked in retail for several years, so she is used to working with people.
雪倫從事零售業多年，所以很習慣和人打交道。

▶ This retail store has a great selection of designer jewelry.
這家零售店有著琳琅滿目的設計師名牌珠寶。

▶ Buying retail is an expensive way to shop.
用零售價來購買物品是相當花錢的購物方式。

▶ Retailing custom jewelry online has been a great way for Susie to make money.
在網路上零售訂製珠寶是蘇西賺錢的絕佳方式。

▶ The new flying cars will be retailed at US$ 1 million, so you better start saving.
新型飛行車的零售價格將會是一百萬美金，所以你最好開始存錢了。

retaliate [rɪˈtæl.i.eɪt] *v.* 報復

實用片語與搭配詞

retaliate against sb. / sth.
對某人 / 事物採取某報復行動

▶ After hearing Gina's hurtful comments, Heather retaliated by insulting her.
聽到吉娜傷人的評語時，希瑟就以辱罵來報復她。

▶ The Bible teaches us not to retaliate against those who have hurt us.
聖經教導我們不要報復那些傷害我們的人。

retort [rɪˈtɔːrt]

① *n.* 反擊；回嘴

② *v.* 反擊；報復；反駁

同 **retaliate**

▶ I thought Paul's retort to Jane's question was a little rude.
我覺得，保羅反駁珍的問題的態度有點粗魯。

▶ I knew Paul would be upset, but I never expected such a sharp retort.
我知道保羅會生氣，只是從沒想到他居然會那麼嚴詞反駁。

retrieve [rɪˈtriːv] *v.* 找出；取回；重新得到

實用片語與搭配詞

retrieve sth. from sb. / sth. 從某人 / 事物那取回某物

▶ I need to retrieve my scarf from the closet.
我需要從衣櫃裡找出我的圍巾。

▶ Many years after the ship sank, divers managed to retrieve crates of gold coins from it.
在沉船多年後，潛水伕們試著在船骸中找回裝著金幣的板條箱。

---

revelation [ˌrev.əˈleɪ.ʃən] *n.* 揭露；啟示

同 **disclosure; revealing**

▶ During the weekly meeting, Tasha made the revelation of her plans to get a new job.
在每週的會議中，塔莎透露她計畫找個新工作。

---

revenue [ˈrev.ə.nuː] *n.* 歲收；收入；營收

同 **earnings; income**

▶ The government's revenue increased this year due to a new trade agreement.
因為那個新的貿易協定，使得政府今年的歲收增加了。

---

reverse [rɪˈvɝːs]

① *v.* 使反向；扭轉；顛倒

同 **revert**

② *adj.* 顛倒的

③ *n.* 反向；倒轉

實用片語與搭配詞

the reverse of sth. 與預期的相反

▶ As a nation, we need to reverse spending and focus more on saving.
我們國家應該反向削減支出，並且更著重於儲蓄。

▶ That looks reversed. Let's turn it this way and see how it looks.
那個看起來顛倒了，我們來把它轉向這邊，再看看那樣的話看起來如何。

▶ Hurry! Put the car in reverse and let's get out of here!
快點！倒車好讓我們離開這裡吧！

▶ If you are kind to others, others will be kind to you, but the reverse of this is also true.
如果你對他人和善，他人就會對你和善，但反之亦然。

revival [rɪˈvaɪ.vəl] *n.* 恢復意識；復興；甦醒

同 **renewal; restoration**

▶ The girl's revival occurred quickly after she fainted.
女孩昏倒之後，很快就又恢復意識了。

revive [rɪˈvaɪv] *v.* 恢復精力；甦醒

實用片語與搭配詞

revive old practices / fashion
恢復舊做法 / 流行

▶ That early morning swim really revived me.
晨泳真的能讓我恢復精力。

▶ To preserve their culture, local people have started to revive old practices such as weaving.
為了保存他們的文化，當地居民已經開始復興其古老的習俗，例如編織。

---

revolt [rɪˈvoʊlt]

① *v.* 起義；反叛

實用片語與搭配詞

revolt against sb. / sth.
反抗 / 使某人憎惡某人 / 事物

② *n.* 反叛；起義

同 **rebellion**

反 **obey**

▶ The citizens revolted after the king raised taxes.
國王增稅之後，民眾憤而起義。

▶ The poor people revolted against their government for not helping them enough.
窮人們因為政府沒有積極協助他們而起身反抗。

▶ There was a small revolt when mom made us do housework on a sunny day.
媽媽強迫我們在陽光普照的晴天裡做家庭作業，而引發我們小小的反叛。

---

revolve [rɪˈvɑːlv] *v.* 旋轉；自轉

實用片語與搭配詞

revolve around / round sth.
以某物為軸繞行

▶ The planets revolve around the sun.
那些行星都繞著太陽轉。

▶ Petro thinks the world revolves around her and she gets angry when things don't go her way.
珮卓非常自我中心，當事情不合她的意時便發怒。

---

rhetoric [ˈret̬.ɚ.ɪk] *n.* 善於言辭；雄辯；修辭

同 **oratory**

▶ The lawyer is famous for his rhetoric and being able to convince a judge just by speaking.
這位律師以巧言雄辯著稱，光是靠說話就足以說服法官。

---

rhinoceros / rhino [raɪˈnɑː.sɚ.əs / ˈraɪ.noʊ]

n. 犀牛

▶ Look at the cute little rhino! I wonder where its mother is?
看看那隻可愛的小犀牛！不知道牠的媽媽在哪裡？

rhythmic [ˈrɪð.mɪk] *adj.* 有節奏的

▶ Jake likes to tap rhythmic beats on the table with his pencil.
捷克喜歡用鉛筆有節奏地在桌子上敲。

---

rib [rɪb] *n.* 肋骨

▶ That basketball game was pretty violent. Linda broke one of her ribs!
那場籃球賽相當暴力，導致琳達一根肋骨斷裂！

---

ridge [rɪdʒ]

① *n.* 屋脊；山脊

② *v.* 作壟；使成脊狀

▶ You'll find there's a beautiful view at the top of that ridge.
你可以在那山脊的頂端看到優美的風景。

▶ Let's ridge the garden with these bricks.
我們用這些磚頭在庭園裡作壟吧。

ridicule [ˈrɪd.ə.kjuːl]

① *n.* 嘲笑

反 **respect**

② *v.* 嘲笑

同 **jeer; mock**

實用片語與搭配詞

an object / target of / for ridicule
被嘲弄的對象

▶ The professor received a lot of ridicule when people found out his research results were false.
當人們發現那個教授的研究結果是假造的時候，他就被大大地嘲笑。

▶ Don't ridicule people for minor mistakes.
不要因為小錯誤就嘲笑別人。

▶ The woman became an object of ridicule at work after she colored her hair orange.
那位女人染了橘色頭髮以後，她在公司便成為被嘲弄的對象。

---

ridiculous [rɪˈdɪk.jə.ləs] *adj.* 荒唐的；可笑的

同 **absurd; foolish**

▶ You want me to loan you a million dollars? That's a ridiculous idea!
你想向我借一百萬美元？那個主意實在太荒唐了！

Exercise 54

I. Derivatives

1. In recent years, with the promotion of fine arts from the government and a few enterprises whose CEOs like classical music, there seems to have been a ___________ (revive) of public interest in ancient music.
2. To many experts in education in the Western countries, the Asian culture of sending children to cram schools since early age at the sacrifice of family quality time is in every way ___________ (ridicule).
3. The boss of the chain suit store provided a few job openings to those applicants who had had experience in ___________ (retail) in the hopes of increasing each chain's business.
4. Facing the greatest recession in a decade, the ambitious manager refused to give in and strove with the hope to ___________ (reverse) the decline in the company's business.
5. Finding herself unable to respond to her brother's quick wit of kind-natured irony toward her new relationship, Mary could only ___________ (retorted), "Shut it, will you?"

II. Vocabulary Choices

(A) retrieve	(B) restrained	(C) revelation	(D) revived
(E) revolted	(F) retailed	(G) rhetoric	(H) restoration
(I) rhythmic	(J) retaliated		

1. After the typhoon devastated the island and brought much dirt into the dam, the first task for the government following the disaster was the ________ of clean water supplies.
2. As the demonstration went out of control, the crowds started to throw stones at the police, who ________ by firing Lachrymatory Bomb, which emitted tear gas.
3. Nowadays many people stored files on the cloud drive, and ________ the files whenever necessary, without having to carry heavy USB-drives.
4. In Taiwan, there is still room for democracy to improve since most campaign ________ before the election fails to be realized by the politicians.
5. Having been under oppression for many years, the people finally ________ against the regime and established their own government.

Unit 55

rifle [ˈraɪ.fəl]

① *n.* 來福槍；步槍

② *v.* 匆忙地翻找；用步槍射擊

同 **ransack; search through**

▶ As the bear approached, Dave raised his rifle and took aim.
那隻熊靠近時，大偉舉起來福槍，瞄準牠。

▶ The thief rifled through my stuff, but, thankfully didn't take anything valuable.
小偷匆忙地翻找了我的東西，幸虧沒有帶走任何貴重物品。

---

rigid [ˈrɪdʒ.ɪd] *adj.* 嚴格的；堅固的

同 **unbending**

反 **pliable**

▶ The teacher has rigid rules for writing research papers.
老師針對撰寫研究報告設定了嚴格的規定。

---

rigorous [ˈrɪg.ɚ.əs]

adj. 嚴謹的；縝密的；嚴格的

同 **rigid; strict**

▶ Scientists are conducting a rigorous study of the disease to learn everything they can.
科學家正在進行嚴謹的研究，希望能了解有關那種疾病的一切。

---

rim [rɪm]

① *n.* 邊緣

同 **border; edge**

② *v.* 裝邊於…

同 **fringe; margin**

▶ The rim of this glass is dirty. Please get me another one.
這個玻璃杯邊緣很髒，請幫我換一個。

▶ OK everyone, next we rim the cake with chocolate stars, like this.
大家聽好，接下來我們把巧克力星星裝飾在蛋糕的邊緣，就像這樣。

---

riot [ˈraɪ.ət]

① *n.* 暴亂

實用片語與搭配詞

run riot 發生暴動

② *v.* 群眾鬧事；暴動

同 **uprising**

反 **peace**

▶ Several people were injured during the riot. Police were called to stop further damage.
在暴動中有幾個人受傷了。警方被召來阻止進一步的破壞。

▶ After the dictator died, people ran riot for a few weeks.
當獨裁者去世後，民眾發起長達數週的暴動。

▶ People were rioting in the streets and destroyed several shops.
人們在街上鬧事，破壞了幾家商店。

rip [rɪp]

① *v.* 撕；扯

實用片語與搭配詞

rip sb. off 騙 / 偷走某人的錢財

② *n.* 裂口；破洞

▶ Could you please rip me off a piece of paper? I need to spit my gum out.

你可不可以幫我撕下一張紙？我吐口香糖要用的。

▶ It is easy to get ripped off by sellers at the market if you don't know the prices on the items.

如果你不清楚商品的實際價格，便很容易被市場小販敲竹槓。

▶ Oh no! There's a rip in my pants!

糟了！我褲子有裂口！

---

ripple [ˈrɪp.əl]

① *n.* 漣漪；波浪

② *v.* 起漣漪；輕輕盪漾

▶ Look how calm the lake is. There's hardly a ripple.

看看那座湖，幾乎平靜無波。

▶ Uncle Joe's rude comment quickly rippled through the family gathering.

喬叔叔粗魯無禮的評語，迅速在家庭聚會裡掀起波瀾。

---

rite [raɪt] *n.* 儀式

實用片語與搭配詞

marriage / funeral rites 婚葬儀式

▶ The pastor explained the rite of baptism to the new Christians.

牧師向剛信主不久的基督徒解釋洗禮的儀式。

▶ Different cultures have different marriage and funeral rites and you should know them so you don't offend locals.

不同的文化有不同的婚喪儀式，你要熟知禮節，才不會冒犯當地人。

---

ritual [ˈrɪtʃ.u.əl]

① *n.* 儀式

同 **ceremony**

② *adj.* 儀式的

同 **ceremonial**

▶ The couple decided to follow the wedding ritual of exchanging rings during the ceremony.

那對未婚夫妻決定在典禮過程中遵循交換戒指的婚禮儀式。

▶ The priest wore his ritual garments during the ceremony.

神父在典禮當中穿著儀式用的服裝。

98

rival [ˈraɪ.vəl]

① *n.* 對手

同 **opponent**

▶ Josh has few rivals on the basketball court.

喬許在籃球場上少有敵手。

② *v.* 可以媲美；和…不相上下

▶ Wow! Honey, this chocolate cake recipe rivals my mom's recipe!
哇！親愛的，這個巧克力蛋糕的食譜可以媲美我媽媽的了！

---

rivalry [ˈraɪ.vəl.ri] *n.* 相互較勁；對抗；競爭

同 **competition**

▶ There was a clear rivalry between the teams during the championship game.
在冠軍賽中，兩個隊伍之間的相互較勁明顯可見。

---

roam [roʊm] *v.* 遊蕩；漫步；散步

實用片語與搭配詞

roam through sth. 漫步於某處

▶ Please don't let your dog roam around in the streets.
請不要放任你的狗在街頭遊蕩。

▶ When I have nothing to do, I love to roam through the streets and watch people.
當我沒事做的時候，我喜歡在街道上漫步並觀察路人。

---

robin [ˈrɑː.bɪn] *n.* 知更鳥

▶ When you see the season's first robin, you know spring has finally arrived.
當你第一次看到這個季節的知更鳥時，就曉得春天終於來臨了。

---

robust [roʊˈbʌst] *adj.* 強健的

同 **vigorous**

反 **weak**

▶ One brother is skinny while the other is robust.
那兩兄弟的其中一人骨瘦如柴，另一人則相當強健。

---

rod [rɑːd] *n.* 竿子；棒子

同 **bar; pole**

▶ Do you really believe that you can use a wooden rod to detect water?
你真的相信你能用一根木竿偵測到水源？

---

rotate [ˈroʊ.teɪt] *v.* 旋轉；轉動

同 **spin; revolve**

▶ Please rotate your chairs to face the back of the room.
請旋轉你的椅子，好讓它朝向房間的後方。

---

rotation [roʊˈteɪ.ʃən] *n.* 旋轉；轉動

同 **revolving**

▶ One rotation of the earth takes 24 hours.
地球旋轉一周要花二十四個小時。

---

royalty [ˈrɔɪ.əl.ţi] *n.* 王室

▶ This golden crown was worn by royalty several hundred years ago.
這頂金皇冠是好幾百年前的王室人員所戴的。

rubbish [ˈrʌb.ɪʃ] *n.* 垃圾；廢物

同 **garbage; junk**

▶ Don't forget to take the rubbish on your way out the door.
別忘了出去時順便把垃圾帶走。

---

ruby [ˈruː.bi]

① *n.* 紅寶石

同 **garnet**

② *adj.* 紅寶石色的

▶ Lucy bought a ring that has a beautiful, red ruby in the center.
露西買了一個戒指，中央鑲有美麗的紅寶石。

▶ That ruby dress would look great on you. Red is definitely your color.
那件紅寶石色的洋裝你穿一定很好看。紅色絕對是適合你的顏色。

---

rugged [ˈrʌg.ɪd] *adj.* 高低不平的；粗糙的

同 **rocky; rough**

▶ This road looks very rugged and hard to travel on.
這條路看起來相當崎嶇難行。

---

rumble [ˈrʌm.bəl]

① *v.* 發出低沈的連續聲響；隆隆作響

同 **roar; growl**

② *n.* 隆隆聲；低沈的連續聲響

▶ Mom, my stomach is rumbling. When's dinner?
媽，我肚子在咕咕叫了，什麼時候才能吃晚餐啊？

▶ Did you hear that rumble? Was it thunder?
你有沒有聽到隆隆聲？是打雷嗎？

101

rustle [rʌsəl]

① *v.* 發出窸窣聲；沙沙作響

實用片語與搭配詞

rustle sth. up 倉促準備 / 提供某些東西

② *n.* 窸窣聲；沙沙聲

同 **crackle; crunch**

▶ Could you please not rustle the newspaper so much when you read it?
可不可以請你在看報時，不要發出那麼大的沙沙聲？

▶ Lucia was not prepared for her dinner guests, but she rustled up a feast in no time.
露西亞並未預期要接待晚餐的賓客，但她在匆忙中馬上做了一桌好菜。

▶ The dogs created a huge rustle last night when the thief broke into the house.
昨晚竊賊闖入家中時，那些狗發出很大的窸窣聲。

---

sacred [ˈseɪ.krɪd] *adj.* 神的；神聖的

同 **holy**

反 **profane**

▶ OK, kids, this is a sacred burial site, so please don't shout or run around.
孩子們注意，這是一處神聖的墓地，所以請不要大聲喊叫或跑來跑去。

saddle [ˈsæd.əl]

① *n.* 馬鞍

② *v.* 裝馬鞍；使負擔

實用片語與搭配詞

saddle sb. with sth. 讓某人承擔困難的責任

▶ This old Mongolian saddle once belonged to Genghis Khan.

這個年代久遠的蒙古馬鞍曾一度為成吉思汗所擁有。

▶ OK everyone, saddle up your horses. We'll be heading out in fifteen minutes.

大家聽好，請為馬裝上馬鞍，我們十五分鐘內就會出發。

▶ It is unfair to ignore your responsibilities and saddle someone else up with them.

逃避責任並且連累他人是非常不公平的。

Exercise 55

I. Derivatives

1. Since the job openings were quite attractive with a salary twice the average amount, serious ____________ (rival) could be perceived among applicants.
2. Usually the earth completes 365 ____________ (rotate) about its axis in a year, but for a leap year, it is 366.
3. Though Thomas could ride on the horse without a ____________ (saddled), he equipped his horse with one for better maneuvering.
4. My mom's daily life pattern is not predictable, while my dad always reads newspaper and drinks coffee as his morning ____________ (rite).
5. Inner city ____________ (rioting) erupted as an old lady selling tea-leaves was gunned down by the vicious policemen.

II. Vocabulary Choices

(A) rustled	(B) roam	(C) rugged	(D) rumble
(E) robust	(F) sacred	(G) rigorous	(H) rubbish
(I) royalty	(J) ripped		

1. As a company with good reputation, the I-Nei Co. puts top priority on the food safety and adopted _________ examining methods on processing.
2. After the bar closed, the unemployed man was kicked out, and he could only _________ the streets, not knowing where he should go.
3. As a hiker who traversed a lot on rough paths, Josh always bought _________ boots that could stand the wear and last longer.
4. In a heavy mood, the vagrant got on a bus heading out the city, and the sound made by the bus seemed to _________ all the way, adding to his sorrow.
5. "Moses quickly removed his sandals because he was standing on the _________ ground of God."

Unit 56

safeguard [ˈseɪf.ɡɑːrd]

① *n.* 保護；防衛

同 **precaution; shield**

② *v.* 保護；防衛

實用片語與搭配詞

safeguard sb. against sb. / sth.
保衛某人不受某人 / 事物的侵犯

▶ Stephanie is taking vitamin C as a safeguard against catching a bad cold.
史蒂芬妮服用維生素 C 來保護自己避免得到重感冒。

▶ The president is discussing a new plan to safeguard his citizens from attacks.
總統正在討論能保護人民避免遭受攻擊的新方案。

▶ As a safeguard against typhoon damage, the villagers build a storm shelter.
村民們建造了能夠抵擋颱風侵襲的暴風雨避難所。

---

saint [seɪnt / sənt]

① *n.* 聖徒

② *v.* 封為聖徒；承認…為聖徒

▶ There's a statue of the patron saint in the middle of the old town.
那座歷史悠久的城鎮中央，矗立著守護聖徒的雕像。

▶ Many people believe Mother Teresa should be sainted for her good works.
很多人認為德蕾莎修女應該因她的善行而被封聖。

---

salmon [ˈsæm.ən]

① *n.* 鮭魚

② *adj.* 鮭肉色的；淺橙色的

▶ This place makes a pretty good fried rice with salmon.
這裡做的鮭魚炒飯很好吃。

▶ That salmon tie goes well with your shirt. Nice!
那條鮭肉色的領帶和你的襯衫很配，真好看！

---

saloon [səˈluːn] *n.* 酒館

同 **bar; gin mill**

▶ The men went into the saloon to get a drink.
那些男人去酒館裡喝酒。

---

salute [səˈluːt]

① *n.* 敬禮；致敬

② *v.* 向…行禮；向…致敬

同 **greeting; toast**

▶ A salute is a form of honor and respect.
敬禮是一種用來表示敬意和尊重的方式。

▶ Frank, we salute you and all the hard work you've done.
法蘭克，我們要向你和你付出的辛勞致敬。

salvation [sælˈveɪ.ʃən] *n.* 救助；救恩

同 **redemption**

▶ Sue's salvation from the rockslide came from a rescue worker removing rocks.

一位救援工作人員搬走了岩塊，使蘇從落石堆中獲救。

---

sanction [ˈsæŋk.ʃən]

① *n.* 批准；認可

② *v.* 批准；認可

同 **approve; permit**

反 **interdict**

▶ The boss gave official sanction to increase the number of vacation days for employees.

老闆正式批准增加員工度假的天數。

▶ Timmy's plan to make a deal with the other company was sanctioned by his boss.

提米和另一家公司簽訂協議的計畫獲得老闆的批准了。

---

sanctuary [ˈsæŋk.tʃu.er.i]

① *n.* 聖堂；聖所

② *n.* （動物）保護區；收容所

▶ Please do not eat or drink in the sanctuary of the church.

請不要在教會聖所內飲食。

▶ Bob went to the bird sanctuary to take photos.

巴伯到鳥類保護區拍照。

---

sandal [ˈsæn.dəl] *v.* 涼鞋

實用片語與搭配詞

high / low-heeled sandal / shoes
高 / 低根的涼鞋 / 鞋子

▶ If you're going to the beach, you should wear sandals.

如果你要去海灘的話，就應該穿涼鞋。

▶ People who stand a lot while they work should wear low-heeled shoes.

工作時必須長時間久站的人應該要穿低跟的鞋子。

---

sane [seɪn] *adj.* 神智正常的；頭腦清楚的

同 **logical**

反 **insane**

▶ John can be a little weird at times, but he is definitely sane.

約翰有時有點怪異，但他絕對神智正常。

---

sanitation [ˌsæn.əˈteɪ.ʃən] *n.* 公共衛生

▶ The city is in charge of sanitation, so they have to take care of trash collection.

那座城市掌管公共衛生，所以他們必須處理垃圾收集。

S

savage [ˈsæv.ɪdʒ]

① *adj.* 兇殘的；兇猛的；野蠻的

同 **ruthless**

反 **civilized**

② *n.* 野蠻人

③ *v.* 兇猛地攻擊；激烈抨擊

▶ Look at all those bite marks on her arm. That was a savage attack!
看看她手臂上那些咬痕，就知道那實在是很兇殘的攻擊！

▶ The explorers were afraid of savages.
探險家們很害怕野蠻人。

▶ It was a terrible time in history; the whole village was savaged by the barbaric invaders.
那真是歷史上相當可怕的一段時期，全村人都遭受野蠻的入侵者兇猛地攻擊。

scan [skæn]

① *v.* 審視；掃描

同 **examine; inspect**

② *n.* 掃描；審視

▶ I couldn't see any smoke or fire, but let me scan the horizon one more time.
我沒看到煙或火，不過再讓我仔細審視地平線一次吧。

▶ The scan results are back. No broken bones!
拿到掃描結果了，沒有任何骨裂現象！

---

scandal [ˈskæn.dəl] *n.* 醜聞

同 **disgrace**

反 **praise**

▶ The tax scandal forced the mayor to resign from office.
稅收醜聞逼得那位市長辭職下台。

---

scar [skɑːr]

① *n.* 疤；傷痕

同 **mark; wound**

② *v.* 留下創傷；留下傷疤

▶ The scar on Frank's arm was from a car accident ten years ago.
法蘭克手臂上的傷痕是十年前一次車禍所遺留下的。

▶ Timmy's tragic childhood scarred his memory.
提米悲慘的童年在他的記憶裡留下創傷。

---

scenic [ˈsiː.nɪk] *adj.* 風景的；風景秀麗的

實用片語與搭配詞

a scenic railway 賞景小鐵路

▶ The scenic designs used for the performance were very beautiful.
那場表演的舞台設計相當優美。

▶ A great and relaxing way to see Europe is via the many scenic railway routes.
其中一個很棒且愜意的遊歐方式就是乘坐不同賞景路線的火車。

scent [sent]

① *n.* 氣味；香味

同 **fragrance**

反 **stench**

② *v.* 嗅出

同 **smell**

▶ I love the fresh scent in the air after it rains.
我很喜歡下雨過後空氣中的清新氣味。

▶ If there's blood in the water, a shark can scent it.
如果水裡有血，鯊魚就能嗅到。

---

scheme [ski:m]

① *n.* 計畫

② *v.* 策劃；密謀

同 **contrive; conspire**

實用片語與搭配詞

scheme against sb.
和某人密謀反對某人

▶ Watch out! John has another get-rich-quick scheme!
小心點！約翰又想出了一個快速致富的計畫了！

▶ Janet is always scheming about how to find her sister a rich boyfriend.
珍娜老是在密謀幫自己的姊妹找個有錢的男朋友。

▶ The students scheme against their teacher to het out of the test.
這些學生瞞著老師，祕密籌劃著跳掉那場考試。

---

scope [skoʊp] *n.* 眼界；範圍

同 **extent; range**

▶ You should broaden your scope by reading more non-fiction books.
你應該透過閱讀更多非小說類的書籍來擴充你的眼界。

---

scorn [skɔ:rn]

① *n.* 嗤之以鼻；輕蔑

實用片語與搭配詞

be filled with scorn for sth.
對某事十分鄙視

② *v.* 輕蔑；不屑

同 **contempt; despise**

▶ Peter felt the scorn of the fans after he missed the game-winning basket.
彼得那記原本可以贏得比賽的投籃沒投進之後，就感覺到球迷對他嗤之以鼻。

▶ The scientist was filled with scorn for his colleague who stole his research and became famous.
這位科學家的同事竊取了他的研究報告並且一舉成名，他為此感到不齒。

▶ My wife scorned me because I didn't leave a tip for the waiter.
我太太對我感到相當不屑，因為我沒有給服務生小費。

scramble [ˈskræm.bəl]

① *v.* 倉促地行動；爬行

同 **hurry; bustle**

② *n.* 爭搶；爬行

▶ Every morning I scramble out the door so I can catch the 7:15 train.
我每天早上都倉促地出門，以便趕上 7 點 15 分的火車。

▶ Right as the store opened, there was a scramble by the crowd to be first in line.
那家店一開門，群眾就爭先恐後地搶著要排在最前面。

---

scrap [skræp]

① *n.* 碎屑；小片

同 **crumb**

② *v.* 把…拆毀；把…作為廢物

實用片語與搭配詞

scrap a car 報廢汽車

▶ Honey, I forgot, where do we put the food scraps?
親愛的，我忘了該把廚餘放到哪裡了？

▶ It broke down again! I think this old car is ready to be scrapped!
這輛舊車又拋錨了！我看它要面臨被拆毀的命運了！

▶ I scrapped that old car after the car accident.
車禍後，我將那輛老舊的車子報廢了。

---

scrape [skreɪp]

① *v.* 磨破；擦傷

同 **rub; scratch**

② *n.* 擦傷；破皮

▶ Johnny scraped his knee on the playground.
強尼在遊樂場上擦傷了膝蓋。

▶ Where did you get that nasty scrape on your leg?
你腿上嚴重的擦傷是在哪裡受傷的？

---

script [skrɪpt]

① *n.* 筆跡；腳本；劇本

同 **writing**

反 **prina**

② *v.* 把…改編為劇本

同 **edit; rearrange**

▶ Lisa's script is very clear. You can easily understand everything she writes.
莉莎的筆跡很清楚，你很輕易就能了解她所寫的一切內容。

▶ The TV show is being scripted now.
那個電視節目正被改編成劇本。

---

scroll [skroʊl]

① *n.* 卷軸；書卷

同 **roll**

② *v.* 滾動；捲起

▶ Do you think you can read what it says on this ancient scroll?
你能看懂這幅古老卷軸上寫了什麼內容嗎？

▶ Use the mouse and scroll down the page a little more.
用滑鼠滾動到這頁下面一點。

Exercise 56

I. Derivatives

1. It was truly a miracle that Michelle only ___________ (scrape) her knees and elbows a bit in that serious car accident.
2. Many nations, following the statement of the UN, ___________ (sanction) this country for the testing of nuclear bombs.
3. The scientists recently discovered an alienated island where the islanders, due to the geographical separation from other civilization, remain ___________ (savage) and lead a primitive life style.
4. Due to the increasing violence on campus, the principal is ___________ (scheme) a new discipline to cope with this phenomenon.
5. Since this kidnapping for ransom is a matter of life and death, it's necessary for the president of the company to calculate ___________ (sane) the significance of his decisions.

II. Vocabulary Choices

(A) scandal	(B) scraped	(C) scrambled	(D) scope
(E) sanitation	(F) scented	(G) sanctuary	(H) salmon
(I) salvation	(J) sandal		

1. With the couple both yearning to talk and refusing to listen for years, their marriage finally came to a state beyond ________ and led to divorce.
2. Because the illegal immigrants couldn't find a shelter to spend the night in, they could only take ________ in a local church.
3. Due to inadequate ________ in this flood-stricken region, even more people died afterwards from the resulting illnesses.
4. The president's ________ with his secretary was finally reported by a local newspaper, for which a lot of paparazzi worked.
5. Without due measure to control the disease from spreading, the ________ of its devastation may be broadened beyond imagination.

Unit 57

sculptor [ˈskʌlp.tɚ] *n.* 雕刻家

▶ My grandfather used to be a sculptor. He loved working with stone and wood.
我祖父從前是雕刻家，他喜歡用岩石和木材作為素材。

---

sector [ˈsek.tɚ] *n.* 領域；行業

實用片語與搭配詞
business / manufacturing / market sector 商業 / 製造 / 營銷部門

▶ The business sector has seen positive developments this year, so many jobs are being created.
那個商業領域今年出現正向的發展，也產生了很多工作機會。

▶ It is difficult for a country to have economic growth without a strong manufacturing sector.
一個國家在沒有強大製造業的狀態下是很難有經濟成長的。

secure [səˈkjʊr]

① *adj.* 安全的
同 **safe**
反 **anxious**
② *v.* 扣緊；使安全
同 **fasten**

▶ The thief got in because the house was not secure.
因為這棟屋子不夠安全，使得竊賊趁虛闖入了。

▶ Please be sure to secure your safety belt before driving.
請務必在開車前先扣緊安全帶。

---

seduce [səˈduːs] *v.* 引誘
同 **lure; tempt**

▶ Orville was seduced by the advertisement and decided to buy the useless product.
歐維爾受到那個廣告的引誘，而決定買下那個毫無用處的產品。

segment [ˈseg.mənt]

① *n.* 部分；片；段
同 **division; fraction**
② *v.* 分成；分割

▶ This opera was written in four separate segments.
這齣歌劇分為四個段落。

▶ The story was segmented into five chapters.
這個故事分成五章。

selective [sə'lek.tɪv]

adj. 嚴格篩選的；有選擇性的

實用片語與搭配詞

be selective about sb. / sth.

慎選某人 / 事物

► That is a very selective college, so don't be upset if you don't get accepted there.

那所大學會嚴格篩選學生，所以如果你沒有申請到入學許可也不要難過。

► If you do not have a lot of money, you should be more selective about the things you buy.

如果你沒有很多錢，購物時就應該慎選商品。

---

seminar ['sem.ə.nɑːr] *n.* 研討課；研討會

實用片語與搭配詞

conduct / attend a seminar

主持 / 出席研討會

► Samantha is attending a seminar on French art history this semester.

莎曼沙這學期選修了一門法國藝術史的研討課。

► Cindy's company sent her to Australia to attend a seminar on human resource practices.

辛蒂的公司派她去澳洲出席一場關於人力資源訓練的研討會。

---

senator ['sen.ə.t̬ɚ] *n.* 參議員

► One of our senators is retiring, so there will be an election to select a new one.

有位參議員要退休了，所以還會舉行選舉好選出一位議員。

---

sensation [sen'seɪ.ʃən] *n.* 感覺；知覺

同 **feeling**

► I can't explain it, but I have a strange sensation that it's going to rain tonight.

我無法解釋為什麼會這樣，可是我有種奇怪的感覺，覺得今天晚上會下雨。

---

sensitivity [ˌsen.sə'tɪv.ə.t̬i]

n. 敏感度；善解人意

► No wonder Bob has no friends! He could use some sensitivity training.

難怪巴伯沒有朋友！他需要訓練察言觀色的能力。

98

sentiment ['sen.t̬ə.mənt] *n.* 感情；情緒

► Grace had a sentiment of pity for the beggar.

葛雷絲對那個乞丐起了憐憫之情。

---

sentimental [ˌsen.t̬ə'men.t̬əl]

adj. 情感上的；多愁善感的

同 **affectionate; emotional**

► Johnny has sentimental attachments to that old blanket.

強尼對那個老舊的毯子在情感上有很深的依附。

101

sequence [ˈsiː.kwəns]

① *an.* 順序；次序

同 **series**

反 **severance**

② *v.* 排序

同 **sort**

反 **mix up**

▶ You must enter the numbers in the correct sequence to open the door.
你必須按照正確的順序來輸入數字，才有辦法打開門。

▶ The scientist sequenced his results from the most important to the least important.
科學家把他的成果從最重要的到最不重要的依次加以排序。

---

serene [səˈriːn] *adj.* 平靜的；祥和的

同 **peaceful; tranquil**

▶ Violette felt serene as she looked at the flowers in the field.
維歐萊望著田野裡的花朵，感覺平靜祥和。

---

serenity [səˈren.ə.t̬i] *n.* 平靜；祥和

同 **peace; tranquility**

▶ Serenity is a great quality to have, especially when you are going through difficult times.
平靜是很棒的特質，尤其是當人經歷困境之際。

---

sergeant [ˈsɑːr.dʒənt] *n.* 中士

▶ The drill sergeant yelled at the soldiers to run faster.
中士教官向士兵們大喊，要他們跑得更快一點。

---

series [ˈsɪr.iːz] *n.* 系列；連續

同 **serial**

▶ Well, we may have lost this one, but there are still three more games in the series.
雖然我們輸掉了這場比賽，可是整個系列賽事還有三場比賽。

---

sermon [ˈsɝː.mən] *n.* 佈道；説教

同 **lecture; talk**

▶ Little Billy fell asleep during the pastor's sermon.
牧師講道時，小比利忍不住打瞌睡了。

---

server [ˈsɝː.vɚ] *n.* 服務生

▶ I found the servers at that restaurant to be a little rude.
我覺得那家餐廳的服務生有點粗魯無禮。

---

serving [ˈsɝː.vɪŋ] *n.* 一份；一客

▶ Carol eats 3 servings of fruit every day.
卡羅每天吃三份水果。

session [ˈseʃ.ən] *n.* 開庭；會議；研討會

同 **meeting; conference**

▶ The session will begin in five minutes, so please enter the courtroom and sit down.

將在五分鐘內開庭，所以請進入法庭內坐好。

---

setback [ˈset.bæk] *n.* 挫折

同 **obstruction**

▶ There was a setback in the business deal when the company presidents started arguing.

兩家公司總裁開始爭吵起來之後，讓彼此的商業交易也遭受重挫。

---

setting [ˈset̬.ɪŋ] *n.* 設定；背景

同 **configuration; background**

▶ The setting of Linda's novel is India.

琳達的小說背景設在印度。

---

sewer [ˈsuː.ɚ] *n.* 下水道

▶ The city is currently repairing part of the sewer, so it smells bad there.

該市目前正在維修部份下水道，所以導致臭氣沖天。

---

shabby [ˈʃæb.i] *adj.* 破舊的；衣衫襤褸的

同 **tattered**

反 **decent**

▶ You're not really going to the wedding wearing those shabby clothes, are you?

你不會真的想穿著一身破舊的衣服去參加婚禮吧！

S

Exercise 57

I. Derivatives

1. The latest model of this car features an extra fortified system that could demobilize the whole car for more ___________ (secure) against theft.
2. To make the whole concept of marketing clearer to the students, the professor ___________ (segmentation) this topic into separated parts on the syllabus, and the course today is about 4Ps.
3. Joy was a ___________ (sentiment) girl, and she would particularly value little stuff she got from others as a gift.
4. In comparison with the hustle and bustle of city life, the ___________ (serene) here in this village seems like heaven.
5. If there is no particular ___________ (sequential) in which you have to perform these tasks on the list, why not start from the easy ones?

II. Vocabulary Choices

(A) seminar	(B) seduce	(C) setback	(D) sewer
(E) session	(F) senator	(G) series	(H) sergeant
(I) serving	(J) sensation		

1. The neglected wife of the boss laid her eyes upon the young fellow fixing the door, and she tried to ________ him.
2. The side effect of the medicine may include a temporary loss of ________ in keeping balance, so please take it with caution.
3. As the first episode of the ________ adapted from Sherlock Holmes went popular, many fans started to get the novels for themselves.
4. The athlete got sprained ankle during the training ________ last week, and he had to wait till full recovery before he could join the race.
5. Though the agents were confronted with a serious ________ in their plan, they were not frustrated and kept going on with plan B.

Unit 58

sharpen [ˈʃɑːr.pən] *v.* 加強；削尖

▶ If you want to be a scientist, you're going to need to sharpen your math skills.
如果你想當科學家，就得加強數學技能。

---

shatter [ˈʃæt̬.ɚ] *v.* 粉碎
同 **break; smash**

實用片語與搭配詞
shatter sth. into pieces 粉碎某物

▶ The glass got knocked off the table and shattered on the floor.
那個玻璃杯不小心被推到桌下，在地板上摔得粉碎。

▶ I accidently bumped into the antique vase at the museum and it shattered into a thousand pieces.
在博物館裡，我不小心撞到一個古董花瓶，它就被摔成碎片了。

---

shed [ʃed]
① *n.* 分水嶺
同 **spread**
② *v.* 流出

▶ Daniel is working to protect the shed so that the river water will remain clean.
丹尼爾致力於保護分水嶺，以便讓河水能維持潔淨。

▶ Long-haired cats can shed a lot of fur.
長毛貓很會掉毛。

---

sheer [ʃɪr]
① *adj.* 透明的；純粹的
同 **transparent**
② *adv.* 近乎垂直的；陡峭的

▶ I love sheer curtains because they let in plenty of sunlight.
我喜歡透明窗簾，因為這樣就能讓很多陽光透進來。

▶ We watched the rocks falling sheer into the valley below.
我們看著岩塊幾乎垂直地掉落到下方的山谷中。

---

sheriff [ˈʃer.ɪf] *n.* 警長

▶ I need to call the sheriff. Someone just tried to break into my house.
我要通知警長，因為有人剛剛試圖闖進我家。

---

shield [ʃiːld]
① *n.* 盾

▶ The soldier used his shield to protect himself from the flaming arrows.
那名士兵用盾保護自己不被火焰箭射中。

S

② *v.* 保護
同 **defend; guard**

實用片語與搭配詞
shield sth. / sb. against sth.
保護某人 / 物不受某物的侵害

▶ Too bright outside? Use sunglasses to shield your eyes from the sun.
外面陽光太刺眼了嗎？用太陽眼鏡來保護你的眼睛不會受到太陽直射。

▶ To protect and keep your skin beautiful, you should shield it against the sun by wearing a hat.
為了保護並保持你肌膚的美麗，你應該要戴帽子遮陽。

---

shilling [ˈʃɪl.ɪŋ] *n.* 先令（貨幣單位）

▶ John wondered what he could buy with the five shillings in his pocket.
約翰想知道他口袋裡的五先令能買到什麼。

---

shiver [ˈʃɪv.ɚ]

① *v.* 發抖；打顫
同 **quiver; shake**

② *n.* 顫抖
同 **tremble**

▶ Look, it's so cold, the poor dog is shivering!
你看，真的很冷，那隻可憐的小狗都在發抖了！

▶ Simon's scary story sent a shiver down my back.
賽門的恐怖故事讓我起了一陣寒顫。

---

shoplift [ˈʃɑpˌlɪft]
v. 在商店內行竊；在商店內順手牽羊

▶ The girl was caught shoplifting a pair of earrings from the store.
女孩被逮到在商店內順手牽羊偷了一對耳環。

101

shortage [ˈʃɔːr.t̬ɪdʒ] *n.* 缺少；不足
同 **deficit; lack**

▶ The government says we can't take a shower because of the water shortage.
政府表示，因為水源短缺，所以民眾不能淋浴。

---

shortcoming [ˈʃɔːrtˌkʌm.ɪŋ] *n.* 缺點；短處
同 **defect; deficiency**

▶ Everybody loves Jane, but they don't know about her many shortcomings.
大家都很喜歡珍，可是他們卻不知道她有很多缺點。

---

shove [ʃʌv]

① *v.* 推；擠

實用片語與搭配詞
shove up / off 再擠一下 / 走開

▶ Teddy shoved the sandwich into his mouth and then ran out the door to catch the school bus.
泰迪把三明治猛塞進嘴裡，然後就衝出門外趕搭校車了。

▶ You had better shove off home before your mother comes looking for you.
你最好在你媽媽進門找你之前離開家裡。

② *n.* 推；撞

▶ Peter was afraid to jump so I gave him a little shove.
彼得很害怕跳下去，所以我就輕輕推了他一下。

---

shred [ʃred]

① *n.* 極少量；碎片

同 **slice; mince**

② *v.* 切割成條狀

▶ The dog tore the newspaper into shreds.
那隻狗把報紙扯成碎片了。

▶ These old business records can't simply be thrown away; they need to be shredded.
這些老舊的業務檔案不能就這樣扔掉，還必須用碎紙機碎掉才行。

---

shrewd [ʃru:d] *adj.* 精明的

同 **sharp; clever**

反 **dull**

▶ People like to ask Sam for advice because he makes shrewd decisions.
大家喜歡諮詢山姆的建議，因為他能做出精明的決定。

---

shriek [ʃri:k]

① *v.* 尖叫；喊叫

同 **howl; scream**

② *n.* 尖叫聲

▶ Mary shrieked when she saw the spider.
瑪莉看到那隻蜘蛛時不禁尖叫了。

▶ Did you hear that shriek? Sounds like someone is in trouble!
你有沒有聽到那聲尖叫？聽起來像是有人出事了！

---

shrine [ʃraɪn] *n.* 聖壇；神殿

▶ This museum is a kind of shrine to the best baseball players in history.
這座博物館堪稱是紀念史上最佳棒球手的聖殿。

---

shrub [ʃrʌb] *n.* 灌木

同 **bush**

▶ I'm going to plant some shrubs next to the swimming pool.
我要在游泳池旁邊種一些灌木。

---

shudder [ˈʃʌd.ɚ]

① *v.* 發抖；戰慄

同 **quiver; shake**

② *n.* 發抖；戰慄

▶ I shuddered at the thought of getting my tooth pulled.
光是想到要拔牙，就讓我忍不住發抖起來。

▶ Horror movies give me the shudders.
恐怖片讓我嚇得發抖。

shun [ʃʌn] *v.* 避開

同 **avoid**

▶ Carol is shunning dessert because she wants to lose weight.
卡羅刻意避吃甜點，因為她想減重。

---

shutter [ˈʃʌt̬.ɚ]

① *n.* 百葉窗；（相機）快門

實用片語與搭配詞

rolling shutters 捲門

② *v.* 裝百葉窗

▶ After thirty years of neglect, the shutters finally got a new coat of paint.
那扇百葉窗在三十年來乏人照管之後，終於被上了一層新油漆。

▶ Most of the shops along the street have rolling shutters to protect the goods after closing time.
為了在非營業時間保護商品，這條街上大部分的商店都有鐵捲門。

▶ The new owner of the house doesn't want to shutter the windows.
新屋主不想裝上百葉窗。

---

siege [siːdʒ] *n.* 包圍；圍攻

▶ The invading army's siege of the castle lasted two days.
入侵的軍隊持續圍攻城堡已經兩天了。

---

signature [ˈsɪg.nə.tʃɚ] *n.* 親筆簽名

▶ This document will need a signature.
這份文件需要親筆簽名。

---

signify [ˈsɪg.nə.faɪ] *v.* 代表；表示；意味著

反 **nullify**

▶ The boss's announcement signifies a change in policy.
老闆的宣佈代表政策的改變

---

silicon [ˈsɪl.ə.kən] *n.* 矽

▶ Many pieces found inside a computer are made from silicon.
電腦裡面的很多零件都是用矽製成的。

---

silkworm [ˈsɪlk.wɝːm] *n.* 蠶

▶ Many elementary school students raise silkworms for science projects.
很多小學生都會養蠶來做科學研究。

Exercise 58

I. Derivatives

1. A tough guy as Robert might appear to be, he ___________ (shedding) tears at his daughter's wedding when he gave his girl to the lucky young fellow.
2. The vagrant wandering the streets on a cold, drizzling evening couldn't help but ___________ (shivering).
3. At the thought of the challenge she was about to face as a rookie in the forensic examination where there was brutally severed corpse waiting for her, Jane ___________ (shudder) a little.
4. Despite all the failures the team had experienced since the beginning of the project, they still held on to one last ___________ (shredded) of hope.
5. If you wish to conceal more heat within the room, you may consider equipping all your windows with ___________ (shuttering), which would do just that.

II. Vocabulary Choices

(A) shoved	(B) shields	(C) shrub	(D) shunning
(E) shortage	(F) shrewd	(G) shrieked	(H) signified
(I) siege	(J) shattering		

1. The moment Julian stepped into the house, he witnessed his cat, chased by his dog, dashing around wildly and accidentally knocking down the mirror, ________ it.
2. To take precaution against the prospect of riots throwing anything to attack, the police held up the ________ while they held their position.
3. This summer observed a dramatic change in the weather pattern, and the lack of currents and rains led to a serious water ________ .
4. As a senior official, Nelson was quite ________ in giving talks with unclear stance in order to avoid offending any parties.
5. The police ignored the marking on the walls at the crime scene as they considered it nothing more than graffiti, but the detective knew it ________ a message to be delivered to the victim.

Unit 59

simmer ['sɪm.ɚ]

① *v.* 燉；煨

實用片語與搭配詞

simmer with sth. 醞釀；積聚

② *n.* 燉；煨

同 **stew**

▶ Let the broth simmer for another hour.
把那鍋湯再多燉一個小時。

▶ My mom simmered with anger after I told her that I wanted to quit my studies at university.
在我告訴母親我想要自大學輟學，她的憤怒一觸即發。

▶ Put the sauce on a slow simmer and then add the cheese.
先慢慢燉煮調味醬，然後再加入起司。

---

simplicity [sɪm'plɪs.ə.t̬i] *n.* 簡單；簡明

實用片語與搭配詞

relative / apparent simplicity
相對 / 明顯簡單

▶ The simplicity of this painting is very obvious. There's only one color.
很明顯就可以看出這幅畫的簡單，因為只用了一種顏色。

▶ The relative simplicity of putting the DIY table together turned out to be a big nightmare for me.
自己動手組裝桌子看似相對簡單，但竟然會演變成一場噩夢。

---

simplify ['sɪm.plə.faɪ] *v.* 簡化；使單純

反 **complicate**

▶ Can you please simplify your explanation? I don't understand.
你能不能簡化你的解釋？我聽不懂。

---

simultaneous [ˌsaɪ.məl'teɪ.ni.əs]

adj. 同時發生的

同 **co-occurrent; concurrent**

▶ The simultaneous announcements of increased pay and fewer vacation days left employees with mixed feelings.
同時宣佈了加薪和休假減少的兩個消息，讓員工心情很複雜，一則以喜，一則以憂。

---

skeleton ['skel.ə.t̬ən] *n.* 骸骨；骨骼

同 **frame**

▶ Is that skeleton in science class real or fake?
自然科學課裡的那副骸骨是真的還是假的？

---

104 103 99

skeptical ['skep.tɪ.kəl] *adj.* 懷疑的

同 **doubting; skeptical**

▶ Vince was skeptical of Carly's promise to pay back the money she borrowed.
對卡麗答應會歸還她借的錢的承諾，文斯抱持懷疑的態度。

skim [skɪm]

① *v.* 去除表面浮物；去除表面浮沫

同 **brush; glide**

② *n.* 掠過（表面）

- ▶ Rick used a net to skim his pool to remove leaves from the water.
  里克把游泳池表面的浮葉用網子撈出去。
- ▶ The bird made a skim across the top of the lake, barely touching the water.
  那隻鳥飛掠湖面，只輕輕碰到水而已。

---

skull [skʌl] *n.* 頭蓋骨

實用片語與搭配詞

a fracture of the skull 頭骨的裂痕

- ▶ Scooter helmets are designed to protect our skulls from injury.
  機車用安全帽是設計來保護頭蓋骨避免受傷的。
- ▶ After falling off the roof, Jeremy suffered a fracture of the skull and was admitted to hospital.
  從屋頂上摔下以後，傑若米的頭骨碎裂，並且被送入醫院救治。

---

slam [slæm]

① *v.* 砰地關上

同 **bang; shut**

② *n.* 砰聲；巨大聲響

- ▶ Karen slammed the door behind her because she was so angry.
  凱倫因為很生氣，就砰地關上身後的門。
- ▶ The slam was so hard that both cars were stuck together.
  相撞事故嚴重到兩輛車都幾乎黏在一起了。

---

slang [slæŋ]

① *n.* 俚語

同 **colloquial speech**

② *v.* 用俚語；用粗話罵

- ▶ Gary uses a lot of slang when he talks with friends, but not when he talks with his boss.
  蓋瑞和朋友講話時會用很多俚語，但和老闆講話的時候就不會這樣。
- ▶ Since they were slanging and not using formal English, I didn't understand them.
  由於他們都在用俚語，而不是正式的英文，所以我聽不懂他們說什麼。

---

slap [slæp]

① *v.* 用手掌打；摑…耳光

同 **smack; hit**

② *n.* 摑；拍擊聲

- ▶ Nancy slapped her boyfriend on the arm after he made a rude comment.
  南西的男友出言不遜後，她就打了男友手臂一下。
- ▶ Keri felt her sister's unwillingness to help was like a slap in the face.
  凱瑞覺得自己姊妹都不願意出手幫忙，等於是狠狠打了自己一巴掌。

③ *adv.* 正好；恰好；不偏不倚

▶ Kay wasn't paying attention and ran slap into the wall.
凱因為心不在焉，就這麼不偏不倚地撞上牆了。

slash [slæʃ]

① *v.* 猛砍；亂砍

同 **cut; slice**

實用片語與搭配詞

slash at sth. with sth. 以某物砍某物

② *n.* 猛砍；亂砍

▶ Karen slashed her way through the thick growth of the jungle.
凱倫在叢林裡濃密的樹叢中猛砍而砍出一條路。

▶ The workers slashed at the trees with their machetes to make a path through the jungle.
這些工人用砍刀在樹叢中劈出一條通道。

▶ The fighter made a slash with his sword.
鬥士用劍亂砍。

slaughter [ˈslɑː.t̬ɚ]

① *n.* 宰殺；屠殺

同 **butchery; killing**

② *v.* 宰殺；屠殺

▶ All the villagers were killed by their enemies. It was a complete slaughter.
所有村民都被敵人殺死了。那真是一場屠殺。

▶ Manny works for a company that slaughters and packages chickens.
曼尼工作的那家公司專門宰殺雞隻並包裝雞肉。

slavery [ˈsleɪ.ɚ.i] *n.* 奴隸制度；奴役

反 **liberty**

▶ Slavery was once common, but now it is illegal to own other people.
奴隸制度曾一度相當常見，但如今視其他人為財產屬於非法。

slay [sleɪ] *v.* 殺死；殺害

同 **exterminate; kill**

▶ Jenny loves the story about the young prince who slays the dragon.
珍妮很喜歡那則有關年輕的王子殺死了龍的故事。

104

sloppy [ˈslɑː.pi] *adj.* 潦草的；草率的

同 **messy**

▶ Sometimes Gary can't even read his own sloppy handwriting.
有時就連蓋瑞自己都看不懂他潦草的字跡。

slot [slɑːt]

① *n.* 狹槽；狹縫；投幣孔

▶ Drop your letters in the mail slot, and the postman will pick them up later.
把你的信放到郵筒的狹槽中，郵差稍後就會來拿走。

② *v.* 開孔；開槽

▶ Jerry needs to slot the wood before he can add legs to the tabletop.
傑瑞先要在木材上開孔，才能在桌子上裝桌腳。

---

slum [slʌm]

① *n.* 貧民窟

② *v.* 去貧民窟

▶ Shannon's family was very poor, and she grew up in the slums on the other side of town.
珊儂家裡很窮，而且她是在城裡另一頭的貧民區長大的。

▶ The teenagers went slumming to see what life was like for people in the poor neighborhood.
那群青少年去貧民窟觀察貧困地區民眾的生活樣貌。

---

slump [slʌmp]

① *n.* 衰退；暴跌

同 **decline; drop-off**

實用片語與搭配詞

slumped down onto / into sth.
瞬間倒 / 陷落在某物上

② *v.* 倒下；下降

同 **fall**

▶ Ever since the war started, the economy has been in a slump.
自從戰爭爆發之後，經濟就陷入衰退。

▶ After working for 24 hours, I went home and just slumped down on the sofa.
在工作了 24 小時之後，我回到家就癱倒在沙發上。

▶ After crossing the finish line, Paul slumped to the ground in exhaustion.
保羅跨越終點線之後，就精疲力盡地倒在地上。

---

sly [slaɪ] *adj.* 狡猾的

同 **sneaky**

反 **frank**

▶ Be careful playing cards with Nancy. She's pretty sly!
和南西一起玩牌要小心，她相當狡猾！

---

smack [smæk]

① *n.* 砰的一聲；啪的一聲；猛擊

② *v.* 咂（嘴）；打；撞

同 **crack; whack**

③ *adv.* 正好；恰好

▶ The door closed with a loud smack that made everyone jump.
那個門發出砰然巨響而關上，讓大家都嚇得跳起來。

▶ Stuey happily smacked his lips as he ate the ice cream cone.
史都伊吃冰淇淋甜筒時，一邊高興地咂嘴。

▶ The little boy fell smack on his face and started crying.
小男孩正好跌得臉朝地，痛得他開始大哭起來。

smallpox ['smɑːl.pɑːks] *n.* 天花

同 **variola**

► Smallpox was once one of the most feared diseases in the world.
天花一度曾是全球最可怕的疾病之一。

---

smash [smæʃ]

① *v.* 砸碎；粉碎

同 **crash; crush**

② *n.* 砸碎；粉碎

► The naughty kids smashed all of farmer Miller's pumpkins.
頑皮的孩子們把農夫米勒全部的南瓜都砸爛了。

► You can use a hammer and give it a quick smash.
你可以用鐵鎚迅速把它砸碎。

---

smother ['smʌð.ɚ]

① *v.* 悶死；使窒息

同 **choke; suffocate**

② *n.* 令人窒息之物（如濃煙、灰塵等）

► It looked like the cat was smothering her kittens, but she was actually keeping them warm.
雖然看起來那隻貓好像是在悶死她的孩子，但事實上她是在幫小貓保暖。

► The land was covered with a smother of smoke that made it difficult to breathe.
大地覆蓋著令人窒息的濃煙，令人呼吸困難。

---

smuggle ['smʌg.əl] *v.* 走私

實用片語與搭配詞

smuggle sb. / sth. into / out of
走私某人 / 物進 / 出某處

► The men were caught trying to smuggle birds into the country.
那些男子企圖走私鳥入境時被逮。

► During the war, the hero smuggled a lot of people out of the country to save their lives.
戰爭期間，這位英雄夾帶了許多人逃出這個國家，以拯救他們的性命。

Exercise 59

I. Derivatives

1. The old man living next door, after having experienced so much throughout his life, now opted for a lifestyle of ____________ (simplify).
2. Because the manager was in a hurry to his next meeting, he only ____________ (skim) through the letter that was delivered to him on his way to the briefing room.
3. After the terrorists besieged this little town, no one escaped the merciless ____________ (slaughtered), and thus there was no survivor.
4. The machine must be broken because no matter how hard I pressed the button after putting the coin into the ____________ (slotted), nothing came out.
5. Ever since the verbal humiliation from her boss right in front of many other colleagues at the meeting, Patricia had been ____________ (simmer) with resentment.

II. Vocabulary Choices

(A) slammed	(B) skeptical	(C) simultaneous	(D) slum
(E) slashed	(F) slapped	(G) slavery	(H) slew
(I) smother	(J) sloppy		

1. The terrorists had planned the attack since long ago, so all the five explosions in different regions were nearly _________ , rendering the police force to scatter for the convenience of their next attack.
2. Though this young scholar has brought forth several convincing statistical evidence, other experts are still _________ toward the validity of the researching methods.
3. With a veteran mountain-climber leading the team, through the long grass was our way _________ to clear out a path for the followers to proceed.
4. Even though there are quite many advanced countries with democratic social systems, _________ still exists in many parts of the world, and poor people have to making a living that way.
5. For fear that the abrupt sound might distract the speaker, who was reaching the climax of his speech, I tried with all my might to _________ a sneeze.

Unit 60

snare [snɛr]

① *n.* 陷阱

② *v.* （用陷阱）捕捉

同 **hook; trap**

▶ The hunter set a snare on the ground to catch rabbits.
獵人在地上設置陷阱想要捕捉兔子。

▶ The goose was snared by the hunter.
那隻鵝被獵人用陷阱捉到了。

---

snarl [snɑːrl]

① *n.* 吠叫；咆哮

同 **growl; grumble**

② *n.* 吠；咆哮

▶ There's a mean dog in the park that snarls at me whenever I pass it.
公園裡有隻惡犬，每次我經過牠都會向我吠叫。

▶ If you hear a snarl, don't worry. It's just the old guard dog.
如果你聽到狗吠聲，別擔心，那只是隻年老的看門犬。

---

snatch [snætʃ]

① *v.* 搶走；奪走

同 **grab; grasp**

② *n.* 搶；奪

▶ Little Mickey snatched a cookie from his baby sister's hand.
小米奇從妹妹手中搶走了一塊餅乾。

▶ The thief just took her purse. That was a quick snatch!
竊賊剛才拿走她的錢包，他搶得超快！

---

sneak [sniːk]

① *v.* 偷偷地走

同 **creep; lurk**

② *n.* 鬼鬼祟祟的人；偷偷摸摸的人

同 **creep; lurk**

▶ I hate it when Carl sneaks up on me and scares me!
我很討厭卡爾偷偷摸摸地靠近我，然後嚇我！

▶ Gary is such a sneak! He ate the last piece of cake last night while everyone else was sleeping!
蓋瑞真是個鬼鬼祟祟的人！他昨晚趁其他人都在睡覺時，偷吃了最後一塊蛋糕。

---

sneakers [ˈsniːkɚ] *n.* 運動鞋

▶ Jack likes to wear sneakers on weekends.
傑克喜歡在週末穿運動鞋。

---

sneaky [ˈsniːki] *adj.* 偷偷摸摸的；鬼鬼祟祟的

▶ Cheryl tried to be sneaky by planning a surprise party for her husband.
雪柔試圖秘密的地為丈夫籌辦一場驚喜派對。

sneer [snɪr]

① *n.* 冷笑；嘲笑

② *v.* 嗤之以鼻；嘲笑

同 **mock; scoff**

▶ A sneer appeared on the man's face when he started yelling.
那名男子開始喊叫時，臉上浮現一抹冷笑。

▶ Thomas sneered at the idea that he was wrong.
對於認為他錯了的想法，湯瑪斯嗤之以鼻。

---

sniff [snɪf]

① *v.* 聞；嗅

同 **smell**

② *n.* 聞；嗅；吸氣聲

▶ Here, sniff this flower. Isn't that just the most amazing smell ever?
來，聞聞這花。是不是你聞過最香的味道？

▶ Give this a sniff and tell me if you think it's rotten.
聞聞看這個，然後告訴我你覺得那有沒有壞掉？

---

snore [snɔːr]

① *n.* 打呼聲；鼾聲

② *v.* 打呼；打鼾

▶ Wow! Is that snoring I hear in there? It sounds like a train!
哇！我在這裡聽到的是不是打呼聲啊？聽起來簡直和火車一樣大聲。

▶ My roommate snores every night.
我室友每天晚上都會打呼。

---

snort [snɔːrt]

① *n.* （類似豬叫的）鼻哼聲

② *v.* 發出（類似豬叫的）鼻哼聲

▶ I'm glad you liked my joke, but your laugh sounded more like a snort!
我很開心你喜歡我講的笑話，可是你的笑聲聽起來比較像豬叫聲！

▶ Harry made everyone laugh when he snorted like a pig.
哈利發出像豬叫一樣的鼻哼聲，惹得大家全都笑開了。

---

soak [soʊk]

① *v.* 浸泡

同 **sop**

反 **dry**

實用片語與搭配詞

soak sth. into / through sth.
把某物浸泡入某物中

② *n.* 浸泡

▶ Who wants to go soak in the hot spring?
有誰想去泡溫泉嗎？

▶ Julie spilled some wine on the floor and it soaked through the carpet.
茱莉撒落了一些紅酒在地板上，紅酒便浸濕了地毯。

▶ What a rough day! Let's go to the hot springs. I could use a good soak.
真是辛苦的一天！我們去溫泉吧，我需要好好泡個湯。

soar [sɔːr] *v.* 高飛；驟升

同 **fly; ascend**

▶ Look at the large birds soaring in the sky.
看看那些大鳥在空中高飛。

---

sober [ˈsoʊ.bɚ]

① *adj.*. 清醒的；沒喝醉的

同 **clear-headed**

反 **drunken**

② *v.* 使酒醒

▶ I don't want to talk to him unless he's sober.
除非他很清醒，否則我不想跟他講話。

▶ After the party, Henry tried to sober up with a hot pot of coffee.
派對結束之後，亨利試著喝一壺熱咖啡來讓自己更清醒。

sociable [ˈsoʊ.ʃə.bəl] *n.* 社交的；善交際的

同 **gregarious**

▶ Joe is very sociable and loves talking to people.
喬善於社交，喜歡和人交談。

---

socialism [ˈsoʊ.ʃəl.ɪ.zəm] *n.* 社會主義

反 **capitalism**

▶ Tasha thinks socialism is a good idea and that the government should control the economy.
塔莎認為社會主義是不錯的理念，而政府應該對經濟加以掌控。

---

socialist [ˈsoʊ.ʃəl.ɪst] *n.* 社會主義者

同 **socialistic**

▶ Karl Marx is a famous socialist.
卡爾・馬克斯是知名的社會主義者。

---

socialize [ˈsoʊ.ʃə.laɪz] *v.* 交際；參加社交活動

實用片語與搭配詞

socialize with sb. 與某人社交

▶ Jaqueline enjoys going to parties and socializing with people.
賈克琳喜歡參加派對，和人們交際應酬。

▶ Making friends requires socializing with people at work and at parties.
交朋友有賴於在職場及派對上與人交際。

---

sociology [ˌsoʊ.siˈɑː.lə.dʒi] *n.* 社會學

▶ Doug is studying sociology and learning about how people organize their societies.
道格正在研修社會學，並學習人類規劃社會的方式。

---

sodium [ˈsoʊ.di.əm] *n.* 鈉

▶ There is a lot of sodium in that snack, so it tastes very salty.
那個零食裡含有大量的鈉，所以吃起來很鹹。

soften [ˈsɑː.fən] *v.* 緩和；使變軟

反 **harden**

▶ The boss had to let Carl go, but he softened the blow by giving Carl three months' salary.

老闆不得不資遣卡爾，可是他也加發了三個月薪水來減緩對卡爾造成的衝擊。

---

sole [soʊl]

① *n.* 鞋底；腳底

② *v.* （給鞋）裝鞋底

③ *adj.* 唯一的；單獨的

▶ Oh no! The sole on my shoe just fell off!

糟了！我鞋子的鞋底剛剛脫落了！

▶ I hate to throw these shoes away. Maybe I should have them resoled.

我不想把鞋子扔掉，也許我該重新裝鞋底繼續穿。

▶ After the horrific gun battle, Johnson emerged as the sole survivor.

在可怕的槍戰過後，強生成了唯一的生還者。

---

solemn [ˈsɑː.ləm] *adj.* 嚴肅的

同 **serious**

反 **frivolous**

▶ My brother's funeral was a very sad and solemn time.

我兄弟的葬禮期間是一段相當悲傷而嚴肅的時刻。

---

solidarity [ˌsɑː.lɪˈder.ə.t̬i] *n.* 團結

實用片語與搭配詞

a gesture of solidarity 團結一致的姿態

▶ After the disaster, people showed their solidarity by donating their time and money.

災難過後，民眾獻出時間和金錢，展現出大家的團結一致。

▶ In a gesture of solidarity, all the staff quit their jobs when their boss was laid off.

當老闆被革職時，全體員工也團結一致地請辭。

---

solitary [ˈsɑː.lə.ter.i]

① *adj.* 單獨的

同 **isolated**

反 **bustling**

② *n.* 獨居者

▶ The criminal was sentenced to six months in solitary confinement.

那名歹徒被判單獨監禁六個月。

▶ Tom lives by himself in the woods. He is a solitary.

湯姆自己一個人住在森林裡，他是獨居者。

---

solitude [ˈsɑː.lə.tuːd] *n.* 孤獨

同 **aloneness; loneliness**

▶ The writer worked in solitude, so he wouldn't be disturbed while writing his book.

那位作家獨自工作，因此寫書時就不會受到打擾。

Exercise 60

I. Derivatives

1. Even though throughout history people blamed ____________ (social) for injustice taking place, one basic element of it is equality, not discrimination.
2. The insurance contract is full of wordy ____________ (snare) for those who are not very careful in examining the obligations and rights.
3. Joseph happened to grab his sister's smart phone on the desk and started to read out loud her messages, only to experience a fierce ____________ (snatched) from Maria.
4. Judy has a preference for fancy stuff, and she ____________ (sneer) at my accessories because most of them were bought at a pretty low price.
5. Though there are several people whom you can turn to for inquiry on the details of the project, Jessica is the ____________ (sole) manager in charge and thus you should go to her first.

II. Vocabulary Choices

(A) snarl	(B) sober	(C) soaked	(D) sneaked
(E) sodium	(F) solemn	(G) sniffed	(H) snorted
(I) solidarity	(J) softened		

1. Seeing the cat appearing out of nowhere, the dog lying at the front gate started to _________ , ready for a strike that could take place anytime.
2. Because Rebecca had come home much later than she was requested, she _________ in through the back door in case she woke up anyone.
3. Compared with other friends of mine who were drinking to their hearts' content at the party, I didn't drink at all, and I was stone _________ and drove them home.
4. At the scene of the horrible car accident where the victim had been seriously wounded for being dragged over a long distance, everybody looked _________ , including the police officer and the medical staff.
5. The fact that a consensus among the votes failed to be reached clearly raised important questions about _________ among member states of the United Nations.

Unit 61

solo [ˈsoʊ.loʊ]

① *n.* 獨唱（奏）；獨唱（奏）曲

同 **alone; unaccompanied**

實用片語與搭配詞

solo flight 單飛

② *v.* 獨唱；獨奏

③ *adv.* 單獨地

- ▶ The opera singer's solo was the highlight of the concert.
  歌劇演唱家的獨唱是那場演唱會的高潮。
- ▶ Many people have tried to do solo flights around the world in small planes, but they failed.
  許多人都曾經嘗試用小飛機獨自飛行環遊世界，但他們都失敗了。
- ▶ Everyone was surprised when the guitarist soloed with the guitar behind his back!
  那名吉他手把吉他放在背後的獨奏，帶給全場觀眾意外的驚喜！
- ▶ He likes to go solo. He never likes to have people with him.
  他喜歡單獨行動，從來不喜歡和別人一起。

---

soothe [suːð] *v.* 安慰；撫慰

實用片語與搭配詞

soothe sb.'s ache 使某人的疼痛減輕

- ▶ I soothed my daughter by giving her a hug.
  我擁抱女兒來安慰她。
- ▶ If you want to soothe a friend's ache after a break-up, the best thing to do is be there for her.
  如果你想要緩解朋友分手後的傷痛，最好的作法就是陪伴在她的身邊。

---

sophisticated [səˈfɪs.tə.keɪ.t̬ɪd]

adj. 處事練達；精於世故的；見多識廣的

同 **unsophisticated**

- ▶ Ariel is a very sophisticated woman who knows a lot about our world today.
  艾瑞兒是個處事練達、精於世故的女子。

---

sovereign [ˈsɑːv.rən]

① *n.* 元首；最高統治者；君王

同 **supreme ruler**

② *adj.* 主權獨立的；最高統治的

同 **supreme**

- ▶ The nation's sovereign stepped down from power due to years of poor health.
  那個國家的元首因為多年來身體狀況一直欠佳而辭職下台。
- ▶ Whether or not the Southern states could have succeeded as a sovereign nation is still debated.
  南方各州是否能成功成為主權獨立的國家仍有爭議。

S

sovereignty [ˈsɑːv.rən.i] *n.* 統治權

同 **reign**

▶ The government has maintained its sovereignty over the area for more than 50 years.
那個政府維持在當地的統治權超過五十年之久。

---

sow [soʊ] *v.* 播種

同 **distribute**

反 **reap**

▶ If you sow bean seeds, why would you expect to get watermelons?
如果你播種的是豆子的種子，怎麼能期待採收西瓜呢？

---

spacecraft [ˈspeɪs.kræft] *n.* 太空船

同 **capsule**

▶ It will take six days for the spacecraft to reach the moon.
那個太空船要花六天的時間才能飛抵月亮。

---

spaceship [ˈspeɪs.ʃɪp] *n.* 太空船

同 **starship**

▶ It will take six days for the spaceship to reach the planet.
那個太空船要花六天的時間才能飛抵那個行星。

---

spacious [ˈspeɪ.ʃəs] *adj.* 寬敞的

同 **capacious**

▶ Kyle wants to buy a spacious house for his large family.
凱爾想買個寬敞的房子給自己的大家庭居住。

---

span [spæn]

① *n* 跨度；一段時間

同 **interval; period**

實用片語與搭配詞

a short span of time 短暫的一段時間

② *v.* 橫越

▶ The span of the bridge is 30 meters.
橋的跨度是三十公尺。

▶ The manager completed the project in a short span of time and his boss was happy there were no delays.
這位經理在短時間內完成了這個專案，他的老闆樂見一切如期進行。

▶ Timothy's time as a musician spanned more than 60 years.
提摩西擔任音樂家的生涯超過六十年。

---

specialist [ˈspeʃ.əl.ɪst] *n.* 專家

同 **expert**

▶ The diet specialist told me I need to cut down on sugar.
那位飲食專家告訴我，我需要減少糖分的攝取。

---

specialize [ˈspeʃ.ə.laɪz] *v.* 專攻；專門研究

▶ Queenie specializes in treating heart conditions in dogs.
昆妮專攻治療狗的心臟病。

實用片語與搭配詞

specialize in sth. 專攻某事物

▶ My friend specializes in setting up websites; I can ask her for help.
我的朋友專門從事網站架設；我可以請她幫忙。

---

specialty [ˈspeʃ.əl.ti] *n.* 專長；專業

同 **expertise**

▶ Hazel's specialty is entertaining people with magic tricks.
海柔的專長是以魔術娛樂民眾。

---

specify [ˈspes.ə.faɪ] *v.* 具體指定；明確說明

同 **indicate; detail**

▶ Sukie asked her boss to specify how much time she had to complete the project.
蘇琪要求上司明確說明她有多少時間來完成那個專案。

---

specimen [ˈspes.ə.mɪn] *n.* 樣本

同 **representative; sample**

▶ The astronauts were asked to collect moon rock specimens.
那些太空人被要求去蒐集月球岩石的樣本。

---

spectacle [ˈspek.tə.kəl] *n.* 公開展示；壯觀

同 **manifestation; display**

▶ Did you see the group of clowns walking down the street? What a spectacle!
你有沒有看到那群小丑在街上走？好壯觀啊！

---

spectacular [spekˈtæk.jə.lɚ]

① *adj.* 壯觀的

同 **dramatic; magnificent**

② *n.* 奇觀

實用片語與搭配詞

a spectacular victory 輝煌的勝利

▶ The sunset's variety of colors looked spectacular.
夕陽西下的萬般色彩十分壯觀。

▶ The fireworks spectacular will begin at 9 p.m.
煙火奇觀秀將在晚上九點展開。

▶ After a spectacular victory at the World cup, the Brazilian soccer team returned home as heroes.
在世界杯獲得輝煌的勝利後，這支巴西足球隊衣錦還鄉。

---

spectator [spekˈteɪ.t̬ɚ] *n.* 觀眾；旁觀者

同 **witness**

▶ All the spectators ran for cover when it began to rain.
開始下雨時，所有觀眾都跑去找避雨的地方。

---

spectrum [ˈspek.trəm] *n.* …譜

▶ Humans can only hear a limited portion of the entire sound spectrum.
人類只能聽到全部聲譜的一小部份而已。

S

實用片語與搭配詞

a spectrum of opinion 一系列的想法

▶ There has always been a wide spectrum of opinion about legalizing gay marriage, making it a controversial issue.
人們對於同性婚姻總是有廣泛的意見，這便成為一個具有爭議性的議題。

95

speculate [ˈspek.jə.leɪt] *v.* 推測；推斷；思索

同 **guess**

▶ Nancy speculated that her assistant wanted to quit his job, but she had no evidence.
南西推測她的助手想辭職，可是她卻沒有證據。

---

sphere [sfɪr] *n.* 球體

實用片語與搭配詞

out of one's sphere 超出某人的範圍 / 領域

▶ Jack loves spheres and has several globes and marbles on his desk.
傑克喜歡球體，桌上有好幾種球體和彈珠。

▶ One should not talk about politics or religion if it is out of one's sphere of knowledge.
當談論的政治或宗教議題已經超出你的知識範圍，就別發言了。

---

spike [spaɪk]

① *n.* 大釘；尖刺

② *v.* 用大釘釘牢

同 **pierce; stab**

▶ The rail worker drove the spike into the railroad track.
鐵路工人把尖釘釘進鐵軌裡。

▶ Kara spiked the base of her tent against the ground.
卡拉用大釘把帳篷底部釘緊地面。

---

spine [spaɪn] *n.* 脊椎

同 **backbone; spinal**

▶ I severely injured my spine when I fell down the stairs.
我從樓梯上跌下來時，脊椎受了重傷。

---

spiral [ˈspaɪr.əl]

① *adj.* 螺旋的

同 **twirl**

② *n.* 螺旋

同 **twist**

實用片語與搭配詞

spiral staircase 螺旋式樓梯

▶ Don't pull on the phone's spiral cord.
不要拉扯電話的螺旋線路。

▶ Looking at the spiral on her shirt makes me feel dizzy.
望著她裙子的螺旋形讓我覺得頭昏。

▶ The old castle has a beautifully handcrafted spiral staircase going up to the top.
這座古堡有一座由手工製作的美麗螺旋梯直通城堡頂端。

③ *v.* 盤旋；使成螺旋形

同 **escalate**

▶ The clouds spiraled around the top of the mountain.
雲層在山頂盤旋。

---

spire [spaɪr]

① *n.* 尖塔

同 **steeple**

② *v.* 給…裝尖頂；塔狀矗立

▶ The spire on the church is very tall.
教堂的尖塔高聳入雲。

▶ The designer decided to spire the roof of the house to make it look like a castle.
那位設計師決定給房子的屋頂裝尖塔，好讓它看似城堡。

S

Exercise 61

I. Derivatives

1. The ___________ (sovereign) of Taiwan remains in dispute over nearly a century, for people and officials all have their own perspectives toward the history and the legitimacy of who reigns over the island.
2. Joshua's computer broke down, the major problem lying in the hard-disk, and I advised him to turn to the companies which ___________ (specialist) in retrieving the data.
3. At the peak of the mountain, hikers as well as professional photographers often gather for the ___________ (spectacle) view of the sunset.
4. This writer is quite famous in that he always reflects recent social and political events in his writings, ___________ (spike) them with sarcasm and humor.
5. Cutting down prices to attract more customers may seem an effective way, but it can lead to a downward ___________ (spiraled) where all the competitors follow.

II. Vocabulary Choices

(A) specified	(B) soothed	(C) spacious	(D) sowed
(E) sophisticated	(F) spanned	(G) speculated	(H) spectrum
(I) specimen	(J) spectacle		

1. The antagonism between the two neighbors stems from their complicated backgrounds, and thus a ________ approach is needed if anyone wishes to appease their hostility.
2. Melody is from a wealthy family, and all her friends who have been to her place were all impressed with the ________ living room where they could play hockey.
3. It is wise to follow what is ________ in the contract before making any decision on adjustments in case you violate it.
4. Over the mysterious murder case, many people, including talk show hosts, all ________ on who the murderer and what the motivation was.
5. In order to attract more audience to the theater, the manager dedicated a lot of resources making the stage a grand ________ resembling a true colosseum, the oval amphitheater in the center of the city, Rome.

Unit 62

splendor [ˈsplen.dɚ] *n.* 光輝；壯麗

同 **glory; magnificence**

▶ The splendor of the queen caused everyone to bow in respect.
王后的雍容華貴，使得大家都不禁俯首致敬。

---

spokesperson [ˈspoʊks.pɝː.sən]

n. 發言人（男女通用）

▶ The company plans to hire a spokesperson to promote its new product.
公司打算僱請發言人來推廣新產品。

---

sponge [spʌndʒ]

① *n.* 海綿

② *v.* 用海綿吸取、抹掉

實用片語與搭配詞

sponge sth. off / out 用海綿清除某物

▶ Mark quickly grabbed the sponge and wiped up the spilled milk.
馬克很快拿起海綿來，擦掉濺出去的牛奶。

▶ Don't worry, spills happen. Use this to sponge up the milk.
別擔心，水濺出去的情況難免會發生。用這個海綿來把牛奶吸掉。

▶ Mindy had such a high fever that her mom had to sponge her off with cold water throughout the night.
敏迪嚴重發高燒，因此她的母親必須整晚用海綿沾冷水擦拭她。

---

sponsor [ˈspɑːn.sɚ]

① *n.* 主辦者；贊助者

同 **backer; supporter**

② *v.* 主辦；贊助

同 **fund**

▶ Randy needs to find a sponsor for his education costs.
藍迪需要找到贊助人來支付他的教育費用。

▶ The company is sponsoring several interns this summer.
那家公司今年夏季贊助了幾名實習生。

---

spontaneous [spɑːnˈteɪ.ni.əs]

adj. 自發的；自然的

同 **automatic**

反 **compulsory**

▶ The bird made a spontaneous movement and flew from the tree.
那隻鳥自發性地動了起來，然後從樹上飛走了。

99

spotlight [ˈspɑːt.laɪt]

① *n.* 聚光燈；備受矚目的焦點

同 **focus**

▶ The spotlight should always be on the lead dancer.
聚光燈應該總是打在首席舞者身上。

S

② *v.* 用聚光燈照亮；使突出醒目

同 **highlight; focus on**

▶ It's too dark in that corner. We need to spotlight that area.
那個角落實在太暗了，我們需要用聚光燈照亮那個區域才行。

---

spouse [spaʊs] *n.* 配偶

同 **mate**

▶ Tina is Aaron's spouse. They have been married for five years.
提娜是亞朗的配偶，他們結婚五年了。

---

sprawl [sprɑːl]

① *v.* 攤開四肢；不規則擴展、蔓延

同 **stretch out; slouch**

② *n.* 雜亂無序地擴展、蔓延

▶ The child sprawled out to take a nap and took up all the space on the couch.
那孩子攤開四肢躺著小睡片刻，一個人把沙發佔滿了。

▶ There was a sprawl of books all over the floor.
地板上散落著一地的書。

---

sprint [sprɪnt]

① *v.* 短距離快速奔跑；衝刺

實用片語與搭配詞

break into a sprint 突然開始衝刺

② *n.* 短距離賽跑；短時間竭力工作

▶ Before we go, just let me sprint upstairs and get my phone.
在我們離開之前，先讓我快跑到樓上拿我的手機。

▶ Peter didn't want to be late for work, so he broke into a sprint as soon as he got off the bus.
彼得不希望上班遲到，所以他一下公車便開始飛奔。

▶ Rachel won the sprint event by a full five seconds!
瑞秋以整整五秒之差在短距離賽跑中獲勝！

---

spur [spɝː]

① *n.* 踢馬刺；刺激

② *v.* 用馬刺策馬前行；鞭策

同 **provoke; urge**

▶ Let's go everyone! Use your spurs to get those horses going!
我們出發吧！用馬刺來讓馬前進！

▶ Spurring alone won't make you a better rider.
單靠用馬刺策馬前行，並不會讓你變得更會騎馬。

---

squad [skwɑːd] *n.* 小隊

同 **troop; team**

▶ We will be sending a squad of people to lead a training camp next week.
我們將派出一隊人手來帶領下週的訓練營。

squash [skwɑːʃ]

① *n.* 南瓜屬植物的果實

② *v.* 壓制；壓扁

同 **crush; mash**

③ *n.* 果汁飲料

▶ Squash is delicious and can be added to many dishes such as pasta or salad.
南瓜很好吃，可以加入很多菜餚中，像是義大利麵或沙拉都行。

▶ With a team as strong as yours, you are sure to squash the opposition.
像你們那樣強的團隊，一定能壓制對手。

▶ The vegetable squash is full of nutrients.
那蔬果汁飲料富含營養素。

---

squat [skwɑːt]

① *v.* 蹲下

同 **crouch**

② *adj.* 矮胖的；蹲著的

③ *n.* 深蹲；蹲坐

▶ Alright kids, if you can't find a seat, just squat on the floor.
孩子們，如果找不到座位，就蹲在地上吧。

▶ The boxer was short and squat.
這個拳擊手身材矮胖。

▶ The coach ordered the players to do squats.
教練下令選手們作深蹲。

95

stability [stəˈbɪl.ə.t̬i] *n.* 穩定；安定

同 **constancy; stableness**

▶ The building's stability was tested during the earthquake.
地震讓那棟建築的穩定度受到測試。

---

stabilize [ˈsteɪ.bə.laɪz] *v.* 使穩定

同 **steady**

▶ Toby's one-year old daughter is learning to walk. He stabilizes her by holding her arms.
東尼一歲大的女兒正在學走路。他扶著她的手臂來穩定她的步伐。

---

stack [stæk]

① *n.* 乾草堆

同 **heap; pile**

② *v.* 把…疊成堆

實用片語與搭配詞

stack sth. up 將某物堆起

▶ If you ever need to take a nap, that stack of hay makes a nice bed!
如果你需要小睡片刻，那乾草堆可以充當床，還蠻舒服的！

▶ Here, help me stack these dirty dishes next to the sink.
來幫我把這些髒盤子疊在水槽旁。

▶ The store always stacks their products up to the highest shelf where no-one can reach them.
這間店總是把存貨高高的堆到沒有人可以拿到的架子上。

stagger ['stæg.ɚ]

① *v.* 搖搖晃晃；蹣跚而行

同 **sway; tumble**

② *n.* 搖晃；蹣跚

▶ The defeated soldiers staggered back to their camp.
打敗仗的士兵們腳步蹣跚地回到營地裡。

▶ The actor plays a drunk in the movie and has a funny stagger.
那位演員在電影中飾演醉漢，有著搖搖晃晃的滑稽步伐。

---

stain [steɪn]

① *v.* 弄髒；沾污

同 **spot**

反 **cleanse**

實用片語與搭配詞

stain sth. with sth. 使某物沾染上某物

② *n.* 汙漬

實用片語與搭配詞

fabric stain 布上的汙漬

▶ I'm sorry, I spilled my grape juice and stained your carpet!
很抱歉，我把葡萄汁灑出來了，弄髒了你的地毯！

▶ In the old days, people used to stain cloth with colors taken from nature, such as blueberry juice.
以前的人們利用大自然中的天然色素將布料染色，例如藍莓汁。

▶ The stain wouldn't come out of his shirt.
他襯衫上的污漬除不了。

▶ The best way to get rid of fabric stain is to use salt and lemon juice.
去除布料上污漬的最佳方法是使用鹽和檸檬汁。

---

stake [steɪk]

① *n.* 樁；棍子

同 **peg; post**

② *v.* 用樁圍住；用樁支撐

實用片語與搭配詞

stake in sth. 與某事利害攸關

▶ Don't forget to bring the stakes. We'll need them to secure the tent.
別忘了帶樁，我們需要用它們來拴牢帳篷。

▶ We need to stake this piece of property if we really want it.
我們如果真想要那塊地，就要用樁把它圍起來。

▶ We need to work hard, because we all have a stake in the process of the project.
我們必須努力工作，因為我們全體都跟這個專案進程有著利害關係。

stalk [stɑ:k]

① *n.* 莖；悄悄跟蹤

實用片語與搭配詞

cyberstalking 網絡跟蹤

② *v.* 偷偷靠近；悄悄地跟蹤

同 **follow; track**

③ *n.* 稈；莖

同 **stem; twig**

▶ The stalk of the sunflower was thick and hard to cut.
向日葵的莖很粗，很難割斷。

▶ Today one has to be very careful about talking to strangers online; you might become a victim of cyberstalking.
如今人們在網路上與陌生人交談時必須格外小心；你可能會成為網路跟蹤的受害者。

▶ The hunter quietly stalked the herd of elk through the mountains.
獵人悄悄地靠近山上的馬鹿群中。

▶ The typhoon destroyed every last stalk of rice.
颱風摧毀了所有稻稈。

---

stall [stɑ:l]

① *n.* 廄；攤位

同 **booth**

② *v.* 把…關入畜舍

同 **block**

▶ Wow, this night market has so many food stalls!
哇，這個夜市有好多小吃攤！

▶ Go stall the animals. It looks like a big storm is on its way.
把那些動物關進畜舍裡。看起來好像有一場大風暴要來了。

---

stammer [ˈstæm.ɚ]

① *v.* 結結巴巴地說

同 **stumble; stutter**

② *n.* 口吃；結巴

▶ Derek was so nervous that he stammered when he tried to confess his love to Emmy.
迪瑞克試圖向艾美表達愛意時，因為太緊張而結結巴巴。

▶ The judges took off points during her speech because of her stammer.
她演講時因為口齒結巴，所以被裁判扣分了。

---

stanza [ˈstæn.zə] *n.* 詩的一節

同 **verse**

▶ OK class, now let's look at this poem's third stanza on page 9.
同學們，現在請大家看第 9 頁這首詩的第三節。

---

staple [ˈsteɪ.pəl]

① *n.* 主要作物；主食；釘書針

實用片語與搭配詞

staple food / diet 主食

▶ Rice is the main staple in this farming region.
稻米是這處農業區的主要作物。

▶ In many countries, corn is part of the staple diet of most people because it is the cheapest food source.
在許多國家，玉米是大多數人主食中的一部分，因為它是最便宜的食物來源。

② *v.* 用釘書針固定

同 **bind**

▶ Janice stapled the papers together.
珍妮絲把紙張用釘書針固定在一起。

---

stapler [ˈsteɪ.plɚ] *n.* 釘書機

同 **stapling machine**

▶ The office stapler can be used to fasten 100 sheets of paper at a time.
辦公室的釘書機一次可以用來釘牢一百張紙。

Exercise 62

I. Derivatives

1. Many student clubs in senior high school will seek resources outside the campus, such as brand-name product enterprises, to ___________ (sponsored) their performance.
2. After a month spent in the hospital, the patient's condition ___________ (stability) and was gradually on its way to recovery.
3. Alfred was recently dumped by his girlfriend, and this night, he drank again to the extent that he could not walk straight but ___________ (stagger) all the way home.
4. White sweater and a big fast-food meal with French-fries sprayed with ketchup are a bad combination since it is quite easy to ___________ (stained) the sweater, and the tomato sauce is difficult to wash off.
5. For fear that the druggies and dealers might notice, the police force ___________ (stalk) them in secret for weeks before arresting them.

II. Vocabulary Choices

(A) spur	(B) spotlight	(C) stammer	(D) squad
(E) spontaneous	(F) sponge	(G) splendor	(H) sprawl
(I) spouse	(J) stack		

1. With the auctioneer at the beginning of the musical coming to his line of "illumination," the broken chandelier got slowly lifted up, and the surrounding interiors of the theater were restored to its original ________ .
2. The famous talk show host always gives the audience the impression that his hilarious jokes are ________ improvisation while actually they are well-prepared beforehand.
3. For those who are traveling abroad or reapplying for a new ID, there will be blanks to fill in, such as the space for ________ , where one should enter the name of his/her wife or husband.
4. The victim in the video tape could be seen to read out, under the threat of a gun on the side of his head, the terrorists' demands, but he could only ________ out of extreme fear.
5. The newly made policy of lowering taxes for the sales is generally expected to ________ the economy of the country.

Unit 63

starch [stɑːrtʃ]

① *n.* 澱粉

同 **amylum**

② *v.* （用澱粉）上漿

▶ There is a lot of starch in this meal - potatoes, corn, rice and bread.
這餐飯裡含有大量澱粉質，包括了馬鈴薯、玉米、米和麵包。

▶ The cleaner starched the collar of the shirt to make it stiff.
乾洗店把衣領上漿好讓它變挺。

---

startle [ˈstɑːr.t̬əl] *v.* 使驚嚇；使嚇一跳

同 **shock; surprise**

▶ The dog startled the mailman.
那隻狗把郵差嚇了一跳。

---

starvation [stɑːrˈveɪ.ʃən] *n.* 飢餓；挨餓

同 **famishment; starving**

▶ Starvation is a problem in many parts of the world where people don't have enough food.
世界很多地區都有飢荒的問題，人們沒有足夠的食物可吃。

---

statesman [ˈsteɪt.smən] *n.* 政治家

▶ The statesmen spent countless hours trying to create peace between the two warring countries.
那位政治家花了很多時間試圖讓那兩個交戰國締結和平。

---

stationary [ˈsteɪ.ʃə.ner.i] *adj.* 不動的

同 **firm; steady**

▶ Ned bought a stationary bike to put in his living room.
奈德買了一台健身車放在客廳裡。

---

stationery [ˈsteɪ.ʃə.ner.i] *n.* 信封信紙；文具

▶ Jeana's job is to write and send letters, so she needs a lot of stationery.
珍娜的工作是撰寫和寄信，所以她需要很多信封信紙。

---

statistic(s) [stəˈtɪs.tɪk]

n. 統計數據；統計資料

▶ Where can I find birth rate statistics for all the European countries?
怎樣才能找到所有歐洲各國的出生率統計數據？

97

statistical [stəˈtɪs.tɪ.kəl]

adj. 統計的；統計學的

▶ This baseball team had the statistical advantage, but they still lost.
這個棒球隊雖然在統計數據上佔有優勢，可是最後還是輸球了。

---

stature [ˈstætʃ.ɚ] *n.* 身高；身材

同 **height; physique**

▶ Vincent will probably have a large stature since both of his parents are tall.
文生的身材可能會長得很高，因為他爸媽都很高。

---

steamer [ˈstiː.mɚ]

① *n.* 汽船；輪船

▶ When my grandfather was young, he took a steamer from Italy to the U.S.--all by himself.
我爺爺年輕時，自己一個人搭輪船從義大利去到美國。

---

steer [stɪr]

① *v.* 掌舵；駕駛

▶ The pilot steered the ship through the dangerous channel.
船長掌舵讓船穿越危險的海峽。

實用片語與搭配詞

steer a boat into 把船駛進某處

▶ In the old days, lighthouses were the best way to steer a boat into the harbor during a storm.
以前當暴風雨來襲時，燈塔是幫助船員們將船駛進港口的最佳指引。

② *n.* 指點；建議

同 **direct**

▶ The new team needs a good steer from their department supervisor.
新團隊需要部門主管善加指點。

---

stereotype [ˈster.i.ə.taɪp]

① *n.* 刻板印象；成見

▶ That all Asian-American students are good at math is just a stereotype.
認為所有亞裔美籍學生的數學都很強，其實只是一種刻板印象。

實用片語與搭配詞

stereotyped images 刻板印象

▶ It is difficult to get rid of stereotyped images such as that all Americans are wealthy.
消除人們心中的刻板印象並非易事，例如人們總以為美國人都很富有。

② *v.* 對…有成見；對…形成刻板的看法

▶ It's not a good thing to stereotype people.
對人抱有成見不是件好事。

S

stern [stɝ:n] *adj.* 嚴格的

同 **harsh**

反 **gentle**

▶ My math teacher is a stern but caring teacher.
我的數學老師是一位很嚴格卻很有愛心的老師。

---

stew [stu:]

① *v.* 燉；煮

同 **simmer; poach**

② *n.* 燉肉；燜菜

實用片語與搭配詞

make a stew 做一道燉菜

▶ The meat needs to stew for a few more hours before it's ready to eat.
那塊肉需要再燉幾小時才能吃。

▶ The beef stew was very good. May I have more?
那道燉牛肉很好吃。我能不能再多吃一點？

▶ In winter, the best kind of food to cook is to make a stew from vegetables, beans and beef.
在冬天，最應景的料理便是用蔬菜、豆類以及牛肉做一道燉菜。

---

steward / stewardess [ˈstu:.ɚd / ˈstu:.ɚdɪs]

n. （男）服務員 /（女）服務員 / 服務員

同 **attendant**

▶ The stewardess just announced that we all need to fasten our seat belts and hang on!
那名女空服員剛才宣佈，我們大家都必須繫上安全帶，緊緊抓牢！

---

stimulate [ˈstɪm.jə.leɪt] *v.* 刺激；激勵

實用片語與搭配詞

stimulate sb. / sth. to sth.
刺激 / 激勵某人 / 事物

▶ The government hopes to stimulate spending to help the economy.
政府希望能刺激消費來拉抬經濟。

▶ If you want to stimulate yourself to exercise, you should do something you like with a friend.
如果你想要激勵自己運動，你應該要跟朋友一起從事自己喜歡的運動項目。

stimulation [ˌstɪm.jəˈleɪ.ʃən] *n.* 刺激；激勵

實用片語與搭配詞

a lack of stimulation 缺乏刺激

▶ The approaching deadline provided her with stimulation to finish the report.
即將來臨的截止日期刺激她趕快寫完報告。

▶ Many children get bored in school due to a lack of stimulation, not because they are lazy.
許多孩子們在學校感到無聊不是因為他們懶惰，而是因為缺乏刺激。

95

stimulus [ˈstɪm.jə.ləs]

n. 刺激（物）；激勵（物）

同 **input**

▸ The biggest stimulus for her desire to be an actress is her love of performing.
她想要當女演員，最大的激勵就來自於她對表演的熱愛。

---

stink [stɪŋk]

① *v.* 發出惡臭

同 **stench**

② *n.* 惡臭

▸ Our neighbor downstairs is cooking fish and stinking up the place -- again!
樓下鄰居在煮魚時，又把這裡弄得很臭。

▸ Oh my! Did something die in your closet? What is that stink?
天啊！你櫃子裡有死什麼東西嗎？為什麼那麼臭？

---

stock [stɑːk]

① *n.* 儲備；貯存

② *v.* 儲備；貯存

同 **accumulate; store up**

③ *n.* 股票

實用片語與搭配詞

a good stock of sth. 庫存充足的某物

▸ That store has a large stock of canned goods.
那家店貯藏了大量罐頭食物。

▸ They stocked the warehouse with books that will be for sale next week.
他們在倉庫裡儲備了下週要販售的書籍。

▸ My stocks did really well this year. Let's go on vacation!
我持有的股票今年行情很好，我們去度假吧！

▸ Don't blame others for your failures -- you should take a good stock of your own efforts first.
別將你的失敗怪罪在他人身上，你必須先好好累積自己的實力。

---

stoop [stuːp]

① *v.* 彎腰；屈身

同 **crouch; squat**

② *n.* 彎腰；屈身

▸ Come on, kids. Don't be afraid to stoop down and pet the dog.
孩子們，別這樣。彎下腰去撫摸那隻狗，別怕。

▸ Why are you in a stoop? Are you feeling okay?
你為什麼彎腰？哪裡不舒服嗎？

---

storage [ˈstɔːr.ɪdʒ]

n. 儲藏；儲存

▸ Where am I going to put all this stuff? I need more storage!
我該把那些東西放在哪裡？我需要更多儲藏空間！

S

stout [staʊt] *adj.* 強壯結實的

實用片語與搭配詞

a stout heart 堅定的意志

▶ I know it's heavy, but Jack's a really stout fellow; he'll be able to lift it!
我知道那很重，可是傑克那麼強壯，他能抬起來的！

▶ A true hero is not someone without fear, it is someone with a stout heart.
真實的英雄並非無懼的人；而是具有堅定心志的人。

---

straighten [ˈstreɪ.ən] *v.* 把…弄直；使挺直

同 **unbend**

▶ Here, let me help straighten your tie before you go and give your speech.
來，在你出門演講前，讓我先幫你把領帶拉直。

---

straightforward [ˌstreɪtˈfɔːr.wɚd]

adj. 直率的；坦誠的

同 **frank; uncomplicated**

▶ Peter is a straightforward kind of guy. He'll always tell you what he really thinks.
彼得真的很直率，他總是會說出他真正的想法。

Exercise 63

I. Derivatives

1. The professors in the thesis defense advised the presenter that though ___________ (statistic) evidence is compelling, more variants should be taken into consideration or analysis.
2. The sudden outburst of an explosion-like sound outside the campus ___________ (steer) everyone's attention away from the blackboard, including the teacher.
3. Failures, frustrations, competitions, or even verbal humiliation, sarcasm, indifference, should all be taken as ___________ (stimulate) that spur one's self-reflection and progress forward.
4. My brother is such a lazy couch potato that he can leave the trash and leftover untouched for months until it ___________ (stink) so terribly that the neighbors protest.
5. My sister likes to eat so much, so I always ___________ (stocked) the fridge with plenty of her favorite food before she comes to spend a few nights with me.

II. Vocabulary Choices

(A) straightforward	(B) starch	(C) statesman	(D) stern
(E) stout	(F) startled	(G) steamer	(H) stationary
(I) stature	(J) stooped		

1. Just when Oscar scattered the toast crumbs onto the side of the road for the pigeons and was enjoying the peaceful sight, a car rumbled by and ________ all the birds, making them fly about for their lives.
2. Abraham Lincoln is considered a great ________ because what he did for the country was not based on economy but humanity.
3. In the novel of Harry Potter, two of Ron's brothers, the twins, Fred and George, were described as short and strong in ________ , but in the movies, two tall and thin guys were taking the roles instead.
4. Mr. Anderson was a carpenter who liked to drink and eat, and his figure was quite ________ because of the muscles built in chopping woods and of the fat he gained from eating too much.
5. This historical event was intertwined with many complicated backgrounds, and there is no ________ answer as to right or wrong.

Unit 64

strain [streɪn]

① *v.* 拉緊；繃緊

反 **relax**

② *n.* 張力；壓力

同 **tension**

實用片語與搭配詞

a bit of a strain 有點壓力

▶ The cables are too tightly strained. I'm afraid they'll snap.
纜線繃得太緊了，我擔心它們會斷掉。

▶ I'm afraid these money problems are putting a strain on our relationship.
我擔心這些財務問題會讓我們之間的關係緊張。

▶ If you have a bit of a strain at work, you will actually perform better, than if you have no pressure at all.
比起工作時完全無壓力，稍有一點壓力將能幫助你表現得更好。

---

strait [streɪt] *n.* 海峽

▶ It takes two days to cross the strait by boat.
搭船穿越這處海峽需要花兩天的時間。

---

strand [strænd]

① *v.* 使擱淺

② *n.* 海灘；河岸；湖濱

▶ The ship got stranded in the sand.
那艘船擱淺在沙灘上了。

▶ This strand of beach is the most beautiful in the country.
這處海灘是國內最優美的海灘。

---

strangle [ˈstræŋ.gəl] *v.* 勒死

同 **smother; suffocate**

▶ The victim had marks around his neck and appeared to have been strangled.
受害者脖子上有痕，看似是被勒死的。

---

strap [stræp]

① *n.* 帶子

② *v.* 用帶捆綁

同 **belt; bind**

▶ Oh no, my strap broke! Could I borrow one of your shoelaces?
糟了！我的帶子斷掉了！能不能向你借一條鞋帶？

▶ Can you help me strap this luggage to the roof of the car?
你能不能幫我把行李綁在車頂？

---

strategic [strəˈtiː.dʒɪk] *adj.* 策略的；戰略的

同 **strategical**

▶ Marilyn made strategic plans about her future before applying for jobs.
瑪麗琳在申請工作前，已經對未來的生涯做出策略性的規劃。

stray [streɪ]

① *n.* 迷路

實用片語與搭配詞

stray from sth. 偏離某物

② *n.* 走失的寵物

③ *adj.* 流浪的；走失的

實用片語與搭配詞

stray cat / dog 流浪貓狗

▶ Don't stray too far Jonny, we're having dinner in half an hour!
強尼，別跑太遠喔，我們半小時內就要吃晚餐了！

▶ The Bible warns that one should not stray from the righteous path, but if you do, God will help you.
聖經警示人們不該偏離正途，但即使你真的走偏，神也會幫助你。

▶ I don't know who this dog belongs to. I think it's a stray.
我不知道這隻狗是誰養的，我覺得牠是隻走失的流浪狗。。

▶ Daddy, I feel sorry for these stray cats. Can we take them home?
爸，我覺得這些流浪貓好可憐喔，我們能不能把牠們帶回家？

▶ The old lady feeds the stray cats and dogs every day to make sure they get something to eat.
那位老太太每天都餵食那些流浪貓狗，以確保牠們不會挨餓。

---

streak [stri:k]

① *n.* 條紋

同 **stripe**

② *v.* 挑染；在…留下條紋

▶ Why are there streaks on these windows? I just washed them!
窗戶上怎麼會有條紋？我才剛洗過啊！

▶ Hey Heather, who streaked your hair? I like the color!
希瑟，是誰幫你挑染頭髮的，我好喜歡那種顏色喔！

---

stride [straɪd]

① *v.* 大步走

實用片語與搭配詞

stride across / over sth. 跨越某物

② *n.* 大步；闊步

▶ If Brandon thinks he's just going to stride back in here as if nothing happened, he is mistaken!
如果布蘭登以為他可以假裝好像什麼事都沒發生一樣地大剌剌地回來，就大錯特錯了。

▶ If my boss strides across the office to my cubicle, I know I am in trouble.
如果我的老闆大步橫跨整個辦公室向我的辦公隔間走來，我就知道有麻煩了。

▶ Jenny, we'll need to pick up our stride if we want to make it home before dark.
珍妮，如果我們想趕在天黑前回到家，就必須大步快走。

S

stripe [straɪp] *n.* 條紋

▶ Look, you can tell what kind of snake this is by the stripes on its back.
你看，從這條蛇背上的條紋就能判斷是哪種蛇。

101

stroll [stroʊl]

① *v.* 散步

同 **stride; amble**

② *n.* 散步

▶ After dinner, let's stroll down to the beach, OK?
晚餐後，我們去海灘上散步好嗎？

▶ That's an interesting question. Mind if we take a stroll and talk about it?
那個問題相當耐人尋味。我們可不可以一起去散步，討論一下？

---

structural [ˈstrʌk.tʃɚ.əl]

adj. 結構上的；建築上的

▶ The earthquake caused a lot of structural damage to the bridge.
那場地震對那條橋造成了很多結構上的損壞。

---

stumble [ˈstʌm.bəl]

① *v.* 絆倒；絆跌

同 **stagger; tumble**

實用片語與搭配詞

stumble over / through sth. 被某物絆倒

② *n.* 絆倒；絆跌

▶ Be careful you don't stumble over the cat!
小心別被那隻貓絆倒了！

▶ I don't like speaking in public because I always stumble over my words, no matter how hard I practice.
我不喜歡公開發表演說，因為無論多努力地練習，我當場都會結巴。

▶ Karen, I think you should go to the hospital; you took a big stumble.
凱倫，我覺得你應該去醫院，你跌得不輕！

---

stump [stʌmp]

① *n.* 樹樁；殘幹

② *v.* 問倒；砍去…的幹

▶ How do you suggest we remove this giant stump from the ground?
你建議我們該怎麼把這個大樹樁從地上拔出來呢？

▶ Sam's question stumped the teacher.
山姆的問題問倒老師了。

---

stun [stʌn] *v.* 使震驚；使驚訝

同 **shock; surprise**

實用片語與搭配詞

stun sb. into silence
使某人驚訝得說不出話來

▶ Everyone was stunned when Jenny shared the news that she was leaving.
珍妮透露她要離職的消息時，大家都很震驚。

▶ Mark stunned us all into silence when he announced his resignation.
馬克宣布辭職時，我們都驚訝得說不出話來。

stunt [stʌnt]

① *v.* 阻礙發育；表演絕技
② *n.* 特技動作；矮化病

▶ His growth was stunted because he didn't eat healthy food when he was young.
他因為年輕時沒有攝取營養的食物，而導致發育受阻。

▶ The actor performed many stunts in his new action movie.
那演員在他的新動作片中表演了很多特技動作。

---

sturdy [ˈstɝː.di] *adj.* 牢固的；健壯的

同 **firm; solid**

▶ I wouldn't put that big soup pot there; the table doesn't look very sturdy.
我不會把那一大鍋湯放在那裡，桌子看起來不太牢固。

---

stutter [ˈstʌt̬.ɚ]

① *v.* 結結巴巴地說話
同 **firm; solid**
② *n.* 口吃
同 **stammer**

▶ John stutters when he has to speak in front of strangers.
約翰在陌生人面前講話就會口吃。

▶ Pauline speaks with a slight stutter.
寶琳講話有點口吃。

---

stylish [ˈstaɪ.lɪʃ] *adj.* 時髦的；漂亮的

同 **fashionable**

▶ Hey Jimmy, I like your new shoes. They're so stylish!
喂，吉米，我喜歡你的新鞋。好時髦喔！

---

subjective [səbˈdʒek.tɪv] *adj.* 主觀的

反 **objective**

▶ What is considered polite is highly subjective and varies from country to country.
所謂的客氣有禮其實是很主觀的觀點，對此各國各不相同。

102

submit [səbˈmɪt] *v.* 提交；呈遞；屈服；服從

同 **comply**
反 **resist**

▶ Alright everyone, I need you all to submit your reports by Friday at five o'clock!
大家注意，我要所有人都在星期五五點以前繳交報告！

---

subordinate [səˈbɔːr.dən.ət]

① *adj.* 次要的；下級的
同 **inferior; secondary**
② *n.* 部屬

▶ That is a subordinate project, so you can work on it after you finish this one.
那是次要的專案，你可以在完成這個專案之後再做。

▶ The manager had a meeting with her subordinates.
經理和她的部屬一起開會。

subordinate [səˈbɔːr.dən.eɪt]

v. 使居於較低的地位

實用片語與搭配詞

subordinate sth. to sth.
將某事物置於次於另一事物的地位

- By subordinating his peers, Peter felt like he was more important.
  彼得藉由讓同僚屬於較低的地位，而讓自己顯得更重要。
- Sometimes you have to subordinate getting a higher salary to being happy at work.
  有時候你必須將快樂工作擺在獲得更高的薪水之上。

---

subscribe [səbˈskraɪb] *v.* 訂閱；訂購

- I've subscribed to Studio Classroom for 20 years and receive a new magazine each month.
  我訂閱《空中英語教室》雜誌已經二十年了，每個月都會收到一本新雜誌。

---

subscription [səbˈskrɪp.ʃən] *n.* 訂閱；訂購

- I need to renew my newspaper subscription soon.
  我不久就需要重新再訂閱那家報紙了。

---

subsequent [ˈsʌb.sɪ.kwənt]

adj. 其後的；隨後的

同 **following**

- We already met this morning, but there will be a subsequent meeting tomorrow.
  我們今天早上已經會面過了，可是明天還會有後續的會議要開。

Exercise 64

I. Derivatives

1. The couple had tried to communicate with each other but ended up arguing all the time, which kept putting a ____________ (straining) on their marriage.
2. Two frantic fishermen were so concentrated on fishing on the rocks slightly offshore that they didn't notice the tide coming in and were finally ____________ (strand) on the rock.
3. A sudden strike of an unpredicted storm aroused huge waves, making the small ship ____________ (strayed) off the original course.
4. Those naughty boys liked to tease the shy girl, mimicking the way she ____________ (stutter) in front of the boy she had a crush on.
5. After Gareth grew fond of the Japanese girls idol group, he decided to take out a ____________ (subscribe) to a fashion magazine for which the idols worked as models.

II. Vocabulary Choices

(A) strangled	(B) subjective	(C) streaked	(D) strapped
(E) strides	(F) stumble	(G) strategic	(H) stripe
(I) strait	(J) subsequent		

1. The breaking of the windows must have been ________ to our departure since we didn't hear anything resembling the shattering of glasses.
2. To increase raters' reliability, more objective and less ________ grading policies must be made for all the raters to follow.
3. After Japan lost the battle in World War II, this country made impressive ________ in improving the society in nearly every aspect.
4. The creative drive of the great artist has been ________ by the cruelty of reality.
5. Since the bombs were not sufficient, the military always place them in ________ positions to cause as much as chaos and undermine as much force for counter strike as possible.

Unit 65

substantial [səb'stæn.ʃəl] *adj.* 多的；大量的

同 **affluent; prosperous**

▶ Jess, you better be careful walking around with such a substantial amount of cash!
傑希，你帶著那麼多現金四處走，最好小心點！

96

substitute ['sʌb.stə.tu:t]

① *n.* 代替人；代替品

實用片語與搭配詞

a substitute for sb. / sth. 代替某人 / 事物

② *v.* 取代；替代

同 **replace**

▶ I'm going to be a substitute at the high school all next week.
我下個星期每天都要在那所高中當代課老師。

▶ Watching television at home all day is not a substitute for a good friend.
整天在家看電視不能取代與好友互動的快樂。

▶ How do you like the cake? I substituted honey for the sugar.
你覺得那個蛋糕味道如何？我用蜂蜜取代糖來製作的。

---

substitution [ˌsʌb.stə'tu:.ʃən] *n.* 取代；替換

▶ The substitution of natural materials with man-made products has become common.
以人造產品來取代天然素材相當常見。

---

subtle ['sʌt̬.əl]

adj. 隱約的；不明顯的；微妙的

同 **delicate**

▶ The food has a subtle taste of lemon.
這食物嚐起來略微有檸檬的味道。

---

suburban [sə'bɝ:.bən] *adj.* 郊區的；近郊的

▶ Claire loves her suburban neighborhood. It's quiet but not too far from the city.
克萊兒很喜歡位於郊區的房子，不但很安靜，而且離都市也不遠。

---

succession [sək'seʃ.ən] *n.* 接連；連續

同 **sequence; series**

▶ The contest results were announced in succession from third place to first.
比賽的結果是從第三名到第一名接連宣佈的。

---

successive [sək'ses.ɪv] *adj.* 連續的

同 **consecutive; sequential**

▶ It rained for nine successive days, so we were happy when it finally stopped.
連續下了九天的雨，因此終於雨停時，我們都覺得好高興。

successor [sək'ses.ɚ] *n.* 繼任者；後繼者

反 **predecessor**

▶ The young prince is the king's only successor and will rule the country after his father dies.
年輕的王子是國王唯一的繼任者，將在父親駕崩後統治國家。

103

suffocate ['sʌf.ə.keɪt] *v.* 使窒息

同 **choke; smother**

▶ Make sure there are small holes to allow air inside the box, or the bird will suffocate.
一定要讓盒子留有小孔好讓空氣進入，否則那隻鳥就會窒息。

suitcase ['su:t.keɪs] *n.* 手提箱；旅行箱

同 **traveling bag**

▶ Honey, pack your suitcase. We're going to Hawaii!
親愛的，打包行李。我們要去夏威夷了！

suite [swi:t] *n.* 套房；隨員

同 **entourage**

▶ The movie star stayed in the most expensive suite of the hotel.
這位電影明星住宿在飯店裡最貴的套房。

sulfur ['sʌl.fɚ] *superficial.* 硫磺

▶ No wonder it smells like sulfur. We're at a hot spring!
難怪聞起來的味道像是硫磺，我們到一處溫泉了！

104

summon ['sʌm.ən] *v.* 命令⋯到；召喚

實用片語與搭配詞

summon the courage 鼓起勇氣

▶ Marty, Mr. Meinman is summoning you. I think you're in trouble!
馬提，棉門先生叫你去找他。我想你慘了！

▶ Liz wanted to ask her boss for leave, but she could not summon the courage to do so.
麗姿想要請她的老闆離開，但是她無法鼓起勇氣這麼做。

superb [su:'pɝ:b] *adj.* 極好的

同 **excellent**

▶ This dessert is superb! I've never tasted anything so good.
這甜點超好吃的！我從來沒吃過那麼好吃的東西。

superficial [ˌsu:.pɚ'fɪʃ.əl] *adj.* 表面的

同 **surface**

反 **deep**

▶ Don't cry dear, it's just a superficial scratch.
親愛的，別哭。只是表面刮傷而已。

superiority [sə,pɪr.iˈɔːr.ə.t̬i] *n.* 上級；優越

反 **inferiority**

▶ Charlie has superiority, so you'll have to ask him to approve your request.
查理是你的上級，所以你必須請他核准你的要求。

---

supersonic [ˌsuː.pɚˈsɑː.nɪk] *adj.* 超音波的

▶ The supersonic jet flew through the sky and set a new speed record.
超音波噴射機飛越天際，創下了新的速度記錄。

102

superstition [ˌsuː.pɚˈstɪʃ.ən] *n.* 迷信

實用片語與搭配詞

an ancient superstition 古老的迷信

▶ You really believe the number thirteen is bad luck? That's just superstition!
你真的相信 13 這個數字代表厄運？那只是迷信而已！

▶ Fear of the number 13 is an ancient superstition rooted in historical events.
對數字 13 的恐懼是起源於歷史事件的古老迷信。

---

superstitious [ˌsuː.pɚˈstɪʃ.əs] *adj.* 迷信的

▶ My grandmother is very superstitious and thinks the number 13 is unlucky.
我祖母非常迷信，她認為 13 這個數字不吉利。

---

supervise [ˈsuː.pɚ.vaɪz]

v. 監督；管理；指導

同 **administer**

▶ Sorry dear, I don't want you to go if there's no adult there to supervise.
親愛的，很抱歉，如果沒有大人在場監督，我就不能讓你去。

---

supervision [ˌsuː.pɚˈvɪʒ.ən] *n.* 監督

同 **oversight**

▶ Children need supervision at the playground to make sure they don't get hurt.
孩子們在遊樂區必須要有人監督，這樣才能確保他們不會受傷。

---

supervisor [ˈsuː.pɚ.vaɪ.zɚ]

n. 監督者；管理人；指導者

同 **director; manager**

▶ Let's celebrate! I just got promoted to supervisor!
我們一起慶祝吧！我剛獲得晉升為主管！

---

supplement [ˈsʌp.lə.ment]

① *n.* 補充；增補

▶ John includes vitamin supplements in his diet because he thinks they improve his health.
約翰在飲食中添加了維生素補充錠，因為他認為它們能增進健康。

實用片語與搭配詞

vitamin supplement 維他命補充品

② *v.* 補充；增補

同 **augment; fortify**

▶ Tom takes vitamin supplements to ensure he consumes enough nutrients.
湯姆服用維他命補給品，以確保攝取足夠的營養。

▶ Today's discussion on economics supplements what we discussed last week.
今天針對經濟學的討論，可以作為我們上周所討論內容的補充。

---

suppress [səˈpres] *v.* 壓抑；鎮壓

同 **repress; restrain**

▶ The prince sent his guards to suppress the angry villagers.
王子派守衛鎮壓憤怒的村民。

---

supreme [suːˈpriːm] *adj.* 最大的；最高的

同 **greatest; utmost**

▶ The soldier made the supreme sacrifice when he died on the battlefield.
那名士兵戰死沙場，做出了最大的犧牲。

S

Exercise 65

I. Derivatives

1. Because one of the players had made too many critical mistakes resulting in losing many points, the coach decided to make a ___________ (substitute).
2. The team that got second place last year has undergone extremely strict training, and this year looks promising for them since so far they've won 7 ___________ (succession) matches and not lost even one.
3. What seems ___________ (superstition) to one may be merely a way of following the tradition for another, like stabbing and erecting chopsticks in a bowl of rice.
4. The interns are not allowed to handle the machines without proper guidance and ___________ (supervise) from a senior engineer.
5. Seeing the need for the patient to be well-nurtured for quick recovery, the doctor advised for her to take vitamin and protein ___________ (supplement).

II. Vocabulary Choices

(A) superb	(B) summoned	(C) subtle	(D) suite
(E) suburban	(F) suffocated	(G) superiority	(H) substantial
(I) suppress	(J) supreme		

1. A cross-reference on the data gained from the poll revealed a ________ difference between the opinions of men and women.
2. This story contains many hidden messages for readers to read between lines, being too ________ for young kids to read and comprehend.
3. Over the decades, with the housing price soaring, a growing number of citizens have been moving to ________ areas for more affordable and more reasonably charged residence.
4. While people generally thought the victims had died in flames, the forensic report suggested that they had ________ from the fumes.
5. The manager held an emergency meeting and ________ all the employees to his office, demanding that no absence was allowed.

Unit 66

surge [sɝːdʒ]

① *n.* 大浪

同 **flood; wave**

② *v.* 高漲；（海浪）洶湧；激增

▶ The surge crashed against the houses along the shore.

大浪衝擊到岸邊的房子。

▶ During the storm, the tide surged as high as Delancey Street. It was a terrible flood!

在暴風雨期間，浪潮漲到德蘭西街那麼高。那洪水真的好可怕！

98

surpass [sɚˈpæs] *v.* 勝過；超過

同 **exceed; excel**

▶ Candace surpassed her older sister's record and was named the new record holder.

甘達絲超越了姊姊的記錄，被稱為新的記錄保持者。

---

surplus [ˈsɝː.pləs]

① *n.* 過剩；剩餘

② *adj.* 過剩的；剩餘的

同 **excess**

反 **deficit**

▶ The toy store is having a sale because they have a surplus of stuffed animals.

玩具店正在舉行特賣會，因為店裡有很多填充動物玩具。

▶ The surplus corn will be stored for later use.

過剩的玉米將會被貯存下來以供日後使用。

97

suspend [səˈspend]

v. 使休學；使停課；使暫停參加活動

同 **postpone; defer**

▶ John broke the rules and got suspended from school for three days.

約翰違反規定，結果被罰停課三天。

---

suspense [səˈspens] *n.* 懸疑；懸而未決

同 **dangling**

▶ The performers couldn't stand the suspense as they waited for the winners to be announced.

表演者等待宣佈獲勝者時，都忍受不了那種緊張懸疑的氣氛。

---

suspension [səˈspen.ʃən] *n.* 懸吊；停職

同 **intermission**

▶ There will be a suspension of this project until further notice. Please stop all work immediately.

這項專案將暫停進行，以待進一步通知。請立刻停止所有工作。

sustain [sə'steɪn] *v.* 維持；支撐

同 **maintain; stand**

▶ Honey, if we want to sustain a balanced budget, we'll need to spend less money.
親愛的，如果我們想要維持預算平衡，就必須減少開支才行。

---

swamp [swɑ:mp]

① *n.* 沼澤

同 **flood; marsh**

② *v.* 使忙得不可開交；使陷入沼澤

實用片語與搭配詞

be swamped by sb. / sth.
為某人 / 事物應接不暇

▶ Locals say the swamp is full of mosquitoes and scary monsters!
據當地人說，那沼澤裡有很多蚊子和可怕的怪物！

▶ Sorry, I can't make it to the game. I'm swamped this weekend.
很抱歉，我不能去參加比賽。我這個週末忙得不可開交。

▶ Modern day students are so swamped by homework that they have no time to digest what they learn.
現在學生們的功課多到難以招架，以致於他們根本沒有時間消化所學的知識。

---

swap [swɑ:p]

① *v.* 交換

同 **exchange**

② *n.* 交換

同 **switch**

▶ Ronnie swapped his chips for Frankie's cookies.
郎尼用洋芋片交換法蘭奇的餅乾。

▶ Nicole plans to do a house swap and trade houses with someone for a week.
妮可打算交換房子，下週要和別人互換自己的房子。

---

swarm [swɔ:rm]

① *n.* 蜂群；一大群

同 **crowd; gather**

② *v.* 簇擁；成群移動

實用片語與搭配詞

swarm with sb. / sth. 擠滿人 / 物

▶ Be careful, there's a swarm of bees over by that bush.
小心點，灌木叢那裡有一大群蜜蜂。

▶ You should have seen those teenagers swarm around that movie star. Crazy girls!
你真該看看那些青少年簇擁著那位電影明星的德行，真是瘋狂的女孩！

▶ The mall was swarmed with people trying to buy Christmas presents.
那間購物中心擠滿了想買聖誕禮物的人們。

---

symbolic [sɪm'bɑ:.lɪk] *adj.* 象徵的

▶ This symbolic statue represents a mother's love for her children.
這個具有象徵意義的雕塑代表了母親對子女的愛。

symbolize [ˈsɪm.bə.laɪz] *v.* 象徵

同 **represent; signify**

▶ Some people believe owls symbolize wisdom.
有些人認為貓頭鷹象徵智慧。

---

symmetry [ˈsɪm.ə.tri] *n.* 對稱

同 **balance**

▶ Today we will look at the symmetry of the human face.
我們今天會觀察人臉的對稱情形。

---

sympathize [ˈsɪm.pə.θaɪz] *v.* 同情

同 **understand**

▶ Danny's upset because he doesn't feel like anyone sympathizes with him.
丹尼很難過，因為他覺得沒有人同情他。

97

symptom [ˈsɪmp.təm] *n.* 症狀

同 **indication**

▶ Eric's symptoms include a bad cough and fever.
艾瑞克的症狀包括嚴重咳嗽和發燒。

---

synonym [ˈsɪn.ə.nɪm] *n.* 同義字

同 **antonym**

▶ Large is a synonym for big.
大型的和大的是同義詞。

---

synthetic [sɪnˈθet̬.ɪk]

① *adj.* 合成的；人造的

同 **artificial; man-made**

② *n.* 合成纖維；合成物

▶ This shirt is made from plastic that went through a synthetic process.
這件襯衫是用塑膠經由合成過程所製成的。

▶ Alan's company sells synthetics to many other businesses.
亞蘭的公司販售合成纖維給很多其他的公司。

101

tackle [ˈtæk.əl] *v.* 著手處理

同 **undertake; deal with**

▶ We don't have time for this right now. Let's tackle this problem tomorrow.
我們現在沒有時間處理這件事。明天再處理這個問題可以嗎？

---

tact [tækt] *n.* 老練；圓融

同 **diplomacy**

反 **awkwardness**

▶ Annie needs to use more tact when talking to customers so that she won't offend them.
安妮和客戶講話時，需要更加圓融，才不會觸怒他們。

98

tactic [ˈtæk.tɪk] *n.* 戰術；手法

同 **maneuver**

▶ The basketball coach spent a lot of time planning the team's tactics for the upcoming game.
籃球教練花了很多時間規劃球隊下一次比賽的戰術。

S

tan [tæn]

① *n.* 淺棕色；曬成古銅色的皮膚

② *adj.* 淺棕色的

同 **bronze; burn**

③ *v.* 曬成古銅色

► Instead of brown, why not choose a lighter color? Why not choose tan?
與其選棕色，何不選個淺一點的顏色？為什麼不選棕黃色呢？

► Your new tan shoes look really stylish.
你那雙淺棕色的鞋看起來真時髦。

► I am going to tan the hide of the bear and make a rug.
我要去把那張熊皮染成淺棕色，然後製成地毯。

---

tangle [ˈtæŋ.gəl]

① *v.* 使糾纏

同 **twist**

反 **disentangle**

② *n.* 糾結的一團；混亂

► Our headphone wires were tangled together.
我們的頭戴式耳機的線纏在一起了。

► You will need a lot of patience to undo this tangle.
你需要很有耐心地解開這糾結的一團。

---

tar [tɑːr]

① *n.* 柏油；瀝青；焦油

② *v.* 用瀝青覆蓋

► They used tar to fill in the cracks in the highway.
他們用柏油填補公路上的裂縫。

► The road workers tarred the cracks in the highway.
修路工人用柏油填補公路上的裂縫。

---

tariff [ˈter.ɪf] *n.* 稅率；關稅

同 **duty; tax**

► The government placed a new tariff on fruit so now apples are more expensive.
政府針對水果課徵新關稅，導致現在蘋果變得更貴了。

---

tart [tɑːrt] *n.* 餡餅

► I would like to have a cup of coffee with this tart.
我想來杯咖啡來配這塊餡餅吃。

Exercise 66

I. Derivatives

1. The experts appealed to the government to enact the ___________ (suspense) of a chemical fertilizer that is capable of jeopardizing people's health.
2. In many stories and films, the presence of white doves can be seen as a ___________ (symbolic) of peace and serenity.
3. In the making of clothes, more and more merchants opt for ___________ (synthetically) fibers rather than natural ones, which costs more.
4. A sign was erected some distance away from the alligator-infested ___________ (swampy), warning people to keep off for their safety.
5. As the mega-star of a rock band announced that their final concert of the year would be held in a park free of charge, tens of thousands of fans ___________ (swarm) to it.

II. Vocabulary Choices

(A) tangled	(B) surge	(C) tariff	(D) sustain
(E) tactic	(F) synonym	(G) symmetry	(H) swap
(I) suspended	(J) sympathized		

1. After accidentally finding a letter hidden among the books on her shelf, which was from her ex-boyfriend, Nancy read with a ________ of remorse, missing him a lot.
2. Joe's leg was broken in a car accident, and it was quite uncomfortable for him to lie on the hospital bed with his leg ________ in the air.
3. Still single in his forties, Ben seems to find it difficult to ________ relationships with the women he loved.
4. In this story, the main character was portrayed as someone who always ________ with others, putting himself in their shoes, and thus won many friends at last.
5. Melody's boyfriend was a selfish, self-centered man, and thus her friends and family all considered him the last man they want to get ________ with, but she would not listen.

Unit 67

taunt [tɑːnt]

① *n.* 嘲笑；嘲弄；奚落

同 **jeer; mock**

② *v.* 嘲笑；嘲弄；奚落

實用片語與搭配詞

taunt sb. with sth. 嘲弄某人

▶ The taunts of the bully were enough to make Jack cry.
那個霸凌者光是嘲弄就害傑克哭了。

▶ The bully taunted his younger classmates.
那個霸凌者嘲弄了年紀比他小的同學。

▶ I had to study for a test, but my friends tried to taunt me with images of the party they were going to.
我必須讀書準備考試，但是我朋友們秀出他們要去的派對的照片，試圖逗弄我。

---

tavern [ˈtæv.ɚn] *n.* 小酒館

同 **bar; pub**

▶ The tavern was full of people, eating and drinking.
那家小酒館坐滿了客人，大家在裡面吃吃喝喝。

---

tedious [ˈtiː.di.əs] *adj.* 單調乏味的；無趣的

同 **boring**

反 **exciting**

▶ Doing the same thing every day can be very tedious.
每天重複做同樣的事可能會相當單調乏味。

---

teller [ˈtel.ɚ] *n.* 敘述者；說故事者；出納員

同 **narrator; storyteller**

▶ The teller filled us with wonder as he told stories of the past.
說故事的人訴說著從前的故事，讓我們聽得驚奇萬分。

---

temperament [ˈtem.pɚ.ə.mənt]

n. 氣質；性情

同 **disposition**

▶ Benny has a calm temperament and always seems very relaxed.
班尼個性平穩，似乎總是一副很放鬆的模樣。

---

tempest [ˈtem.pɪst] *n.* 暴風雨

同 **storm**

▶ Going outside in that tempest is a bad idea. The wind and rain are too strong.
在暴風雨中出門是很差的主意，風雨太強了。

---

tempo [ˈtem.poʊ] *n.* 節奏；速度

同 **pace**

▶ This song is too slow. We need one with a faster tempo.
這首歌太慢了，我們需要聽首節奏更快的歌。

103

tempt [tempt] *v.* 誘惑；吸引

同 **attract**

▶ Please don't tempt me with those donuts. I've already eaten too much.
請不要用那些甜甜圈來誘惑我，我已經吃太多了。

99

temptation [temp'teɪ.ʃən] *n.* 誘惑（物）

同 **seduction**

▶ It was difficult to resist the temptation to continue playing video games.
實在很難抗拒繼續打電玩的誘惑。

104

tenant ['ten.ənt]

① *n.* 房客

同 **inhabitant**

反 **landlord**

② *v.* 租；居住於…

同 **dwell**

▶ The reason she is a good tenant is because she keeps the house clean.
她是個好房客，因為她把房子維持得很乾淨。

▶ Almost all of the houses on this block are tenanted.
這條街上幾乎所有房子都出租。

---

tentative ['ten.t̬ə.t̬ɪv] *adj.* 嘗試的；暫時的

同 **provisional**

▶ He has tentative plans for the weekend.
他想好了度週末的暫定計畫。

---

terminal ['tɝː.mə.nəl]

① *adj.* 末端的

同 **terminus**

② *n.* 末端；終站；航站大廈

▶ His final exam is tomorrow. It will be the terminal moment of his school year.
他明天期末考，也就是他本學年尾聲的時刻了。

▶ The terminal of the school year often includes many exams.
學年末往往會有很多考試。

---

terminate ['tɝː.mə.neɪt] *v.* 使停止；使終止

同 **end; finish**

▶ The meeting terminated with a surprise birthday for one of the employees.
會議結束時，為一位員工舉行了驚喜生日會。

---

terrace ['ter.əs]

① *n.* 露台

同 **patio**

② *v.* 使有露台；使成梯形地

▶ The wooden terrace surrounded the house.
房子四周環繞著木質露台。

▶ The workers agreed to terrace the house.
工人答應為房子建造露台。

T

textile [ˈtek.staɪl]

① *n.* 紡織品

同 **cloth fabric**

實用片語與搭配詞

handwoven textile 手工織品

② *adj.* 紡織的

▶ This store supplies textiles to dressmakers.
這家店為服裝廠商供應紡織品。

▶ Handwoven textiles, especially carpets, are very expensive.
手工編織品是非常昂貴的，特別是地毯。

▶ Mark works in a textile factory.
馬克在一家紡織工廠工作。

texture [ˈteks.tʃɚ]

① *n.* 質地；結構

同 **surface**

② *v.* 使…具有…的紋理；使具有特殊結構

▶ Ken loves the texture of loose-knit sweaters.
肯恩喜歡寬鬆毛衣的質地。

▶ Cynthia textured the walls of her living room to make them slightly rough.
辛西亞讓客廳牆壁具有特殊紋理，使它們看起來有點粗糙的質感。

---

theatrical [θiˈæt.rɪ.kəl] *adj.* 戲劇的；劇場的

▶ There will be a theatrical performance at the high school on Saturday.
週六那所高中將舉行戲劇表演。

---

theft [θeft] *n.* 竊盜

同 **stealing**

▶ This store uses security cameras to try to discourage theft.
那家店用安全監控攝影機試圖防止竊盜發生。

---

theoretical [ˌθiː.əˈret̬.kəl] *adj.* 理論上的

同 **empirical**

▶ The speaker will discuss the theoretical ideas that support the theory of gravity.
講員將探討支持重力理論的理論上的概念。

---

therapist [ˈθer.ə.pɪst] *n.* 治療師

▶ Nick is seeing a therapist to help him overcome his anger issues.
尼克在看治療師，來幫助自己克服發怒的問題。

therapy [ˈθer.ə.pi] *n.* 治療；療法

▶ After breaking her leg, Shelly needed therapy to help her walk again.
雪麗斷腿之後，需要治療才能再度行走。

---

thereafter [ˌðerˈæf.tɚ] *adv.* 此後

同 **thenceforth**

▶ Angie attended college from 1998 to 2002, thereafter, she worked as a secretary.
安吉從 1998 年至 2002 年就讀大學，之後她就擔任秘書的工作。

thereby [ˌðerˈbaɪ] *adv.* 因此

▶ The mayor announced a new holiday for the city, thereby making many people happy.
市長宣佈該市有新的假日，因此讓很多民眾都感到很開心。

95

thermometer [θɚˈmɑː.mə.t̬ɚ] *n.* 溫度計

▶ The doctor placed the thermometer in her patient's mouth to check his temperature.
醫師把溫度計放入患者的口中，以便測量他的體溫。

thigh [θaɪ] *n.* 大腿

同 **second joint**

▶ During the race, John pulled a muscle in his thigh.
約翰在比賽時拉傷了大腿。

Exercise 67

I. Derivatives

1. Though the ___________ (tempt) of fame and wealth was so great, this young singer still resisted and decided to quit her career in the show business at the peak of her life.
2. Bullying can come in various forms, not just in fist fights but also in verbally abusing and publicly ___________ (taunt) someone, making fun of him/her in a humiliating way.
3. Paul fell asleep on the bus for he had stayed up all night, and the moment he woke up, he found himself at the bus ___________ (terminate) with no one in sight but the bus driver.
4. In this mountainous county, there was no plain for farmers to grow food, and the ___________ (terrace) came as an alternative to that problem, transforming the slopes into small pieces of farmland ·
5. The newly-invented artificial fabric has, to the surprise of many, the ___________ (texture) resembling that of silk and was smooth to the touch.

II. Vocabulary Choices

(A) tentative	(B) theoretical	(C) tavern	(D) thereby
(E) temperament	(F) textile	(G) theft	(H) tedious
(I) therapy	(J) theatrical		

1. After a long day trekking through the dense forest, the protagonist in the novel came to a small village, where there was only one small ________ for them to get something to drink.
2. Though jogging is a good form of aerobics, many people find it ________ to carry out in that it is not competitive in nature but mechanically repetitive.
3. Fierce-looking as Mr. Hoffman was, he was, as a matter of fact, of a rather gentle and tender ________ and could take good care of others.
4. The ________ construct of this experiment is feasible, but in reality, there are many other influences that one should take into consideration in its conduction.
5. Among the major-crime convicts that were being transferred to another jail, it seemed weird that Nicholas, who was accused of ________ , a relatively minor crime, was also in the queue; he wouldn't dare to steal from them.

thorn [θɔ:rn] *n.* 刺；有刺的植物

同 **prickle**

▸ Roses are beautiful but have many thorns.
玫瑰雖美，卻有很多刺。

---

threshold [ˈθreʃ.hoʊld] *n.* 門檻

同 **doorway; gateway**

▸ Be careful not to trip on the wooden threshold when you walk through the door.
你走進門時，小心別被木門檻絆倒了。

---

thrift [θrɪft] *n.* 節省；節約

反 **waste**

▸ Marge was very impressed by her sister's thrift and ability to buy many things at low prices.
瑪吉相當佩服姊妹的節省和以低價買到很多東西的能力。

---

thrifty [ˈθrɪf.ti] *adj.* 節儉的

同 **prudent**

反 **wasteful**

▸ Dennis is teaching his kids to be thrifty, so they will have good spending habits in the future.
丹尼斯正在教導孩子力行節儉，好讓他們未來培養出良好的花錢習慣。

---

thrill [θrɪl]

① *n.* 興奮；引起激動的事

同 **excitement**

② *v.* 使興奮

同 **excite**

▸ It gave John a thrill to score the goal for the team.
約翰為球隊進了一球，而感到興奮無比。

▸ Anna was thrilled when she got the promotion.
安娜獲得升遷時，感到非常興奮。

---

thriller [ˈθrɪl.ɚ]

n. 使毛骨悚然的東西；恐佈小說或電影

實用片語與搭配詞

best-selling thriller 暢銷驚悚小說

▸ The thriller was very scary to watch.
那部恐怖片觀賞起來真的很嚇人。

▸ That best-selling thriller will be made into a movie.
那本暢銷驚悚小說會被拍成電影。

---

thrive [θraɪv] *v.* 生長茂盛；興旺；繁榮

同 **flourish**

反 **decline**

▸ This flower thrives in hot, humid environments, so make sure it doesn't get cold and dry.
這種花在炎熱潮溼的環境中生長茂盛，所以不能讓它處於寒冷和乾燥之中。

T

throb [θrɑːb]

① *v.* 跳動；脈動

同 **beat; pulsate**

② *n.* 跳動；脈動

▶ Katie's heart throbbed when she saw her boyfriend get down on one knee.
看到男友單膝下跪時，凱蒂心蹦蹦跳。

▶ After running 10 kilometers, Anna could feel the throb of her heart throughout her body.
安娜跑了十公里之後，全身上下都能感受到心臟蹦蹦跳。

---

throne [θroʊn] *n.* 王座；王權

實用片語與搭配詞

an heir to the throne 王位繼承人

▶ The king sat on his throne.
國王坐在他的王座上。

▶ If the king dies without an heir to the throne, then his brother or nephew might become king.
如果國王在駕崩前未指定王位繼承人，那麼他的兄弟或外甥可能會成為國王。

---

throng [θrɑːŋ]

① *n.* 群眾；人群

同 **crowd; gather**

② *v.* 擠滿；湧入

同 **jam**

▶ The throng of people gathered in the square.
群眾集結在廣場上。

▶ The audience thronged the area in front of the stage.
舞台前方的那塊區域擠滿了聽眾。

---

thrust [θrʌst]

① *v.* 插入；推擠；刺

同 **shove; propel**

② *n.* 猛推；推力

同 **push**

▶ They started digging the hole by thrusting the shovel into the ground.
他們將鏟子插入土中，開始挖洞。

▶ The thrust of the bus caused many people to lose their balance.
巴士突然猛地一動，導致很多人失去平衡。

---

tick [tɪk]

① *n.* 滴答聲

② *v.* 發滴答聲

▶ The tick of the clock slowed down because the battery was low.
鐘的滴答減緩了，因為電池電量很低。

▶ The clock kept on ticking throughout the night.
那座鐘整晚都不停地發出滴答聲。

---

tile [taɪl]

① *n.* 瓷磚

▶ The tile had come loose from the floor.
那塊瓷磚從地板上脫落了。

實用片語與搭配詞

floor tile 地磚

② *v.* 鋪磁磚

▶ Jo loves marble floor tiles, but her husband feels that they are too hard to keep clean.
喬喜愛大理石地磚，但她的丈夫認為它很難維持潔淨。

▶ The bathroom floor was tiled.
浴室地板鋪了瓷磚。

---

tilt [tɪlt]

① *v.* 使傾斜；翹起

同 **incline; slope**

實用片語與搭配詞

tilt to one side 向某一方倒 / 一面倒

② *n.* 傾斜

▶ He tilted the bowl of soup.
他端的那碗湯傾倒了。

▶ The ferry disaster happened when the boat tilted to one side too much and started sinking.
當渡輪朝一邊過度傾斜並開始下沈時，那場船難便發生了。

▶ It was difficult to eat soup because the dining table had a tilt.
因為餐桌傾斜了，所以很難在上面好好地喝湯。

---

tin [tɪn]

① *n.* 錫

② *v.* 把…裝罐；在…上鍍錫

▶ Most cans are made of tin.
大多數罐頭都是用錫做的。

▶ The fish will be sent to the factory where they will be tinned.
那些魚會被運到工廠裝進罐頭裡。

---

tiptoe [ˈtɪp.toʊ]

① *n.* 躡手躡腳地走；踮著腳走

② *v.* 躡手躡腳地走；踮著腳走

③ *adv.* 踮著腳尖

▶ Because they are asleep, you need to tiptoe.
因為他們已經睡了，所以你必須躡手躡腳地走才行。

▶ I tiptoed into the room as quietly as I could.
我躡手躡腳走進房間，盡量靜悄悄地不發出聲音。

▶ The short boy had to stand tiptoe just to be able to see.
小個子的男孩必須踮著腳尖才能看清楚。

---

toad [toʊd] *n.* 蟾蜍

同 **toad; frog**

▶ The slimy toad lived in the swamp.
那隻身上滿是黏液的蟾蜍住在沼澤裡。

toil [tɔɪl]

① *v.* 辛勤工作；辛苦工作

同 **labor**

反 **rest**

② *n.* 辛勞；辛苦；苦工

同 **labor**

反 **rest**

▶ The mother toiled over making dinner.
那位母親很辛苦地做晚餐。

▶ Making dinner requires a lot of toil.
做晚餐相當辛苦。

---

token [ˈtoʊ.kən] *n.* 表示；象徵；紀念品

同 **symbol**

▶ The mother's sacrifice was a token of how much she loved her children.
母親的犧牲代表她對子女莫大的愛。

---

toll [toʊl]

① *v.* 收（通行等）費；敲鐘

同 **charge**

② *n.* 收費站；通行費

同 **fare; fee**

③ *n.* 鐘聲

▶ The city tolls cars as they enter through the main road.
該市向進入主要道路的車輛收通行費。

▶ There is a toll on this road, so make sure you stop and pay it.
這條路上有收費站，所以一定要停車付通行費。

▶ We could hear the toll ringing throughout the city.
我們可以聽到鐘聲響徹市內各地。

---

topple [ˈtɑː.pəl] *v.* 使倒塌；推翻

同 **stumble; tumble**

▶ Walter bumped into the desk, and his glass of water toppled to the floor.
華特撞到桌子，導致他的那杯水就倒到地上了。

---

torch [tɔːrtʃ]

① *n.* 火把；火炬

同 **lamp; lantern**

實用片語與搭配詞

carry lighted torches 拿著點燃的火把

② *v.* 引火燃燒

▶ The torch made a bright light.
那個火把發出了很亮的光芒。

▶ Protesters against the electricity price increase symbolically carried lighted torches on their night march.
那些不滿電費調漲的抗議人士象徵性地在夜間遊行中高舉火把。

▶ All of the unwanted waste was torched.
所有廢棄的垃圾都被燒掉了。

---

torment [ˈtɔːr.ment]

① *n.* 痛苦；苦惱

▶ I don't like this movie. It's a torment to keep watching it.
我不喜歡這部電影，一直盯著看是很痛苦的事。

② *v.* 折磨；使痛苦

同 **agonize**

反 **comfort**

▶ Stop tormenting me by playing that awful song.
不要播放那首可怕的歌，別再折磨我了。

104

tornado [tɔːrˈneɪ.doʊ] *n.* 龍捲風；颶風

同 **hurricane; whirlwind**

▶ The winds of the tornado were so strong that it carried a house down the road.
颶風的風強烈到把一棟房子都刮到路上了。

---

torrent [ˈtɔːr.ənt] *n.* 洪流；（雨的）傾注

同 **flood**

▶ The torrent of water poured down.
洪水奔流而下。

T

Exercise 68

I. Derivatives

1. Beginning as a poor teenager, Dustin is now a wealthy businessman, but he still stays ____________ (thrift) for it's the key factor contributing to his success.
2. Julia advised her sister Janet to be wary of boys' invitation to a movie, saying that if it was a ____________ (thrill), it was likely that they desired physical touch.
3. In the occasions like parties, there are songs with good ____________ (throb) bass, constituting the base rhythm, which is great to dance to.
4. At the front gate of the court, a lot of reporters swarmed over and ____________ (thrust) the microphones at the accused official, firing questions.
5. Though depriving people of their lives is not something that should be approved, some would agree that euthanasia is a humane way to end ____________ (torment) for patients in critical conditions.

II. Vocabulary Choices

(A) tornado	(B) threshold	(C) token	(D) ticked
(E) throne	(F) torrent	(G) topple	(H) toil
(I) thrived	(J) tilted		

1. Most young people nowadays earn a salary well below the _________ for the standard of minimum wage, not even able to pay the rent.
2. Though his family didn't expect his business of chocolate candy to come any closer to success, it _________ with his innovation in creating new flavors.
3. As the only heir in the royal family, Charles ascended the _________ when his father died in the battle.
4. With days of incessant rain, the accumulated heavy rainfall turned the river into a raging _________ , drowning the villages nearby.
5. A small gift from the cats, as the story goes, was offered to the little girl who saved their Prince Cat, as a _________ of gratitude and trust.

Unit 69

torture ['tɔ:r.tʃɚ]

① *n.* 拷打；折磨

實用片語與搭配詞

the tortures of suspense
內心疑慮 / 恐懼的折磨

② *v.* 拷打；使難過

同 **persecute; torment**

▶ The soldiers were trained to be able to withstand torture.
那些士兵接受過訓練能夠忍受拷打。

▶ The tortures of suspense, whether someone loves you or not, is too hard to bear.
無論對方是否愛你，內心疑慮所帶來的折磨都是難以忍受的。

▶ The soldiers tortured the enemy in order to get information.
那些士兵拷打敵人，以便獲得情報。

---

tournament ['tɝ:.nə.mənt / 'tʊr.nə.mənt]

n. 比賽；錦標賽

同 **contest**

▶ Our soccer team is going to the national tournament this year!
我們的足球隊今年要參加國家錦標賽！

---

toxic ['tɑ:k.sɪk] *adj.* 有毒的

同 **poisonous**

▶ The toxic trash was causing people to be sick.
有毒的垃圾導致人們生病。

---

trademark ['treɪd.mɑ:rk] *n.* 商標

同 **hallmark**

▶ The company's name was protected from being copied by a trademark.
那家公司的名稱有註冊商標的保護以防被仿冒。

---

trait [treɪt] *n.* 特性；特徵

同 **attribute**

▶ I think Cindy's best trait is her willingness to help others.
我認為辛蒂最好的特性就是她樂於助人。

---

traitor ['treɪ.t̬ɚ] *n.* 叛徒；賣國賊

同 **betrayer**

▶ He had joined with the enemy and was now considered a traitor to his country.
他加入了敵人的陣營，如今被視為賣國賊。

---

tramp [træmp]

① *v.* 沈重行走

同 **vagrant**

② *n.* 沈重腳步聲

▶ We tramped through the forest.
我們腳步沈重地穿越森林。

▶ Did you hear that? It sounded like a tramp!
你有沒有聽到那聲音？聽起來像是重重的腳步聲！

T

104

trample [ˈtræm.pəl]

① *v.* 踐踏

同 **tramp down; tread down**

實用片語與搭配詞

trample on sb.'s dignity 踐踏某人的尊嚴

② *n.* 踐踏（聲）

▶ He was almost trampled by the crowd of people coming into the store.
他幾乎要被衝進店裡的人群踐踏到了。

▶ When you trample on someone's dignity, you not only destroy their spirit, but also yours.
當你踐踏他人的尊嚴，你不僅是摧毀了他人的心靈，也摧毀了你自己的。

▶ Although the horses are far away, you can hear their trample.
雖然那些馬離這裡很遠，但可以聽到馬蹄的踏地聲。

---

tranquil [ˈtræŋ.kwɪl] *adj.* 安靜的；平靜的

同 **quiet**

反 **noisy**

▶ We hope to spend the weekend at a tranquil location away from the city.
我們希望週末能在遠離都市的安靜地點度過。

---

tranquilizer [ˈtræŋ·kwəˌlɑɪ·zər] *n.* 鎮定劑

▶ The doctor recommends using music as a tranquilizer to calm nervous patients.
醫生建議運用音樂來鎮定安撫緊張的患者。

transaction [trænˈzæk.ʃən] *n.* 交易

同 **deal**

▶ The two companies completed their business transaction after months of discussion.
經過長達數月的商議，那兩家公司終於完成了商業交易。

transcript [ˈtræn.skrɪpt] *n.* 副本

同 **copy**

▶ The government office keeps a written transcript of all of the verbal requests it receives.
那個政府單位會針對所有收到的所有口頭要求都保存書面文字記錄。

---

transformation [ˌtræns.fɚˈmeɪ.ʃən]

n. 徹底改觀；轉變

同 **shift**

▶ The old house went through a major transformation and now looks very modern.
那棟老房子歷經大幅裝修，如今外觀非常現代。

---

transistor [trænˈzɪs.tɚ] *n.* 電晶體

▶ The electrician connected the transistor to the board to act as a switch.
電工把電晶體連接到板子上作為開關之用。

transit ['træn.zɪt]

① *n.* 通過；經過；運輸

② *v.* 通過；經過；運輸

同 **pass; through**

▶ We saw many animals during our transit through the mountains.
我們通過山區時，看到了很多動物。

▶ The ship transited the Atlantic Ocean in two weeks.
那艘船在兩週內就穿越大西洋。

transition [træn'zɪʃ.ən] *n.* 轉變；過度

同 **change; shift**

▶ The shop plans to make a transition from selling bread to selling cake.
那家店計畫從賣麵包改為販售蛋糕。

transmission [træns'mɪʃ.ən] *n.* 傳輸；傳送

實用片語與搭配詞

simultaneous transmission 同步播放

▶ The transmission of sound is slower than that of light.
聲音的傳輸速度比光的傳輸更緩慢。

▶ The election outcome was broadcast world-wide through simultaneous transmissions to all television stations.
這場選舉的結果藉由所有電視台的同步播放，被散佈至全世界。

transmit [træns'mɪt] *v.* 傳輸；傳送

同 **dispatch; send over**

▶ The message was transmitted by email.
那個訊息透過電子郵件傳送出去了。

101

transparent [træn'sper.ənt] *adj.* 透明的

反 **opaque**

▶ The paper was so transparent, you could see through it.
那張紙透明到幾乎可以一眼看穿。

transplant [træn'splænt]

① *v.* 移植

同 **relocate**

② *n.* 移植

實用片語與搭配詞

a heart transplant operation
心臟移植手術

▶ Gayle transplanted the flowers into a larger pot.
蓋爾把那株花移植到更大的花盆裡。

▶ The transplant of the tomatoes from the pot to the garden was successful.
番茄成功地從花盆移植到園子裡了。

▶ The first successful heart transplant operation was done in the 1960s and since then it has become fairly common.
從 1960 年第一起成功的心臟移植手術以後，至今該手術已變得相當普遍。

T

trauma [ˈtrɑː.mə] *n.* 外傷；創傷

反 **injury**

▶ Jerod suffered head trauma from the car accident.
傑若發生車禍之後深受頭部創傷所苦。

---

tread [tred]

① *v.* 步行；走；踩；踏

同 **step**

② *n.* 步行；走；踩；踏

實用片語與搭配詞

tread on sb.'s toe 踩到某人的地雷

▶ The hikers treaded along the path through the woods.
健行者沿著路走，穿越森林。

▶ We're going to take a tread through the jungle.
我們將會步行穿越叢林。

▶ Jenny tread on her boyfriend's toes by mentioning her ex-boyfriend and now he is not talking to her.
珍妮提及她的前男友時踩到了現任男友的地雷，導致他現在拒絕跟她說話。

---

treason [ˈtriː.zən] *n.* 叛國罪；謀反罪

反 **betrayal**

▶ The man was charged with treason for selling secret government files to another country.
那名男子被控叛國罪，因為他販售國家機密檔案給別國。

---

treasury [ˈtreʒ.ɚ.i] *n.* 國庫；寶藏

▶ The country stored it's money in the treasury.
那個國家把錢都存進國庫裡。

---

treaty [ˈtriː.t̬i] *n.* 協定；條約

反 **agreement; arrangement**

▶ The two countries made peace by signing a treaty.
兩國簽署協定，和平共處。

Exercise 69

I. Derivatives

1. During the earthquake, the stadium collapsed, the crowd rushed out onto the football pitch, and a few were ____________ (trample) to death.
2. After her husband died in a car accident and her only son was recruited to the battlefield, Maria had been on ____________ (tranquil) for long.
3. The explosion of the power plant seemed to let out some kind of invisible wave that hindered the ____________ (transmit) of text messages on cell phones.
4. The heart ____________ (transplantation) surgery, though taking a lot of time, was successful in that the patient's body didn't show signs of rejection.
5. Throughout history, there is no lack of examples in which a country perished not because its military force was not strong enough but because there were ____________ (traitorous) who were not loyal to the country.

II. Vocabulary Choices

(A) transparent (B) torture (C) tournament (D) toxic
(E) trauma (F) transition (G) tread (H) transaction
(I) treason (J) transcript

1. After the senior officials were invited to the feast held by a country deemed as an enemy, they were charged with _________ when returning.
2. Some childhood _________ can last for a lifetime and influence one to the extent that he/she cannot lead a normal life without counselling.
3. In the frantic artist's next exhibition, a female model was sitting in a _________ enclosure made from plastic, posing slowly and silently for people to watch.
4. The president of that country was impeached for cronyism, and the vice president served as an interim substitute during the _________ until the next election.
5. In a courtroom, everything the witnesses says is important and has to be recorded as a _________ either by typing or writing.

Unit 70

trek [trek]

① *v.* 艱苦跋涉

② *n.* 徒步旅程；艱苦跋涉

▶ We trekked through the wilderness for two weeks.
我們在野外跋涉兩週之久。

▶ The first trek of our journey will take us across this mountain.
我們這次旅行中的第一段徒步旅程就是穿越這座山。

---

tremor [ˈtrem.ɚ] *n.* 震動；顫抖

同 **quiver; shiver**

▶ Everyone was surprised by the tremor because they had never experienced an earthquake.
大家都對震動感到驚訝，因為他們從未經歷過地震。

---

trench [trentʃ]

① *n.* 溝；渠

同 **channel; ditch**

② *v.* 挖溝渠

同 **dig**

▶ The soldiers dug a trench to protect themselves.
士兵們挖掘壕溝來防護自己。

▶ The construction workers will trench the area around the building.
建築工人將在那棟建築四周挖溝。

---

trespass [ˈtres.pæs]

① *v.* 擅自進入

同 **transgress**

② *n.* 侵入；擅自進入

同 **infringe; intrude**

▶ Aaron put up a fence to prevent people from trespassing on his land.
亞倫豎起圍籬，以防止民眾擅自進入他的土地。

▶ The thief was not sorry for his trespass and planned to break into another house.
那名小偷對於他擅自侵入完全不後悔，還打算闖入另一戶人家。

---

tribute [ˈtrɪb.juːt] *n.* 讚揚；敬意

同 **eulogy; praise**

▶ The king gave him a medal in tribute to his bravery.
國王為了讚揚他的勇敢，就頒發獎章給他。

---

trifle [ˈtraɪ.fəl]

① *n.* 少量；小事

② *v.* 玩弄；輕視

▶ His pocket change was a trifle compared to his money in the bank.
和他的銀行存款金額相比，那筆零錢只是小錢而已。

▶ Don't trifle with my feelings!
不要玩弄我的感情！

trigger ['trɪg.ɚ]

① *n.* 扳機

實用片語與搭配詞

pull / squeeze the trigger 扣板機；做決定

② *v.* 引發；扣扳機

同 **fire**

▶ The gun instructor showed his students how to hold one finger against the trigger.
射擊講師向學生示範用一個手指扣住板機的方式。

▶ After months of consideration, the boss pulled the trigger and ended the project.
經過幾個月的思量，老闆決定終止這個專案。

▶ Valerie's mention of free food triggered a happy reaction among the students.
維樂利提到了免費食物，在學生中間引發了快樂的反應。

---

trim [trɪm]

① *v.* 修剪

同 **shave**

② *n.* 修剪

實用片語與搭配詞

trim sth. off sth. 把某物從另一物修剪掉

③ *adj.* 苗條的；整齊的

同 **neat; tidy**

▶ He spent his afternoon trimming the hedges in his yard.
他下午在院子裡修剪樹籬。

▶ The hedges in his yard really needed a trim.
他院子裡的樹籬需要修剪一下。

▶ My article was too long, so my editor told me to trim some words off the end.
我的文章太長了，所以我的編輯要我刪減結尾中的幾個字。

▶ The runner had a trim figure.
那名跑者體型相當苗條。

---

triple ['trɪp.əl]

① *adj.* 三倍的

② *n.* 三倍數；三個一組

③ *v.* 增至三倍

▶ Please give me a triple portion of the soup.
請給我三份湯。

▶ With the shaved ice, you can order the single, the double or the triple.
你可以點一份、兩份或三份剉冰。

▶ The money he put in the bank tripled over ten years.
他存在銀行裡的錢在十年後增為三倍。

---

triumphant [traɪ'ʌm.fənt] *adj.* 勝利的

同 **exulting; rejoicing**

▶ The little girl was triumphant and won first place.
小女孩獲勝了，贏得第一名。

T

trivial [ˈtrɪv.i.əl] *adj.* 不重要的；瑣碎的

同 **insignificant**

反 **important**

▶ Even though the problems were only trivial, Susan was still stressed out.
雖然問題很小，但蘇珊仍然倍感壓力。

---

trophy [ˈtroʊ.fi] *n.* 獎盃；戰利品

同 **award; prize**

▶ Chris had several trophies on display for all the games he had won.
克里斯展示出的幾座獎盃，全都是他贏得比賽的戰利品。

---

tropic [ˈtrɑː.pɪk]

① *n.* 北回歸線

② *adj.* 熱帶的

同 **tropical**

▶ Sam lives very close to the Tropic of Cancer.
山姆住在離北回歸線很近的地方。

▶ Andy lives in a very tropic environment, so he often talks about the hot temperatures.
安迪住在熱帶的環境，所以他常常提到炎熱的氣候。

---

trot [trɑːt]

① *v.* （馬）小跑步；快步走

② *n.* （馬）小跑步；快步走

實用片語與搭配詞

go for a trot 去小跑

▶ The horse trotted over to me.
那匹馬朝我跑來。

▶ That horse has a beautiful trot.
那匹馬小跑步的步態相當優美。

▶ During summers on the farm, I would go for a trot on my favorite horse to enjoy the fresh air.
在夏日的農場，我會騎著我最愛的馬小跑一段，享受新鮮空氣。

---

trout [traʊt] *n.* 鱒魚

▶ The trout jumped out of the water.
那隻鱒魚跳出水面。

---

truant [ˈtruː.ənt]

① *n.* 逃學者

② *adj.* 逃學的

③ *v.* 逃學

▶ The school principal had to discipline the truants for skipping class.
校長必須管教蹺課的逃學者。

▶ Any truant students will have to make up their work during summer school.
所有逃學的學生都必須在暑期輔導補課。

▶ Nathan had to catch up on his schoolwork after truanting from school for several days.
逃學了幾天之後，拿森必須趕上學校課業。

truce [tru:s] *n.* 停戰；休戰

同 **recess**

▸ After many months at war, the Army commanders called for a truce on Christmas Day.

經過很多個月的交戰之後，陸軍指揮官要求在聖誕節停戰。

---

tuberculosis [tu:ˌbɝ:.kjəˈloʊ.sɪs] *n.* 結核病

▸ Since being diagnosed with tuberculosis, Nina must regularly go to the doctor for a breathing treatment.

妮娜自從被診斷罹患了結核病之後，就必須定期看診接受呼吸治療。

---

tuck [tʌk]

① *v.* 把…塞進

同 **insert**

② *n.* 打褶

同 **bend; fold**

▸ He tucked his shirt in.

他把襯衫塞進褲子裡。

▸ The young boy tried to make his bed, but he had trouble with the tuck.

小男孩嘗試自己疊被，可是卻不太會打摺子。

---

tuition [tʊˈɪʃ·ən] *n.* 學費

同 **instruction**

▸ He had just enough money to pay for the school tuition.

他的錢只夠付學費而已。

---

tumor [ˈtu·mər] *n.* 腫瘤

▸ Gary will have surgery next week to remove the tumor on his right lung.

蓋瑞下週動手術，要切除他右肺的腫瘤。

---

tuna [ˈtu:.nə] *n.* 鮪魚

▸ Do you want to order tuna or salmon?

你想點鮪魚還是鮭魚？

---

turmoil [ˈtɝ:.mɔɪl] *n.* 混亂

同 **chaos; disorder**

▸ The city was in turmoil after all of the protests in the streets.

街頭抗議之後，市長陷入一片混亂。

---

twilight [ˈtwaɪˌlaɪt] *n.* 黎明；黃昏

同 **dusk**

▸ Let's go fishing at twilight so the heat won't be as intense.

我們在黎明時去釣魚，因為那時氣溫還不會很炎熱。

---

tyranny [ˈtɪr.ən.i] *n.* 暴政；專制

同 **dictatorship; totalitarianism**

▸ After years of government tyranny, the citizens were finally free to make their own decisions.

歷經多年政府的暴政之後，民眾終於能自由做出決定了。

T

Exercise 70

I. Derivatives

1. It takes about half an hour on a bus from here the downtown to the resort in the suburban area, and if you prefer walking, it's quite a ___________ (trekking) that will take four hours.
2. After examining the reason for the teenager's ___________ (trespass) into private property, the owner forgave him and let him go.
3. The annual reports from the school to the Parent-Teacher Association showed that the vast majority of students' problems were related to ___________ (truant).
4. Though modern facilities are used in Mongolia, many Mongolians would still climb onto horses and head off at a relaxed ___________ (trotting) to places some distance away.
5. Ever since Miller succeeded in his candy business, he further expanded the scale of the factories, and the workforce had ___________ (triple) in size.

II. Vocabulary Choices

(A) tremor	(B) tyranny	(C) trench	(D) truce
(E) tribute	(F) tuition	(G) trifled	(H) trimmed
(I) tumor	(J) trivial		

1. To improve efficiency, Jessica followed her parents' advice and focused on tasks with top priority first, leaving the ________ ones temporarily.
2. On Christmas Eve, the two countries agreed on a temporal ________ for the soldiers on the front line from both sides to have some peace.
3. Though the ________ fee for college is considered quite high by some, studying abroad requires much higher, and yet they could afford that.
4. The family of the patient learned from the doctor, to their disbelief, that a malignant ________ had been found in the liver.
5. A lot of revolutionary wars in history were waged against ________ , under which the people couldn't live in freedom.

Unit 71

tyrant [ˈtaɪ.rənt] *n.* 暴君；專橫的人

同 **oppressor**

▶ Everyone who hated the king called him a tyrant.
痛恨國王的人都稱他為暴君。

---

ulcer [ˈʌl.sɚ] *n.* 潰瘍

實用片語與搭配詞

gastric ulcers 胃潰瘍

▶ All of the stress from Ronnie's new job had given him an ulcer.
朗尼新工作所帶來的壓力，使他得到了潰瘍。

▶ Too much pressure can cause gastric ulcers, and these could be very dangerous if not treated.
壓力過大會導致胃潰瘍，若未治療，將會非常危險。

---

ultimate [ˈʌl.tə.mət]

① *adj.* 最後的

同 **conclusive; final**

② *n.* …的極致；終極；結局

反 **proximate**

▶ The ultimate obstacle in the race involves crawling on hands and knees through the mud.
賽事的最後障礙是以手和膝在泥地中爬行。

▶ Matt had climbed many mountains, but Mount Everest was his ultimate in climbing.
麥特爬過很多座山，但聖母峰可說是他登山的極致。

---

umpire [ˈʌm.paɪr]

① *n.* 裁判員；仲裁人

同 **arbitrator; judge**

② *v.* 裁判；仲裁

▶ The umpire made sure that the rules were kept.
裁判是確保大家都遵守規定。

▶ They decided to let Dave umpire the game.
他們決定讓大偉當比賽的裁判。

---

unanimous [juːˈnæn.ə.məs]

adj. 全體一致的；一致同意的

同 **agreed; concurrent**

▶ After a unanimous vote, the team made Frank the new captain.
投票結果全體一致，團隊選擇法蘭克為新隊長。

---

uncover [ʌnˈkʌv.ɚ] *v.* 揭開…的蓋子；揭露

同 **disclose**

反 **cover**

▶ Mom uncovered the cake, only to find that Billy had already taken a slice.
媽媽揭開蛋糕的蓋子後，發現比利已經拿走一塊了。

underestimate [ˌʌn.də-ˈes.tə.meɪt]

① *v.* 低估

反 **overestimate**

② *n.* 估計不足；低估

▸ Rachel may be young, but don't underestimate her ability to handle tough jobs.
瑞秋也許年紀很輕，但別低估她處理困難任務的能力。

▸ We should order more food if the number of guests coming is an underestimate.
如果來訪的客人人數被低估了，我們就應該叫更多食物才行。

---

undergo [ˌʌn.də-ˈgoʊ] *v.* 接受；經歷

同 **endure; suffer**

▸ After my grandpa undergoes knee surgery, he will need six weeks to recover.
我祖父接受膝蓋手術後，需要休養六個星期來復原。

---

undergraduate [ˌʌn.də-ˈgrædʒ.u.ət]

n. 大學生

反 **graduate**

▸ He was an undergraduate student studying business.
他是大學生，主修商學。

---

underline [ˌʌn.də-ˈlaɪn]

① *v.* 在下方畫線；強調

同 **underscore**

② *n.* 劃在下面的線

▸ He underlined the parts of the book that he didn't understand.
他把那本書裡看不懂的部份都在下面畫線。

▸ The underline shows the main point of the sentence.
下面畫線的部份是句子的重點。

104

undermine [ˌʌn.də-ˈmaɪn]

v. 暗中破壞（名聲等）；侵蝕…的基礎；

反 **destroy; sabotage**

▸ The teacher quit his job because the students undermined him by talking behind his back.
老師辭職了，因為學生在背後說他的壞話，暗中破壞他的名聲。

---

underneath [ˌʌn.də-ˈni:θ]

① *prep.* 在…下面

同 **below; under**

② *adv.* 在下面

③ *n.* 下面

▸ The pillow is underneath his head.
他頭下面墊著枕頭。

▸ He wore a T-shirt with nothing underneath.
他身上的 T 恤裡面沒有穿其他衣物。

▸ The underneath of many school desks are dirty.
很多學校的書桌下面都很髒。

④ *adj.* 下面的

▶ The underneath layers of the paint were a different color.
那油漆下面的幾層是另一種顏色的。

99

understandable [ˌʌn.dɚˈstæn.də.bəl]

adj. 易懂的；可了解的

實用片語與搭配詞

perfectly / wholly understandable
完全能夠理解的

▶ The professor gave a very understandable lecture.
那位教授的講課清楚易懂。

▶ It is perfectly understandable that people get sick of the negative news on TV and prefer to rather watch soap operas.
人們厭倦於觀看負面的電視新聞而偏好收看連續劇，這是完全可以理解的。

---

undertake [ˌʌn.dɚˈteɪk]

v. 試圖；著手做；進行

同 **attempt; try**

▶ Billy is undertaking the tiring job of grading papers.
比利正著手進行批改考卷的累人工作。

---

undo [ʌnˈduː] *v.* 取消；打開；解開

同 **cancel; solve**

▶ You can't undo your mistakes; only learn from them.
你無法取消自己所犯過的錯，只能從中學習。

99

undoubtedly [ʌnˈdaʊ·t̬ɪd·li] *adv.* 無庸置疑地

▶ What he said was undoubtedly true.
他所說的無疑是事實。

---

unemployment [ˌʌn.ɪmˈplɔɪ.mənt] *n.* 失業

▶ After two years of unemployment, Jim was very thankful to have a job.
失業兩年之後，吉姆很感恩能找到工作。

---

unfold [ʌnˈfoʊld] *v.* 展開；攤開

同 **uncover**

反 **fold**

▶ Lisa unfolded the blanket, and we sat down and had a picnic.
麗莎把毯子展開，我們坐上去，享用野餐。

---

unify [ˈjuː.nə.faɪ] *v.* 統一；聯合

同 **merge; unite**

▶ The coach gave the players a pep talk to unify their strategies to score a goal.
教練給選手加油打氣，以便統一戰術好得分。

---

unlock [ʌnˈlɑːk] *v.* 開⋯的鎖；解開

反 **lock**

▶ I can't find my keys to unlock the front door.
我找不到鑰匙來開前門。

unpack [ʌnˈpæk] *v.* 打開（行李）取出東西

同 **unload**

反 **pack**

▶ Freddie unpacked his suitcase as soon as he got back from his vacation.
佛雷迪假期結束一回到家，就把行李箱的東西取出來。

---

upbringing [ˈʌpˌbrɪŋ.ɪŋ] *n.* 養育；教養

同 **fostering; nurture**

▶ Because of his proper upbringing, George had very polite manners.
喬治因為接受了良好的教養，因此舉止相當斯文有禮。

update [ʌpˈdeɪt]

① *v.* 使現代化；更新

實用片語與搭配詞

manually update 手動更新

② *n.* 最新的情況；最新的信息

▶ Most apps have to be updated often.
大多數應用程式必須經常更新。

▶ Our company's internet is down, so we have to manually update all the transactions.
我們公司的網路故障，所以我們必須手動更新所有交易。

▶ Please give me an update on how the project is going so far.
請告訴我那個專案的最新進度。

---

upgrade [ʌpˈgreɪd]

① *v.* 升級

反 **downgrade**

② *n.* 升級

▶ If we pay another $1000, we can upgrade our plane tickets to first class.
如果我們再付一千美元，就可以把機票升等為頭等艙了。

▶ Michelle traded in her phone for the latest upgrade.
米雪把舊手機換新機了。

---

uphold [ʌpˈhoʊld] *v.* 支持；高舉

同 **support**

反 **subvert**

▶ Mike proudly upheld his country's flag high above his head.
麥克自豪地把國旗高舉過頭。

Exercise 71

I. Derivatives

1. This match for the Annual School Celebration was called on at the spot, and the two teams had to ask their coach to ___________ (umpire) the race for them.
2. Though the military had deployed many secret agents to fetch as much data as possible, the enemy's force was still ___________ (underestimate), which gave rise to a devastating loss for the country.
3. Mr. Heathcliff looked stern, but ___________ (underneath) that seemingly severe exterior, he was actually a very warm and genial gentleman.
4. With the spectacular scene of the Grand Canyon ___________ (unfold) before the tour group, all of the tourists consider this trip to America worth it.
5. Jim had ___________ (undergo) a tough path and later became the most influential and prestigious comedian in the field of acting.

II. Vocabulary Choices

(A) unanimous	(B) unfolds	(C) undertake	(D) undo
(E) undermines	(F) unemployment	(G) unpack	(H) uphold
(I) uncover	(J) ulcer		

1. Judy had stayed up late for over a week, and she got mouth ________ afterwards, which hurt a lot whenever and whatever she ate.
2. The board reached a(n) ________ decision accepting the proposal to adopt environment-friendly techniques to produce their products.
3. Some parents have little knowledge on how to foster children's confidence and habitually criticize them, which only ________ them.
4. In an era of economic recession, ________ rates soared, and many people are laid off, losing not only the jobs but their dignity as well.
5. As a law-enforcer, the police officers had to ________ the law whether they agree with it or not.

Unit 72

upright [ˈʌp.raɪt]

① *adj.* 直立的；挺直的；正直的；誠實的

同 **erect**

反 **dishonest**

② *adv.* 挺直地

③ *n.* 垂直

實用片語與搭配詞

upright piano 直立式鋼琴

▶ The post was placed in an upright position.
那根柱子是直立的。

▶ He was sitting upright in the chair.
他在椅子上的坐姿很挺。

▶ For small apartments with limited space, upright is the trend.
對空間有限的小公寓來說，直立式是流行趨勢。

▶ I fondly remember the upright piano on which my grandma played classical music.
我深刻記得祖母彈奏古典樂的那架直立式鋼琴。

---

upward [ˈʌp.wɚd]

① *adj.* 向上的；升高的

② *adv.* 朝上；向上地

▶ This T-shirt has had an upward trend in sales.
這件 T 恤的銷售情況上揚。

▶ He looked upwards to the roof of his house.
他朝上看自己房子的屋頂。

---

uranium [jʊˈreɪ.ni.əm] *n.* 鈾

▶ The specialist is performing a study on the amount of uranium found in nuclear weapons.
那位專家正在發表核子武器含鈾量的研究。

---

urgency [ˈɝː.dʒən.si] *n.* 緊急；迫切

▶ The medical team worked with great urgency to try to revive the patient.
醫療團隊緊急地救治，試圖讓患者甦醒。

---

urine [ˈjʊr.ɪn] *n.* 尿

同 **pee; piddle**

▶ The doctor needs samples of blood and urine to test for diseases.
那名醫師需要血液和尿的樣本來進行疾病檢測。

---

usher [ˈʌʃ.ɚ]

① *n.* 接待員；引座員

同 **guide; lead**

▶ Josh was an usher in the wedding and escorted the groom's sister down the aisle.
喬許在婚禮擔任招待，並陪同新郎的妹妹入場。

② *v.* 引；領

▶ The security guard ushered the singer out of the performance hall.
警衛引領那位歌手離開表演廳。

98

utensil [ju:ˋten.sɪl] *n.* 用具

同 **apparatus; appliance**

▶ Please use your fork or another utensil to eat your food.
請用你的叉子或是其他餐具來進食。

---

utility [ju:ˋtɪl.ə.t̬i] *n.* 有用性；實用

▶ Frank lost the utility of his right hand and learned to write with his left.
法蘭克無法使用右手，就學習用左手寫字。

---

utilize [ˋju:.t̬əl.aɪz] *v.* 利用；使用；應用

▶ In order to utilize her singing talents, Beth joined the girls' choir.
貝絲加入女子合唱團，以便善加利用自己的歌唱天賦。

---

utmost [ˋʌt.moʊst]

① *adj.* 最大的

同 **greatest; most**

② *n.* 極限；最大可能

實用片語與搭配詞

the utmost importance 極為重要的

▶ Once we climb the utmost peak, the rest of this hike will be easy.
一旦我們爬到頂峰，健行的其餘路程就輕而易舉了。

▶ Jennifer sang to the utmost of her ability, even though she wasn't feeling well.
珍妮佛雖然不太舒服，卻盡自己最大能力去唱歌。

▶ The news of the bankruptcy was of the utmost importance, yet the company waited a week before telling shareholders.
公司破產是極重要的消息，然而公司拖了一週才告知它的股東們。

---

utter [ˋʌ.t̬ɚ]

① *adj.* 徹底的；完全的

同 **absolute; complete**

② *v.* 發出聲音；說；表達

同 **say; speak**

▶ His utter disobedience got him into trouble.
他徹底反抗的態度替自己惹了麻煩。

▶ The boy uttered a cry when he saw the wolf.
那名男孩看到了一隻狼就發出了哭聲。

U

97

vacancy [ˈveɪ.kən.si] *n.* 空處；空位

同 **emptiness**

▸ There was a vacancy in my room after I moved out.
我搬出去之後，房間就空出來了。

---

vaccine [ˈvæk.siːn] *n.* 疫苗

▸ The children were given vaccines to prevent diseases.
孩子們都接種了疫苗以預防疾病。

---

102 99

vacuum [ˈvæk.juːm]

① *n.* 真空

同 **void**

② *v.* 用吸塵器清掃

▸ I saw a huge vacuum as I looked into outer space.
我望向太空時，看到了一大片虛空。

▸ It is my job to vacuum my room once a week.
我負責每星期用吸塵器清掃房間一次。

---

vague [veɪg] *adj.* 模糊不清的；不明確的

同 **dim**

反 **clear**

▸ The moral behind the story was quite vague.
這則故事的寓意含糊不清。

---

valiant [ˈvæl.i.ənt] *adj.* 勇敢的；英勇的

同 **brave**

反 **timid**

▸ Because of his courage in battle, David will always be remembered as a valiant soldier.
由於大衛在戰場上的勇敢表現，大家將永遠記得他是位英勇的軍人。

---

valid [ˈvæl.ɪd] *adj.* 有效的

同 **well-grounded**

反 **invalid**

▸ Students should double check their sources to make sure they are valid.
學生應重複檢查資料的來源，以便確認它們是正確的。

---

validity [vəˈlɪdəti] 正確；確實；正當

同 **cogency**

▸ Your story lacks validity, so I doubt anyone will believe you.
你的說法不確實，所以我懷疑會有任何人相信你。

---

vanilla [vəˈnɪl.ə] *n.* 香草

▸ Of all the ice cream flavors, vanilla is my favorite.
在所有冰淇淋的口味中，我最喜歡香草。

---

vanity [ˈvæn.ə.t̬i] *n.* 自負；虛榮心

▸ Her vanity prevented her from being truly happy.
她的愛慕虛榮使她無法感受到真正的快樂。

vapor ['veɪ·pər] *n.* 蒸氣；霧氣

同 **fog; steam**

▶ The water in the cup turned into vapor under the heat.
杯子裡的水經過加熱就化為蒸氣了。

---

variable ['ver.i.ə.bəl]

① *adj.* 易變的；多變的

反 **constant; invariable**

② *n.* 變數

實用片語與搭配詞

highly variable 高度易變的

▶ Amy's variable emotions make her a very unpredictable person.
艾美善變的情緒使她變得相當難以預測。

▶ There are too many variables in our plan to know exactly what will happen.
我們的計畫中有太多變數，所以很難確切預知未來會發生怎樣的結果。

▶ The price of mobile phones these days are highly variable, depending on the brand.
如今行動電話的售價依據其所屬品牌而差距極大。

---

100 95

variation [ˌver.iˈeɪ.ʃən] *n.* 變化

同 **fluctuation**

▶ Of all the variations of the song "Amazing Grace", this arrangement is my favorite.
「奇異恩典」這首歌的所有變化版本中，這個版本是我最喜歡的。

---

vegetation [ˌvedʒ.əˈteɪ.ʃən]

n. （總稱）植物；植被；草木

▶ Vegetation in the field was growing fast.
原野裡的植物生長得很快速。

98

veil [veɪl]

① *n.* 面紗

② *v.* （以面紗）遮蓋；遮住

同 **cover**

反 **unveil**

▶ The groom took the veil off of the bride's face.
新郎把新娘臉上的頭紗拿掉了。

▶ A piece of cloth veiled the woman's head.
有塊布遮蓋了那名女子的頭部。

Exercise 72

I. Derivatives

1. The roar from the trainer shocked the trainees, making them sit ___________ (upright) immediately for fear of any sign of laziness.
2. Enclosed are a few stickers which can be ___________ (utility) to stick the dust away from the screen before you can apply the protection layer on.
3. Mrs. Doris kept two dogs and two cats, and she had to ___________ (vacuum) the floor three times a day to keep it clean of fur.
4. Though the witness' testimony seemed far-fetched, the district attorney could not find any counter evidence to argue against its ___________ (valid).
5. Though there are different versions to this classic novel, readers can find that the ___________ (variable) among them are quite minor.

II. Vocabulary Choices

(A) urgency	(B) vanity	(C) vacancy	(D) urine
(E) ushered	(F) utmost	(G) vaccine	(H) uranium
(I) utensil	(J) valiant		

1. Though weakly radioactive, the chemical element ________ is a toxic metal, which with too much exposure, one's kidney, brain, liver, and heart can get affected.
2. The manager invited the property owner over for a cup of coffee and earnestly ________ him into his office when he arrived.
3. In the novel The Three Musketeers, d'Artagnan, Porthos, Athos, and Aramis were all ________ royal guards who kept their oath to protect the king.
4. The wise parents gave great advice to their teenage son, reminding him to explore deep inside his heart to examine whether it was out of ________ , or pure love, that he pursued the lady from the wealthy family.
5. As an extreme case, this child who suffered from autism must be approached with ________ love and care; any sign of indifference can hurt.

vein [veɪn] *n.* 靜脈；血管
反 **artery**

▶ I could feel the blood pumping through my vein.
我可以感覺到血液在我的血管中流竄。

---

velvet [ˈvel.vɪt] *n.* 天鵝絨；絲絨

▶ The clothes he wore were made from velvet.
他穿的衣服是以天鵝絨製成的。

velvet [ˈvel.vət]
adj. 天鵝絨製的；（像天鵝絨般）柔軟光滑的
同 **velvety**

▶ She went to the store to buy a velvet dress.
她去店裡買了一件天鵝絨的洋裝。

---

vend [vend] *v.* 叫賣
同 **peddle; sell**

▶ Rita is vending delicious cookies at the school fundraiser.
麗塔在學校的募款會上賣可口的餅乾。

---

vendor [ˈven.dɚ] *n.* 攤販
同 **marketer**

▶ The vendor at the baseball game was selling snacks and drinks.
棒球比賽中的小販在賣零食和飲料。

99

venture [ˈven.tʃɚ]
① *n.* 冒險；投機活動
同 **adventure**
② *v.* 冒險去做

實用片語與搭配詞
venture sth. on sth. 以某事物冒險做某事

▶ The climber's venture on the cliff was very risky.
那位攀登者冒險登上峭壁的舉動相當冒險。

▶ We ventured ourselves on a rollercoaster ride.
我們冒險去玩雲霄飛車。

▶ The investor ventured all his money on the housing project, and then he lost everything.
這位投資者冒險砸了所有積蓄在這個住宅區上，但他後來變得一無所有。

---

verbal [ˈvɝː.bəl] *adj.* 口頭上的；言詞上的
同 **spoken**
反 **written**

▶ Each math problem came with a verbal explanation.
每個數學問題都附帶有口頭上的解釋。

V

verge [vɝːdʒ]

① *n.* 邊；邊緣

同 **edge; rim**

② *v.* 處在邊緣

► They approached the verge of the cliff with caution.
他們小心翼翼地靠近懸崖邊緣。

► Based on her perfect scores, Karen is verging on being number one in her school.
由於凱倫得了滿分，所以在學校幾乎穩拿第一名了。

---

versatile [ˈvɝː.sə.t̬əl] *adj.* 多才多藝的

同 **skilled; talented**

► Steve is quite versatile in his job and can thrive in any situation.
史提夫在工作上表現得多才多藝，在任何情況都如魚得水。

---

version [ˈvɝː.ʒən] *n.* 版本

同 **interpretation**

► Erika's version of the story is quite different from Sharon's.
艾瑞卡的說法版本和雪倫的截然不同。

---

versus [ˈvɝː.səs] *prep.* …對…；對抗

同 **against**

► The competition will feature the boys versus the girls.
那是一場男孩對抗女孩的比賽。

---

vertical [ˈvɝː.t̬ə.kəl]

① *adj.* 垂直的；豎的

同 **upright**

反 **horizontal**

② *n.* 垂直線；垂直面

► I made a chart using vertical and horizontal lines.
我用垂直和水平的線條製作了一張圖表。

► If you're looking for Point A, it's on the vertical.
如果你是在找 A 點，它就位在垂直線上。

---

veteran [ˈve.t̬ɚ.ən] *n.* 老兵；富有經驗的老手

同 **experienced; practiced**

► The army veteran didn't like to talk about his previous experiences with war.
那名軍中老兵不喜歡提到過去的作戰經歷。

---

veterinarian / vet [ˌvet.ər.ɪˈner.i.ən / vet]

n. 獸醫

► Holly took her puppy to the veterinarian for a checkup.
荷麗把小狗帶到獸醫那裡去檢查。

---

veto [ˈviː.t̬oʊ]

① *n.* 否決；否決權

► The president's veto of the new bill surprised everyone.
總統否決了那條新法案，讓所有人都大感意外。

② *v.* 否決

同 **deny; refuse**

▶ The proposition of a new law was vetoed in the end.
制定新法案的提議最後遭到否決了。

---

via [ˈvaɪə / ˈviː.ə] *prep.* 經由；透過

▶ Our family traveled to Hualien via Taipei.
我們全家人去了花蓮，途經台北。

---

vibrate [ˈvaɪ.breɪt] *v.* 顫動；震動

同 **quiver; shake**

▶ Strings on a guitar will vibrate if you pluck them.
如果你撥弄吉他的琴弦，琴弦就會顫動。

---

vibration [vaɪˈbreɪ.ʃən] *n.* 震動；振動

同 **oscillation; quiver**

▶ The bass and drums were so loud I could feel the vibrations in my chest.
貝斯和鼓聲實在太大聲，我幾乎可以感受到胸腔都震動了。

---

vice [vaɪs] *n.* 惡習；邪惡

同 **crime**

反 **righteous**

▶ Sam is trying to overcome greed, which is one of his biggest vices.
山姆正式圖克服自己的貪心，那是他最嚴重的惡習。

---

vicious [ˈvɪʃ.əs]

adj. 兇殘的；邪惡的；惡毒的

同 **brutal; evil**

▶ When we heard about the vicious crocodile attack, we didn't want to go swimming.
我們聽說那起兇殘的鱷魚攻擊後，就不想去游泳了。

---

victimize [ˈvɪk.tə.maɪz]

v. 使受害；虐待；迫害

實用片語與搭配詞

victimize sb. for sth. 因某事責罰某人

▶ The school bully victimized anyone who was smaller than him.
學校裡的惡霸會迫害任何個子比他小的人。

▶ Jennifer victimized her opponents for the school president election, so she was disqualified.
珍妮佛在校長遴選中使她的對手受害，她因而失去遴選資格。

---

victor [ˈvɪk.tɚ] *n.* 勝利者

同 **superior; winner**

▶ The victor of this game will move on to the next round.
這場比賽的獲勝者會晉級下一回合。

V

victorious [vɪkˈtɔːr.i.əs] *adj.* 得勝的；戰勝的

▶ It was a hard game, but Oliver's team was victorious.
這場比賽並不好打，可是奧利佛的隊伍獲勝了。

---

videotape [ˈvɪd.i.oʊ.teɪp]

① *n.* 錄影帶

② *v.* 把…錄下來；錄製

▶ We recorded all the film on videotape.
我們把整部片都轉錄成錄影帶了。

▶ My friends videotaped my piano performance.
我朋友把我的鋼琴演奏都錄下來了。

---

viewer [ˈvjuː.ɚ] *n.* （電視）觀眾；觀看者

▶ A lot of viewers watched the basketball game.
有很多電視觀眾都收看了那場籃球賽。

---

vigor [ˈvɪg·ər] *n.* 精力

同 **energy; muscularity**

▶ I always have a lot of vigor when I exercise.
我運動的時候，都會感到精力充沛。

Exercise 73

I. Derivatives

1. Before Antonio worked in the fashion industry, he had been working as a street ___________ (vend), selling clothes and kits.
2. In the evening, the couple went out for a walk beside the riverbank, their figure beautifully silhouetted against the ___________ (velvet) pink clouds.
3. When the military secretly tested their newly developed nuclear bombs, ___________ (vibrate) from ground could be clearly felt by people miles away.
4. The subway bombing incident had injured many commuters not only by explosion, but also the toxic air that followed, and the police said this was the most ___________ (vice) attacks they'd ever seen.
5. The result of the election was ___________ (victory) for the recently emerged party, which won a lot of seats in the congress.

II. Vocabulary Choices

(A) victimized	(B) vein	(C) velvet	(D) versatile
(E) versus	(F) vigor	(G) ventures	(H) verge
(I) vertical	(J) veto		

1. With the increase of domestic limitations, a lot of businessmen had no choice but to look abroad for more lucrative business ________ .
2. As the night approached, the hikers found a safe place on the ________ of the thick forests and set up their camp there.
3. One of the requirements of this company for the job applicants is being ________ in facing various challenges.
4. The chair of the board has the power of ________ over any proposals that he doesn't consider promising or possessing of potentials for thriving business.
5. Whenever there is a case of scandal involving teacher and student, the student always seems to be the victim, and more often than not, it is the teacher who is ________ by the media.

Unit 74

vigorous [ˈvɪg.ɚ.əs]
adj. 精力旺盛的；強壯的
同 **active; energetic**

▶ The vigorous athletes practiced long and hard.
那些精力旺盛的運動員都長時間辛苦地練習。

---

villa [ˈvɪl.ə] *n.* 別墅

▶ My grandpa retired and moved to a villa by the sea.
我祖父退休了，就搬到海邊的別墅去住。

---

villain [ˈvɪl.ən] *n.* 壞人；惡棍
同 **rascal; rogue**

▶ That evil woman is a villain who cheats everyone.
那個惡毒的女人是壞人，她欺騙所有人。

---

vine [vaɪn] *n.* 藤蔓（植物）；葡萄藤

▶ A vine started growing around the front gates.
一株藤蔓植物開始攀爬在前門上。

---

vineyard [ˈvɪn.jɚd] *n.* 葡萄園

▶ Uncle Robert lives on a vineyard where he harvests his own grapes.
勞伯叔叔住在葡萄園裡，並且自己採收葡萄。

---

violinist [ˌvaɪəˈlɪn.ɪst] *n.* 小提琴手

▶ My music teacher is a skilled classical violinist.
我的音樂老師是技巧精湛的古典小提琴手。

---

virtual [ˈvɝː.tʃu.əl] *adj.* 實質上的；虛擬的
同 **essential**

▶ The virtual collapse of the stock market is causing some people to make unwise decisions.
股市實質上的崩盤導致一些民眾做出不智的決定。

---

visa [ˈviː.zə] *n.* 簽證

實用片語與搭配詞
obtain a visa 取得簽證

▶ I'm going to Brazil next month. I need to apply for a visa.
我下個月要去巴西。我需要申請簽證。

▶ If you travel abroad, make sure you do not need to obtain a visa to enter that country.
若你要出國旅遊，先確認你不需要取得簽證就能入境該國。

visualize [ˈvɪʒ.u.əl.aɪz] *v.* 使可見；想像

同 **envision**

▶ I'm having trouble visualizing your idea. Can you explain it again?

我實在很難想像出你的理念，你能不能再解釋一次？

98

vitality [vaɪˈtæl.ə.t̬i] *n.* 活力；生氣

同 **energy**

▶ As I get older, I feel that I'm losing vitality.

隨著我的年紀越來越大，我覺得我也越來越沒有活力了。

---

vocal [ˈvoʊ.kəl]

① *adj.* 暢所欲言的；直言不諱的；聲音的

同 **oral**

② *n.* 主唱

同 **singer**

▶ Kenny is very vocal about his opinion and is always ready to debate.

肯尼往往直言不諱自己的意見，總是隨時準備與人爭辯。

▶ That vocal sounded more like screaming than singing.

那個主唱的聲音更像是尖叫而非唱歌。

---

vocation [voʊˈkeɪ.ʃən] *n.* 職業

同 **occupation; profession**

▶ Before John finishes his second year of college, he hopes to figure out which vocation to pursue.

約翰希望在大二結束前，能先想好想從事哪種職業。

---

vocational [voʊˈkeɪ.ʃən.əl] *adj.* 職業的

▶ James went to a vocational school that specialized in mechanics.

詹姆斯去讀一所專精機械的職業學校。

---

vogue [voʊg] *n.* 流行；風行

同 **fashion; style**

▶ These new jeans are the latest vogue.

這條新的牛仔褲是最新流行的款式。

---

vomit [ˈvɑː.mɪt]

① *v.* 嘔吐

同 **spew; throw up**

② *n.* 嘔吐

▶ Stephen vomited because he ate a big meal right before going running.

史帝芬吐了，因為他去跑步前吃了大餐。

▶ To be a nurse, you have to be willing to clean up vomit and bandage wounds.

你如果想要當護士，必須願意清理嘔吐物以及包紮傷口。

---

vow [vaʊ]

① *n.* 誓約；誓言

同 **swear; vouch**

▶ The bride and the groom said their vows to each other.

新娘和新郎彼此交換誓約。

② *v.* 誓言；發誓

同 **assure; pledge**

► He vowed never to lie to his family ever again.
他誓言永不再對家人說謊。

---

vulgar [ˈvʌl.gɚ] *adj.* 粗俗的

同 **filthy; nasty**

► The girls were not impressed by Jeremiah's vulgar speech and inappropriate jokes.
傑若米亞粗俗的言語和失當的笑話並沒有讓女孩們留下好印象。

---

vulnerable [ˈvʌl.nɚ.ə.bəl] *adj.* 易受傷害的

同 **sensitive; susceptible**

► Kevin is vulnerable to illness because he has poor health.
凱文很容易生病，因為他健康情形很差。

---

wade [weɪd]

① *v.* 涉水而行；跋涉

② *n.* 涉水；跋涉

► Many of the soldiers waded through the swamp.
很多士兵涉水穿越沼澤。

► The wade in the pool felt nice and refreshing.
在游泳池中涉水，感覺不錯，讓人神清氣爽。

---

wail [weɪl]

① *n.* 號啕大哭；慟哭

同 **howl**

反 **joy**

② *v.* 號啕大哭；慟哭

實用片語與搭配詞

wail for sb. 為某人而哭叫

► We heard a wail coming from the back of the room.
我們聽到從房間後面傳來號啕大哭的聲音。

► She wailed for a long time during the funeral.
她在葬禮中嚎啕大哭了很久。

► The baby wailed for his mother when she left the room.
當小嬰兒的媽媽離開房間時，他因為見不到媽媽而嚎啕大哭。

---

ward [wɔːrd]

① *n.* 病房

② *v.* 避開；抵擋

► There are three nurses per ward in this hospital.
這家醫院每個病房可分配到三名護士。

► He tried to ward himself from the heavy rain.
他試圖避雨，讓自己不被滂沱大雨淋溼。

100

wardrobe [ˈwɔːr.droʊb] *n.* 衣櫃

同 **closet**

► Rebecca found some old clothes in the wardrobe that belonged to her grandmother.
蕾貝加在衣櫃裡找到一些祖母的舊衣服。

ware [wer] *n.* 製品；商品

同 **merchandise; product**

▶ I will sell you my wares for half price!
我可以半價把產品賣給你！

---

warehouse [ˈwer.haʊs] *n.* 倉庫；貨棧

同 **storehouse**

▶ All sorts of boxes were stored inside a warehouse.
各式各樣的盒子都被儲藏在倉庫裡。

warehouse [ˈwer.haʊz] *v.* 把…存放到倉庫

▶ The important packages were warehoused away.
重要的包裹都被存放到倉庫裡了。

---

warfare [ˈwɔːr.fer] *n.* 戰爭

▶ After the soldier's traumatic experience in warfare, he was permitted to go home.
那名士兵歷經戰爭的創傷經歷後，就獲准返鄉了。

Exercise 74

I. Derivatives

1. Though there are 13 members in this famous pop-music group, only three share the ___________ (vocal), with the rest doing mainly the dancing.
2. In our country, ___________ (vocation) training lies outside the scope of compulsory education, while many consider that it should be involved.
3. The bridge over the creek was worn out to the state of being visually unreliable, and the hikers had to rely on a barefoot ___________ (wade) to cross the creek.
4. It's the ancient tradition for the Orient to wear a blessed charm like bracelet as a holy object to ___________ (ward) off evil spirits.
5. Owing to the great nationwide strike from the workers, tons of goods had been accumulated in the ___________ (warehouse) for months.

II. Vocabulary Choices

(A) warranty	(B) visualize	(C) vitality	(D) vigorous
(E) virtual	(F) wardrobe	(G) vulnerable	(H) wail
(I) vulgar	(J) villain		

1. The government's new construction plan involved a small scale of deforestation and was faced with ________ oppositions from the environmentalists.
2. The main character in this film, who was both a good guy and a bad guy, said at the beginning of the movie, "You either die a hero or live long enough to see yourself become a ________ ."
3. Having run for several hours over a long distance, the participants in the marathon race gradually lost ________ .
4. Isn't it a bit ________ to invite a bunch of friends to a fancy 3-star restaurant, order far more than necessary, find the cost beyond imagination and start bargaining with the restaurant manager in front of all the friends and guests?
5. Airports are generally ________ to terrorists' attack because once destroyed, aid from overseas cannot be sent, and the next attack on any place within the country will be even easier.

Unit 75

warranty [ˈwɔːr.ən.t̬i] *n.* 保證書

同 **guarantee**

▶ Because Trent didn't have a warranty, he couldn't return his computer after it broke.
特蘭特因為沒有保證書，所以電腦壞掉後不能退回原廠送修。

---

warrior [ˈwɔːr.i.ɚ] *n.* 戰士；武士

同 **fighter; soldier**

▶ A strong warrior would train himself everyday.
強壯的戰士會天天自我鍛鍊。

---

wary [ˈwer.i] *adj.* 唯恐的；提防的

同 **cautious; suspicious**

▶ Everybody was wary of the dangers up ahead.
大家都很怕前方面臨的危險。

---

waterproof [ˈwɑː.t̬ɚ.pruːf]

① *adj.* 防水的

同 **raincoat; waterproofed**

② *v.* 使防水

▶ Luke bought a waterproof watch, so he could wear it while scuba diving.
路克買了防水錶，好在浮潛時戴。

▶ Stanley waterproofed his phone by putting it in a special plastic bag.
史丹利把手機放到特殊的塑膠袋中好讓它能防水。

---

watertight [ˈwɑː.t̬ɚ.taɪt]

adj. 防水的；不透水的

▶ Make sure your bottle is watertight, so it doesn't spill in your bag.
要確保你的水瓶不透水，以免在包包裡漏水。

---

weary [ˈwɪr.i]

① *adj.* 筋疲力盡的；疲倦的

同 **fatigued; tired**

② *v.* 使疲勞；使疲倦

實用片語與搭配詞

weary of sth. 對某事感到厭倦

▶ The weary traveler stopped at a small town to rest.
那名筋疲力盡的旅客停留在一處小鎮上休息。

▶ All the loud noises wearied my poor ears.
所有那些噪音簡直在對我可憐的耳朵進行疲勞轟炸。

▶ Elderly people should be very weary of scammers trying to steal their money.
老年人對於試圖竊取他們存款的詐騙份子感到非常厭煩。

weird [wɪrd] *adj.* 怪異的；不尋常的

同 **peculiar; queer**

▸ Stay far away from that weird stranger there.
別靠近那個怪異的陌生人。

---

wharf [wɔːrf]

① *n.* 碼頭；停泊處

同 **dock; harbor**

② *v.* 停靠碼頭；把（貨物）卸在碼頭上

▸ We visited the wharf to see all the ships.
我們去碼頭欣賞船隻。

▸ The sailors wharfed their boat as the sun came down.
夕陽西下，那些船員們把船停靠在碼頭。

---

whatsoever [ˌwɑːt.soʊˈev.ɚ]

① *adj.* 無論什麼…都一樣；不管什麼樣的

② *pron.* 無論什麼；不管什麼

▸ Nothing whatsoever can stop the determination of our team.
無論任何事物都無法阻撓我們的團隊的決心。

▸ Whatsoever is done in love will have a powerful effect.
無論任何事物，若是以愛心來做的，將會收到強大的效果。

---

wheelchair [ˈwiːl.tʃer] *n.* 輪椅

▸ I had to use a wheelchair after breaking my foot.
我跌斷了腳之後，就不得不用輪椅代步了。

---

whereabouts [ˈwer.ə.baʊts]

① *adv.* 在哪裡

② *n.* 行蹤；下落

▸ Whereabouts can I find a nice restaurant?
我要到哪裡才能找到不錯的餐廳？

▸ My cat's whereabouts could be anywhere now.
現在我的寵物貓可能流落在任何地方。

---

whereas [werˈæz] *conj.* 但是；卻

▸ He likes to drink tea, whereas she prefers coffee.
他喜歡喝茶，而她卻偏好喝咖啡。

---

whine [waɪn]

① *n.* 嗚咽聲；哀鳴聲

同 **cry; whimper**

② *v.* 發出嗚咽聲；發出哀鳴聲

▸ The whining in the room caused a commotion.
那個房間裡的嗚咽聲引發了一陣騷動。

▸ My dog whined in front of my door for more food.
我的狗在門前發出嗚咽聲，想再討點食物吃。

whirl [wɝːl]

① *v.* （使）旋轉

同 **rotate; spin**

② *n.* 旋轉

▶ A group of soldiers whirled flags in their hands.
一群士兵手中揮舞著旗幟。

▶ The whirl of the engine was making a loud noise.
引擎轉動發出了很大的噪音。

---

whisk [wɪsk]

① *v.* 攪打；撢

同 **brush**

實用片語與搭配詞

whisk sth. away / off 清掉某物

② *n.* 攪拌；攪拌器

▶ I whisked the eggs in my mixing bowl.
我用我的攪拌碗打蛋。

▶ The tragedy whisked away Frieda's short-lived happiness in the blink of an eye.
在一眨眼的時間內，這場悲劇抹煞了弗里達短暫的幸福時光。

▶ The baker poured a few things in a bowl and gave it a quick whisk.
糕點師傅把一些材料倒進碗裡，然後迅速攪拌。

---

whiskey / whisky [ˈhwɪs·ki / ˈwɪski]

n. 威士忌酒

▶ My uncle likes to drink whiskey to celebrate.
我叔叔喜歡喝威士忌來慶祝。

---

wholesale [ˈhoʊl.seɪl]

① *n.* 大批；批發

反 **retail**

② *adj.* 大批的；批發的

反 **retail**

③ *adv.* 大批地；以批發方式

④ *v.* 批發（貨物）

反 **retail**

▶ You can buy all your groceries at the wholesale.
你買食品雜貨可以用大批購買的方式。

▶ Wholesale prices are usually cheaper in the long run.
批發價長久來說通常會比較便宜。

▶ All the food supplies were bought wholesale.
全部的食物儲備都是大批購買的。

▶ Instead of selling your goods one by one, why not wholesale them?
與其把產品一個一個賣掉，何不用批發的方式來賣呢？

---

wholesome [ˈhoʊl.səm]

adj. 有益健康的；合乎衛生的

同 **beneficial**

▶ Eating healthy can help lead to a wholesome lifestyle.
健康的飲食習慣有助於導向有益健康的生活方式。

實用片語與搭配詞

wholesome meals
有益健康的餐點

▶ The new law forces schools to provide wholesome meals to students to ensure they get all the nutrients they need.
這條新的法律強制學校提供有益健康的餐點給學生們，以確保他們能攝取所有必需的營養。

---

widespread [ˌwaɪdˈspred]
adj. 流傳很廣的；普遍的

▶ The widespread disease became difficult to handle.
蔓延很廣的傳染病疫情變得難以掌控。

---

widow [ˈwɪd.oʊ]
① *v.* 使成寡婦（鰥夫）；使喪偶
② *n.* 寡婦

▶ My mother was widowed after my father died.
我爸爸去世之後，媽媽就守寡了。

▶ That widow still had three children to provide for.
那名寡婦還要養三個孩子。

---

widower [ˈwɪd.oʊ.ɚ] *n.* 鰥夫
反 **widowman**

▶ The widower chose not to marry another woman.
那名鰥夫決定不再娶妻。

---

wig [wɪg] *n.* 假髮

▶ All the actors wore wigs for their characters.
全部演員都為了所扮演的角色而戴上假髮。

---

wilderness [ˈwɪl.dɚ.nəs] *n.* 荒野

▶ It is easy for people to get lost in the wilderness.
人們很容易在荒野中迷路。

---

wildlife [ˈwaɪld.laɪf] *n.* 野生生物

實用片語與搭配詞
preserve wildlife 保護野生動物

▶ We saw all sorts of wildlife in the mountains.
我們在山裡看到了各式各樣的野生動物。

▶ The best way to preserve wildlife is to promote eco-tourism to boost the economy.
保育野生動物的最佳方法就是推廣生態旅遊以提振經濟。

---

windshield [ˈwɪndˌʃild] *n.* 擋風玻璃

▶ So many bugs hit the windshield that we could hardly see the road.
很多蟲子撞到了擋風玻璃，導致我們幾乎都看不到路了。

Exercise 75

I. Derivatives

1. While many loyal brand-name pursuers believe that this watch is ____________ (waterproof), let me remind you that this function is limited to a certain depth of water.
2. The criminal attempted to flee as far as he could but still got caught, for the police had set a sensor on one of the buttons in his shirt, which revealed his ____________ (whereabouts) on the radar.
3. The scene of the ballet dancer ____________ (whirl) around gracefully under the spotlight was so picturesque and astonished the audience.
4. I only have a vague memory that I was being ____________ (whisk) to the hospital, then I lost my consciousness and couldn't know what happened after.
5. Over the years, I've been going abroad with the same guy, settling for the same pattern of counting every nickel we spent, and I've just grown ____________ (weary) of it.

II. Vocabulary Choices

(A) watertight	(B) widespread	(C) wholesome	(D) wilderness
(E) whining	(F) wholesale	(G) whatsoever	(H) wary
(I) widower	(J) wig		

1. Visitors to foreign countries are advised to be _________ of leaving personal information on any form, including those in the check-in counter.
2. Having been ignored by my family for a whole day, my old loyal dog sits by the door _________ , and I think I'd better take it out for a walk.
3. The _________ suppliers sell goods in great packs to retailers, who in turn divide them into small units and sell them to the customers.
4. In Africa, malnutrition is a _________ phenomenon, since the weather there is not ideal for growing sufficient crops to meet the requirements from the whole population.
5. The gray wolves, once endangered because of the culling policy, were finally redeveloped in population before they were freed into the _________ of the Yellowstone National Park.

Unit 76

wither [ˈwɪð.ɚ] *v.* 枯萎

同 **deteriorate; languish**

▶ The plants started to wither without enough water.
那些植物因為得不到足夠的水分而開始枯萎了。

102

withstand [wɪðˈstænd] *v.* 抵擋；禁得起

同 **endure; oppose**

▶ If you can withstand the discomfort of training, you'll be able to run in the race.
如果你能禁得起訓練期間的不舒服，就能夠跑完賽程。

---

witty [ˈwɪţ.i] *adj.* 機智的

同 **clever; humorous**

▶ Larry's witty words and creative jokes keep everyone laughing.
賴瑞機智的話語和充滿創意的笑話，讓大家都笑個不停。

---

woe [woʊ] *n.* 困難；不幸；悲哀

同 **anguish; misery**

▶ I listened as my friend expressed her woes to me.
我聆聽著朋友向我訴說她的不幸遭遇。

---

woo [wuː] *v.* 追求

▶ Rick used his kind words to woo Rita and gain her affection.
里克用體貼的話語來追求麗塔，並贏得她的芳心。

---

woodpecker [ˈwʊdˌpek.ɚ] *n.* 啄木鳥

同 **pecker**

▶ The woodpecker started drilling into the tree.
啄木鳥開始在那棵樹上鑽洞。

---

workshop [ˈwɝːk.ʃɑːp]
n. 工作坊；專題討論會；廠房

實用片語與搭配詞

hold / host / organize a workshop
舉辦工作坊

▶ Ken likes to attend photography workshops.
肯恩喜歡參加攝影工作坊。

▶ The university hosted a workshop on entrepreneurship and it was very successful.
這間大學舉辦了一個關於創業的工作坊，且它非常成功。

worship ['wɝː.ʃɪp]

① *n.* 敬拜；崇拜

② *v.* 敬拜；崇拜

同 **admire**

反 **contempt**

▶ The worship of God does not have to be in a church only.
敬拜神不一定只能在教會裡進行。

▶ I spend time to worship God in the morning.
我早上會抽時間敬拜神。

---

worthwhile [ˌwɝːθˈwaɪl] *adj.* 值得做的

▶ It is definitely worthwhile to go watch that movie!
去看那部電影絕對值得！

---

worthy ['wɝː.ði]

adj. 有價值的；可尊敬的；配得上的

反 **unworthy**

▶ Donating to a good charity is a worthy gesture.
捐錢給好的慈善機構是相當值得的舉動。

---

wreath [riːθ] *n.* 花圈；花冠

▶ Wreaths hung on every door during Christmas time.
聖誕節期間，家家戶戶門上都掛著花圈。

---

wrench [rentʃ]

① *n.* 板手；扭傷

實用片語與搭配詞

wrench sth. off sth. 把某物從某物拉脫

② *v.* 猛扭；扭傷

同 **sprain; twist**

▶ The mechanic used a wrench to loosen the screws that had rusted.
機械工用板手鬆脫生銹的螺絲。

▶ After the accident, emergency workers had to wrench the truck off the small car trapped under it.
車禍過後，緊急救難人員必須將壓在受困轎車上的卡車猛力拖下。

▶ The roller coaster wrenched us back and forth so quickly that I got a headache.
雲霄飛車把我們快速甩來甩去，害我頭痛了。

---

wrestle ['res.əl]

① *n.* 角力；摔角

同 **battle; fight**

② *v.* 與…摔角

▶ Brad challenged his classmate to a wrestle after school.
布雷德挑戰同學在放學後比角力。

▶ My brother and I used to wrestle on the ground.
我和我兄弟以前會在地上角力。

實用片語與搭配詞

wrestle with sth. 與某事搏鬥

▶ John has been wrestling with the decision to quit his job or not for weeks.
約翰對於辭職與否已在內心交戰了數週。

---

wring [rɪŋ] *v.* 絞；擰

同 **squeeze; twist**

▶ I wrung the bottom of my shirt to get the water out.
我把襯衫下方的水擰掉。

---

xerox [ˈzɪr.ɑːks]

① *n.* 影印；複印機

② *v.* 影印；複印

▶ Judy's job was to make a xerox of important papers to keep on file.
茱蒂的工作是影印重要文件並存成檔案。

▶ Please xerox these papers, and hand them out to everyone at the meeting.
請影印這些文件，並發給所有開會的人。

---

yacht [jɑːt]

① *n.* 遊艇；快艇

同 **boat**

② *v.* 駕遊艇

▶ My siblings rode on a private yacht last summer.
去年夏季，我的弟兄姊妹搭過私人遊艇。

▶ I have always wanted to yacht across a lake.
我一直想搭遊艇遊湖。

---

yarn [jɑːrn]

① *n.* 毛線；紗線

同 **thread**

② *v.* 講故事；長談

同 **spin**

▶ Grandmother likes to use yarn for knitting scarfs.
祖母喜歡用毛線織圍巾。

▶ My grandfather used to yarn to the kids every night.
我祖父以前每天晚上都會講故事給孩子聽。

---

yearn [jɝːn] *v.* 渴望；嚮往

同 **desire; long for**

▶ While the soldier was fighting overseas, he yearned to see his family.
那名軍人在海外作戰時，非常渴望能看到家人。

---

yeast [jiːst] *n.* 酵母

▶ The yeast in the dough caused the bread to expand.
麵團裡的酵母讓麵包膨脹了。

98

yield [jiːld]

① *v.* 結出（果實）；出產

▶ My tree will yield many good apples for me.
我的樹能結出很多品質很好的蘋果。

同 **produce**

實用片語與搭配詞

yield to sb. / sth. 讓給 / 屈服於某人 / 事

▶ If you don't have all the facts during a debate, yield to your opponent before making a fool of yourself.
若你在辯論中未能掌握所有的論據，在自己出醜之前就向對手屈服吧。

② *n.* 產量；收穫量；收益

▶ The yield I received from my hard work was worth it.
我辛勤工作所獲得的收穫，相當值得。

---

yoga [ˈjoʊ.gə] *n.* 瑜珈

▶ Some friends practice yoga when they are stressed.
有些朋友會在壓力大的時候練習瑜伽。

---

zeal [ziːl] *n.* 熱情；熱忱

同 **eagerness; fervor**

▶ The actress delivered a flawless performance, with great zeal and emotion.
那位女星的演技完美無暇，充滿了熱情和情感。

---

zinc [zɪŋk] *n.* 鋅

▶ Zinc intake is important to keep your body healthy.
攝取鋅對保持身體健康相當重要。

---

zip [zɪp]

v. 拉鍊 / 用拉鍊拉上 / （電腦）提供壓縮程式

反 **unzip**

▶ Let me zip up my jacket.
我先把夾克的拉鍊拉上。

---

zip code / zone improvement plan code

[ˈzɪp ˌkoʊd / zoʊn ɪmˈpruːv.mənt plæn koʊd]

n. 郵遞區號 / 區域改善計畫

▶ Please write down your home address and zip code.
請寫下你的住址和郵遞區號。

---

zoom [zuːm]

① *v.* 將畫面推近或拉遠；快速移動

▶ The director zoomed in the camera for a close-up shot.
導演把鏡頭拉近來拍特寫。

實用片語與搭配詞

zoom in / out on sb. / sth.
放大縮小某人 / 物

▶ When Mike arrived at the party, he immediately zoomed in on the food table laden with snacks.
當邁可抵達派對時，他的雙眼馬上聚焦到滿是零食的食物桌上。

② *n.* 變焦鏡頭；嗡嗡聲

▶ David bought a zoom lens to take photos of landscapes.
大衛買了變焦鏡頭來拍風景照片。

Exercise 76

I. Derivatives

1. On this little island, different Gods were ___________ (worship), which was more or less a kind of hindrance for the Christian pastors to preach.
2. The interviewee, when walking out of the court, tried to shun away from the reporters in a rush and tripped over a cord, ___________ (wrench) a microphone along with its holder from where he stood.
3. The teenager who got drugs on his car attempted to escape but was immediately ___________ (wrestle) to the ground by the police officer.
4. The school recently signed a contract with a new ___________ (xerox) machine provider, but the new machines were so complicated in manipulation and brought a great complaint from the teachers.
5. In recent years, with the influence of the climate change, crop ___________ (yield) in this region have descended.

II. Vocabulary Choices

(A) zeal	(B) worthwhile	(C) zinc	(D) witty
(E) yacht	(F) yoga	(G) withstand	(H) yeast
(I) woe	(J) yearned		

1. Classical literature pieces differ from common contemporary pieces in that it is able to ________ the test of time and repetitive reading.
2. In this program designed for a particular pop-music group, the host of the show is featured with his ________ remarks and gentle look.
3. Appearing not so rewarding at first, language learning, for most learners, is a process filled with frustrations no matter how much time and energy they devote, but in the long run they will find it ________ to work hard.
4. Having led many years of life in solitude, Mr. Wang ________ for a wife with whom he could spend the rest of his life.
5. Religious ________ sometimes results in terrible incidents, but it also results in miracles that heal injured minds.

解答
Answer

Answer 解答

Exercise 1

Ⅰ. ① accommodations ② aboriginal ③ abundant ④ acceleration ⑤ abstractions

Ⅱ. ① B ② B ③ D ④ A ⑤ C

Exercise 2

Ⅰ. ① addiction ② administrative ③ adapt ④ acquisitions ⑤ accusations

Ⅱ. ① G ② B ③ A ④ J ⑤ D

Exercise 3

Ⅰ. ① C ② A ③ D ④ C ⑤ B

Ⅱ. ① affectionately ② aggression ③ agricultural ④ alcoholic ⑤ allergic

Exercise 4

Ⅰ. ① alternative ② analytical ③ ambiguous ④ anonymous ⑤ annoyance

Ⅱ. ① B ② F ③ A ④ C ⑤ E

Exercise 5

Ⅰ. ① B ② D ③ C ④ D ⑤ B

Ⅱ. ① assert ② architects ③ applaud ④ anticipation ⑤ applicable

Exercise 6

Ⅰ. ① B ② C ③ A ④ C ⑤ D

Ⅱ. ① attainment ② astonishment ③ assumption ④ attendance ⑤ assessment

Exercise 7

Ⅰ. ① B ② C ③ A ④ B ⑤ C

Ⅱ. ① D ② A ③ C ④ I ⑤ H

Exercise 8

Ⅰ. ① betrayal ② beneficial ③ blur ④ biological ⑤ besieged

Ⅱ. ① D ② A ③ D ④ A ⑤ C

Exercise 9

Ⅰ. ① D ② C ③ A ④ B ⑤ D

Ⅱ. ① E ② D ③ B ④ G ⑤ J

Exercise 10

Ⅰ. ① C ② D ③ A ④ C ⑤ C

Ⅱ. ① J ② A ③ G ④ E ⑤ F

Exercise 11

Ⅰ. ① D ② B ③ C ④ B ⑤ D

Ⅱ. ① J ② I ③ G ④ B ⑤ H

Exercise 12

Ⅰ. ① certainty ② cautious ③ cashier ④ catastrophe ⑤ certify

Ⅱ. ① B ② A ③ D ④ B ⑤ C

Exercise 13

Ⅰ. ① chantable ② characterize ③ charitable ④ chemist ⑤ chatter

Ⅱ. ① D ② A ③ D ④ A ⑤ B

Exercise 14

Ⅰ. ① closure ② clinical ③ coincide ④ clearance ⑤ coherent

Ⅱ. ① H ② C ③ B ④ D ⑤ G

Exercise 15

Ⅰ. ① commitment ② collision ③ Communist ④ collective ⑤ colonial

Ⅱ. ① B ② C ③ C ④ D ⑤ A

Exercise 16

Ⅰ. ① C ② B ③ D ④ D ⑤ A

Ⅱ. ① companionship ② competent
③ compensation ④ comprehensive
⑤ compassionately

Exercise 17

Ⅰ. ① confrontation ② conscientious
③ conceit ④ concession ⑤ conception

Ⅱ. ① H ② G ③ J ④ B ⑤ D

Exercise 18

Ⅰ. ① C ② A ③ D ④ D ⑤ B

Ⅱ. ① contemplation ② consultation
③ contradiction ④ conservation
⑤ consolation

Exercise 19

Ⅰ. ① B ② D ③ C ④ A ⑤ C

Ⅱ. ① C ② B ③ D ④ J ⑤ I

Exercise 20

Ⅰ. ① C ② A ③ B ④ D ⑤ A

Ⅱ. ① credibility ② criteria ③ crooked
④ crumbs ⑤ cowardly

Exercise 21

Ⅰ. ① deceive ② decisive ③ customary ④
declaration ⑤ deadly

Ⅱ. ① G ② B ③ I ④ E ⑤ C

Exercise 22

Ⅰ. ① D ② A ③ D ④ C ⑤ A

Ⅱ. ① defect(s) ② descendants ③ delegation
④ density ⑤ descriptive

Exercise 23

Ⅰ. ① differentiate ② dictation ③ destination
④ diagnosis ⑤ destructive

Ⅱ. ① D ② A ③ C ④ B ⑤ B

Exercise 24

Ⅰ. ① C ② C ③ A ④ D ⑤ B

Ⅱ. ① B ② H ③ A ④ D ⑤ C

Exercise 25

Ⅰ. ① C ② B ③ D ④ C ⑤ A

Ⅱ. ① E ② B ③ G ④ H ⑤ I

Exercise 26

Ⅰ. ① D ② D ③ C ④ B ⑤ A

Ⅱ. ① C ② A ③ F ④ B ⑤ I

Exercise 27

Ⅰ. ① A ② B ③ A ④ C ⑤ D

Ⅱ. ① G ② A ③ H ④ I ⑤ F

Exercise 28

Ⅰ. ① C ② B ③ A ④ B ⑤ C

Ⅱ. ① H ② B ③ A ④ D ⑤ J

Exercise 29

Ⅰ. ① A ② B ③ B ④ C ⑤ A

Ⅱ. ① G ② B ③ F ④ D ⑤ I

Exercise 30

Ⅰ. ① B ② C ③ D ④ C ⑤ A

Ⅱ. ① housing ② horizontal ③ heir ④ heroic
⑤ hurled

Exercise 31

Ⅰ. ① innumerable ② indispensable ③
indifference ④ indulge ⑤ interference

Ⅱ. ① B ② B ③ C ④ D ⑤ A

Exercise 32

Ⅰ. ① C ② A ③ C ④ B ⑤ B

Ⅱ. ① F ② H ③ A ④ J ⑤ E

Exercise 33

Ⅰ. ① liberation ② Lessen ③ lengthy
④ legitimate ⑤ layer

Ⅱ. ① F ② E ③ G ④ H ⑤ B

Exercise 34

Ⅰ. ① C ② D ③ A ④ B ⑤ B

Ⅱ. ① B ② D ③ A ④ J ⑤ H

Exercise 35

Ⅰ. ① C ② C ③ A ④ D ⑤ D

Ⅱ. ① J ② B ③ E ④ C ⑤ H

Exercise 36

Ⅰ. ① mentality ② materialism ③ meditation ④ mastery ⑤ mechanism

Ⅱ. ① B ② D ③ A ④ B ⑤ B

Exercise 37

Ⅰ. ① mocking ② miraculous ③ migration ④ minimal ⑤ missionary

Ⅱ. ① D ② A ③ B ④ D ⑤ A

Exercise 38

Ⅰ. ① D ② D ③ B ④ B ⑤ A

Ⅱ. ① C ② G ③ F ④ H ⑤ D

Exercise 39

Ⅰ. ① D ② B ③ C ④ A ⑤ B

Ⅱ. ① B ② A ③ D ④ I ⑤ G

Exercise 40

Ⅰ. ① notify ② nonviolent ③ nourishment ④ noticeable ⑤ nomination

Ⅱ. ① C ② J ③ D ④ H ⑤ E

Exercise 41

Ⅰ. ① occurrence ② obligation ③ nutritious ④ oppressions ⑤ obscure

Ⅱ. ① I ② C ③ G ④ A ⑤ E

Exercise 42

Ⅰ. ① optional ② orderly ③ originality ④ outfitted ⑤ outlawed

Ⅱ. ① D ② G ③ B ④ I ⑤ H

Exercise 43

Ⅰ. ① overall ② outrageous ③ overflows ④ overwork ⑤ overheads

Ⅱ. ① D ② G ③ J ④ B ⑤ F

Exercise 44

Ⅰ. ① peddlers ② patrol ③ patent ④ patriotic ⑤ patch

Ⅱ. ① E ② B ③ J ④ F ⑤ C

Exercise 45

Ⅰ. ① pensioned ② perseverance ③ perception ④ persistence ⑤ perspective

Ⅱ. ① C ② I ③ J ④ A ⑤ F

Exercise 46

Ⅰ. ① photographic ② piety ③ pistol ④ pleading ⑤ plantation

Ⅱ. ① G ② A ③ B ④ D ⑤ E

Exercise 47

Ⅰ. ① poachers ② precedent ③ potential ④ poking ⑤ pollutants

Ⅱ. ① H ② B ③ C ④ E ⑤ F

Exercise 48

Ⅰ. ① prejudice ② preliminary ③ prescription ④ presidency ⑤ priority

Ⅱ. ① E ② G ③ C ④ J ⑤ A

Exercise 49

Ⅰ. ① prohibition ② propeller ③ prosecution ④ prospective ⑤ provincial

Ⅱ. ① I ② F ③ E ④ B ⑤ A

Exercise 50

Ⅰ. ① purify ② qualification ③ questionnaire

④ radiation ⑤ radical

Ⅱ. ① B ② F ③ I ④ A ⑤ J

Exercise 51

Ⅰ. ① raided ② ravaging ③ recklessly ④ rattled ⑤ reckoned

Ⅱ. ① J ② B ③ F ④ E ⑤ G

Exercise 52

Ⅰ. ① recruited ② referee ③ refinement ④ rehearsal ⑤ reigned

Ⅱ. ① H ② E ③ B ④ F ⑤ G

Exercise 53

Ⅰ. ① relishes ② residential ③ resentment ④ reptiles ⑤ residence

Ⅱ. ① E ② B ③ A ④ I ⑤ F

Exercise 54

Ⅰ. ① revival ② ridiculous ③ retailing ④ reverse ⑤ retort

Ⅱ. ① H ② J ③ A ④ G ⑤ E

Exercise 55

Ⅰ. ① rivalry ② rotations ③ saddle ④ ritual ⑤ riots

Ⅱ. ① G ② B ③ E ④ D ⑤ F

Exercise 56

Ⅰ. ① scraped ② sanctioned ③ savages ④ scheming ⑤ sanely

Ⅱ. ① I ② G ③ E ④ A ⑤ D

Exercise 57

Ⅰ. ① security ② segmented ③ sentimental ④ serenity ⑤ sequence

Ⅱ. ① B ② J ③ G ④ E ⑤ C

Exercise 58

Ⅰ. ① shed ② shiver ③ shuddered ④ shred ⑤ shutters

Ⅱ. ① J ② B ③ E ④ F ⑤ H

Exercise 59

Ⅰ. ① simplicity ② skimmed ③ slaughter ④ slot ⑤ simmering

Ⅱ. ① C ② B ③ E ④ G ⑤ I

Exercise 60

Ⅰ. ① socialism ② snares ③ snatch ④ sneers ⑤ sole

Ⅱ. ① A ② D ③ B ④ F ⑤ I

Exercise 61

Ⅰ. ① sovereignty ② specialize ③ spectacular ④ spiking ⑤ spiral

Ⅱ. ① E ② C ③ A ④ G ⑤ J

Exercise 62

Ⅰ. ① sponsor ② stabilized ③ staggered ④ stain ⑤ stalked

Ⅱ. ① G ② E ③ I ④ C ⑤ A

Exercise 63

Ⅰ. ① statistical ② steered ③ stimulations ④ stinks ⑤ stock

Ⅱ. ① F ② C ③ I ④ E ⑤ A

Exercise 64

Ⅰ. ① strain ② stranded ③ stray ④ stuttered ⑤ subscription

Ⅱ. ① J ② B ③ E ④ A ⑤ G

Exercise 65

Ⅰ. ① substitution ② successive ③ superstitious ④ supervision ⑤ supplements

Ⅱ. ① H ② C ③ E ④ F ⑤ B

Exercise 66

Ⅰ. ① suspension ② symbol ③ synthetic
④ swamp ⑤ swarmed

Ⅱ. ① B ② H ③ D ④ J ⑤ A

Exercise 67

Ⅰ. ① temptation ② taunting ③ terminal
④ terrace ⑤ texture

Ⅱ. ① C ② H ③ E ④ B ⑤ G

Exercise 68

Ⅰ. ① thrifty ② thriller ③ throbbing ④ thrust
⑤ torments

Ⅱ. ① B ② I ③ E ④ F ⑤ C

Exercise 69

Ⅰ. ① trampled ② tranquilizer ③ transmission
④ transplant ⑤ traitors

Ⅱ. ① I ② E ③ A ④ F ⑤ J

Exercise 70

Ⅰ. ① trek ② trespass ③ truants ④ trot
⑤ tripled

Ⅱ. ① J ② D ③ F ④ I ⑤ B

Exercise 71

Ⅰ. ① umpire ② underestimated
③ underneath ④ unfolded ⑤ undergone

Ⅱ. ① J ② A ③ E ④ F ⑤ H

Exercise 72

Ⅰ. ① upright ② utilized ③ vacuum
④ validity ⑤ variations

Ⅱ. ① H ② E ③ J ④ B ⑤ F

Exercise 73

Ⅰ. ① vendor ② velvety ③ vibrations
④ vicious ⑤ victorious

Ⅱ. ① G ② H ③ D ④ J ⑤ A

Exercise 74

Ⅰ. ① vocals ② vocational ③ wade ④ ward
⑤ warehouse

Ⅱ. ① D ② J ③ C ④ I ⑤ G

Exercise 75

Ⅰ. ① waterproof ② whereabouts ③ whirling
④ whisked ⑤ weary

Ⅱ. ① H ② E ③ F ④ B ⑤ D

Exercise 76

Ⅰ. ① worshipped ② wrenching ③ wrestled
④ xerox ⑤ yields

Ⅱ. ① G ② D ③ B ④ J ⑤ A

索引
Index

單字索引

C

E

F

P

Q

S

NOTE

NOTE

NOTE

NOTE

國家圖書館出版品預行編目(CIP)資料

完勝大考英語7000單字. 中高級篇4501~7000字 / 空中英語教室編輯群著. -- 二版. -- 臺北市 : 笛藤出版圖書有限公司, 2024.01
面； 公分
ISBN 978-957-710-909-5(平裝)
1.CST: 英語教學 2.CST: 詞彙 3.CST: 中等教育
524.38 112021293

全新修訂版

完勝大考！英語7000單字

中高級篇 4501~7000字

7000單字雲端服務
專屬序號

2024年8月2日 二版第2刷 定價330元

著　　者　空中英語教室編輯群
封面設計　王舒玗
總 編 輯　洪季楨
編　　輯　林子鈺、葉雯婷
編輯協力　黃昱仁、陳佳文、楊逸婷、林予安
編輯企畫　笛藤出版
發 行 人　林建仲
發 行 所　八方出版股份有限公司
地　　址　台北市中山區長安東路二段171號3樓3室
電　　話　(02) 2777-3682
傳　　真　(02) 2777-3672
總 經 銷　聯合發行股份有限公司
電　　話　(02) 2917-8022 · (02) 2917-8042
製 版 廠　造極彩色印刷製版股份有限公司
劃撥帳戶　八方出版股份有限公司
劃撥帳號　19809050